An Introduction to

PSYCHOANALYTIC THEORY
OF MOTIVATION

An Introduction to
PSYCHOANALYTIC THEORY
OF MOTIVATION

WALTER TOMAN

ASSOCIATE PROFESSOR
BRANDEIS UNIVERSITY
WALTHAM, MASS.

PERGAMON PRESS

OXFORD · LONDON · NEW YORK · PARIS

1960

PERGAMON PRESS LTD.
Headington Hill Hall, Oxford
4 & 5 Fitzroy Square, London W.1

PERGAMON PRESS INC.
122 East 55th Street, New York 22, N.Y.
P.O. Box 47715, Los Angeles, California

PERGAMON PRESS S.A.R.L.
24 Rue des Ecoles, Paris Vᵉ

PERGAMON PRESS G.m.b.H.
Kaiserstrasse 75, Frankfurt am Main

Library of Congress Card Number 60–14191

PRINTED IN GREAT BRITAIN BY PAGE BROS. (NORWICH), LTD., NORWICH

Contents

CONTENTS

Publisher's Preface

THIS book has been written from a number of backgrounds. The author has lived and worked professionally in Europe and in the United States. He has been trained in the theory and practice of psychoanalysis at the Vienna Institute of Psychoanalysis, and in general and child psychology as well as in the philosophy of science at the University of Vienna. He has been in clinical practice as psychoanalyst, psychotherapist and counsellor, has done research also in the fields of perception and cognition before he finally turned to the areas of motivation and personality, and has taught general psychology, child psychology, clinical psychology and psychoanalytic theory at the University of Vienna, Harvard University and Brandeis University. Apart from writing a number of articles for professional American and German journals he is the author of two psychological texts, *Einführung in die moderne Psychologie* and *Dynamik der Motive*, as well as of three books of short stories, *Die eigenwillige Kamera*, *Busse's Welttheater*, and *A Kindly Contagion*. He has also written a book of poetry (*Distelvolk*), and a short novel (*Das Dorf mit dem Drachen*).

The present book is a kind of a confluence of all these interests, experiences and talents. It is theoretical as well as clinical and practical, rigorous in essence as far as the subject-matter permits and, at the same time, more rigorous probably than other treatises available, but also sensitive, intuitive, and diplomatic. It is objective, yet of a certain personal appeal, instructive and constructive, fairly easy to read and yet difficult enough to forbid a glib or purely scanning contact. The reader may get the full benefit only after re-readings and second checks. It is comprehensive and broad, yet in a sense merely opening the subject-matter. To the extent that it does so, however, the reader will perhaps find himself enlightened enough to further pursue the subject independently, whether in everyday life including his own, in clinical work or in his readings. Some experts may be hesitant at first to "buy" certain aspects of the conceptual introduction, but if they do go on with it and even enter the second part, namely the "Theory at Work", they will probably not regret it.

On the college level this book may be useful as supplementary reading in courses such as child development, educational psychology and abnormal psychology, whereas in more advanced courses or seminars on motivation, personality, projective techniques, clinical interviewing or psychoanalytic theory, it could be used more thoroughly and as a major text.

Author's Preface

WITH this book I have tried to do something not too common among writers on the subject. I have tried to keep allegiance to two masters. One is Sigmund Freud and the other is the theoretical system which he has proposed. Freud changed his mind on several issues of his system in the course of his ingenious work of fifty years, and he has left some confusion behind him which his disciples have tried to clear up only with trepidation and an almost irrational, though understandable, adherence to the letter of his writings. But he has also left a theoretical system with enough cohesion so that remaining confusions and obscurities could, in principle, be dispelled by careful reading from its system-properties. The strange thing about his theoretical system is, however, that its best accounts are perhaps not so much to be found in the psychoanalytic literature, but, unspelled-out, in the minds of practising psychoanalysts and psychoanalytically orientated psychotherapists. This has at least become my strong impression through the years of work and professional discourse. One might say that an essential part of psychoanalytic theory has not yet been handed down in writing. By general standards of science and scientific pursuits this would be a deficiency which certain critics of Freud have assailed with some justification.

The present book is an attempt to ameliorate that condition to an extent. It intends to convey to the reader at least a portion of what is commonly conveyed mainly in the course of psychoanalytic training and elaborate supervision of the trainee's own psychotherapeutic work. This seems possible to me because psychoanalysis or psychotherapy, whether exercised or experienced "patients", i.e. as a "patient", is not altogether different from practices and experiences that everyone may encounter and has encountered in his daily life. The differences are of degrees rather than in kind, although of degrees in a number of dimensions. This book does not try to accomplish anything like a psychoanalytic training or treatment of the reader. That could not possibly succeed. The contention is, though, that many people are ready to understand more about peoples' lives including their own and capable of dealing more intelligently with them than they are often given credit for by clinicians, and that some of these people may well be able to benefit from a book of this kind. Also that psychoanalytic theory contains more common sense than one might at first be led to expect. Maybe the earlier accounts of psychoanalytic findings and conclusions had to be over-dramatized in order to be noticed at all. But that might have obscured

ix

issues, sometimes antagonised audiences (and even a few patients) unduly, and severed some of its connections to everyday life. This book tries to establish better "diplomatic relations", mainly by bringing out the very general character, indeed, of Freud's theoretical system.

The comment I would like most to elicit is that I have presented psychoanalytic theory and its implications; that I have not hesitated to clarify and elaborate wherever it seemed to contribute to the conceptual consistency without violating the original spirit; that I have drawn on a broad area of *data*, preferably clinical and from everyday life, while continuing to convey something beyond *data*: the click of a theory; and that the didactics was not bad in spite of some initial hardships and apparent ramblings. Perhaps one might also say that I hold a middle line between authors on the subject who, on one extreme, prove little more on ever so many pages than that they have read and can quote, and those, on the other extreme, who convey little more in ever so many words than that they are psychoanalysts or psychotherapists and have seen it all.

PART I

CONCEPTUAL INTRODUCTION

Psychological Forces

THE undefined elements of psychoanalytic theory are psychological forces, drives or desires. The psyche, mind or personality, is a system of desires in which three sub-systems can be distinguished: Id, Ego and Superego.

*   *   *

Psychoanalytic theory is a theory of the mind or the psyche or of personality in a technical sense. More specifically, it is a theory of man's psychic or psychological forces and of the ways in which these forces come about and interact with each other as well as with the givens of the world, whatever they are.

Forces cannot be seen. Yet they are observable in their effects. They can be identified from the behavior we see. In fact, we cannot even see behavior without hypothesising forces. If a person is lifting one leg from the ground and thrusting it forward while pulling the opposite arm back, and then lifting the other leg from the ground and thrusting it forward too while pulling the other arm back, and doing so before the first leg has reached the ground, then lifting the first one again, etc., we are seeing the complicated effects of something that we can name very easily as *running*. We cannot even help seeing it as that. Yet by saying that he is running we are postulating a force. We seem to imply that he desires to get from one place to another fast. What is more, we seem to imply that he will get up again and continue running if, e.g. he should happen to stagger over the curb of the sidewalk; and if the wind blows his cap away, he may run after it and catch it wherever he can, but then he will resume the old direction. As a matter of fact, he can run in different ways, slowly or quickly, with large or small strides, with skips, jumps or occasional somersaults inserted. Many aspects of behavior involved in the execution of a force are interchangeable. They are not irrevocably tied to the force. Which implies that given aspects of behavior may also be in the service of different forces. It is such implications that make it particularly worthwhile to postulate forces. The observer sticking strictly to behavior may still be trying to describe how our runner managed to come to a halt and it may have escaped his notice altogether that his hat flew away, while we, postulating a force, have plenty of time to look, will not miss the hat incident and can assume what will happen thereafter long before he has caught it again.

The concept of "force" comprehends not only impulse, drive, need, motive,

3

desire, wish and striving, but even such specific concepts as intentions or plans, and such broad concepts as attitudes, interests and values. Let us single out the term desire to stand for psychological force in general, but I will not promise that the other terms, especially drives, motives and wishes, will not sneak in here and there, if for no other than aesthetic reasons. They will always mean the same as desire or psychological force. The attribute "instinctual" is unnecessary. We shall see that all desires and all their derivatives would, in principle, deserve the attribute. So we might as well save ourselves some trouble. Intentions, plans, attitudes, interests and values are more complex terms. They manifest compounds of desires, although one or a few specific desires can usually be recognised as the strongest of their determinants.

My preference for the term "desire" stems from its connotation of a full and active experience. It concerns something we do indeed want. One may hurry to ask: "But to use your term, are there not desires that are active against our will, desires that we would rather not have but we cannot help having?" Yes, precisely. We shall see, however, as we go on, that there are no desires in a person that have not at one time been full and active experiences that had his conscious support. Otherwise they could not even have formed.

If psychological forces or desires interact with each other and the "givens" of the world in more than one distinguishable way, we are dealing with a system. The psyche, the mind or personality, *is* a system of forces or desires. At least that was among Freud's first major postulates (Freud, 1900).

What more can one say about that system? Freud, after some revisions, postulated that it is made up of three sub-systems which he finally called Id, Ego and Superego (Freud, 1923). These sub-systems are also systems of forces or desires. In addition, however, they ought to have properties of their own. What are these?

The Id is the system of primitive, unorganised and unspecific desires. They cannot usually be satisfied in reality. Eating up somebody beloved would be such a desire. Usually we cannot and do not do that. However, we may hear a lady say of a little boy: "He is so cute. I could eat him up." Which indicates that there is such a desire, although in the subjunctive. Or we may find Christians of various denominations eating the beloved son of God in the form of the holy wafer. Killing an opponent even over a trifle would be another such desire. We manage ordinarily to abstain from doing so, although somebody may find himself whispering with clenched fists: "I could kill you!" when his boss would not have it any other way than his narrow own, or when a policeman stops the traffic just when that person is coming along in a hurry.

The Ego is that system which has undertaken to organise the primitive desires and to attune them to each other as well as to specific conditions of reality so that they can be satisfied in reality. In another, briefer, though somewhat contradictory version we could say that the Ego simply is the system of complex, organised and specific desires. Our lady will not eat up the cute little boy, but she will, perhaps, kiss him passionately and eat many other things, steak and spinach, bread, apples, etc. The pious Christian mentioned will eat a small piece of wafer and know that it "means" communion with Christ. The rebel against the boss's narrow ways may be able to get his will after a little detour. He may prove his point in figures and not only persuade him to it, but even get a salary raise instead of a death sentence, had he really killed him. Finally even the malicious policeman can be handled otherwise, but let us rather leave him alone altogether. One never knows. Besides he may not even really be malicious.

The Superego, finally, is the system of desires that have been taken over from other people or, more indirectly, from the social system in which the person lives. The first, most powerful and most influential suppliers of such desires are the parents of the person's infancy and childhood. To eat and drink properly, to be dressed and clean in the presence of other people, to keep order among one's things and to treat them gently and carefully, to share with brother and sister, to respect their "property", to say "please" and "thank you", etc., are examples of such desires. They could also be phrased as "Don'ts". "Do not spill and smear food!" refers to the same desire as "Eat and drink properly!" although the first one may be a more primitive and archaic version of it, and the second an advancement. More about that later (see p. 91).

Well, these descriptions do not tell us very much yet. We need to know more. Above all we need to know how these systems form in the first place and how they interact. Let us look at the Id and the Ego first. How does the Ego manage to organise primitive desires so that they can be satified in reality? Or more generally speaking: How does control come about?

Control of Desires, Derivative Desires, Cathexis and Object-Formation

DESIRES form by the process of control, which is a function of the process of formation of derivative desires, which, in turn, is a function of the process of cathexis of conditions under which desires can be satisfied. Cathexis is the major "operator" in psychoanalytic theory. It is learning in a general sense. It goes on all the time as long as the individual is satisfying desires, and it is cumulative. It builds up knowledge in a general sense, knowledge of objects and knowledge of the world, which includes oneself. One may say that cathexis is a function of the Ego by which a person learns about or "cathects" the world, which implies: forms derivative desires, which, in turn, implies: gains control over his desires that, otherwise, might stay primitive or never even form.

*　　　*　　　*

Take a very primitive and ancient desire such as sucking. The infant has a chance to satisfy this desire for the first time soon after birth. He finds he can do it, although it is a great struggle at first. If something touches his mouth, he will surround it with his lips and suck, and if some fluid can be extracted that way and fills his mouth, he will swallow it.

However, his sucking depends entirely on the actual stimulation of the mouth. He does not see or hear it come, although his mother is already rushing around and could be seen and heard doing so, if only our infant could see and hear such things. He does not even feel the approach of the event, when mother lifts him out of the basket and carries him to a place where he can be fed. What is worse: the infant has already started screaming like mad, and mother guesses that he is hungry, but he does not know it yet himself. Something in him registers that something is wrong, but he does not know what. Although he can suck and swallow, he is entirely dependent upon the world to provide the conditions. He cannot even suck his fist as a substitute, because he does not know yet how to move his arm so that the fist will end up in his mouth, and he does not know how to keep it there, if, quite accidentally or by external help, it should already be there.

Obviously our infant cannot go on like that for ever. We find that before too

6

long he does recognise that being lifted and carried brings a feeding. How do we know he recognises? Well, he stops screaming at that point, when before only the breast's or bottle's nipple filling his mouth would stop him. Or he screams particularly hard at this point, demanding impatiently that the world hurry on, whereas before he would just go on screaming as if nothing had yet changed. Then he begins to recognise steps, the noise of a closing door, then the sight of some colors, mother's dress and a fair patch on top of it—her face. Besides, his fist will reach his mouth with some reliability. Finally he can distinguish his desire for feeding from other things such as being freed when caught accidentally in the corner of his crib, wishing to be changed or just wanting the window shades to be lifted in the morning. He can even distinguish between one drink and another, between a sweet one and one into which mother has sneaked castor oil or a bitter medicine. He takes one rapidly and the other with hesitation. He may even spit it out.

The infant has learned a little more about the conditions under which his ancient desire can be satisfied and he has also learned to satisfy it in different ways, rapidly, slowly, or not at all, with a certain kind of food, munching a lot or just a little, etc. He has gained more control over sucking.

Take another example, walking. We find that around one year of age the child begins to make his first steps without support. He could crawl places and stand without support before, and he could walk along the railing of the play pen or while pushing a light chair before him. Now, with all his concentration, he is able to set one foot before the other a few times all by himself. Then he falls to the floor, is delighted over the accomplishment and will try it soon again. Gradually he can walk longer stretches, walk and carry something in his hands, walk rapidly or slowly, take sharp turns around corners, run, etc. He can do all kinds of walking, can do it under all kinds of conditions and may be doing it even for other purposes.

The same trends can be demonstrated for something like bicycle riding or driving a car, for drawing, reading, skiing, public speaking, practising law and many, many other desires. In fact, there is no desire that would not tend to develop that way. An individual controls more and more conditions under which his desires can be satisfied and his desires can be satisfied in an increasing number of ways, whereby control comprehends the slightest inkling of anticipation of an event, judgment of a given condition as inappropriate, anticipation of appropriate potential conditions all the way up to direct and active manipulation of given conditions.

There may be a misunderstanding. We have distinguished conditions under which a desire can be satisfied, and ways in which it can be satisfied (under given conditions). This distinction is somewhat arbitrary, although convenient. Strictly speaking, different ways of satisfying a desire are different conditions too, just as different conditions require different ways of satisfaction. If an infant wants to hold the bottle himself, when before his mother held it, he is changing his way of sucking the bottle. Yet we may also say: he is sucking under a different condition. If a child wants to walk or run in two-feet-deep water he is satisfying a desire under a different condition. Yet this condition will also modify the way in which he does it.

In the first case the infant introduces the condition himself—he is in a familiar situation and tries to change it. Here we might say, he finds a new way of sucking the bottle. In the second case he is in a condition which dictates a change to him. He must walk or run in a different way, if he is to walk or run at all. Here we might say that he satisfies a desire under a new condition. There is a difference; however, it is one of degree.

The increase of control over a desire implies the *formation of derivative desires*. Sucking anything, as long as it fills the mouth and can possibly be swallowed, differentiates into sucking from mother's breast, sucking the bottle, sucking milk, warm water, cold water or orange juice, but also sucking one's fist and feet which, fortunately, cannot be swallowed, although the infant may well regret that in the beginning. Gradually these desires develop into something like a life of their own. One day the infant does not want milk for a change but water, and not the breast but the bottle, particularly if mother has added a little sugar to it. If he has just been nursed, his own hands and feet may be more attractive than any food at all.

The same would hold for walking. A child who has run around a lot will not mind walking slowly and properly for a change. And a child who has been walking and running a lot, but has not climbed stairs for some time may, at the moment, prefer that to any other locomotion. Not even a car ride may win over that.

These examples should illustrate that learning about or gaining control over conditions of satisfaction, is an integral part of the formation of derivative desires. If the infant distinguishes mother's breast from the bottle, or milk from water and orange juice, he has learned something specific about or gained control over the conditions of satisfaction of a desire, sucking. He can, for instance, refuse to take milk and scream until he gets something else. At the same time we may say that derivative desires have been formed. They have begun to be active side by side with the original or primal desire, sucking. They can even substitute to a greater or lesser extent for the latter. In fact, the concepts of "derivative desire" and "substitute desire" refer to the same thing. Hence the formation of derivative desires is a function of the control achieved over conditions of their satisfaction.

The increase of control over a desire also implies cathexis. This term is a translation of Freud's "libidinöse Besetzung" (Freud 1905, 1916–17), which means "libidinal investment" or "investment with libidinal energy". It has led to various misunderstandings, one of which is to treat it as something that can be bestowed and withdrawn at the individual's discretion. Another one is the notion that it "flows".

The *process of cathexis* or *cathecting* means approximately "learning how to like, to appreciate, to love". The infant cathects, or learns how to love, sucking, sucking mother's breast, the bottle, milk, water, sweet milk, etc. He learns how to love walking, running, running through water, climbing stairs, etc. That means, he will have all of these things again and again. Not only that. Each time he has had them again, he will have learned a little better to like or appreciate or love them. This need not mean that he loves them more. It does mean, however, that he loves more aspects and angles of them and that it will be increasingly less of a problem for him to have these things again, sucking, sucking mother's breast, walking, climbing stairs, etc. He knows more and more about them and about how to get them.

In fact, the process of cathexis may be taken to mean learning in a general sense or acquisition of knowledge, provided that we assume that we learn what satisfies desires and that knowledge is nothing academic, but something "dynamic". Whatever we know we have learned about, in principle, while satisfying desires. Those *data* that were most regularly present are even the most likely to be acquired, but they are also most likely to be "instrumental" to our desires. The baby who is breast-fed will not learn too much at first about mother's dresses. They change. But he will learn about the breast which is always present at a feeding, and later also, say, about the voice which does not seem to change.

In that sense, however, the process of cathexis is a function of the control achieved over the conditions under which desires can be satisfied and also a function of the derivatives formed. The more a desire is under control and, consequently, the more derivative desires there are side by side with its primal form, the more cathexis must have taken place. Cathexis might even be viewed as making control of desires and formation of cathexis possible. Hence it might be appropriate to say that the latter are functions of cathexis.

We may be missing something here. After all, one does not only love to suck mother's breast or the bottle, but one also loves mother and the bottle. One does not only love to run through water. One also loves water. Does cathexis apply to that too?

Yes, it does. As a matter of fact, all cathexis of desires is cathexis of the conditions under which they can be, or rather have been, satisfied. Cathexis extends to the "*object*" of a desire. However, there is no object to start with. There is no breast at first that could be separated from sucking. The breast "exists" in the infant's mind only as long as he is busy with it. It is gone again, once he is finished. There is also no difference at first between the breast and the bottle. We may suspect, however, that the infant given both in alternation will soon begin to prefer one, most likely the breast.

Something changes as the child continues to be exposed to the object of a desire. There is no object in his mind at first, but slowly, bit by bit, it "emerges" into existence. Something like the peculiar texture and consistency of the breast comes to the infant's notice. The infant cathects it. He learns that this particular feeling goes with sucking. If he is given a bottle now for the first time, he will not like its feeling. That is not the "thing" he has learned how to appreciate. The same would hold for the taste of human milk versus that of the bottle's milk or water, and for various other aspects. Gradually, the infant will even learn how to like the substitute for mother's breast too, and only the second substitute, say, the pacifier, will be rejected. Finally even that will be liked. A *substitution continuum* will be formed in his mind on which mother's breast ranks highest, the bottle with human milk next, then the bottle with cow's milk, then the pacifier, etc. That is to say that different conditions under which sucking can occur, or different objects of sucking, are being learned about or cathected. The infant learns how to like or love or appreciate them, or he simply learns about them, so that he will eventually turn and stretch his head toward them, begin to scream impatiently, or smile at them upon mere sight.

The same thing holds for walking. The child does not cathect the desire itself. While moving around he happens also to get to places, to different rooms, even to distant corners and dark niches of the house and to the little yard outside. Wherever he goes he finds things to look at and listen to, to touch, pound or scratch, even to put in the mouth. He learns about all these things. He learns how to like them. He cathects them. As a matter of fact, the same holds for desires in general. Their satisfactions bring the individual in contact with the world and he learns, or learns how to like, more and more about the world.

In other words, objects form for the growing individual. But we have not looked at one aspect that is crucial.

If mother's breast, the bottle and the pacifier would offer no other modes of experience or, more precisely, if they would not be satisfying to other desires too, they would not really become objects. As it is, mother's breast suckles the baby, but it can also be felt by touch and friction, it has the scent of soap or human skin and it can be fair or very fair, depending on the illumination. Besides sucking, it satisfies the desires to be touched and touch, by mouth or by hand, to smell, to see, even to listen or to be lifted and carried, although the latter are aspects of the surrounding conditions rather than of the breast itself and will be attributed by the infant to other "parts of mother" later on. "Mother's breast" becomes something holding milk, something that is solid, but soft and smooth, something fair and glimmering, something even of a taste of its own. When confronted with any one of these aspects, the other aspects are co-existent in the infant's mind, so that he can choose with increasing ease and independence which one to take up on its promises. He is no longer so totally seriously engaged in sucking. He can stop and play, i.e. do other things or satisfy other desires, before he goes on sucking.

The child's home becomes an object by the same device. It is an uncanny space of unknown dimensions at first, but already a year later it has become a lively and colorful amusement-center. There are many things one can do now.

The desires to touch and pound or to touch by means of something held in the hand, say a little hammer, or the desires to look, to taste, to listen, can all be satisfied in many different places of the house and almost any place offers satisfactions for more than one desire. There are light curtains which can be pulled, looked through or used for wrapping something, and chairs that can be pushed, sat on or hid under. There is the sofa which lets the hammer bounce back when you beat it, which chairs do not do, and it can be sat on and hid under even better. However, it cannot be pushed. There are colors on the walls, some of which come off on scratching, and windows to look through that cannot possibly be scratched. There is a mirror which tastes like nothing much, feels like a window, but shows another little Tom. And there are doors that do not only open, but can also be hid behind and they squeak, and toys that can be pushed, sat on, though neither hid under nor behind, and they rattle, if you throw them on the floor, or they make a big bang. You can get from everything to everything else by a little walking or running or even by crawling, if you like, by standing on your toes and reaching very high, stepping on a stool or indicating to mother, as the last resort, that you want a lift. Mother, of course, is always somewhere in the house, and if not mother, at least father or, at the very least, the baby-sitter. If you are outside the house, you are outside of everything, of curtains, squeaking doors, sofas and even outside of where mother is. There is no point in looking for any of them outside the house. In fact, you had better remember how to get in again, and do not move away too far, although . . . although the yard with its green, green grass offers something that you will not find anywhere inside the house.

This is how the home may look to a two-year-old. There are many different things that he can do at home and he can do them in many different places, and he knows it all. He knows his way around the house. Any particular engagement does not make him lose sight of others, and some of them may even be quite instrumental in what he is trying to do. Such a home has become an "object". The adult who has planned and furnished his own home with much care, set up his library, a record collection and a system by which he can quickly find any book or record that he knows he owns, etc., is in an infinitely more advanced position. His home is a much more complex, thought-out and thought-about object in his mind than the two-year-old's. He has continued to cathect, or to learn about his home for perhaps twenty-five additional years. He has even lived in several different homes already. However, it is not principally different.

It must be mentioned here, that the process of object-formation comprehends also the person involved. A child becomes more and more of an object to himself, the more he learns about himself. While sucking mother's breast, the bottle, the pacifier, etc., there is one inevitable given: his mouth. He cathects his mouth just as he cathects mother's breast. What is more, to the extent that he discovers other satisfactions to which his mouth is instrumental such as tasting, screaming, producing sounds, calling for mother, or even kissing another mouth, his mouth becomes an object too. It satisfies several different desires. The owner has learned what it can do. The child also cathects his hands in a similar fashion. In fact, the first thing that he comes to know of them is that they can fill his mouth. Then he learns that they can be seen, that they can clasp things, that they can bring those things to the mouth and before the eyes, etc. Again they satisfy, or they are instrumental in satisfying, a number of different desires. Learning how to put on shoes or a shirt, how to walk and run, how to be properly behaved in company, how to skate, read, do mathematics, address an audience or guests, etc., in short, anything that a person can *do* involves cathexis of oneself in addition to cathexis of the "outer" world. I would go as far as to say that, with development, one's own person becomes a part of the outer world, or simply of the world, a part that can be controlled more easily in the long run, or even more intimately, if you like, than all the rest of the world, but a part that is not principally different. However, the reader need not yet follow me on that.

Object-formation occurs where conditions under which desires can be satisfied overlap. It is mother, whether we eat, drink, play, talk or what not, who is with us in early life. There is always the home, whether we play tag, climb stairs, hide in niches or whether we eat, drink, play or talk to mother. And our own body, our eyes, our hands, in short all of us is with us as we are exposed to any condition whatsoever. In other words: those aspects of varying conditions that remain invariant "become" objects. Why there should be invariant aspects at all, however, is up to God to answer. They are givens that we cannot account for psychologically.

Object-formation is a function of the number of desires that the object can satisfy and of the number of ways in which it can satisfy them. We have seen before that the greater the number of ways in which a desire can be satisfied, the more derivatives must have been formed and the better will it be under control. Therefore, object-formation must also be a function of the formation of derivatives and of the degree of control achieved over the conditions under which the desires in question can be satisfied. The more an object has been established in an individual's mind, the more will it appear to him in all its complexity, no matter what particular desires are foremost in his mind at the time. He will perceive it and think of it "objectively". It will not change in the light of changing desires. Mother will not become irrelevant for her son because he has just been fed by her, and the home will not become intolerable after he has just had enough of playing there with a ball. Or, to take another area, music will not be boring to him because he has just listened to some, say to Brahms. He can go right on with Schumann, then take up the violin himself for a little étude and end the afternoon with a study of an essay by von Webern. If objects such as mother, the home or music are well established, consolidated and stable, however, it is conceivable that they are themselves, by virtue of their psychological existence, powerful agents of control over desires.

As might be foreseen, we will end up with human beings as the most diversified and intricate of all objects with which a growing individual is likely to come in contact. No other part of the world tends to offer as many ways of satisfaction for as large a number of desires as does another human being. No dog and no chimpanzee can compare. Even an atomic reactor or the entire universe, with which a physicist or an astronomer, respectively, may be as much as in love, tends to fall short of what they, physicist and astronomer, can get from another human being.

But what has all this got to do with Id and Ego? Well, it has been said that the Id is the system of primitive, unorganised and unspecific desires, whereas the Ego is that system which has undertaken to organise them and attune them with each other as well as with specific conditions of reality, so that they can be satisfied. How does the Ego manage such an undertaking? Through control of desires, formation of derivative desires, learning or cathexis and object-formation. Thereby the Ego manages not only to organise and attune primitive desires to each other and to reality, but it also "creates" this very reality. Psychologically speaking, reality is not an absolute thing, but rather what a given individual has made of it for himself. Reality is what he perceives and knows of the world, or his theory of reality. It grows, it becomes more and more complex and organised as he develops. To the extent that it does so, desires will find times, places and ways of satisfaction.

Where then is the Id? What if the primitive, unorganised and unspecific desires—the demons—have all become cultivated and well-behaved? Does that not mean that the Id is disappearing while a person develops?

In a sense, yes. As we grow older, our primitive satisfactions become rarer. We do not experience a house any more like the child of two does. We hardly see the curtains any more which the child loved to pull or hide behind or even to suck in order to find out what they tasted like. Chairs have become quite functional. They must seat us comfortably, and they must fit into the context and atmosphere of the room, or we throw them out. The house itself is highly functional. If it is no longer in a convenient location for our purposes, we leave it, buy or rent another one and do not spend much thought on what delights, secrets and secret recesses we leave behind. We also do not hop and crawl and run around as ceaselessly and emphatically as the child of two does. If we run at all, we are likely to be engaged in a ping-pong game down in the basement, or the house must be on fire. We do not eat voraciously with our hands any more and we do not hit a friend because he does not want to give us a candy.

Yet our primitive satisfactions do not disappear altogether. Sometimes, perhaps on a late afternoon, when by chance spouse and children are gone and have left us alone in the house, we suddenly might see the long ignored curtains, step up to them and, maybe, rub them between our fingers. We may inspect a chair playfully with our hands. We may pat, tilt or shake it gently. We may stroll from room to room and find a cobweb in a corner, something that we have not seen for years, a loose door-knob on a closet-door—which ought to be fixed, but, please, not now—and look at an old picture in the children's room more closely. If circumstances bring us outdoors for the first time after a long, rainy winter, we may well want to move a little more vigorously, jump across a puddle, or not mind at all, for a change, that the children want us to play tag with them. In the course of this we may get quite hungry and end up having a picnic without manners, a really wild one, and we may even fight over a piece of meat or candy with our children.

That is, under certain conditions we may find ourselves satisfying more primitive desires or satisfying our desires in their more primitive forms. Other and more frequent conditions of that sort: fatigue, as one may feel it at the end of the day and of the week, or when intoxicated with liquor. Under either of them we tend to resort to more primitive, unorganised and unspecific desires, although knowing that we still attempt and succeed to beware of the worst. We take it easy at the end of the day or of the week, read a picture magazine rather than our business correspondence, lie back with a cigarette rather than smoking it hectically—as we did a little while ago in a difficult conference—or crawl around with our children on the floor. And when we have had a little too much to drink we may try to be very silly, to win an argument by shouting louder, not even to win an argument, but just to win, or to make love to one person present after the other, possibly even regardless of sex. Still another such condition is sleep, or rather dreaming. Here too we are inclined to satisfy desires in their more primitive forms. We may meet an old friend in our house regardless of the fact that, in reality, he is across the ocean; which is a more primitive way of satisfying the desire to see him than it would be to do so in waking life (booking for tickets, applying for passports, etc.). We may even summon a grandparent who is dead and we may have him give us a fortune when, in reality, he has disinherited us. In waking life the first would be impossible and the second, acquiring a fortune, much more difficult than that to achieve. We may even shoot that very grandparent in our fright over his appearance when, in reality, we would neither have said a mean word to him nor know where to get the gun in the first place.

If the Id is the system of primitive, unorganised and unspecific desires, and these desires have not really disappeared with an adult although they have become rarer, the Id cannot have disappeared either. In fact, the difference between controlled desires upon which the individual usually acts and the most uncontrolled and unspecific desires that he is capable of admitting to behavior must even increase with development. We might say that relative to the Ego the Id falls more and more behind, although it develops too, at least to some extent. On the average, the most primitive of an adult's desires are not as primitive as the most primitive desires of a child.

But does not the Id disappear after all? Or rather, does it not dissolve into an entirely relational concept? Why keep it at all? Why not speak of a trend of all desires to become more controlled and specific with a person's development and leave it at that?

Well, not all desires do become more controlled and specific with development. Some desires get "arrested". They are denied further satisfactions at some point of a person's development. They have been satisfied so far, such as the desire to suck mother's breast, but some day they can no longer, such as when mother's milk supply stops. They have become impossible to satisfy and remain arrested at that point of control and cathexis which they have reached by that time. Not only that. Any attempt to satisfy these desires at a later point of development creates anxiety.

These desires pertain to or even constitute the Id in a more specific sense. More precisely, they pertain to or constitute the unconscious portion of the Id (see also pp. 31f, 78f). If the Id as a whole may have seemed to dissolve into a purely relational concept before our eyes, this portion of the Id—which is sometimes even taken to be all of it—does not. It is partitioned off from the rest of the mind or personality by an alert guard, anxiety. On the other hand, there is no clear-cut border between this portion of the Id and the Id in general. All primitive, unorganised and unspecific desires have a tendency to arouse anxiety. Just imagine, e.g. that a business executive would decide to read the funnies rather than his business correspondence and not just once, but forever. Or that he would crawl around the floor in a business meeting and invite the participants to do likewise. Well, that man is crazy, or he should feel very queasy and uncomfortable doing so. In fact, he simply does not do those things which, at home and with his children, may be perfectly harmless. Just shift the context a little, move to another situation with a primitive desire that you satisfy even as an adult and you will notice the red light of anxiety go on in you even at the mere thought of it. In that respect, not even the Id as a whole seems to be a merely relational concept. Any primitive desire can do that to us.

Deprivation of Desires and Anxiety

ANXIETY is the automatic consequence of excessive deprivation of one, some, many or all of a person's desires. It is a state of disequilibrium of the psyche as a whole, or of a return of all (acute) desires to increasingly primitive forms. It can come about suddenly or slowly and whether deprivation is anticipated or acute. It will mount to total panic, if the situation of excessive deprivation continues unchanged. (Perceived) danger or threat is an already cathected or familiar condition of anxiety. Anxiety is pain in a general sense. "Physical pain ' is a special case.

*　　　*　　　*

All desires, once they have become recurrent at all, increase in intensity from zero or close to zero immediately after they have just been satisfied to a finally intolerable intensity. Usually, however, they or their substitutes can be satisfied long before things are that bad. Usually we eat again long before we are mad with hunger. We take a walk before we are exasperated sitting still at a desk and we go to bed long before we would fall asleep under almost any circumstances. If, however, deprivation of a desire lasts too long, we get restless, irritable and impatient with everything, provided, of course, that we can do nothing ourselves to end this deprivation. We are in alarm, in a state of anxiety (Freud, 1926). Yet even then opportunities for satisfaction usually appear before too long, so that we eat, walk or sleep after all.

If that is not so, if deprivation continues, the state of alarm or anxiety may increase to maximal intensity which is panic, a wild, violent outcry, a tantrum, something resembling an epileptic fit, during which we may even become insensible and without memory. Early in life, when deprivation can be tolerated only for very short times, alarm may actually increase to total panic. Because of a somewhat delayed feeding, and after trying unsuccessfully to eat with increasing "anger" almost anything at all (see also p. 57 f.), we may find an infant screaming at the top of his voice, shaking his arms and his legs madly, turning and twisting his body, and being insensitive to the sight of mother's breast and even to the nipple right in his mouth. He cannot suck, although deprivation of sucking is the source of his trouble. Tantrum has taken over.

As development proceeds and as the individual gains control over his desires

16

and the conditions of their satisfaction, these extreme states of affairs become more and more unlikely. The individual can catch alarm or anxiety when it is just beginning to mount and do something about it. Alarm or anxiety has begun to function as a signal. It stands for full-fledged panic, or at least for greater intensities of alarm or anxiety. It signals: "Danger! Change your course of action!" Which, generally speaking, the individual can do the better, the more control over desires, the more derivative-formation and the more cathexis of the world he has achieved. This does not mean, though, that conditions of deprivation cannot become tougher than ever before and work up an individual that usually can do better to a full-fledged panic after all.

Is the result of extreme deprivation really panic? Is there not another alternative: resignation? Take a man who has been caught in a plane crash in the desert where nobody happens to come to his rescue. Does he not give up at some point and accept his fate, death? Well, yes, but he has had his panic before. As a matter of fact, this is approximately what panic can do. It can bring about resignation. It can "knock out" the deprived desire for the time being and will do so again as soon as the individual "wakes up" from his "knock-out" to reality. If nothing has changed there will soon be another panic. In fact, there will be panic after panic until the desire to drink, to quench his intolerable thirst, cannot "rise" any longer, or until all possibility of obtaining something to drink is erased. "There is no water whatsoever anywhere at all!" is the fact which panic helps our plane-wrecked individual establish in his mind. From here on he can be resigned. If a kind Samaritan comes along later and offers him a bottle of water, he may not know what it is nor what that man wants. This is also what happened to prisoners of war and those in concentration camps who had been starved too long. They were offered food, but they simply could not eat it, at least not for some time. Panic need not be as dramatic as the situation itself. The plane-wrecked pilot in the desert may well miss the overt tantrum and slide into resignation quietly. The more control a person has achieved over his desires, or the farther developed he is psychologically, the more likely is he to be able to miss it even in matters of life and death. Yet something like panic, some terrifying realisation of his plight, some tacit cry, must have preceded his eventual resignation.

Panic, whether full-fledged or subdued, tends to bring about resignation with a mature adult, unless a friendly environment provides the deprived with an object after all. But resignation is a very complicated and mature thing itself. What does panic do to the immature child or to the infant, provided, again, that the environment or the parents cannot be tantalised into giving the badly desired? Well, in principle it does the same thing. It precipitates something like a very primitive resignation. Whereas the pilot in the desert established in his mind that "there is no water whatsoever anywhere", the infant, say, upon weaning, must do likewise with mother's breast. "There is no breast in this whole world!" is what he has to get used to. Otherwise the intolerably intense desire will throw him into an accelerating sequence of panics. We could even assume that they will have retro-active effects on his memory. They might destroy memory traces. They might erase cathexes so that, bit by bit, cumulatively, the feeding breast disappears from his mind.

This process of invalidation of cathexis may be called unlearning or, better, repression, or counter-cathexis. It is automatic. The infant does not intend to do it. He has no choice, for it happens to him. This process is repression in its most primitive form.

This form is so primitive that we wonder whether it exists at all. It might be equivalent to death, but even if it does exist it might no longer occur when the infant is weaned at the age of six months or later. Derivative desires have been formed by that time and other objects such as the bottle or the infant's own hands have been cathected. As a matter of fact, they must have, or panic will be perennial and the child ultimately dies. They can substitute for mother's breast. They will be less satisfying. The desire to suck will not be reduced to zero by bottle feeding, and therefore the infant will be "hungry" again sooner than before, But if he can suck his fist right afterwards and tease his mother, say, into carrying or holding him longer than usual, things may soon be all right. If weaning should occur before any derivative desires and substitute objects have been formed, repression in its most primitive form may be the only way out. The same would hold when a desire drops out (becomes impossible to satisfy) that simply does not have an adequate substitute. An infant may, e.g. turn blind. His desire to look may be deprived for ever.

This will be elaborated below. For the time being we have been side-tracked and should get back. We have said that deprivation of a desire beyond a certain point—of time or intensity—triggers off alarm or anxiety which may grow to full-fledged panic if nothing changes. We have also indicated that alarm or anxiety can be understood and used by an individual as a signal of danger, the danger being his own panic. In either case alarm or anxiety has been viewed as a direct consequence of deprivation of a desire beyond a certain point. Now one may wonder whether that is the only condition under which alarm or anxiety and eventual panic can arise. My answer is Yes. But what about alarm or anxiety as a consequence of an objective danger, or as a consequence of physical pain? Is that not what anxiety means even by common sense?

Well, common sense is certainly right in a common sense, but not necessarily in every sense. Not that I want to deny the existence of objective danger. But what is it in the first place, psychologically speaking? How does it come about? How can such a concept be formed in an individual? Let us remember that the child of two years of age is not afraid to crawl around on the window-sill of an open window of his home, an apartment on the tenth floor of a sky-scraper. However, we will not let him do so. Even the child of three is not afraid of traffic and might walk right into a busy highway. And let us remember that this same child may be afraid of a lion, although it is safe behind bars, or even afraid of a dog, although we know the dog to have been nothing but sweet and friendly.

And the child of two may be afraid to be left alone for half an hour, while we, his parents, know that there is no danger in that. As a matter of fact, the infant of one year of age may scream desperately over such an occasion, thinking, perhaps, that they are going to let him starve to death, while his mother is already preparing a nice meal for him in the kitchen with haste and knows that there is not the slightest danger of that sort.

Danger is always *perceived* danger. Threat, as we may also say, is perceived threat. As such it is related to what the individual has done and experienced. More precisely: it is always related to desires. Danger is any situation in which one, some, many or all of one's desires are impossible to satisfy. That is, as far as the individual can tell. This covers a wide range of situations. Let us inspect a few examples.

If a person accustomed to smoking regularly and heavily goes all by himself on a camping trip to the virgin forests of Canada, he may be in danger of running out of cigarettes. Therefore he is likely to take precautions. He would take several cartons along. He would have to get hopelessly stuck with his jeep in order to really come into trouble with smoking. He may be in a similar danger having to make a longer trip on a bus or plane where smoking happens to be forbidden. There is only one desire involved. Yet its deprivation beyond a certain point is a danger or threat. It entails anxiety or alarm that may mount to panic or something close to it.

If a person is driving a car downhill and notices that his brakes are not working, he is in danger too. This situation implies possible collision with rocks, a building or another car, getting injured, possibly being killed. Collision will imply wreckage of the car. Getting injured may mean losing an arm and hence being incapable of handling things, washing, dressing, writing, etc. with the same ease as before. Certain desires cannot even be satisfied without another person's help. Think of driving, or eating with knife and fork. One might also—believe it nor not—lose one's legs. This implies incapacity to walk, run, climb stairs, hike through mountains and forests, play tennis, football, dance, etc. Both injuries imply being mutilated, ugly, a cripple, unattractive, even repulsive, and all of these may have drastic effects on one's relations with other people, foremost with one's spouse-to-be, husband or wife. Finally one may even be killed—to drag the story still further—and that means not only being deprived of gratification of all desires mentioned, but of all desires whatsoever that a person has developed, and of all objects he has established in his mind, including parents, siblings, spouse and children. The entire world and all one can do in it will be lost for good.

This is not saying that the person in danger should be fully aware of all this. Yet the degree of danger that he perceives himself to be in will be a function of what he might lose. A person who thinks he has less to lose will be less alarmed in a given situation. Consequently people with supposedly less to lose—above all with no spouse and children—are more likely to volunteer for dangerous enterprises. In turn, dangerous enterprises such as combat-flying, parachuting, Arctic or tropical expeditions, secret service in enemy land, etc. tend always to be on the look-out for such volunteers.

The degree of danger that a person perceives is also a function of the abruptness with which the situation changes into a dangerous one. Failure of the brakes on a downhill drive would be a very sudden change of the situation. Danger "jumps" on the driver. Our plane-wrecked pilot, on the other hand, may even enjoy his situation for a day or two, assuming that he must be discovered and rescued any moment. Thereafter, however, he will not only be miserably thirsty, but also afraid of never seeing his home and family again, never sitting in his garden in the evening, plunging into the cool blue pond nearby and into the ocean over weekends, or never even drinking a glass of ice-cold lemonade. Danger "creeps up" on him. Somebody might even say that, in the pilot's case, danger is determined by the absence of a change of situation. No change in some respect, however, does not mean that the psychological situation remains unchanged. The pilot remains unrescued, yes. But he gets hungrier, thirstier, lonelier all the time. If that is not a change of the situation . . .!

The point of the matter is that so-called objective danger is a situation in which one's desires, a few, many, or all, become impossible to satisfy. That is, unless one succeeds in doing something about it. Objective danger is not principally different from deprivation of desires beyond a certain point of time or intensity. In either case alarm or anxiety is triggered off and will increase to panic unless the situation changes after all or substitute desires can be satisfied instead.

How does the concept of stress fit in this context ? Well, all danger is stress. What is usually referred to as stress, however, is a more prevailing condition. Stress is a kind of protracted danger or threat, if you like. Being locked up in a tiny, dark prison cell for weeks—and not just for a few hours, which may still be a kind of fun—or being in combat under difficult circumstances—rain, cold, dirt, no social gatherings, no girls (or boys, in the case of females), little food, plus the danger of being injured or killed—would be stress situations all right. But even a much milder condition, psychologically speaking, such as having to pay monthly installments on a huge debt for the next two, or say twenty years could be a stress for the person in question. Will he always be able to pay them ? Even an examination coming on, or a difficult negotiation may be a stress. In fact, any situation triggering off anxiety or alarm at all could be called a stress. Which leaves us with the notion that stress is no absolute thing. It can have any number of degrees of severity, depending on the degrees of danger involved.

But what about pain ? one might say. What about anxiety as a consequence of physical pain ? At the risk of becoming seriously boring I must take the same tack again. What is physical pain in the first place ? The infant is immune to pinching, even to a hard one, or to needle pricks. We adults are surprised about that, because we would consider such things painful. A year later our little one may poke his finger into his eye, grit his teeth, bite on a piece of metal or glass, scratch and break his finger nails or walk in shoes that have a screw inside, and not utter a sound of pain. Yet even the thought of some of these things will send us shivers down our backs. On the other hand, the infant may scream at the top of his lung, because he got himself caught in the blanket, because of a sudden noise, or even because he is a little hungry. Yet we would think that being caught in a blanket deprives him only of a little bit of free movement. There seems to be no pain involved. Nor is there in a sudden noise, and hunger is not exactly painful even when we have had it for quite a while.

I am not talking pain away. Anybody who ever had a toothache would not let me. But I am trying to point out its relativity. Examples could be multiplied. In combat painful injuries are sometimes not felt at all. I happen to know of a young ex-lieutenant who got his arm amputated without anesthesia while talking glowingly about the ongoing battle. On the other hand, sitting through a boring play may become intolerably painful, so much so that we have to flee at last after itching and wriggling unsuccessfully for two hours. Finally it is worth mentioning that even the most extreme pain can be alleviated temporarily by "counter-acting" it violently, by biting on exactly that tooth which is sore, by clamming up, tightening all the muscles, by screaming at the top of one's voice and finally by throwing an absolute tantrum. As long as such a counter-action is on, the pain seems to be gone.

The point of the matter is this: Physical pain is only one aspect of pain. We were all unable to distinguish it in our first weeks and months of life, but we have learned to identify it as "physical" in the course of our development. Pain in general accompanies any loss of anything that we have already begun to have. It accompanies any trauma, as we might also say, if we understand that a trauma may have any number of degrees of severity, and that any loss whatsoever could be called a trauma. Pain is associated with deprivation of any desire or any number of them, beyond that point of intensity at which anxiety is triggered off. Or in other words: All anxiety is painful. I would go as far as to say: All anxiety is physically painful. Literal physical pain, on the other hand, is a deprivation of a desire. Toothache, e.g. deprives us of the satisfaction of the desire to be physically painfree in the literal sense. This desire has been satisfied continuously almost all our life, excluding short interruptions due to previous toothaches, headaches, bellyaches, bruises, cuts, etc. Therefore even a short deprivation is alarming. It has become quite similar to breathing in that respect. However, breathing had to be satisfied continuously from birth on in order even to keep us alive, whereas the desire to be painfree in the literal or specific sense took a little longer to develop and circumstances that constitute a deprivation tended soon to have a wider range.

Other points could be made. For one thing, no matter what we desire to do and no matter how we act, pain might not go away. Something like morphine may be the only remedy. Also there is no physical pain that would not turn pleasant if stimulation were only a little milder. That applies even to a toothache that comes on only when the tooth is being touched in a certain way. We soon find ourselves touching it every now and again before, out of sheer reason, we decide to consult the dentist. A bellyache, in a milder form, may be the fine feeling of a full belly and a bruise may stem from the excessive pressure of something that we might otherwise call a pat on the head. Stimulation, in turn, is always satisfaction of some desires. Therefore we may say that we even *desire* pain in its mild form. Think of a loving squeeze, a spicy goulash, hot tea or an orgy of back-scratching. However, let us not complicate the issue beyond what is necessary.

Hence, pain too, even in its strictly physical sense, is not principally different from anxiety which, in turn, is the immediate, automatic consequence of deprivation of desires beyond a certain point of intensity or time. Granted, however, that physical pain, once it has been distinguished from any other pain, is often the simplest and most fool-proof indicator of something like objective danger.

One may ask at last: What is that certain point you have been harping on for a while now, the point, at or just beyond of, which deprivation of desires triggers off anxiety? Can you be a little more specific about it? Well, if I have to, we could define it as that intensity of a desire, or that length of deprivation, which has never been reached before under comparable circumstances. We shall see, however, that intensity increments of desires change with development. They decrease. And we shall also see that the lengths of deprivations that are tolerated on the average by a given individual increase with development (see pp. 26, 93f). This would have to be considered in calculating the point in question. Besides comparable circumstances may often be difficult to obtain. After all, a multitude of desires is involved in our behavior. They are all increasing in intensity from zero or close to zero right after satisfaction to intensities at which they are usually satisfied again, and past those, and they meet widely different degrees of opportunity of satisfaction during any given period of time. Therefore the point of intensity of any particular desire at which anxiety is triggered off may not be easy to establish in practice, to say the least.

However, anxiety mounts, if the condition of deprivation lasts. It mounts as a direct function of the increase of the deprived desire. In fact, one could even say that the growing disequilibrium in a person's state of motivation is equivalent to mounting anxiety or, at least, to a major aspect of it, and that a great disequilibrium is not principally different from any disequilibrium at all. Since, furthermore, being alive means being motivated, and being motivated being in disequilibrium, our question of the point at which anxiety is triggered off might be a moot one altogether. There is always anxiety, no matter how negligibly small, one could say. Yet we shall see that our distinction does have theoretical and practical value. Only a disequilibrium of a certain degree or greater, has specific consequences, such as the eventual renunciation of the desire through "defense" or attempts at satisfaction through "aggression". Besides, even when we cannot easily catch the point at which anxiety is being triggered off, we can always catch it sooner or later thereafter.

Counter-Cathexis or Defense

DEFENSE or counter-cathexis is "unlearning" of conditions under which given desires can no longer be satisfied. This is achieved by cathexis of substitute conditions or by satisfaction of substitute desires, or both. Counter-cathexis is cathexis of what is left after desires have become impossible to satisfy henceforth. It prevents the occurrence of anxiety. Only exceptionally high degrees of opportunity to satisfy counter-cathected desires can arouse anxiety again and precipitate further counter-cathexis. One may say that, like cathexis, counter-cathexis is a function of the Ego. It is that function by which a person learns not to try situations that have led to excessive deprivation and anxiety. The counter-cathected desires as a whole can be said to form the Id in its narrower sense, or the unconscious Id. Cathexis as an on-going process has stopped with these desires, whereas with all others it has not.

*   *   *

We have already indicated that anxiety, once aroused, will mount to full-fledged panic, provided that nothing happens to stop it. Panic has an erasing effect on cathexis. The object of the desire involved tends to crumble a little. This is the beginning of the process of repression. If deprivation of the desire involved persists, panic will recur, and if that happens often enough, the object of the desire will eventually "collapse" altogether. It will be blotted out from the person's psychological world. Repression has been achieved and the object is annulled, psychologically speaking (see p. 16).

Repression of this kind is the most primitive of all counter-cathexes or defenses. We shall see that all other forms of counter-cathexes or defenses use, among other things, substitution of another object or of a derivative desire. Repression in its most primitive form does not. However, this kind of repression is also hard to find. It is almost contingent upon death. Suppose a baby has to be weaned from the bottle and the breast at two weeks of age because of some unlucky illness that permits only intravenous or ventral feeding. What on earth can this baby substitute for sucking? It would seem nothing. Yet on closer inspection we would find that he can, of course, suck "his own mouth". He can move his lips, jaws and tongue, will produce saliva and can fool around with that even if he cannot swallow; he does have some substitute after all.

C

We have said that the process of cathexis, or cathecting, means "learning how to like, to appreciate, to love" (see p. 9). Correspondingly, the process of counter-cathexis, or counter-cathecting, means "learning how to avoid" or "learning how to fear". Avoid what? Avoid what has been cathected so far. In paraphrase: You may have had fun with it, say, with mother's breast, but you will no longer. Change your course of action. Search for something else! "Why?" the victim asks. Well, remember that mother's breast has been available neither last night nor last noon nor last morning nor the day before. "But it has been ever available until then!" That is why you cling so desperately to the bottle that they have given you instead. As if you could, thereby, summon mother's breast to emerge from the bottle.

Counter-cathecting in its most primitive form would be literal un-learning. Generally, however, it is learning where and when not to try to learn any more. In fact, even its most primitive form is probably somewhat of that nature. And how does it come about?

At the root of it is a desire that has become impossible to satisfy for one reason or another; be it that mother simply does not have any more milk of her own, or be it that a heavy smoker with a heart condition is told that he must not smoke. In one case there is no alternative. In the other there is one, but then there is no alternative with respect to something else. Tobacco shops are loaded with cigarettes, and a few cents will buy them, but if he does so and continues smoking, he will die.

The desire will grow in intensity, like all desires that have been satisfied recurrently until that day, and reach a point at which it was usually satisfied before. Now, however, nothing happens. There are other things around. There is bottle milk and, in the other case, there are plenty of candies and chewing gums for sale. But our heroes are looking for something else, and time does not stop. Consequently, the intensities of their desires increase further. From a certain point on our heroes get anxious. What is worse, anxiety will continue to mount until it reaches the volume of panic. Under such a prospect and, so to speak, pressed from every corner of the system, our heroes will take to reason and accept the bottle or candies. Something second rate, if it is available, is better than nothing at all.

Satisfaction of a substitute desire can do something for the original desire. In fact, a desire that can do something for another desire *is* a substitute desire. It can reduce the other's intensity to a certain extent, although not by as much as satisfaction of the original desire would. Sucking the bottle satisfies sucking mother's breast, and so does eating candies with the desire to smoke. Yet, neither one of the original desires is fully satisfied or, in other words, reduced to zero intensity. Consequently, the desires to suck mother's breast or to smoke a cigarette will be back to their old intensities sooner than before. Therefore, the infant will need the bottle more often than he needed mother's breast and the ex-smoker-to-be may eat more candies than he ever smoked cigarettes.

There is an additional trouble. The substitute desire has had its own rate of recurrence before it was called upon for help. Now it is satisfied more frequently than before. This implies that it loses satisfaction value. It is being satisfied before it has reached that intensity at which it was usually satisfied before. There is less intensity to be reduced by satisfaction. Concretely speaking: the bottle tasted wonderfully when given once a day in addition to regular breast-feeding, and a piece of candy may be gorgeous for a smoker once a week. However, the bottle loses much of its taste when offered five times a day, and so do candies that one eats in a row.

If that happens, if a substitute desire that has come to the original desire's rescue, loses satisfaction value, it needs help in turn. Sucking the pacifier, e.g., and sucking the fist may be called upon by the infant, and our ex-smoker may resort to drinking lemonade, coffee and say humming songs in addition to his fervor for candies. All these extra desires will also lose satisfaction value as they are called upon more frequently than before.

It would be difficult to pursue the changes in detail that the drop-out of a desire produces on various substitute desires. What we might say, however, is that the *substitution continuum* or drive system as a whole is affected. Some desire will recur more frequently. Its interval between successive satisfactions will become smaller or, in other words, its intensity increment will increase (rate of intensity increase is a reciprocal function of the interval between successive satisfactions; see also p. 26 f). What is worse: this "acceleration" spreads out. Other desires will be affected too. The *substitution continuum* as a whole will end up "accelerated".

That is, the *substitution continuum* or drive system will reach some kind of balance after all. Until then, however, we may say that anxiety prevails. The individual in question will try to satisfy substitute desires in a more haphazard fashion and sequence. Satisfactions will be sought under inappropriate conditions. That means that control over desires will be lessened. Desires will become more primitive (see also p. 57 f). The infant may try to suck anything at all that he can get hold of, and the ex-smoker-to-be may chew on or fumble with pencil, pen, note-book, tie, keys, a rubber band and what not in between more frantic meals, drinks, and candies.

For the sake of conceptual clarity it may be worth risking a little further elaboration (see also Toman, 1957). We can characterise a *substitution continuum*, among other ways, as

$$\sum_{i=1}^{n} \epsilon_i = c \qquad (1)$$

In this formula ϵ_1 stands for intensity increment of desire 1, say, sucking mother's breast, ϵ_2 for that of desire 2, say, sucking the bottle, ϵ_3 for that of sucking the thumb, etc.; n stands for number of desires that constitute the *substitution continuum* in question, c is a given quantity. Formula (1) in words: The intensity increments of all n desires that constitute a *substitution continuum* at a given time of development add up to a given quantity c. Since we assumed that the drop-out of one of the desires increases the intensity increments of at least one and possibly all the others of that *continuum*, it would be compatible, in principle, to assume c constant over a given period of time. In fact, this would be the simplest of all possible assumptions about c (see also p. 93 ff). Therefore

$$\sum_{i=1}^{n-1} \epsilon_i = c \qquad (2)$$

In words: The intensity increments of $n-1$ desires that constitute a "decimated" *substitution continuum* add up to c too. However, intensity increments cannot change at the snap of a finger, although they can change slowly. In fact, they do change with development. Formula (2) would not make sense unless we assume that it describes the end-state of the trouble. As long as the *substitution continuum* has not reached the state described by formula (2), it is in "acceleration". Anxiety prevails. To the extent that the *substitution continuum* approaches formula (2), anxiety declines. Anxiety is zero and defense or counter-cathexis has been established, when this state is reached.

This is not the only way in which counter-cathexis or defense can be brought about. It is also possible to form new derivative or substitute desires. Our ex-smoker may begin to carry an empty pipe in his mouth and, say, chew gums in addition to eating candies. And the baby may take to sucking a little teddy-bear, the blanket and the pillow-case, neither of which he has done before. In such a case formula (2) would have to be replaced by formula (3), namely

$$\sum_{i=1}^{n-1+m} \epsilon_i = c \qquad (3)$$

whereby m represents the number of desires that are newly recruited for the *substitution continuum*.

Both formulas, (2) and (3), describe the state of affairs when anxiety has become zero and counter-cathexis or defense has been established. Formula (2)—which, incidentally, is formula (3) when m is zero—describes the end-state of a "decimated" *continuum* while no new substitute desires are being added. "Acceleration" has come to an end, but the end-state is somewhat accelerated itself compared to the state of the *continuum* just before decimation occurred. The *continuum* has assumed a lower level of functioning. It has "regressed" to an earlier state of its development. Formula (3) describes the end-state of a decimated *continuum* to which new substitute desires have been recruited. This end-state may or may not be accelerated compared to the state before decimation occurred. ϵ_k may be larger than $\sum_{i=1}^{m} \epsilon_i$, whereby ϵ_k is the intensity increment of the desire that has dropped out. However, since derivative-formation occurs all the time, and since the number of desires that can be distinguished on a *substitution continuum* increases steadily in the process of development, m must eventually become so large that $\epsilon_k = \sum_{i=1}^{m} \epsilon_i$, and larger. In fact, only then is the disturbance really overcome.

Before we meet those of our readers again who left us on page 25, I would like to take up two issues that the critical reader may want to raise. Are you assuming, he might ask, that the intensity increments of the desires that constitute a *substitution continuum* become smaller on the whole, as the *continuum* "matures"? Yes. I would even formulate it the other way around: As derivative desires are formed or, in other words, as a *substitution continuum* of a given c increases in number of desires that constitute it, and as, according to formula (1), the intensity increments decrease, we say that the *continuum* grows or matures.

The other issue concerns the intensity increments themselves. Is there not a measurement problem? How can we possibly get hold of something like the intensity increment of a desire without looking into the brain of the person. Well, if we were to wait for that, we probably might not live long enough to see it. But things are not quite as tough. It has already been pointed out that intensity increments are in a reciprocal relationship to the intervals between successive satisfactions of a desire (see p. 25). Hence, if a person's average interval between successive cigarettes is 2 hours (a *datum* that should not be too difficult to obtain), the average intensity increment per hour will be one half. If the interval between successive cups of coffee is 8 hours, the intensity increment will be one-eighth. We can also estimate the intensity increments of a desire from the range of intervals (i.e. the difference between the largest and smallest interval) between a given number of successive satisfactions of that desire. The intensity increments estimated by means of these ranges will also be their reciprocals.

One may finally wonder at this point, how we can possibly add different desires such as, say, a desire to smoke and a desire to have a cup of coffee. That is, after all, what formula (1) requires. Is that not like adding apples and plums? Well, we are not adding desires, but their intensity increments. Furthermore they are supposed to be on the same *substitution continuum* and able to do something for the *continuum* and for each other. Both, smoking and drinking coffee, are forms of sucking. Something like "sucking" or "oral satisfaction" could be the common denominator. Thirdly, their increments, as estimated empirically, say, from the average interval between successive satisfactions, are expressed as a fraction of that intensity, at which the desire is usually satisfied. That intensity is unity. In 1 hour the desire to smoke will increase to one half, and the desire to drink coffee to one eighth of that intensity which, in our example, "mobilises action". This mobilisation of action or of satisfaction, no matter which kind, could also be the common denominator, just as "fruit" or "weight" might be the term under which we could add apples and plums after all. For further reasons see p. 93 ff.

We have shown how a *substitution continuum* or drive system from which a desire has dropped out can regain its equilibrium, i.e. establish counter-cathexis or defense, no matter whether on a lower level than before or on the same level. If no new substitute desires are recruited for the one that has dropped out, the *substitution continuum* will "regress". "Acceleration" or anxiety will come to a stop, but the *substitution continuum* will be on a lower level. It will remain somewhat more accelerated than it was just before decimation occurred, that is just before the desire dropped out. Only when new substitute desires are recruited or, more precisely, only when the newly recruited desires are powerful and/or numerous enough to make up for the deficit, can the *substitution continuum* be restored to its state before decimation. And since new derivatives are being formed all the time in the course of a person's development, the latter is likely to happen eventually. In either case, however, counter-cathexis or defense will be established.

But can one not give up desires without a deficit? Can one not simply outgrow them? In principle, no. We would assume that any desire that has ever formed on a *substitution continuum* is there for keeps unless it *has* to be dropped. Then, however, counter-cathexis is indispensible. If the infant were not weaned, e.g., he would continue to desire to drink from mother's breast, if only once a month or even less often at last. Should a desire that has formed find a substitute that is more gratifying than it was itself, then it may seem to disappear. Adolescent masturbation, for example, tends to be given up in favor of heterosexual intercourse once the latter has begun to be enjoyed. But all it takes to revive it would be some deprivation of heterosexual intercourse beyond the usual or rather maximal intervals. So it has not really been "outgrown". While a counter-cathected desire, whether it is drinking from mother's breast or masturbation, would not be sought to satisfy even under extreme conditions of deprivation.

It is not too difficult to deduce some of the relationships implicit in what has been said so far. First of all, the drop-out of a desire—which is, to give a reminder, the impossibility to satisfy it in the future, when so far it could be satisfied—well, the drop-out of a desire will be the more severe, the closer that desire is to the primal or original desire of the *substitution continuum*. The closer it is to the "father" of the *continuum*, the greater will be its satisfaction value, and the more difficult will it be to make up for the loss, i.e. to end anxiety and to establish counter-cathexis or defense. The worst would be the loss of "father" himself. However, that happens rarely. A child who loses mother's breast will nevertheless continue to suck, whether bottle, pacifier or pillow-case. Sucking mother's breast was already a derivative—although an early one—of the desire to suck, no matter what. The point is, however, that losing mother's breast will be more difficult to make up for than losing the pillow-case. Or, to take another and much more complex *substitution continuum*, people: the loss of mother will be much more difficult to make up for than the loss of an aunt or a nurse (provided that aunt or nurse have not become "mothers" and mother a "stranger" in the child's eyes). Aunt or nurse, in turn, may be more difficult to replace than, say, a teacher.

"Closer" refers to the power of substitution. The more a desire can do to satisfy the original desire (although, by definition, it cannot satisfy it completely), the closer it is. In fact, the more it can do to satisfy any desire "before" it on the *substitution continuum*, the closer is it to that desire. "Closer", however, may also refer to time of genesis and frequency of satisfaction. The closer a desire to the original desire, other things being equal, the earlier in life must it have been formed and/or the more frequently must it have been satisfied.

Another relationship that we can deduce exists between the drop-out of a desire and the size of the *substitution continuum* in question. The greater the *continuum* has become in the course of its development, or the more derivative desires it comprises, the smaller will be the effect of loss of a given one. Weaning will be easier when the infant is already able to suck the bottle, the pacifier, his fist, a doll and the blanket, than if he can just suck the bottle and the pacifier. To lose a friend of a given intimacy will be easier for a person who has thirty others than, other things being equal, for a person who has only three. Even losing the best friend will be easier for the first than for the second.

Still another relationship that we can deduce is this: The more desires have already dropped out in a *substitution continuum*, and the more recently they have done so, the more difficult will it be to cope with the loss of a given one. If a smoker must not only give up smoking, but also sweets, milk, and any form of liquor, he will have more trouble than a person who has to quit just smoking, or a person who had to quit sweets, milk and liquor years ago. Similarly, loss of the third in a row of one's ten friends will be more difficult to handle than the loss of that person alone, or his loss, when the other two dropped out long ago.

One may wonder whether there is not such a thing as a partial loss or drop-out of desires. A desire can, from a certain point of development on, be satisfied under some conditions only, but not under others. That is possible, of course. In such a case, however, we will be dealing with two desires before too long, one that can be satisfied, and one that cannot. This would be easy in weaning. Finally sucking mother's breast will have dropped out, whereas sucking the bottle and others remain. And it would be more difficult when, say, a mother is inconsistent. Sometimes she lets the child have candies during a morning and at other times not. But even then a distinction will emerge as long as there is consistency from some angle or the desire will drop out even though it *could* be satisfied at times and occasions.

Since control over desires is a function of derivative formation, and since both of them are a function of cathexis, we may say the following: The more cathexis has been formed within a *substitution continuum*, the easier will it generally be to establish a given counter-cathexis or defense. As a matter of fact, this would not only hold for a particular *continuum*, but for all *continua* that a person has established, or for the person as a whole.

Like cathexis (see p. 9), counter-cathexis is an automatic process over which the individual does not have any direct control. Therefore it cannot be undone at his discretion, even though the situation may have changed. The desire that had been counter-cathected because it had become unobtainable may be objectively capable of satisfaction again. For the individual in question, however, it remains unobtainable. This is precisely what counter-cathexis does. It obliterates those aspects of the world that the individual *believes* inaccessible. Counter-cathexis has been successful for the weaned child, if he believes that there is no breast, or at least no feeding breast; and it has been successful for the ex-smoker, if he thinks and acts as if there were no cigarettes whatsoever anywhere, at least for him.

It is obvious, then, that an unexpectedly or unusually high degree of opportunity to satisfy such a counter-cathected desire may set the red light of anxiety blinking again. This is what is meant by a "seductive" situation. For a moment the individual may think that, perhaps, there is a chance to get the "deprived of" after all. This possibility would overthrow the balance established in the *substitution continuum* or, in other words, it would overthrow counter-cathexis. The desire whose deprivation was intolerable enough to trigger off anxiety and precipitate the establishment of counter-cathexis some time ago, has remained deprived ever since. That should not *decrease* its intensity. In fact, admitting to it at all may make it so painfully intense and bring the individual so close to panic in such a short time, that even the highest degree of opportunity to satisfy the desire may not work rapidly enough to quench it in time. If satisfaction should materialise, by a surprise attack or what not, a first step toward the removal of counter-cathexis may have been taken. Anxiety which has disappeared with the establishment of counter-cathexis will be revived, but if it is not too severe, the counter-cathected desire may, often under tears, become a member of the *substitution continuum* again. It may be on probation, but it would be in. The child may dare, for instance, to insist on taking a sip from mother's breast at the time when the little baby-brother is being nursed. Or the ex-smoker may take up smoking after all, although, say, pipe smoking.

Ordinarily, however, the red light of anxiety does its purpose. It signals danger. Something counter-cathected is being tapped on. There has not been enough "learning how to avoid or to fear" (see p. 23 f.) Therefore the pursuit of those desires that brought the person into the seductive situation to begin with must stop. Anxiety precipitates counter-cathexis of those desires. The red light is turned off, when counter-cathexis has been established. The child must stop trying even to look while his little baby-brother is being fed. He must not even see mother's breast. And the ex-smoker must not enter a drugstore nor stay in a smoke-filled room. This has been called the "attraction" which counter-cathexes wield on other (later, or newer) counter-cathexes (see also pp. 31, 38).

Maybe we can venture a first tentative summary of the process of psychological development. Achievement of control over desires, derivative formation and cathexis are steady and continuous processes. As we satisfy desires—and we are always doing that—we are gaining control over conditions of satisfaction, forming new derivatives, and establishing further cathexis. This may already imply drop-outs of desires. All conditions of satisfaction that have been learned to be inappropriate could be called counter-cathected in a certain sense. Sometimes, however, desires drop out in a more specific and radical sense. They have been capable of satisfaction until then, and now they are no longer. That triggers off anxiety which subsides only when counter-cathexis has been established. Counter-cathexis cannot annul previous, but it can prevent all further cathexis. It is learning how to avoid and fear or learning where to learn no more. All of cathexis and counter-cathexis, or at least all of the relevant portions of either, determine how any given situation will be perceived. We scan automatically in terms of where to continue cathecting and counter-cathecting, whereby the crucial cue for the latter is anxiety. Whenever this red light goes on, some counter-cathexis has been insufficient, and additional counter-cathexis is necessary.

As might be expected, the amount of counter-cathexis in relation to the amount of cathexis will give us an important over-all clue of a *substitution continuum's* development. In fact, computing this proportion for all of a person's *substitution continua* will give us an important over-all clue about the person as a whole. It will tell us how much defense has infiltrated a person's world as a whole. However, these matters will concern us at a later time (see also p. 96 f.).

One of the sad things about our discourse on counter-cathexis is that we have been simplifying. Things get more complicated relatively soon after birth. Desires that we identify as such are nearly always on more than one *substitution continuum.* While sucking mother's breast, the infant is also satisfying desires to be touched all over the body, but also to touch (mother) with his own hands, the desire to look, to listen, etc. A smoker does not only suck and inhale cigarettes, but also manipulates them with his hands. If a desire drops out, it leaves more or less of a hole in other *substitution continua* too. Anxiety and subsequent counter-cathexis extend beyond the *continuum* involved in the first place.

This is why a mother can ease weaning for her baby even though she is or may have to be adamant about it. While feeding the bottle she can duplicate the breast-feeding situation as closely as is still possible. She can continue to hold the child rather than handing him the bottle in the crib. She can talk to and handle the child as before, change it from one side to the other (faking the change from one breast to the other). Generally speaking, she can try to stay as much the same person for the child as the changed circumstances permit her to. Similarly, the ex-smoker-to-be can help himself by allowing his hands to be more active. Doodling on a piece of paper, handling the pencil to do it with or even bringing its tail-end to his mouth from time to time for a little (thoughtless) nibble may do a bit of the trick.

This is also why certain *substitution continua* can be affected by counter-cathexis in spite of their apparent irrelevance to the dropped-out desire. The infant may take to the bottle all right after weaning, but keep a peculiar aversion to being lifted or changed from one position to the other. And the ex-smoker may find himself getting over smoking all right, but cannot do so well with his hands any longer. No matter what he tries, he soon becomes too fidgety. As once before (see p. 30), we may say that counter-cathexes "attract" other counter-cathexes.

In general we might say that drop-outs of desires are always drop-outs of objects too (see also p. 9 ff.), and objects are invariant conditions under which desires of *different substitution continua* can be satisfied. Therefore the drop-out or loss of an object will be more severe, i.e. more difficult to substitute, the greater the number of different *substitution continua* that is affected, and the more severely they are decimated (the closer the dropped-out desires are to their respective primal desires, and the greater, relative to all desires already formed, the number of desires affected). More about this later. The chapter on quantitative aspects (see p. 92 ff.) will provide some ideas about how to treat more than one *substitution continuum*, or even how to treat all of a person's *substitution continua* at once, at least in principle. And the second part of the book, "The Theory at Work", will implement the matter *expressis verbis* as well as by implication.

One may wonder at this point once more, what all this has got to do with Ego and Id. Well, both cathexis and counter-cathexis are functions of the Ego. They are, in fact, *the* functions of the Ego. By means of cathexis the Ego manages to make well-behaved citizens out of savages or to control primitive desires so that they can be satisfied under an ever increasing range of conditions. One may even say: the Ego builds up a person's world or reality in which desires can be satisfied. By means of counter-cathexis it manages to arrest those desires that have one day become incapable of satisfaction. These desires form the Id in a specific sense, or the "unconscious" Id, whereas the other portion of the Id is in harmony with the Ego. It is "conscious" Id and, therefore, Ego. And there is not even a clear border that separates them. Between the unconscious Id and the conscious Id (which the Ego has undertaken to satisfy) or Ego there are all those desires that can be satisfied under some, many or almost all, but not under other conditions. They are counter-cathected too, although to very different degrees. Accordingly they are "conscious" to a greater or lesser extent, or can become so with greater or lesser ease. Those desires that have become incapable of satisfaction under any circumstances are highly "unconscious" and can be made conscious only with great difficulty or, in other words, against great "resistance". They are the unconscious Id in a radical sense, or the core of the unconscious Id in a broader version. (See also the chapter "A Comment on Consciousness", p. 72 ff.)

I hate to juggle terms that way after a treatise of some kind of precision, but this has been their traditional fate. Readers who are familiar with psychoanalytic literature have been accustomed to thinking in animistic ways about such things as the Id and the Ego, and I would at least *try* not to lose them. I even suspect some secret and implicit wisdom in the juggling as well as in the animisms. Most experts have a better working knowledge of psychoanalytic theory than they could possibly convey in a discussion or in a systematic treatise. They have been taking care of conceptual inconsistencies in some fashion without being able to tell how. There may be as much wisdom, however, in articulating this secret and implicit wisdom. After all, not everybody is in the fortunate position of those experts. Some only *think* they have got such a theory in their heads, and others do not even think so.

Whilst on this subject, I may as well take up another notion that the reader would know from psychoanalytic literature: the notion of primary and secondary process (Freud, 1900, esp. ch. 7; also Rapaport, 1951). Where do they fit? Well, we can equate primary process to primitive desire and secondary process to controlled desire with all that these terms, in turn, entail. One may object on the grounds that primary and secondary process refers to thought rather than action. They are cognitive rather than dynamic terms. Well, there just is not anything cognitive that would not be something dynamic too. Thought is wish, was among Freud's first and most ingenious mottoes. There is, in principle, no thought without a specific desire, just as there is no desire without some cognitive concept of the conditions under which it can, or could, be satisfied. This is at least how these terms have been understood and defined by Freud.

Let me give an example, not to prove the point, but to illustrate what is meant. A person who has been deprived of food and wants to eat very badly is likely to think about food, to have images of all kinds of simple and fancy dishes pass through his mind and to talk about food, if there is a person to talk to. The idea of food pre-occupies him. This, however, is the automatic consequence of the desire to eat, once it has mounted to a certain intensity.

Let me also give an example of the other extreme, a desire of so slight an intensity that we have to put ourselves to work in order to trace it. Say, in the midst of a coffee-break conversation about the economic situation in England one of the discussants notices much to his surprise that a thought of strawberries had flashed through his mind. Where did it come from? Well, as they were talking about the (then, i.e. 1957) declining exports of British cars, which he regretted or, in other words, which he wanted to counter-act, he had an inkling of a thought of helping by consuming British goods. But what? To buy a British car was far too much of an expense. May be, he could buy something little, a bottle of whiskey, or food, strawberries perhaps. "But that is ridiculous. We do not import strawberries from England. Oh, we do import Old English Strawberry Preserves, and they are better and cheaper than the American equivalent." He had sometimes wondered when eating them before: How do they do it? How can they produce them so cheaply? Do they have such an abundance of strawberries? Maybe they stumble across them wherever they go. And here is where the image of strawberries came in.

Although the idea of strawberries seemed to come from nowhere and certainly from no desire, there was a desire behind it after all. In fact, a number of desires. One was to help the British, for whatever reasons. It was controlled by a few others: Do not offend them by a gift. Buy something from them that you can use. And do not waste money. Spend just a little, since you cannot afford more. All of which fuses into: purchase a little bit from the British. With this desire the discussant scans possibilities, rejects a car, may be a suit or shoes too, rejects even whiskey although he has come on a good track: edibles. Then he hits upon strawberry preserves which he loves, yet they may be too little to really help the British. Unless, of course, strawberries do not cost them anything at all, because they are in such abundance. Thus the final desire is to get their strawberries. Which should not mean that they really have them in abundance. I just would not know.

But is there not knowledge involved, knowledge of the world, of geography, economics, food, etc.? Of course there is. But knowledge is the result of cathexis and cathexis occurs as we satisfy desires. Knowledge is certainly not equivalent to desires, but we only come to experience that we have knowledge as we satisfy desires, and every satisfaction of a desire, no matter how small a satisfaction it is, adds a little more to our knowledge of the world. In fact, the world or "reality" *is* our knowledge of it, as has been pointed out before (p. 13). It is ever increasing, which might suggest that there is an objective or "real" reality from which to draw. Our knowledge, or our concept of reality, matches it better and better, as we grow up, but we can never fully succeed. Some physicist even claimed that the size of the unknown increases with the amount of what we know.

One may object that our discussant has not really satisfied a desire. He has not yet bought the strawberry preserves. All right, but he has done something else. He has done everything that he is willing and able to do at the moment. He has found a solution. He will, or may at least, remember this solution when he eats or misses his next strawberry dish, or when he passes by the preserves shelves of a foodstore the next time.

One may also object—or have objected a while ago—to the statement that we learn as we satisfy desires. What desires am I satisfying when I study chemistry or rather when I keep some particular formula in mind, say, of some nuclein-acid in which I have no interest at all? Well, why are you trying to keep it in mind in the first place? I need it for the examination. But then you want to pass the examination, and that is a desire. Yes, but I learn many other formulas with the same desire and the desire will not be satisfied until two months from now. Our young man is certainly correct. But there are other desires that he is satisfying right then. He is probably in a nice and quiet room, in a comfortable temperature and position, in an armchair, say, or at a desk, perhaps also walking up and down as he looks at the formula, talking aloud or to himself, maybe, writing or drawing it in his mind or on a piece of paper. All these desires are probably being satisfied to some small degrees as he learns the formula. In fact, satisfying some of these desires is kind of instrumental to "exploring" the formula, tasting it, so to speak, from all angles—tasting how it looks, how it writes, how it sounds—until he discovers that it "sticks". Cathexis has been achieved or an "object" formed: the formula. If we make life tough for the student, if we give him a cold room, tie him to his chair, expose him to loud noise and fill the room with tear gas, he is being deprived of the satisfactions of some very primitive and steadily satisfied desires and, by our reasoning, likely to learn much more poorly. This is indeed what happens.

But does a student of chemistry not take one look at a formula and remember it? That may be true at times. But then he has taken millions of looks at formulas and chemical conditions before, and not only looks. He may know a lot about acids and an even greater lot about proteins by the time he comes across the formula in question. He will compare it to formulas he knows already and just "place" it, so to speak, rather than "build it up", in his mind. He may know so much that this formula is new to him only in a single aspect. Thousand other aspects such as the very use of symbols, the ways in which elements form connections, their positions in the periodic system, their valences, weights, empirical properties, etc., are all familiar. They have all become knowledge.

That holds for everybody in every field. Wherever we remember something new with little or no effort, we have known the overwhelming majority of what there is to be known already. To illustrate that I shall present the reader with a somewhat more unfamiliar task than he is usually faced with, although even here everyone who can speak, read, and count at all has enough previous knowledge. Every sound of the long strange word spelled below has been used by us, spoken, written or read, a million times, and the same holds for the figures of the long strange number shown below. Even the combinations of any two sounds (d–w, w–i, i–l, etc.) or figures (4–0, 0–6, 6–3, etc.) are not new to us. For one thing, any pair of sounds is pronounceable, to say the least, and we can probably find any pair of figures shown below in our note-book of telephone numbers. Both the word and the number are just a little longer than anything like it that we ordinarily have to learn in everyday life. Yet the reader will find it difficult to remember the word or the number. He will be surprised as to how many readings are necessary to reproduce either one correctly, and how quickly they will be forgotten again. It is quite unlikely that a person can do it after one reading only. In fact, the publisher has consented to my request of paying ten dollars to every owner of this book who can remember either or, for the matter of proof, comparable duplicates after one reading. And who would not wish to get ten dollars that easily? Hence there would even be an unquestionable specific interest. May I add that word as well as number have been taken from a book of ancient Eastern magic claiming for either one to be keys to all the wisdoms of the world provided they are never forgotten again. Whoever believes in that claim should have an even greater interest. Here is the word and the number:

dwilabemechkoteisdaupetwoushagu

4063272314968947586870593150251

I hope I have not annoyed the reader. I am ready, in any case, to hear one more objection, namely: "You are giving the patient candidate a task, and a task is not a desire." Well, in order to make it more of a desire ten dollars have been mobilised. Besides, we shall see a little later (p. 90 f), that tasks are desires too, although a special kind. They have been adopted from the "outside world", preferably from other people.

But your candidate is not even *satisfying* that desire while he is supposed to learn a figure or number. He just *has* that desire! Yes, indeed. And that is why he cannot make it.

Defense Mechanisms

DEFENSE mechanisms are specific types of counter-cathexis or defense. The following have been distinguished so far: repression, projection, introjection-identification, sublimation, reaction-formation, regression. Furthermore: displacement, denial, isolation, turning against the self, undoing, reversal, identification with the aggressor, rationalisation, conversion.

*　　　*　　　*

Among the infinite varieties of ways in which counter-cathexis can work on different occasions and with different people, there are some forms that can be easily identified and distinguished from others on qualitative grounds. In fact, they are relatively few. We might compare this state of affairs to the infinite variety of ways in which, say, three, four, five, six, etc. points can be arranged in relation to each other. There are some outstanding arrangements such as that of a triangular position with equal distances from each other, or of a square, a regular pentagon, hexagon, etc. They would correspond to the defense mechanisms. Even so, however, we will attempt to analyse them in terms of the more general framework outlined in the previous chapter as well as to establish their apparent specificity.

Let me enumerate them first: repression, displacement, introjection, sublimation, reaction-formation, identification (a form of introjection, or vice versa) and regression. There is an additional group of defense mechanisms that can be subsumed, in principle, under those mentioned. They are either specific forms and compounds, or specific pathological manifestations. Their names: denial, isolation, turning against the self, undoing, reversal, identification with the aggressor, rationalisation, conversion into a physical manifestation; perhaps also phobia, compulsion, obsession and "acting-out".

Repression has been discussed already to some extent (see pp. 16, 23). In its most primitive form it would take care of a desire that has become unobtainable and does not yet have any substitute or derivative desires. Whatever cathexis has been formed in connection with the desire may be annulled in this case. That is quite rare, though. Besides there may be a question as to whether any cathexis can have taken place if no substitute desire has yet been formed. We have seen that one is a function of the other (see p. 9). For all practical purposes we can treat it as the very rare, if not *a priori* impossible, extreme of the general case of repression in which substitute desires such as sucking the bottle, the pacifier, the fist, etc., take the place of, or make up for, the desire that has become impossible to satisfy, say, sucking mother's breast. When the *substitution continuum* has found its new balance, counter-cathexis is established. The object of the desire, or that aspect of the object which satisfied the desire, has been repressed. It does not exist any more in the person's world, provided repression has been successful. In our example the infant would wish and act as if there were no mother's breast in the whole world, and as if there had never been one.

A more complicated example: A child loses a dog whom he has had for a year. Suppose it was killed by a car and suppose the parents cannot give him another dog. The dog satisfied many different desires, such as touching him, wrestling with him, being recognised, caressed or generally liked by him, feeding him, lying in bed with him, watching him do things, making him yowl, fight another dog or even another child, etc. All these desires which, apparently, are on several different *substitution continua*, become impossible to satisfy, at least with respect to the dog. They drop out, as we have said, and the decimated *substitution continua* have to regain balance. Once counter-cathexis has been established, the dog is "forgotten" or repressed. Anxiety or the "pain of loss" has abated in every one of the *substitution continua* involved. Generally speaking, repression will be the more difficult to achieve, the greater the number of desires that are involved and the greater the amount of cathexis that has already occurred. The more difficult it gets, the more will it take on the character of "mourning". If all repressions have been completed, mourning is over.

One more example to illustrate the process of repression at a later stage of development when, we might say, all basic or primary repressions have been achieved more or less successfully and repressions become necessary thereafter. Think of a girl who has been slighted at a party by another guest. So she feels, at least, and that is what matters psychologically. She has not been given enough attention by the person in question. Say, the person, a respectable older man, has turned away from her in the midst of a comment she was making. A desire has not been satisfied, and circumstances forbid her to try to get that attention by a little push. Hence the desire becomes impossible to satisfy for the time being and, may be, for some time to come. She may feel irritated. However, flinging herself into another on-going argument or even into some little flirtation may quickly get her over the disappointment. She is getting the attention she wanted after all, although from a different person. The *substitution continuum* "being liked"—a rather complex *continuum*, by the way—is in balance again. Yet, as a consequence she may not only have forgotten the incident soon afterwards, but even the name of the person when, the other day, she was asked for them in some other context. She has repressed the person and the event.

The difference between this repression and something like the repression of mother's breast upon weaning is that the latter can hardly be revoked, no matter how hard the person or anybody tries, whereas the former can be lifted relatively easily. A day later the name may be back and even the event, although with a tiny flare of pain. Repression at this later stage may be called after-repression (*Nachverdrängung*). In fact, most of the repressions that we can trace in our daily lives, either by inference or by lifting them a little, are of that nature. Primal repressions are those that are difficult to trace and even more difficult, if not impossible, to lift.

Repressions closer to a primal repression on the *continuum* "being liked" or "being liked by an older male" would be the experience, say, that father was available to our heroine and would pay attention to her provided that there were no guests in the house. If there were any, he was likely to talk shop with them and even send her up to her room. "Father in company"—and even mother's company would be enough—was the condition under which she learned not to try to get his attention. She repressed that particular desire. Had she sought to satisfy it after all, she could have done so only with anxiety (see p. 29f). Repression, in order to remain intact, would have made her even look for a disappointment. That would be a reason not to try. Repression would tend to "teach" her: "This is what happens when you do try. Quit fishing for older men. If you cannot do that, quit older men altogether!" Well, this is precisely what happened to her much later in life at that party.

This state of affairs has been paraphrased as the "attraction" which old repressions (or old counter-cathexes; see pp. 30, 31) wield on younger ones. At this point, however, it would be more accurate to say that old repressions, or counter-cathexes in general, determine together with all pertinent previous cathexes, how a given situation will be perceived in the first place. A neutral event becomes a little trauma and will have to be repressed, or after-repressed, as we might also call it, because a repressed desire had some small opportunity of satisfaction. This ought to be disappointing or a well-established measure against the desire would be rendered silly.

Displacement is the substitution of one desire by another or of one object of satisfaction by another. If I would like to hit my father, but do hit the dog instead (yet, why do I *not* hit my father?), or if I would want to kiss mother (who does not let me), but I kiss my little sister or my teddy-bear instead, I am displacing or substituting. Displacement refers to some acute impossibility to satisfy one desire and its ready substitution by another. There is no reference as to what will become of the desire in the long run. However, there is a reference to the degree of control involved. It is a more primitive desire that gets satisfied, be it for no other reason than that the object matters less than were I to satisfy the original desire. If it is not the dog that I hit, it may be the chair, or I may break a window. If somebody has lost a friend and picks another person for a friend that same day, a person whom he has not known before, we might say he is displacing. We will feel safer calling it so, the less the new-found friend matters as a person and the shorter that new friendship lasts. This should not be confused with an attempt to find another friend after a period of mourning. This would not be called displacement, but rather the search for a new object, which is a long-range and complicated endeavor.

Projection is the substitution of a desire by a "non-existent" external desire, or the transfer of a desire to the "outside world", preferably to other people. A child who is mad at his parents, i.e. who could hit, beat, kick, mutilate or kill them, may one day, or even that very same day, perceive his parents as if they would want to do these very things to him. Or a young and shy secretary who is in love with her boss, but too afraid to do anything about it, may perceive the boss as being in love with her, although trying not to show it to her nor to others. In both cases, a desire within oneself is perceived in the outside world or, more specifically, in another person. This projected desire helps to check the desire within oneself. More precisely speaking: that substitute satisfaction, which is sought in the disguise of another person seems not only to reduce the intensity of the desire within the person to some extent, but also to make it more dangerous to satisfy the desire directly. While the person was wishing intensely for a state of affairs that could not be had, he or she was anxious. And let us remember that anxiety is the direct consequence of a desire that has become too intense. Now that another person is supposedly wishing for the same thing with respect to him or her, there is something to be afraid of. Anxiety meets a reason, so to speak, and becomes fear. Fear of the parents or fear of those forces in the environment that the secretary's boss must fear too. Otherwise he would act on his love. Fear of another person or something outside, however, can be handled more easily than anxiety *per se*. A feared person can, after all, be escaped, whereas anxiety would inevitably come along with the escapist.

Projection, like all defense mechanisms, is automatic and involuntary. We are not aware that this is what we are doing. The child really sees his parents as threatening people, and the secretary really believes that her boss is in love with her. We would not call it projection, if the child were just trying out in his imagination, whether his parents would hit him or, say, put him out in a huge forest because he has been bad. Nor would we call it projection if the secretary thinks about how nice it might be to have her boss in love with her. Nor are we projecting when we try to understand what another person wants. This should rather be called *interpretation* in its most general sense. Only to the extent that we are "off the beam" with what we perceive, may we be projecting.

Projection, almost like displacement, refers to a more or less transitional condition. Repressions are already operating by the time projection becomes necessary. Why should our child, otherwise, not undertake to really hit, beat, etc. his parents? And why should our secretary not make a pass at her boss? Further repressions will take care of the desire that, for the time being, requires projection. The child will either learn that his parents do not want to hit or kill. That implies that he will have repressed his desire to do just that himself. Otherwise he could not permit himself to see them different. Projection would

D

have to be maintained and prevent him from learning any better. His fears would continue beyond reason. Or he may have learned that his parents are indeed quite ready to beat him (because they do), in which case he would have had to repress all those desires in addition that earned him a beating, at least as far as he could tell. Similarly, our secretary will be able to repress her desires better after a while and see that her boss does not at all respond. Or she will become odder and odder in her behavior and perhaps have to quit the job. In which case we should not be surprised to find her on another job in the same situation before too long.

Introjection is the substitution of a desire by an "existent" external desire, or the adoption of a desire of the "outside world", preferably of other people, to replace one's own. The infant wanting mother to suckle him and catching hold of his fist instead (by means of his mouth, that is) will be suckling himself that way and thereby introject mother's desire. He is not only substituting for sucking, but also for suckling. In a sense, he "is" not only himself, but, for the moment, he "is" mother too. If he wants mother to hold him, but she is not around, he may hold one of his hands by the other or—what is more likely and functions earlier in life as well as more safely—take something in his mouth again, preferably his fists, and "hold" them with his mouth. If he wants to hear mother's voice and she is not around, he will produce his own sounds. Since the mouth seems to play such an integral part, introjection in its earliest forms has also been named "oral incorporation". In which case introjection has often been used interchangeably with identification. Whereas otherwise it is frequently introjection that refers to the primitive form, and identification that refers to the later, more complicated and articulate, form of adopting desires of the outside world, preferably of other people. Our main consideration: they are not principally different from each other.

Identification, therefore, will also be the substitution of one's desires by "existent" external desires, although by desires that are more complicated and articulate, and by a method, so to speak, that is more adequate. What the person adopts will come closer to what he means to adopt. A little girl may, e.g., want mother to play with her. Instead mother has work to do in the kitchen. So the little girl may play kitchen herself. In fact, she may do so when mother is not even in the house. If she, the little girl, plays kitchen—and she does so quite well, quite a bit like mother in more than one respect—she *is* mother herself, and her unavailability is less painful. Or a little girl notices what mother can get from father and what she can make him do for her. She would like to be in the same position with father and will, therefore, i.e. for the sake of expediency, try to be like mother in various ways. She will, say, desire to dress orderly rather than sloppily, extravagantly or not at all, to wash without splashes all over the bathroom, to eat properly and not just any old way, to use no bad language, to say "please" and "thank you", to be polite, etc. There are more satisfying ways of dressing, washing, eating, etc. Yet, she would not be mother, or be like her.

Besides the parents and, perhaps, especially father would not like those ways, and that may entail that he would do even less for her, she feels, than he is already doing. She would lose out altogether to mother.

One may wonder what the child does with desires that the parents have for the child, but that they do not entertain themselves. Say, mother wants her girl to speak French as well as behave like, and develop the taste of, a little Parisienne, but she does not even speak French herself. Or she wants her to be a pianist, but she neither plays an instrument herself, nor does she understand anything about music. Well, mother cannot be identified with for those matters. Not only that: the girl, in some likelihood, will neither become a little Parisienne nor much of a pianist, unless, of course, mother provides her with a true Parisienne as a governess or a devoted and enthusiastic piano teacher to spend her life with, or at least a fair part of it. Those would be the people to identify with.

One may also wonder, whether some of these examples were not cases of imitation. While, however, it is external desires that are being adopted in identification, it is more or less just the behavior that is being adopted in imitation. One may doubt, though, whether there is such a thing as behavior without desires involved. In fact, I would doubt it myself. I have indicated already (see p. 3) that we cannot even recognise behavior without hypothesising, inadvertently, the desires that guide it. If we say somebody is running we are naming a complex sequence of behavioral events by the desire that we can make out. We can make out that this somebody wishes to get from one place to the other, to a place ahead of him, faster than usual. There may be more to it. He may run away from a person or try to get to a person. He may be an Olympic candidate training for the marathon race and, therefore, running for its own sake of sorts, or he could even have a kind of an epileptic fit that makes him do that. Yet even then our hypothesis would not be wrong. We would only need to make additional specifications. In fact, we would want them anyway. A person dashing past us in the street will probably arouse our curiosity automatically. We would look, e.g., whether a policeman is coming behind him, or whether he is behind a policeman. Well, not exactly behind a policeman, but behind somebody whom he wants to apprehend for an offense.

So what *would* be the difference between imitation and identification? They are different by degree. A person imitating another is less serious about wanting to be that person or wanting to do what he does instead of something else. A youngster imitating Charlie Chaplin need not really want to *be* him (although one is tempted to ask: why does he pick him to begin with?). In fact, he can stop the game any time, whereas he could not stop identifying with his mother who happens, say, to be a nasty, aggressive person. He would have to adopt her violent, primitive fashion of doing things in order to defend against everything that he cannot get because of such a mother. He would probably continue to "carry that mother within him" even after he has left home and set up one of his own. Imitation is something passing. Identification, like all counter-cathexis, lasts. Desires for tender contact with other people may be counter-cathected by identification with his untender mother, and any effort to satisfy them after all will trigger off anxiety and stop the effort.

Similarly, one may wonder whether identification of an adult person with a football team or, say, a great actress would belong here. In principle, yes. While watching a game, or sitting in a movie theater, we cannot help identifying. But if identification is a defense mechanism, where is the desire that cannot be satisfied? Well, to be on that football team in reality and earn all the glamor and fame and whatever either may entail would be one, and to be that actress, or any actress, as long as she is beautiful and admired by many, or even just admired by many, would be the other of the desires that cannot be, or are not being, satisfied. However, these identifications, too, may be passing affairs, although even a passing identification with a team that has lost may give us trouble for some time after.

Not all identifications of later life are necessarily of that nature. A person who enters an apprenticeship for many years with a painter of his choice, with a great mathematician, or even with a master watch-maker, is likely to adopt many of that person's desires, so many in fact that we might say he takes much of the entire person into himself. I happen to know a writer myself who, at his sixtieth birthday was, and even considered himself, still an apprentice of another writer ten years his senior, and an economist in his middle forties of excellent reputation who has at last, he says, succeeded being what he had always dreamed of: the assistant of a university professor; although the professor had, in the meantime, become the state secretary of finances and he his right hand. In fact, I myself may be looked at as a specimen of a person who, at thirty-eight, is still trying to learn from master Freud, although I have also claimed allegiance to another master: articulate reason and rationale, or something like the inherent logic of the system.

Apparently identification can be viewed as a powerful means of learning and cathexis too, not only as a specific device of counter-cathexis. The world in which we grow up happens to be crowded with people who can do things and see things better than we can. We might even say more appropriately: in another world we could not even hope to survive and grow up. By identification we learn from these people. We gain more and better control over the world by having them show us how to do it. Only if we never try to do it ourselves will we be missing the point and using identification mainly as a defense. All this can be said of other defense mechanisms too. They too have "positive" aspects, although to different degrees according to the level of development on which they occur. A little more about that later (see p. 56)

Can we also identify with persons or objects who do things and see things more poorly than we do, say, with a little child? Well, a child may also identify with a smaller child, say his little sister. She may be such an authority in getting attention and fun from mother and such an obstacle to his own pursuits, that he would want to be her or like her, at least in some ways. He may wet his bed or pants again, may want to drink from the bottle, etc. Of course, parents will not let him get by on it too long, and he will even learn by himself that this does not bring him what he wants. His sister is an authority in some respects. Yet in many others she is not. So identification will probably be a passing affair. Or take a mother who puts her little child to bed at seven o'clock in the evening and has still a lot of work to do herself. She may think with a sigh: "If I could only be her, without worries, having everything taken care of!" But soon she will go about her work after all. "Who would take care of my child ? And who would take care of me in the first place ?" will be her second thoughts. If her identification would not pass quickly, but last, we may be dealing with something more serious altogether: regression (see p. 48 ff.). Yet one delight in having children is that they are still simple, dependent, happy, fervent, etc. in ways that *we* have had to give up long ago. We see them do what we can do no more.

What about understanding another person ? Which means in our context: understanding his desires, we might add. Does identification not play a part too ? Yes, it does. Yet this may be a very, very passing affair. For all practical purposes we would not refer to that as identification, but rather as interpretation in its most general sense. By adopting another person's desire for as little as a fleeting moment and testing, so to speak, where it would lead us, we might know what he (possibly) wants. Just as we might by "projecting" momentarily the most appropriate of our desires into the other person (see p. 39). This is, in fact, where identification and projection may be hard to distinguish, or where they "touch" each other, as they have done inevitably in the early stages of development (see pp. 83, 87 f).

Finally one may wonder whether identification is also automatic and involuntary like the other defense mechanisms or all counter-cathexes in general (see p. 29). Yes, it is. But can I not choose my object of identification or my ideal ? Certainly not in early life. Mother and father, or whoever takes their place, are the most immediate and inevitable givens of the first years of life. The infant and child has no choice at first, and little thereafter. But even much later in life will what might appear to us as a possible object of identification be determined by our previous identifications and cathexes and counter-cathexes in general. The writer-to-be will choose a writer for his ideal, and not just anybody. In fact, a person choosing Hemingway for his idol at some time of his development might reject Faulkner and, perhaps, despise Evelyn Waugh. He would not have anything to do with them, indeed will refuse to be like them. One may also think that a little girl whose mother is out of the house for a while could choose whether to identify with mother and play kitchen, or whether to play just anything and tolerate the deprivation of her presence. Yet here too there is little choice about how to perceive the situation. Whether she thinks she can tolerate the deprivation or not, and even whether she can tolerate it or not irrespective of what she thinks she can do, will be determined by previous cathexes and counter-cathexes and especially by her previous experiences with mother's absences.

This is not denying the fact that we often feel free to choose. Increasing control over conditions under which we can satisfy our desires means more choice by definition. Hence we even *grow* "freer" as we develop. "Freer", however, has a technical meaning, namely that the process of choice becomes more difficult to disentangle psychologically. Consequently we should also *feel* freer, as we develop. We are disregarding increasingly more whenever we are not bothering to disentangle our choices psychologically or, in other words, whenever we just make them. This is, fortunately, what we are almost always doing. I am not advocating philosophical determinism. However, a theory of the mind or, more specifically, of motivation must be deterministic, i.e. able to determine in principle the genesis of any choice and decision, or it is an inadequate theory and, perhaps, none at all.

Sublimation, like displacement, is substitution of one desire by another. The difference is, however, that the substitute desire is socially acceptable and more controlled than in displacement. Besides it does not refer so much to a momentary as to a long-range solution for a desire that has become impossible to satisfy. The person who is mad at his parents and, therefore, goes into the basement and chops wood is not necessarily sublimating, although this is more acceptable socially than doing anything violent to the parents, and it may also be more controlled. It is not just chopping up anything, but something specific, and for a specific purpose. Even so, it looks more like displacement than sublimation. If, however, the person makes wood-chopping, wood in general, forests, forestry, sawmills, carpentry, etc. his special or even his professional interest, we could say, with greater confidence, that he is sublimating. Something that started out as a defense against a desire has, apparently, developed a "life of its own".

In the same fashion painting may be called the sublimation of desires of smearing or of treating some amorphous material crudely with one's hands. A desire to produce forceful sounds may be sublimated, or transform, into public speaking, a desire to collect things and keep them in order into banking, a desire to tear up things into surgery. But are we not becoming ridiculous? Are we saying anything at all, when we speak of sublimation in these cases?

We are certainly leaving out a long genesis of derivative-formation. The examples of sublimation given are late, complicated, and even compound, derivatives of primitive desires. Substitution of a desire by another is a complicated affair and may not be completed years after the original desire has become unobtainable. In fact, one may even question, whether there has to be a forbidden or impossible desire at all. Could not smearing become painting without any deprivation of smearing at all, or could not tearing and cutting apart become surgery without deprivation of the former, etc.?

No. In the first place, control, derivative-formation, and cathexis implies that certain things have become impossible in given contexts. The painter cannot dip his hands into a pot of paint and splash or smear it all over anything in the house. Nor can the surgeon continue to operate on a patient afcer the operation required is over, no matter how much he likes to operate. As a matter of fact, control over a desire implies that the person would not even get such an idea to begin with. In the second place there are desires that do become impossible to satisfy even though they have come under some control. The infant who has been suckled for five months will no longer search for mother's breast just anywhere, say, in the center of her face, or as far away from her body as he can bend, nor will he try to produce sounds while swallowing. Yet at weaning he has to give up that desire with all there was to it. And he is not alone at that. I would almost bet that every reader has been weaned by now, at least literally, whether from the breast or from the bottle. Similarly, everybody has to give up the desire to play with a substance ideal for primitive manipulation or smearing, namely one's excrements. Someone may claim that he, or she, or their child, has never had such a desire. Well, considering that the child defecates once, twice and sometimes three times a day and has to be taken care of in some ways and considering that the child likes to touch things that are new, and even take them into his mouth, it is just about impossible for anybody not to have had such a desire. It is almost equally impossible, of course, to grow up without learning to renounce it, and without doing so relatively early in life.

The two points of the matter (which could, perhaps, be boiled down to one, if we took the trouble) are that control of desires in general implies tacit, unconspicuous renunciation of certain conditions of their satisfaction, and that there are certain desires that everybody has had to give up under more dramatic circumstances at some point of his development. There is no person who has not had to counter-cathect some desires. In fact, there is no person who has not had to counter-cathect desires on any one of the basic or primary *substitution continua* or drive systems. We shall see later (p. 116 ff.) which those are. Suffice it for the time being to check on our examples. Can we pinpoint at least one desire on each *continuum* involved that would clearly appear to us as generally forbidden or impossible to satisfy?

We have indicated one for the *continuum* "smearing-painting", namely smearing (human and especially our own) excrements. We must not do it. We must dispose of them as neatly and rapidly as we can, flush them away, use toilet paper, wash our hands and emerge from the bathroom as well-trimmed as at all possible. What about the *continuum* "producing forceful sounds—public speaking"? Well, we all have given up screaming in order to get food, and food was one of the brighter aspects involved in our early screams. We have given up hope and even the thought of impressing anybody by a violent bark or a burp. Yet as babies we must have done either with good success. Mother was not happy, e.g., until we had made our burp after eating. As concerns "collecting and ordering things—banking", we have stopped collecting pebbles, rotten twigs, marbles, slugs, shells, etc. Even as bankers we would not be collecting and piling up coins. And as concerns "tearing up—surgery", we have given up desires such as destroying toys, cutting them up where our bare hands would not do the job, or cutting off noses, pigtails and the like. The latter we did not even get a chance to try literally. We were not given knives or scissors as long as these desires *had* not yet been given up.

These examples may not seem too convincing. However, as long as we can see for the time being that all *substitution continua* have suffered at least some losses during their development, we are somewhere. Development of a *substitution continuum* is equivalent to the formation of derivative desires. Sublimation *is* derivative formation. Therefore we can say that some desires have dropped out in every area of sublimation or, in other words: sublimation has always counter-cathectic or defensive aspects too, no matter how small they may be. It is with this connotation in mind that derivative formation has been called sublimation.

Is sublimation not a redundant concept after all? Is it not covered already by the concept of derivative-formation and counter-cathexis? Yes, but so are the other defense mechanisms. They all are specific forms of substitution. Yet we have to show, I believe, in what fashion and to what extent they can be brought on a common denominator and why, of all things, they were different in the first place.

If everybody has to give up some desires while enjoying others, what distinguishes the painter, the public speaker, the banker or the surgeon from any other person?

That is just the point: nobody is psychologically different from anybody else except by degrees. That is what a general theory of the human mind must assume. Otherwise it would hardly be a general theory nor, perhaps, even a theory. These "specialists" have not only given up similar things as everybody else, but everybody else is also a little bit of such a "specialist". We paint a chair, a room, a house or, if female, our lips and fingernails. We speak in the family (which is a small public). We keep track of our own finances and we carve meat or remove a splinter. The "specialists", however, do much more of it. That we can safely say. What we cannot be so sure about is how much they have had to give up. That may be as much or more, or less, than a comparable "non-specialist". The fact that they are painters, public speakers, etc. does not tell us which. If we would know their talent—i.e. the ease with which they learn about or cathect conditions under which they satisfy the desires in question —and if we could take a look at their work, we may be able to get a first idea. A painter who has almost no people in his compositions and is painstakingly meticulous and slow in his work is likely, other things being equal, to have had to give up more than a colleague who prefers to have people in his compositions and works elegantly and fast. Similar relationships would hold for the others.

Reaction-formation is the substitution of a desire by another one of the same *continuum* that is as distant in satisfaction value as possible. More briefly: it is the substitution of a desire by an "opposite" one; whereby "opposite" means greater than usual difference in satisfaction value. Instead of taking to the next-best derivative desire, the least best of all pertinent derivative desires, or just about the least best, steps in.

If a little boy wants to smear things very badly and have new supplies of dirt, plasticine or the like all the time, but cannot have them, he may begin to treat things very daintily, to keep them in order and not to waste any. In fact, while smearing would have occupied him for only, say, about an hour a day, this occupies him ten hours a day or more. He has chosen a desire of small satisfaction value and must therefore satisfy it much more frequently, perhaps "excessively". Again, if that same little boy has wanted to hit his little sister off and on, but never could, he may have developed instead a desire to touch her only tenderly or, at any rate, lightly, so lightly indeed that he would not touch her directly at all. He may touch her by handing her things to play with, by picking up anything she drops or leaves on the floor or by touching, say, the chair she sits on. Again he will have to do a lot of this in order to make up for a desire that he would, circumstances permitting, satisfy perhaps once a day.

Other examples are the pretty girl who dresses miserably and declines to use make-up, the spendthrift who turns miser or the warrior who becomes a pacifist. What they do is not just substitution. They *overdo* the substitute by more than what substitution in general would account for. The pretty girl who does not want to be pretty may not even comb or wash her hair. The miser may come close to starvation and illness, because he will not permit himself to eat properly, and the ex-warrior may be a pacifist to the point of outright suicide. In addition to over-doing the "opposite", the original desire may be satisfied occasionally after all in some unconspicuous context. Our turned-neat-and-orderly little boy may love to smear with and waste soap in the bathroom or he may become peculiarly awkward and break things around the house, while being so very kind to his sister. The pretty girl, who does not want to be pretty may yet go to every party or invitation that she can dig up. The miser may one day make a donation in which he gives away all he has accumulated with greed, and the pacifist may love to "kill" people in debates, or may demand outrageous penalties for slight offenses.

Like in sublimation, the substitute desire is more controlled and socially more acceptable than the original desire. In fact, *much* more so. Sometimes, however, reaction-formation appears to be the reverse, such as in the case of a spend-thrift who has been a tough miser before. It looks as if a controlled desire had been substituted by a primitive desire. This may happen, indeed, and if it is not just temporary as in displacement, but if it lasts, we may be dealing with regression. However, it could also be a reaction-formation to a reaction-formation. In this case the primitive desire would look more premeditated. The person may be sloppy and filthy only under certain conditions, say, when in company of very proper people, or the spendthrift may waste his money only in restaurants and bars, but nowhere else.

Regression is the return of one or more *substitution continua* to an earlier level of development. In its mildest form it is the result of a drop-out of a desire without any replacement by new substitute desires (see also p. 26, formula (2), and p. 27). In all other defence mechanisms new substitute desires are likely to be recruited to a *continuum* in order to make up for the loss of a given one. In regression no new substitute desires have been found. It is the last alternative. The *substitution continuum* or drive system regains its balance on a lower, i.e. somewhat more accelerated, level.

Regression may range from very mild forms that may be hard, if not impossible to distinguish from ordinary repression to very drastic and severe forms. Regression will be the more severe, the closer the dropped-out desires are to original or primal desires, the greater the number of desires that have dropped out before, the more are dropping out right now, the less developed the *substitution continuum* in question, and the greater the number of *substitution continua* that are affected in any of these ways (see also p. 28 f.). Examples of the most severe forms can be found among certain psychotic end-states in which the victim lives literally like an animal, only duller. A mild form may be the regression of the person who, for some reason, has to leave out certain foods from his diet. As a consequence he may eat a little more frequently and be more pre-occupied with food in his thinking, but that could be all. Other *substitution continua* may be unaffected. More specific examples: An infant who is weaned from mother's breast, but continues to get human milk from the bottle is better off than an infant who gets cow's milk instead, and both are better off than an infant who gets weaned from the bottle at the same time and is left with cup- and spoon-feeding only which, say, all three infants have been enjoying as extras. Other things being equal, regression will be severest with the last. All three of them will be worse off, if things take place at an earlier age. And all three of them will be worse off, if they are weaned because mother has been lost altogether. That affects more than one desire. In fact, loss of mother means "drop-outs" of desires on just about all *substitution continua* there are, and that is likely to be worse, other things being equal, than almost any trouble into which a particular *substitution continuum* may get.

Any *substitution continuum* that has been subject to regression may, through further derivative-formation, develop to its former level and beyond it. In fact, everything can be fine thereafter, provided that no further "drop-outs" occur. Even so this *substitution continuum* will lag a little behind that of another person who, other things being equal, has not suffered that regression. Regression that now belongs to the past may be, and has been, called *fixation*. It might not be noticeable other than by the lag, and the lag is not always easy to make out in practice. If regression has been severe enough, however, fixation will be noticeable. A person who must eat a lot and drink, smoke or chew gum incessantly between meals may have suffered regressions or be fixated on the *continuum* "oral gratification". A person who is always busy with his hands without ever achieving much if he tries to use them for a technical, artistic or household job may be fixated on the *continuum* "manipulation"; choosing a more complex example, a person unable to tolerate a lengthy talk with anybody, but in need of people to talk to at every time of the day may have had set-backs in his experiences with people that he could tackle only by regression.

There could be other reasons too. The person who eats a lot and drinks, smokes or chews gum incessantly may have suffered regressions in *other* areas, say, in "manipulation". He may be so pre-occupied with oral gratification because he had to give up too many aspects or desires of manipulation. And the person who always wants to do things with his hands, but is not too successful, may have suffered set-backs in his contacts with people and, therefore, "turn to his hands". In either case a given *substitution continuum* has been called upon for rescue of another. Yet to the extent that it can do something at all for the other, it may be "overburdened". That must not be so of necessity. If the person who "uses his mouth" instead of his hands discovers the enormous possibilities of talking, things may get into shape again, particularly when he discovers in addition that he can, thereby, manipulate things and people after all. He may even stick to food for that matter, learn about all the dishes of the world and become a remarkable cook, which too could win him great friends. Again, the person who is not so successful with his hands could be sufficiently successful hammering on a typewriter and may, by what he writes, even establish contacts with more or more cherished people and do so in a more gratifying form than he could otherwise have done.

A given *substitution continuum* might appear as if it had suffered fixation on still another ground. The person consuming oral gratifications so greedily may be engaged in a very difficult task. Once it is over, the apparent trouble with eating, smoking, etc. may be over too. Our man with the jitter in his hands may gain steady and efficient hands, and even our restless nibbler of social contact may be all right as soon as the acute stress, say, combat or a contest with a fortune at stake, has passed.

The more dramatic and conspicuous cases, however, are those where many or all of a person's *substitution continua* have suffered "drop-outs" that could only be met by regression. It is more or less the entire person that is fixated on an earlier level of development. What is worse: it will take him much longer to regain the level where he left off, or to recover from the trauma. It may take so long, in fact, that he could well suffer another trauma in the meantime and that may throw him back again. He may even regress below the previous level. The worst, however, would be a second trauma occurring while he has not even regained his lower-level balance after the first trauma or, in other words, while regression is still in the making. If the second trauma hit him while he is still in a state of anxiety over the first one, anxiety may mount to such an extent that he can hope to catch himself and establish regression only on a very low level of development. In this case we may see what we usually do not witness directly:

the actual slipping of a person. If a child has lost his father and loses his mother too this could well happen. If the second loss occurs after regression has, so to speak, captured the anxiety over the first loss, things are bad enough, but not quite as bad as if the second loss occurs before regression after the first one has been achieved. The child may be close to panic and it may take very long to make the child believe that the world is still capable of providing some kind of company or even food. We may be lucky, if the child comes out of it withdrawn and heavily subdued, but willing to answer questions or to eat, at least upon sufficient urging.

Just as repressions "attract" later repressions (see p. 38), or counter-cathexes other counter-cathexes (see pp. 30, 31), we would expect that regressions of the past or fixations "attract" regressions of the present. Speaking more accurately, we should say that old regressions will co-determine how a given situation will be perceived. It may be perceived as a trauma, because such a situation was a trauma and required regression before. Being left by a friend may make a girl feel similarly anxious as when she felt she was left as a child by her father who was often on business trips, would have no time for her when around, or both. As a consequence, she may begin to eat a lot of candy, and be particularly lazy and unsociable. She could get out of it, though, if she finds a new friend. This is more likely, the less severe regression of the past was (on the *substitution continua* involved) or, in other words, the milder her fixation is. If she loses a friend, regresses and does not recover for a very long time, we would assume that fixation has been quite severe. We would ask ourselves: what loss in the past has taught her to take the loss of a friend in the present so seriously. Things also depend, of course, on the kind of friend she loses.

We have seen that all defense mechanisms discussed so far can be described as a form of substitution. In repression, other and new desires substitute for a given one for good, whereas in displacement they do so for the moment. Therefore displacement is perhaps just a preliminary to a defense mechanism and should have been mentioned with those discussed below. In projection, a "non-existent" outside desire substitutes for a given one. In introjection and (more articulate) identification, it is an "existent" outside desire that does that. In sublimation, it is a number of socially acceptable and controlled desires, and in reaction-formation it is a distant though still related, or an "opposite", desire that substitutes for a given one. In regression, finally, no new desire has been found to substitute for a given one. The whole *substitution continuum* drops to a lower level.

What remains to be shown is that all other defense mechanisms can be subsumed under the ones discussed. They are specific forms and compounds, or specific pathological manifestations.

Denial refers to *data*, givens, or "facts" of a situation that the person does not want to perceive. A child who has lost a dog may pretend that the dog is still around after all. He may put food in his bowl and insist, upon confrontation with the facts, that the dog just went out of the house and will be back any moment. He is denying that there was a loss, and this is what everybody who has suffered a loss and will have to repress may find himself doing at first. A dear person who died *cannot* be dead, we feel. Yet this will subside very soon and repression be established. If it does not, the "facts" or "reality as a whole" would have to be repressed; which would, of course, be extremely difficult. Denial is the more or less futile attempt to do that, unless regression to a much lower level of reality supports the process.

Isolation concerns desires that have become impossible to satisfy, but also impossible to repress completely. They may find opportunities for satisfaction, but can be satisfied only if the person feels that these desires simply overtook him against his better intentions. They did not really belong to him. A woman, unhappily married, who has spells of street walking and is amnestic about her adventures may be satisfying, or trying to satisfy, some of her genital desires in isolation. A young man who has been subdued by his powerful father forever may feel haunted by frequent thoughts of homicide or patricide. These thoughts come against his will. The desires behind them have nothing to do with him. This is the only way he can have it. Apparently, the desires in question are insufficiently repressed. Isolation is the attempt to repress at least their connection with oneself, one might say.

Turning against the self is the diversion of certain desires to oneself. A person wishing to hit or derogate somebody may hit or derogate himself instead for wishing to do so. The term has been used preferably in connection with aggressive desires. As we shall see later (p. 57 ff), aggressive desires are desires the satisfaction of which deprives other people's desires. Not only that; aggressive desires arise or desires become more aggressive, because some of one's own desires are being deprived. One could say that "turning against the self" is a specific kind of displacement, particularly since, as in displacement, we do not know yet what will become of this momentary solution in the long run. We do not even know for what reason the person wished to hit, derogate, etc. somebody in the first place. Sometimes we may even find that two or more of the other defense mechanisms combine in order to produce a turning against the self: the person wanting to derogate another person may suspect that that person wants to derogate him (projection) and adopt that desire, i.e. derogate himself, as a substitute for the original desire (introjection or identification).

Undoing refers to the revocation of the effects of a desire that has been, or was attempted to be, satisfied. A cleanly boy who has been seduced by an opportunity to get himself really dirty may "wash the dirt off" for several days in a row by being excessively neat, orderly and clean. A pretty girl who wanted to make herself attractive to a particular boy by means of wearing an extravagant dress, but failed, may be dressing miserably thereafter in order to undo her original wish. Comparison with previous examples (see p. 47) will show that undoing is quite intimately related to, if not equivalent with, reaction-formation. To the extent that it is different, it may be reaction-formation in the making.

Reversal is the substitution of a desire or an object of a desire by its "opposite". If a person wants to smear and washes instead, or if he wants to bite and, therefore, kisses, or if he wants to marry a tall and heavy woman and marries a short and light one, he is supposedly exercising reversal. Yet if we can trust our senses, this is reaction-formation too. Some cases that have run under reversal in the literature resembled also sublimations, and others repressions. Sometimes a combination of projection and introjection was referred to as reversal, and sometimes reversal was just the last try to account for psychological phenomena when all other attempts had failed.

Identification with the aggressor would be the substitution of one's desires by outside aggressive desires. A child who is punished by mother often and severely will attempt to be such a punisher himself, whether with respect to others or, by turning against the self, to himself. A psychologically milder example: a boy has been tortured by a dentist and, thereafter, likes to play dentist himself. Obviously this is just a special case of identification in general.

Rationalisation could be called a denial of internal psychological "facts". If a person wants to play a dirty trick on an opponent who happens to be a Jew, and he does so "because the Jews killed Christ", he would obviously be rationalising. So would be the child who is not supposed to leave the house, but drops a ball from the window and therefore "must" go out. Rationalisation avoids what will be shown to be guilt or introjected desires for punishment (see also p. 86 f). In politics somebody may say that a certain measure is not what the people of that country want and intervene by force. Here it may already be rather difficult to distinguish between reality and what one wants to see of it, particularly since reality itself is nothing absolute, psychologically speaking (see also p. 13). But in all likelihood he is rationalising too.

Conversion into a physical manifestation refers to a physical malfunction or disorder with a specific psychological meaning. The malfunction or disorder satisfies and/or prevents from satisfaction a desire that has become incapable of satisfaction under given circumstances. A girl who feels close to fainting in the presence of some particular and attractive man may have to leave the occasion and thereby get out of the seductive situation. Or, by almost fainting, she may catch his attention and get his assistance which she feels she could or must not get in other ways—or she may be doing both. A person having to make a difficult and challenging speech may find his voice failing just when he was going to crush down on some faulty reasoning of others. A child may get sick before a difficult test in school.

These physical manifestations are still within the range of what anybody could experience, especially earlier in life. More pathological forms would be paralyses of arms or legs (that can be revoked under certain conditions such as hypnosis), rashes that come and go, tics, stutters, etc. All of these manifestations are to be distinguished from those that accompany psychological conditions as a matter of course, but do not have a specific psychological meaning themselves. Anybody can, under certain conditions, develop a headache or a stomach-ache. They may come up with an unexpected annoyance or a sudden disappointment, respectively. They become so-called psychosomatic disorders, when the psychological condition turns more or less permanent. The constantly annoyed person may develop high blood-pressure and the constantly disappointed his painful stomach ulcers.

Perhaps it should also be mentioned that all desires, but certainly and most obviously the more primal or basic ones, have their regular physical manifestations as they are being satisfied. We chew and taste, as we eat, and that is surely something physical. We feel temperature, pressure, softness, as we touch. We move our eyes and see, as we look, etc. Therefore we might also say: Conversion into a physical manifestation means substitution of an irregular or unusual physical manifestation for a more regular and usual one.

Finally a remark may be necessary about the "and/or" of our definition of conversion given at the beginning. "Does such a formulation not give way to any possible turn of events and, therefore, explain nothing?" one may ask. "And have you not taken a stand against that kind of obscurity in your preface?" (See Author's Preface.)

Well, if I am to be pinned down, I would say: cancel the "or". It has been indicated before (p. 30) that we are always, whether we want to or not, scanning any situation in the light of all pertinent cathexis and counter-cathexis that have accumulated. What we do in a situation has to be all right in either light. The red one of anxiety has to become toned down and the green one of "go ahead" become as bright as the situation allows for at all. Our action will be a compromise. In fact, all our actions always are as are all our phantasies in waking life as well as in dreams and all so-called neurotic symptoms. In the above definition of conversion, the "and" would be correct. However, on quick inspection, a particular conversion, compulsion, obsession, or other neurotic symptom may appear predominantly to satisfy a desire, while another may rather seem to prevent it. It is for cases of such quick inspection that the "or" has been added.

Phobia is a fear which, on first glance, does not make sense. A person fears, e.g. heights, closed rooms, open places, women, authority figures, people in general, etc. More precisely: he fears all those situations in which some specific repressed or counter-cathected desires find degrees of opportunity for satisfaction that are too high for the repression or counter-cathexis achieved so far. Staying away from such a situation altogether, or running away when he finds that such a situation has sneaked up on him, may be his only solution. That solution, however, is the phobia. There are milder and "more sensible" forms too, such as the child who has learned that the stove must never be touched, even when it is unheated, or the driver who has had an accident and does not dare to drive for a while thereafter. In fact, all counter-cathexis could be called phobic. Counter-cathexis, by definition, is learning how to avoid and fear.

Compulsion refers to a rigidly repetitive action in which a relatively isolated desire is satisfied and/or prevented from satisfaction. A compulsion to wash may satisfy the desire to get dirty—even if I do not feel that I am dirty, I must be; otherwise I would not wash—and/or prevent that desire by washing. A milder and more popular compulsion would be touching wood whenever I have thought or said something that I do not want to happen—that is why I touch wood—and/or do want to happen. Otherwise I would not have thought of it in the first place. Yet we may be reasonable and rational people for all possible concerns. The more isolated, the more pathological is a compulsion. The less isolated, the more will a compulsion have mitigated its rigidity of recurrence and approximate what happens with the satisfaction of any desire. All desires except those that are still in the process of formation are repetitive and become compulsive, i.e. more compelling or intensive, as they go unsatisfied.

Obsession is the thought-analogon of a compulsion. A man who feels strangely bothered by ever-repeating thoughts of rape is preventing a desire to rape from satisfaction by admitting it only as a thought, and even a strange one, he feels. It comes against his will. Yet he is also satisfying the desire to some very small degree by having the thought in the first place. Hearing himself say: "I'll rape you", or having a brief vision of how he would do it, reduces the intensity of the isolated desire by some small quantity. A little later, however, the intensity may be up again, and another one of these thoughts will intrude on him.

"Acting-out" is a kind of a short-circuit acting. If somebody has lost a dear friend and is making friends with a number of strangers the very same day he is probably acting out. Or somebody wants to hit his older brother, who is much stronger, and hits the dog instead. The more obvious displacement is in a person's actions and the more rapidly he has to displace in order to avoid the mounting of anxiety over the deprivation of a desire, the more likely is he to be "acting-out" rather than acting. One could also say, acting out is an "insincere" acting. What the person does is not really what he means to do. He does not really care for his new friends. He cares for the lost one. And he does not really want to hit the dog. He wants to hit his brother. Acting-out ranges from a single instance of acute substitution for a single desire all the way up to a general way of handling any one of one's desires. If a person can only act impulsively and on the spur of the moment, switches from person to person in his relationships, runs from place to place in his work, and from subject to subject in his interests, we might say that he is acting out all around, or even that he is an "acter-out".

I think we can see that all defense mechanisms are cases of substitution for a desire that has become incapable of satisfaction. At the same time they are all satisfactions of other desires themselves. In repression, reaction-formation, sublimation and, if we ought to mention it separately at all, displacement, other and new desires of the *substitution continuum* take over. In introjection-identification and projection desires "come from" and "wander to" someone other than oneself, respectively. In regression other, though no new, desires of the *substitution continuum* take over. Denial and isolation may be seen as related to repression; turning against the self as a kind of displacement or rather as a combination of projection and introjection, undoing and reversal as a kind of reaction-formation, identification with the aggressor as a kind of identification and rationalisation as a kind of denial. Conversion may be called a displacement within one's physique or a substitution of the customary physical aspects of a desire by other physical aspects. Phobia is avoidance and fear of situations that are too seductive (in preference to a re-arrangement within the *substitution continuum* in question or to the establishment of a more radical and efficient defense mechanism). Compulsions and obsessions are satisfactions of desires in isolation, and acting out is a displaced satisfaction or, more frequently, a compound and sequence of such displaced satisfactions.

Is not suppression a defense mechanism too? No. The desire that is being suppressed at the moment will get satisfied later. Its satisfaction is delayed. Opportunity to satisfy it has to be awaited or even brought about. That, however, is what happens to all of our desires continuously. We are satisfying only one or few desires at a time, while many others are quietly mounting in intensity until their opportunities come in turn, or until they are so intense that we must see to it that these opportunities come about quickly (see also p. 16).

"But what about a desire such as to tell somebody off who has insulted me, a desire which I hold back and later on forget altogether?" Well, if you do forget, you have satisfied the desire in a substitute form. Maybe, you have successfully blackmailed your offender to a person who matters. Or you have told somebody innocent off instead. Or, perhaps, you do not even recall a month later that you ever met that person. You have repressed, displaced, etc. or, in any case, counter-cathected the desire. The whole event may have been so insignificant that this took very little trouble. As a matter of fact, I would not want to be asked to trace just any little incident like that as to where the desire went. Besides, if a person had really forgotten the incident, he could not offer it to me for such a test in the first place. The other alternative is, that you tell him off when you meet him again a month later. In which case you get what you want after all.

Am I implying that there is no forgetting? Of course there is. But it is harder to forget some things than others, and the harder it gets to forget, but also the harder it is to revive the forgotten, the more will counter-cathexis be involved as an "active process".

Are these all the defense mechanisms there are? Can we expect new discoveries? Possibly. However, they would not matter very much in principle. Even the ones that we know and that have been discussed do not form a clear-cut system. Historically speaking they have trickled into the literature and into clinical thinking one by one more or less haphazardly.

E

Maybe they could be ordered, say, by the developmental level that a *substitution continuum* must have reached before a particular defense mechanism becomes possible. Each one of the major defense mechanisms alone (repression, projection, introjection-identification, sublimation, reaction-formation and regression), however, covers a wide range of phenomena. Therefore such a classification or order may not be easy and perhaps not even too meaningful. We would assume, e.g., that repression is the first defense mechanism that can be observed in the development of any *substitution continuum* (although not directly nor by the naked eye), and it may well have characteristics of regression at first. It will be followed by reaction-formation and sublimation, both of which require larger and, therefore, more differentiated *substitution continua*. In sublimation, however, the burden of substitution is more evenly distributed among a large number of derivative desires than in reaction-formation. Therefore sublimation may be said to come later than reaction-formation.

Well, this would be a kind of a classification. We have said at the beginning of this chapter that there are infinite varieties of ways in which counter-cathexis can work. Defense mechanisms are only a few easily distinguishable examples. If we would want to trace any particular case of counter-cathexis concretely, we would have to do more than put on a tag. Introjection-identification is a *continuum* of its own altogether. We cannot even put on the tag without specification, say of the object of identification. And projection is on the same *continuum* with "interpretation of outside or, more specifically, other people's desires". Therefore projection may refer to all possible degrees of mis-perception of a situation. Again, we would have to specify our label or we might not be saying anything at all.

So why did I spend so much time on them to begin with? For one thing, they are in the professional literature. Even the most popularised versions of psychoanalytic theory and many of its hybrid forms make sure that they deal with defense mechanisms. Secondly, coming to grips with them is probably a worthwhile, though perhaps redundant and somewhat devious, conceptual exercise after all.

Aggression

AGGRESSION is an aspect of desires. More primitive desires, or more primitive forms of satisfying given desires, are also more aggressive or destructive. Aggression is the "twin brother" of anxiety. Anxiety is a state of the psyche in which more primitive, hence aggressive, desires than usual prevail. If they are acted upon, one may speak of aggression. If they are not acted upon, counter-cathexis or defense becomes necessary. Aggressiveness of desires in general decreases with development. It does so as a function of the overall amount of cathexis that has accumulated. Behavior to implement aggressive desires becomes more efficient with development. Other people, however, become more intolerant of a person's aggressive desires as he develops. Feelings of aggression are feelings of aggressive desires. All feelings are feelings of desires, satisfactions, and/or fears.

*   *   *

Before we discuss the third sub-system of the psyche or personality, the Superego, we have to take up an issue that has led to some confusion: aggression. We call it just that and leave out Freud's philosophical or even metaphysical concept of the "death drive" or "death instinct" (*Todestrieb*) altogether (Freud, 1920; also Menninger, 1938). Aggression manifests itself in aggressive desires, and only in those. But what are those?

Well, first of all they are relatively more primitive desires. Or rather, as a desire becomes more primitive for whatever reason, it becomes more aggressive. Tender kissing is a highly controlled desire that, a long time ago, was sucking and biting. To the extent that tender kissing becomes more angry or violent, such as when the partner is teasing the kisser, or even, say, when the lovers involved see each other for the first time after an imposed separation, it takes on features of sucking and biting again. It becomes more aggressive. Touching or stroking may become punching and slapping, when the other does not let us touch and stroke him or her, and running a competitor out of business, in a more primitive form, becomes hitting him over the head.

For what reason however, or under what conditions, do desires become more primitive? Our examples seem to have indicated already that desires are being deprived of satisfaction for some time or to some degree. This is, indeed, the general condition: deprivation of a desire beyond a certain point of intensity or time.

Which point? That point which triggers off anxiety. Does this mean that this triggers off aggression too? In a sense, yes. Anxiety and aggression are something like twin brothers. More precisely speaking however, we would have to say that deprived desires "become" more primitive and aggressive as anxiety mounts. Not only that: if deprivation continues unchanged and anxiety keeps mounting, it will reach panic. (See also p. 16 ff.) At this point desires have become so primitive and so aggressive that they cannot be satisfied in any way other than by a motor storm, by a tantrum or an epileptiform fit.

Usually, however, something has been done about the situation one way or another long before the worst happens. Substitute desires have taken over, and the *substitution continuum* is working toward a new balance, i.e. toward termination of anxiety and the establishment of counter-cathexis. (See also p. 23 ff.) Or, otherwise, the individual has satisfied a more primitive and aggressive desire, a desire closer to the primal desire of the *substitution continuum*, and has, thereby, also satisfied the desire that has been deprived in the first place. The reluctant partner may bleed from his lips, but our friend has robbed from her or him the desired kiss. The person who did not want to be touched has been punched, and the business competitor is lying on the floor knocked out. The resultant satisfaction experienced by our friend may well be even greater than it would have been, had he been granted his wish in the first place. In general, satisfaction of a more primitive desire means more to the *substitution continuum* and to the person than satisfaction of a more controlled desire. Its capacity to reduce desire intensity, or its satisfaction value, is greater. Anxiety occurs in both cases. In fact, anxiety itself may be seen as an attempt to satisfy the deprived desire in more primitive forms (see also p. 16), or as a regression of the *substitution continuum*, although a temporary and unstable one. It is more at the mercy of given opportunities than established regression or established counter-cathexis in general would be. This temporary regression has been called "acceleration" of the *substitution continuum* (see pp. 26, 27). In one case, however, anxiety is not acted upon—except by sad or resigned crying—and leads to the establishment of counter-cathexis, whereas in the other, a more primitive and satisfying desire than the deprived one is being satisfied, or anxiety, i.e. temporary regression, *is* acted upon, though sometimes by no more than "angry crying" until satisfaction arrives. Thus counter-cathexis becomes unnecessary.

But what determines which will be the case? The given situation, as we have learned to perceive it. And what determines how we have learned to perceive it? Previous situations and our experiences with them or, more technically speaking, all of our previous cathexes and counter-cathexes of conditions under which given desires could and could not be satisfied, respectively. And what determines that? In the end it is the "objective" world and, above all, "objective" people who will let us get by in some instances and not in others. And what determines that? Their desires. They happen to have desires just as we do, and if they can help it, they would rather give up the satisfaction of none, again just as we would.

Finally they tend not to give up any desires merely because of us, and we tend not to give up any merely because of them. Yet the "objective" world and "objective" people are such that we must all give in somewhere. From birth on, and even before, we are hopelessly dependent upon other people even for our mere survival. More specifically, the satisfactions of all of our desires depend on other people's desires, and wherever that is so, there is room for *conflict*. When the baby wants to eat, mother must quit sleeping, and when mother is asleep, the baby must wait until she wakes up and comes. When the baby wants to eat, he must let mother leave him and get food, and no matter how much she loves to play with her baby, she must let him sleep much of the time. Later in life, on a bright sunny spring day, we would rather be out in the country than on our job, but the boss will not permit us to do so. And he, the boss, might want to get our labor for a dollar an hour, or thousand a year, less than he does in reality, but we would walk out on him, and so on. Generally speaking, satisfactions of *our* desires may deprive other people of satisfactions of *theirs*. They may be suffering anxiety or pain from deprivation because of us. Satisfactions of our desires may be *destructive* to theirs, and vice versa. Moreover, satisfactions of our desires will be more destructive in general, the greater the concomitant deprivations of other people, i.e. the greater the number and importance of desires that another person has to give up, and the greater the number of people who have to do so. The importance of a desire refers to its position in the *substitution continuum*. The closer it is to the primal desire of a *substitution continuum*, the greater its importance. (See also p. 28 f.) Other people who have their own desires and thereby obstruct ours will let us get by with ours in some instances since they will sometimes let us "scare them", and will renounce or counter-cathect their own desires. In other instances they will not let us get by. They will rather "scare us" and insist that *we* renounce. In fact, in every instance whatsoever they will let us get by with some things and not with others, depending on how aggressive or destructive our desires are to theirs. Accordingly, we have to learn how to control our desires. We will generally cathect those conditions of satisfaction that are relatively less destructive, and counter-cathect all those that are more destructive to other people or to the world in general. The latter includes animals, plants, and "inanimate" things, at least to the extent that they are instrumental to the desires of other people. They may be their property, for instance.

This has implications. One is that destruction or destructiveness is not an absolute, but a relative thing. We cannot do anything at all without being destructive to somebody's desires, no matter how slightly. What is more: we cannot even do anything destructive at all without being also destructive to ourselves in some respects, no matter how minor they may be. In fact, there was a time in our development when we had not even learned yet how to make the distinction between ourselves and somebody else and, consequently, could not even tell who it was that was being hurt. However, destructiveness can be minimised.

Indeed, if God were to ask me what he should install in man so that a happy life, or even life at all, could be guaranteed without his constant guard and interference, I would say: "Install a gadget by which men can live *together* or, more specifically, one by which men's desires become steadily less destructive as they develop." That would be enough. They never need to reach values of zero destructiveness. God, of course, must see to it that there are men to start with.

This brings us to another implication. Destructiveness is not only an aspect of those desires that are related to other people, but of all our desires. Why? Because, provided we live at all, everyone of our desires *is* related to other people. People are inevitable and indispensible conditions of all satisfactions that we can ever hope to attain. This is particularly evident in early life. A baby cannot get his first meal without somebody to feed him, in fact, he would not even be in the position of wanting one, had it not been for something between his father and mother that brought him into existence in the first place. God must have provided the other people already. Things seem to change, as we grow older, but they do so only in degree. Even late in life there is no desire that is unrelated to other people, if for no better reason than that it *has been* related to people in earlier life. Whatever *has been*, psychologically speaking, *is*. All cathexis and counter-cathexis is cumulative. Every single satisfaction of a desire does something that will last to the *substitution continuum* in question, and possibly to others too. Even the hermit has people in mind when he lives in a dreary forest on snails and berries; in fact it is especially true for his very decision to become a hermit, since complete seclusion from people is the way in which, according to all his experiences with them, he thinks he can come to terms with them best.

What about the desire to breathe? Is this also inevitably related to other people or is not that just dependent on the presence of air? Well, remember that I specified: "provided we live at all'. Shut the air off, and even our modest reflections will collapse at once. Besides we could claim that other people depend on air the same way as we do, just as we and they depend on the earth's gravity and on food and other necessities of life, and this common dependence is in itself a form of relationship.

If aggressiveness or destructiveness is an aspect of all our desires, and control of desires, derivative formation, cathexis and counter-cathexis and object-formation, are all pervasive aspects of our desires too, there must be a relationship between them and destructiveness. In fact, if God were to ask me what the gadget should be like that would guarantee that man's wishes become less destructive with development, I would say: "Here you have one. The capacity to cathect and counter-cathect conditions under which desires can or cannot be satisfied, respectively, is enough to make for control of the destructive aspects of all our desires. Give man a chance to develop, to learn how to like and to fear, and aggressive- or destructiveness of his desires will diminish automatically."

Are we not jumping to conclusions prematurely? Are there not primitive desires that do not harm other people at all? For instance to lie down on the floor during a business conference, to soil one's clothes for the fun of it, or to pick one's nose in public? Are these not primitive desires, the satisfaction of of which leaves other people unaffected? My counter-question would be: "Provided we have such desires at all, why *do* we usually not satisfy them? Who stops us?" One might retort that "these things just are not being done," in which case how did we learn that these things are not being done? Somebody must have taught us. There are no physical obstacles to stop us. Somebody must have wished us not to do these things, before we decided not to do them. Doing them would, therefore, counteract the desires which somebody had concerning us. Such actions deprive him of the satisfaction of such a desire. Somebody, e.g. our parents, would be displeased. In fact, even the people involved at present, the members of the business conference, the person taking care of our muddy suit, or the people before whom we pick our noses, would all be displeased with us, and before long we would know whether we could scare them into tolerance of our behavior or whether they would scare us into renouncing it.

When we come to the discussion of the Superego, we shall see why we would not indulge in any of these primitive desires even when we are alone and nobody seems to be affected by our doing so. Some time ago somebody was affected, and that is enough. The Superego, like all cathexis and counter-cathexis, is cumulative. It carries into the future. It determines how we perceive any given situation to begin with.

But let us get back to our latest thesis: Give man a chance to develop at all, to cathect and counter-cathect, and aggressiveness or destructiveness of his desires will diminish automatically. Why should that be so? Just because there are "objective" people around him whose desires conflict with his?

We have indicated before that we cannot do anything destructive at all without being destructive to some extent to ourselves too. If a person, say a jealous lover, destroys his beloved by stabbing her, not only does he satisfy his desires to control, overpower, or "rape" her, but he also deprives himself of having any more fun with her thereafter. In other cases of aggressive or destructive satisfactions this may not be so apparent. What harm would that same person be doing to himself, if he kicked his dog instead of killing his beloved? Or what, if he just tore up the letter in which she told the infuriating news that she was through with him? Well, the dog may run away if things get too bad for him, or at least be a little less affectionate with his master, so that he will be deprived a little, unless he keeps the dog exclusively for kicking purposes. And if he tears up the letter and wants to read it once more he has to go through the trouble of piecing it together. In other words, one can probably find some self-destructive consequences, no matter how minor, of desires that are destructive to others, or to objects in general. The question remains, however, whether these consequences would be apparent and evident enough to guarantee that desires become automatically less destructive with development.

Although we are primarily concerned with desires, we have not forgotten, I hope, that desires guide, and manifest themselves in, behavior. We settled for desires, because behavior in situations and conditions as complex as we are interested in would be impossible to trace in detail. Besides desires are not unambiguously tied to any one form of behavior (see also p. 3 f). In order not to get hopelessly lost, we have made desires our elements of theorising. Now, all behavior is the result of cathexis. So is all we know about the world. As a matter of fact, only through behavior do we come in contact with the world. We cannot learn about it unless we behave in it in some fashion. What is more, all behavior has something to do with the satisfaction of desires. More specifically: there is no form or aspect of behavior that would not be satisfying to some extent, no matter how small, for some identifiable desire. While holding and reading a book, for example, we are also satisfying the desire to lie on the couch or to sit in an armchair, to be comfortably warm and under a pleasant light, to stretch and relax our legs, etc. These satisfactions would be insignificant compared to those of reading or, more appropriately, even to those satisfied by what we read about. Some of these insignificant desires may not even be satisfied. We may want to stretch our arms too, but we cannot, we have to hold the book. In fact, all of these insignificant desires mentioned may be deprived: we may have to sit upright on a wooden chair, be cold, have poor illumination and too little room for our legs to move. The book may fascinate us nevertheless. One could even argue that sitting on a wooden chair with little room for our legs, being cold or having little, although some, light, may be satisfactions of desires themselves. Somebody may want to be, or give himself the illusion of being, hard-working and ascetic, and these conditions may suit such desires.

For all practical purposes, however, we tend to ignore these so-called insignificant desires. Their satisfaction values may be quite small compared to the major desire that is being satisfied: namely "reading" or "reading about something special". They are simply referred to as behavior, or as behavior instrumental to the satisfaction of the most prominent desires. Similarly, we are satisfying all kinds of desires to minor degrees when we undertake, say, to write a letter to a dear friend far away. We are doing something with our hands, putting something on paper, watching what our hands do, producing words, etc. Yet the important thing is the letter. We will tend to relegate everything else to the ranks and files, to behavior in general, or to behavior instrumental to "letter writing".

If, however, behavior is the result of cathexis, and cathexis of conditions under which desires can be satisfied accumulates steadily, as a person develops, the number of forms of behavior that are distinguishable from each other should also increase. In another version: if all behavior that we can identify is a manifestation of desires, and desires form ever new derivative desires, behavior should develop ever new forms. Now, if the "objective" world were such that no condition, under which desires could be satisfied, had anything to do with any other, we would go on developing new forms of behavior indefinitely without ever getting anywhere. That is, we would keep cathecting, but whatever we have cathected or learned would have no bearing on future conditions. It has been indicated before, however, that, for reasons unaccountable for in terms of our theory, the "objective" world provides conditions that are invariant at least to some extent as they recur. In fact, that is the very reason why we can say that they recur. The nursing mother is perhaps the most invariant thing in most people's early lives, although there is enough in her that does change indeed: her dress, her voice, as she says different things, the illumination under which she appears, such as daylight, electric light, shades down, her behavior in response to changes occurring in the baby, etc. The room in which the baby lives is another such relatively invariant condition. Mother's breast or the bottle is highly invariant, by its looks and touches as well as by what it produces. Milk is mixed according to formula, either by nature or by the pediatrician's recipe, by the guidebook of young mothers, or by Grandmother in person. And there is an even more invariant condition than all of these, namely oneself.

Insofar as we behave, we are a part of the "objective" world too. And insofar as we are invariant, to whatever extent, our behavior must be recurrent in some ways. The behavior involved in sucking, in closing our hand, in kicking our legs, etc., must remain more or less the same under different conditions. There is an even stranger thing about us: the fact that through behavior we can *influence* the conditions which the objective world outside of ourselves provides. In fact, this is the very reason why we are a part of the objective world. We can even summon the recurrence of conditions as a whole. We can scream, for example, and that will bring mother for whatever satisfactions we may desire to use her.

Now, supposing we have n recurrent conditions and m recurrent ways of behaving with a given individual. Then there are nm ways of behaving under n conditions. A baby can try any one of m forms of behavior such as kicking, groping with the hands, stretching the fingers, turning the eyes, screaming, groping with the mouth, etc. and it can try them in any one of n recurrent conditions, such as being in the crib, on the table for changing, in mother's arm, close to mother's breast, etc. Yet due to the peculiarities of the "objective" world, only certain ones of these m forms of behavior will do anything to a given one of n conditions. Only groping with the mouth, but no screaming or kicking, will bring about sucking, when the baby's face is already close to mother's breast.

Obviously, the more often n conditions and m forms of behavior have recurred, the farther can all pertinent cathexis and derivative-formation have progressed, and the greater the likelihood that the instrumental desires, or those forms of behavior that can influence and even bring about any of these conditions, are among the cathected. In fact, one of all the aspects of any conditions that can be cathected is its relation to other conditions, or its "instrumental" aspects.

These aspects are, perhaps, the most important of all, if on no other grounds than that they would tend to be the most regularly occurring of all. How, otherwise, could they have become "instrumental" in the individual's mind?

Suppose there are two recurrent conditions and three recurrent forms of behavior. And say, only one form of behavior can be tried at a given recurrence of the conditions. Would that not mean that the first recurrence of a given form of behavior under a given condition might not come about before the seventh occasion? Therefore, if n and m are large enough, would it not take extremely long, to say the least, before a given occasion would recur even for the first time?

Actually, it does take extremely long for some combinations of recurrent conditions and recurrent forms of behavior to occur for the first time so that cathexis can begin. Take for example "sitting and stepping on a pedal", a thing which we have done while riding a scooter, a tricycle, or a bicycle long ago, and the condition of "sitting in a moving car," a condition we have been in many times while our parents did the driving. Learning how to drive a car oneself can only begin when these two are combined in one occasion for the first time. We have to be sixteen before we *should* even have such an occasion. Or think of "mother" who is psychologically the most important of all recurrent conditions. There is nothing more steadily recurrent at first, nothing to which she would not be instrumental as far as the baby is concerned, and yet she will have to have dealt with the baby many, many times and, to be sure, practically all those times at which the baby screamed, before the baby can do something as simple as "scream for mother". On the other hand, there is no reason why as few as three or even many more forms of behavior could not be tried out or recur while a given recurrent condition lasts. As a matter of fact, the first feedings of a baby show him diffusely active in about every possible way. Arms, legs, fingers, trunk, neck, head, even the eyeballs are moving. We may say that he is exercising just about all muscles that will ever be engaged in any form of behavior yet to develop. Of course, only sucking proves constructive, so the general and diffuse motor activity will gradually subside in favor of sucking as his feeding experience increases.

Apparently, there is no danger of n and m being too large (larger than the number of occasions at which they recur). Allowing for all forms of behavior that can be distinguished from each other with an individual to occur while any given one of n conditions lasts, we can refute the argument even on logical grounds. If there are n different recurrent conditions, there must have been at least $2n$ occasions at which they occurred, or they would not be recurrent.

Thus as cathexis of conditions under which desires can be satisfied progresses, those forms of behavior that can influence and even create any of these conditions are more and more likely to be among the cathected. In other words, as the formation of derivative desires goes on, the likelihood increases that among those there are desires that are instrumental to the satisfactions of other desires.

Therefore behavior becomes more efficient as cathexis continues to accumulate, or as derivative formation proceeds. *Behavior becomes more efficient with a person's development.* It looks as if a person's world and what he can do in it gets ordered into a network of "instrumentality", as he grows up. Part of a person's knowledge of the world as a whole, which includes himself, is to know in ever so many ways what leads to what.

This makes for one of the two regulatory trends that guarantee, better than individual experience and foresight, that man's desires become less destructive with development. At a time of development when desires are still primitive, the efficiency of behavior is very small. Primitive desires would be correspondingly aggressive or destructive desires, if only our ways of implementing them were more advanced. Since they are not, primitive desires on the one hand and aggressive or destructive desires on the other hand do not seem on brief inspection to be aspects of the same thing. Yet the factor which prevents the infant of six months old from devouring his mother, if she keeps him waiting too long, or even merely for the fun of it, is his literal inability to do so. The two-year-old may have times when he could kill his father and does not for the same reason. Primitive desires are aggressive and destructive desires by all intentions. They are meant to be, even though they cannot destroy in effect.

This is different when "primitive" does not refer to the level of development in general, but to particular desires on a given level of development. We have seen that any condition of deprivation beyond a certain point triggers off anxiety which may be defined as a condition of temporary regression. More primitive desires of the same *substitution continuum* are sought to be satisfied. (See p. 58.) These desires that are more primitive in relation to the level of development reached can count on an efficiency of behavior in general that is appropriate to the level of development. Hence in any such case they can become aggressive or destructive in reality. A woman who has been badly betrayed by her lover may, by clever scheming, succeed in bringing him into an untenable situation, in making her rival leave him, in trying to ruin and perhaps even in killing him, depending on the severity of the loss as well as on the general efficiency of her behavior. Even a child may already be able to retaliate for a particular deprivation, not by ruining or killing his parents, but by breaking a piece of furniture dear to them, by bringing home from school a bad report, or by embarrassing them in public. The potential destructiveness of behavior increases with development. Therefore desires of a given primitivity and destructiveness tend to be more dangerous, the later in development they still occur.

The second trend which guarantees that a man's desires become less destructive with development is produced by the behavior of his neighbours. We have already said that their desires come in conflict with his, and vice versa. We must add now, that they will become increasingly more intolerant of deprivations of their desires by a given individual as he develops.

The crudest kind of evidence would be something like the amount of time a mother has to be with her child in the course of a day. She is on a twenty-four hour schedule with the new-born and sees him, say a boy, go off to college on his own, sometimes as long as a year at a time, when he is eighteen. She is pretty much off schedule with him by that time. He does not need her any longer. She is "free" again to do as she pleases. But there is other evidence too. In fact, no matter where we look for it, there is this trend. By a certain age a child is supposed to be able to eat by himself or to take care of himself in the bathroom rather than engage the parents. He is supposed to walk to school by himself, or to get along with other children so that the parents or other adults will not have to come to his rescue all the time. He must know better and better how to behave in traffic, so that at sixteen he can even be entrusted with a car. He ought to be able to read and write by the age of seven or eight, and still better by sixteen. He is supposed to fix things for himself, or to use smaller and later also larger amounts of money sensibly. One day he even has to earn it himself. Other people, preferably all those who are his seniors by a distance, and especially those who are his parents' generation or older, will let him get away with less and less as he grows older. Unless, of course, he is mentally ill or retarded, physically handicapped, and the like. But even then he must usually grow up in some ways.

We have indicated before that this trend, too, cannot be accounted for by means of psychoanalytic theory alone. If we postulate the existence of social systems, however, we are in a better position. This is postulating a little more than that there is a multitude of men rather than just the individual in question. Yet the existence of social systems is not too remote from that. If men can live together at all, which, apparently, they do, we have some kind of a system already. Anyway, if social systems are to exist at all, they must last. If they are to last, there must be new generations of men or children. And if they are to be of any use in making the system last, they must learn to take the places of those of the older generation who step out or, as it sometimes happens nowadays, who drop dead right on the spot. They must learn what their elders had to learn, even a trifle more, and the more they approximate that level, the less can they be permitted to fuss about it. Otherwise the social system might be in danger, and the danger is, that it might *not* last.

If the other people become more intolerant of deprivations of their desires by a given individual as that individual develops, and if an individual's desires are defined as aggressive or destructive when their satisfactions do deprive the desires of others, we might also say: *other people become increasingly more intolerant of an individual's aggressive or destructive desires as he develops*. And that, precisely, is the second regulatory trend that guarantees that an individual's desires do, indeed, become less destructive as he grows up. The other trend mentioned and discussed, the relatively slow increase of efficiency of behavior, as well as an individual's foresight of consequences of what he wants to do tend to make desires less destructive in general and in the long run. This trend, however, the increasing impatience of other people with one's destructive desires, takes care of more acute affairs. If, in a condition of deprivation beyond a certain point, the individual would tend to *act* on anxiety or temporary regression, he will be forced with increasingly greater insistence to renounce or counter-cathect instead. If he beats a child that annoys him while a child himself, perhaps even the smaller of the two, other people will not mind. He may learn his lesson straight from the other child. If he beats a child violently when he is an adolescent himself, or even an adult, other people will usually not let him get away with it. If he cannot resist after attempts at persuasion or psychotherapy have failed, he may have to be committed to some kind of an institutional seclusion for everybody's protection including his own. But even smashing things such as dishes or a doll or using bad language over an annoyance—i.e. over a deprivation of some desires beyond a certain point—or, if you like, all "acting-out" and displacement of destructive desires becomes more and more forbidden as we grow up, even though we are already foregoing direct attacks. Temper tantrums, which are very crude ways of acting on anxiety and usually inefficient as far as the physical environment is concerned, efficient only with respect to the parents or people in the physical environment who respond, temper tantrums may be forbidden as early as two or three years of age. In any case, however, they fail very soon to have effects. If they do not, the parents are heading for trouble.

What about aggressive or destructive desires that are activated in response to a sudden insult, to a physical injury, to threats such as that of losing one's money, one's wife or life, say, in a hold-up. Are they not different from those referred to so far? No, not in principle. They all are conditions of deprivation of one, a few, many or even all of a person's desires, whether that condition is existent or impending. However, the situation may change into a depriving one suddenly or slowly, the deprivation may be more or less of a danger to the person and physical pain may be involved to a greater or lesser degree. This makes for a large variety of possible conditions of deprivation that trigger off aggressive or destructive desires or, as a matter of fact, anxiety in general, whether it is acted upon or not. Anxiety and aggression are twin brothers, we said (see p. 57 ff), or even the same thing looked at from two different angles. They are conditions of a temporary regression that is ameliorated by the establishment of counter-cathexis in one case and by more aggressive or destructive satisfactions in the other. Therefore the determinants of anxiety as discussed before (p. 16 ff) will be determinants of aggression as well.

We have let a term get into our discussion without adequately introducing it: annoyance. There are related terms such as anger, hate, revenge and hostility. "Do these terms not refer to specific aspects of aggression, or even to feelings?" one may ask and continue: "Where are affects, emotions, and feelings anyway? They have not come up in your discourse so far."

Let me take up the general question first and ask a question in return: "What do you mean by affects, emotions, or feelings? Give me a few examples." Since we cannot very well wait for his reply, our discussant is the reader, I will provide some examples myself. Let us say, somebody may feel anxious, angry or elated, in love, fond of someone, moved by a person's distress, by another person's greatness, or feel just very lazy. How can we account for these feelings ?

Well, when I feel anxious, I must be feeling a condition that we described and explained as anxiety (see p. 16 ff). I am feeling something, when I am a smoker but without cigarettes, when I am driving downhill in a car and noticing that the brakes are not working or when I have a toothache. I feel anxious to get cigarettes, to bring the car to a stop safely or to end the toothache by whatever means I have. A person may also feel diffusely anxious. He might not be aware of what he wants, such as when he gets restless in his room or at his work. Whatever he can think of or feels like doing, however, may tell him what he had been anxious about. If he feels like being with people, he has been deprived of their company or some aspect thereof too long, either altogether or in relation to the particulai condition he is in, say hard work in some kind of isolation. If he feels like eating or drinking something or like eating something very special such as truffles, then this may be what he got anxious about. Being with people or eating truffles may make him less anxious. Yet it may also not or may do so insufficiently.

At any rate, we are feeling desires, especially those that are in a state of deprivation beyond a certain point, when we feel anxious. We will feel them even more clearly when we are "at rest" or, rather, when we can do little to speed up our pursuits. When sitting on a train or while our car is being stopped by a traffic light, we tend to feel how anxious we are to get to our destination. At the same time we feel less while running to our destination at top speed or while actively managing our way through the city traffic. We feel very anxious in a dangerous situation that we can do nothing about but just await, such as an oncoming battle, whereas we feel less so, if we do something about it, say, fight or run. In fact, when very much at ease, e.g. relaxing in an armchair after the day's work has all been done, one may notice even relatively light (deprivations of) desires such as to contact an old friend across the Atlantic by a letter, to take out one's wife, or to be taken out by one's husband, for dinner, etc. In fact, we will feel desires that are still far from the point at which anxiety is being triggered off. We will just feel what we would like to do. We would not have to be anxious yet to do them.

What about feeling angry ? The same story applies. We feel what we desire to do, and what we desire to do will be more primitive and destructive than other times. We may feel like hitting a person for a particular remark he made. Should we hit him, we will not feel angry any more. We may even feel sorry that we did. If we do not or must not or cannot hit him, however, we will feel how much we would like to do it. We have not even given up the idea yet of doing something to him in some fashion, perhaps pay him back by an even nastier remark on the very next occasion. If we are to convey to somebody else, how angry we feel, we will find ourselves referring to desires automatically. We will say: "Oh, I could kill him!" or: "I could beat him up!" or: "I am just waiting for the occasion when he wants a favor of me. He will not get a penny!" and if we just say: "I am very angry!" the other person will tend to appraise it in terms of desires, in terms of what we would be likely to do as a consequence, or of what is meant by "very angry". Even poetry has no better device, in principle, than to describe what a person would do—that is, what desires he would try to satisfy in what fashion—in order to convey what he feels. It would be said beautifully and with sophistication, of course. Take Baudelaire, for example, who describes the incredible beauty of his beloved and what he would do to honor it until, at last, he donates to her the most precious and beautiful of all presents, a dagger, and does so right into her heart. That is, he stabs her. Thus revealing superbly what he also and altogether felt.

What about feeling elated or happy? Well, every satisfaction of any desire is presumably pleasurable, although to very different degrees. We feel elated and happy to the extent that we are satisfying our desires and will generally do so the more, the greater the satisfaction value of a desire and the greater the intensity of the desire by the time it is being satisfied. Since we are always satisfying some desires, we should feel happy or elated at every moment of our life or at least of our waking life, although to different degrees. Hence elation would clearly come to our own notice—and to those of others, say, through our smiles—only when the degrees of satisfaction are high or the waiting has been long, but also when satisfactions or even their mere promises come about unexpectedly. Mother appearing before the crying infant of six months may mean that "everything is well again" for the little one. Receiving a proposal from the man she had been waiting for will make a girl smile, at least inside, when she saw it coming, and be jubilant with happiness when it came out from nowhere. And a farmer seeing his crops thrive or a millionaire watching his fortunes grow further will not be unhappy either as he is rubbing his hands.

These three feelings, anxiety, anger and elation, have been known as primary emotions outside of psychoanalytic theory and they do assume a distinguished position within psychoanalytic theory too. They are those feelings that participate to some extent in all other feelings we can possibly have and, at the same time, those which relate most directly to the prototypes of all situations in which we can possibly desire and act: pursuit and satisfaction of desires (elation), and deprivation of desires, whereby one alternative of the latter is renunciation (anxiety leading to counter-cathexis) and the other aggression (more primitive and destructive satisfaction). These feelings or emotions have also been known as affects, although "affect" has taken on different connotations ranging all the way from standing for just one or two of the three emotions, anxiety, anger or elation, to any kind of feeling in general. I would rather use it as equivalent to emotion, but we do not really have to make a decision on that matter. Feelings, emotions and affects accompany all motivation, but they are not entities in themselves. They derive meanings only from specific conditions of motivation, and it is the latter that we have been, and shall be, concerned with mainly.

What about a person who is in love? What is the condition of motivation that he feels? Well, I would suppose, for the time being, that such a person wants to talk, listen and perhaps even sing to his beloved, to see, touch, kiss her, make love to her, etc. He may want to build her a house on a cliff and watch sunsets and the surf of the ocean with her. He may wish to take her to Cuba, Europe, mountains, a lake. He may desire to see her face forever, rather to die than lose her, simply to marry her, to see her beauty in hundreds of different displays, to have children with her, two, three, well, many, but not so many that her beauty would suffer, etc. In fact, if such are his desires we would tend to believe him when he tells us he is in love. If he does not want to marry her nor even keep up with her for long, or if he does not want to have children, if he does not want to touch or kiss her, we will have serious doubts about what he says his feelings are. Probably he will too.

If a person feels fond of someone, he is likely to desire some, although not necessarily a literal physical, contact and he may do so rather infrequently. He will probably wish him good luck, though, i.e. wish him to be able to satisfy his desires, and he will even be ready to make some sacrifices to him, if necessary. If he is moved by another person's distress, this is likely to be a person of whom he is fond, perhaps also a person whom he identifies with, but at any rate a person whom he would want to help. He would want to sacrifice the satisfactions of some of his own desires in order to make the other person's losses smaller, and it is losses that the person's distress is about. He will be moved, other things being equal, in proportion to the calibre of that person's losses, and the more he himself falls short of making up for them by what he can, or is reasonably willing, to do. He will also be moved in proportion to how dear, or how highly cathected, the stricken person is. To be moved by another person's greatness is likely to involve desires which that person can satisfy, whereas the person moved cannot, or can only to a limited degree. A great violinist may impress the person who is an amateur violinist himself. The amateur would know how much talent and work went into the virtuoso's performance. In fact, the more he is impressed, the more likely would he desire, among other things, to be that person himself. That would solve all his problems in that area. If he were him, he could have such performances every day and perhaps many other things too. As it is, he must wait until the artist comes to town the next time or until the radio or record companies employ his services. However, that is not quite the same. This impressive greatness can, of course, also come from a tragic hero. If only I could take blows as well as he can! If only I were as strong as he is! Such may be the desire that the person moved feels. . . . And if we feel very lazy, we feel the desire to rest or sleep. We have been deprived of its satisfaction for some time or we are generally deprived of it. We may get too little chronically.

Let us finally look at a few "versions" of aggression mentioned before, such as anger, annoyance, hate, hostility and revenge. They too are, or derive meaning from, specific conditions of motivation. Anger and annoyance refer to a deprivation of desires beyond a certain point irrespective of whether it came about suddenly or slowly. Hate and hostility do so too. Yet one may say that they are more specific. The object perceived as the source of deprivation is the goal of the more primitive and destructive desires that make up aggression. In revenge, finally, the individual tends to satisfy more primitive and destructive desires with that person who, usually, did something similar to him.

Are we talking away feelings, affects and emotions ? On the contrary. We want to understand them better. We want to understand them not as isolated phenomena of introspection. We want to understand what man or any particular individual perceives, desires, and does in all kinds of situations. We grant him that he feels, of course. But feelings without context are not enough to go by. Or are we simply reducing feelings to underlying desires ? May be, yes. But that is not necessarily a reduction. If we can really trace all the desires involved in a particular feeling, we have enriched rather than reduced our concept of that feeling. In fact, if we managed to pick up only the most prominent desire, we have probably said more about a feeling than the person who tells us in ever so many words in what parts of the body the feeling under investigation caused him or anybody what kinds of itches. I doubt, however, that even that person can really refrain from referring to desires.

F

A Comment on Consciousness

OF ALL desires that are active and effective in a person at a given time only some are conscious. Others are preconscious, i.e. potentially conscious. Still others are unconscious, i.e. not even potentially conscious. They can become conscious only with various degrees of difficulty. Hence consciousness can be said to be an epiphenomenon. Perception and behavior are conscious and preconscious for most practical purposes, although even they can, in principle, become unconscious, at least in some of their aspects.

* * *

Let us take up the terms "conscious", "preconscious", and "unconscious" (Freud, 1900, esp. ch. 7). In our context they refer, first of all, to desires. We can be conscious of them. We can feel them and comment about them. Yet we need not necessarily be conscious of all of those that determine what we think or do in a given situation. Consciousness provides us with a picture of something, but not necessarily with all there is to be seen. In fact, the picture it provides may sometimes be rather inadequate.

Let us take a concrete case. Say, two boys, John and Stanley, are courting the same girl, Marilyn, who is pretty, but not exactly a beauty, bright, but not terribly so, and charming in her manners. Some say her charm derives from her mother who is French. Others say she simply is an amateur nurse with upbringing and imagination. John is a tall and handsome boy, a member of the basket-ball and swimming team of the co-educational college where all three of them (Marilyn, John and Stanley) are students. The two boys are even roommates. John comes from a family of four boys. He is the third oldest and wants to become a lawyer like his father and his oldest brother who is in law school. Stanley is the only child of parents who had a large wool-manufacturing business from which they have retired a few years ago. He wants to study history of art after graduation. Marilyn is the daughter of . . . well, it does not matter in this case.

The three of them are having dinner in a downtown restaurant and discussing contemporary paintings. While Marilyn and Stanley are doing much of the talking, John flirts a little with a girl he knows vaguely. She sits at a table across the room in the company of a young man. Then, all of a sudden, John breaks into the conversation of Stanley and Marilyn with a remark to the effect that they should stop talking shop, adding in parenthesis that he had to be back to campus right away. He had to do some reading for to-morrow's class.

What happened? Well, late that evening the two boys try to talk it over in their room. That is, John volunteers: "You know, I suddenly got angry over your conversation. All this business about paintings. The world is not made up of paintings, is it? There must be other things to talk about too." Whereupon Stanley replies: "I am sorry. Marilyn realised too that we had been rude. She wanted to go home as soon as you had left, but then she tried not to be rude to me either. So we stopped at Picorello's before going home."

The boys as well as the girl seem to be conscious of some of the psychological forces that determined the event: the early break-up. Marilyn and Stanley realise that they got carried away by their topic and ignored John at least a little. And Marilyn realises that things would have been worse if she had been inconsiderate of Stanley in addition. But let us focus on John who, after all, precipitated the event. John was conscious of the deprivation of his desire to participate in the conversation. He felt left out in some fashion and finally got angry. But what tipped the balance? Why did he get angry just when he did?

Well, in a quick reply to that question he says: "I don't know!" and says so with a tiny grudge. Upon prodding he may even maintain: "Don't you ever boil over? Just let the heat be on long enough." That comment may close the discussion in everyday life. However, let us play psychological detectives for a while. Let us assume that we have been watching the event. In that case, we will remember, say, that the girl across the room, with whom John had been flirting lightly, left the restaurant with her escort just before John "blew up". Not only that, she left in a manner as if John did not exist. Yet she had been flirting back before. John felt sure until then. But as she was passing rather close by his table, she did not look at him for a moment.

Suppose now, we asked John whether he still remembers that. If we are lucky, he may admit it. "Yes," he might say, "that could have had something to do with it." "What?" "I don't know!" There is this tiny grudge in his voice again. We could help him: "Perhaps because she did not seem to care for you either?" "I don't understand. Who else did not care for me?" "Marilyn. Not necessarily that she really did not. But didn't you think so?" The point being that he felt somewhat let down by that other girl too. That could have tipped the balance, whether he can see it or not.

But how did whatever balance there was come about in the first place? Well, the full story of such an event is much more complicated than that. Remember our assumption that all pertinent previous cathexes and counter-cathexes determine how a given situation will be perceived before any action can even be contemplated (see p. 30). For one thing, John has not just been let down by Marilyn and the other girl. He has been let down in favor of another boy, Stanley in one case and the other girl's escort in the other. He has lost out to another boy, may be a more appropriate paraphrase of how he perceived the situation. Yet, if we offered that interpretation to him, he may well deny it. "What do you mean? Stanley is my room-mate and friend. We would not be in in each other's way, if decisions had to be made." We may let his concept of Stanley ride at that for a moment and ask him: "What about the other girl's escort?" "What about him?" John may ask us in surprise. "I don't even remember him." Does that mean that the other boy did not matter at least in this substitute triangle? Let us see: "Do you mean that you do not remember that there was an escort or that you do not remember what he looked like, or what?" "There was an escort, sure. But I have no idea what he looked like." Upon prodding, however, he reveals that he does remember something about him: "He was a small and thin guy. But what has that got to do with it?"

Well, we cannot go too far or even hope to get too far even if we tried. However, John could have been particularly annoyed about that girl, because he lost out to a guy considerably inferior to him in physique and stature. He himself was a sportsman with well-trained muscles and a going-to-be-lawyer, that is: a man of a man's world. That creature, however, was a sissy, a tender, feminine fellow. Or rather, that fellow did not really matter so much. Who mattered was Stanley. And he, too, is a slim boy, and rather on the small side, at best of average size. And he is a kind of a ... well, almost of a sissy. What, after all, is history of art? That is no profession. Of course, he does not have to look for a profession, for he is taken care of by the fortune of his parents. He will have enough for a lifetime even if he does not stir a finger. How can a girl prefer such a boy to him?

Yet the story is still more complicated. Why is he in such a situation in the first place? Why do Stanley and he himself take the same girl to dinner? What may even be more important: Why do they room together, which they did, before they came to know Marilyn? What is there between Stanley and John that attracts them to each other. I do not mean to intimate anything specific or terribly manifest. But the choice of a room-mate cannot altogether be an accident, at least not, when it has been kept up for the third year in a row. What does John get from Stanley, so that he can say that they "would not be in each other's way, if decisions had to be made" about Marilyn? In other words, Stanley may be even more important to John than Marilyn. In fact, absurd as it may sound, John could have been jealous of Stanley as well as of Marilyn.

We could probe even further. John's very first contact with a woman and men-rivals was, in all likelihood, his own home, and there he had four other males to cope with. Father, a strong and hard-working man, the oldest brother who grew very much after his father, the second-oldest who was a soft and easy-going person, almost a scatter-brain, who went into a salesman job after he barely finished college, and his youngest brother who was the pampered little brat, not exactly physically soft, but lazy in his work and adventures as well as successful with girls. For one thing, he had always been mother's pet, much to John's distress. Now, suppose John tried to become mother's foremost darling, which would not necessarily be an odd desire. And suppose he did not have an altogether thick head. Then he might have seen how father and perhaps his oldest brother succeeded with mother, and how his second-oldest brother, the "weasel-slob", as somebody called him once, failed. But then the youngest succeeded better than anybody. John may have hated him for that. Yet he also may have wished he were him. He was such a lucky guy. John was even quite fond of him, such as when he rolled his eyes in his funny way, or when he made his graceful gestures, or when he smiled. He could floor a person by his smile just as . . . Well, on still further probing he may be able to continue: "Just as mother could floor a person with her smile. Coming to think of it, he looks a bit like mother. He has the same dark hair—whereas he, John, is blond—he is slim, rather on the small side or, at best, of average size, and he has the same melodious voice. I remember somebody even said that he looked and sounded like mother when he was a little boy. I was envious."

All this may have had something to do with the choice of Stanley as a room-mate and the joint courtship. As we, the detectives, come to think of it: Stanley looked somewhat like that too, that is like John's mother (of whom he keeps a photograph in his room) and, consequently, like his youngest brother. John may have been seeing aspects of his brother and of his mother in Stanley when he chose him for a room-mate and stuck with him. To find the two of them "united" in one person may even be particularly attractive. He can satisfy in a substitute form his desire to be very close to mother. He even rooms with "her". And he is protecting himself from further disappointments by "disguising" her into a boy, so that he would not even think of trying to come too close. Should he want too much of "mother" in Stanley, he will be immediately reminded that "she is a boy" after all. Marilyn would exert an attraction of her own on John. Yet if he was not too successful with mother, he would feel safer being not too successful with Marilyn either. She is on the slim and dark side herself. For that matter as well as for her charming manners and warmth she is like mother too. He can switch from mother in Stanley to mother in Marilyn whenever necessary. And he can have Marilyn check him on his intentions with Stanley, and Stanley check him on his intentions with Marilyn. In other words, the triangle could be the delicate compromise between the various desires involved and their various counter-cathexes.

All of this, however, would have been unconscious when John decided to break up the evening with Stanley and Marilyn. He was conscious only of the most immediate and obvious determinants of his behavior. Stanley and Marilyn were getting too close with each other and talking about something of which he understood little. He wanted to end that condition. That much he was aware of. The other desires involved, such as to be like his father and older brother, to be friends with his youngest brother as well as with Stanley, also to be like them rather than a "super-male", to have rich parents like Stanley and to be like him for that matter also, to succeed with mother and to give up trying wherever it seems wise, to succeed and not succeed with Marilyn, to have both Stanley *and* Marilyn, etc., all these desires he was not aware of. They were more or less unconscious. It would have been difficult to various degrees with some and perhaps impossible with others to make him aware of them, at least under ordinary circumstances. Remember how he got impatient and irritated as we questioned him only a little.

Apparently John's conscious account of the desires that determined the event in question is rather incomplete. He gets a very inadequate story of what made him break up the party just at that time and on the occasion he did. Not that there would not be people who could do better than he all by themselves. And not that even John's story would not be sufficient to get by in everyday life. But if we should, for the sake of the argument or for whatever reason, attempt to get at something like the whole story, we will find that his conscious account is but a segment, and not necessarily a very integral one. He did not have to tell us, e.g., that he "blew up". We saw that ourselves. On the other hand, he would not even answer some of our questions—leave alone think of them himself— about those very things that we, and he, would have to know in order to understand what he did.

And what does preconscious refer to? Preconscious means "potentially conscious". Desires that we are conscious of whenever they are intensive enough, but that are not intensive enough at the moment, are preconscious. If we ask John, while he is doing some reading, whether he would want to go out with Marilyn tomorrow, or visit his parents during vacation, or whether he would want to be the captain of the basket-ball team, he would probably have no trouble noticing and admitting to such desires. In fact, all those of our desires that we satisfy recurrently tend to be preconscious right after they have been satisfied, and tend to make themselves known again as time goes by. But they can become conscious even right after they have been satisfied provided that somebody poses the question. And all those of our desires that are not in the state of recurrence yet, that we have not satisfied even for the first time, because they are still in the making, such as marrying a particular person, when we are still unmarried, but in love, obtaining a particular academic degree, owning a house, etc., all those desires can become conscious too whenever there is a call for them.

What about perception and behavior? Do the terms conscious, preconscious and unconscious apply to them too? Well, all motivation requires the perception of a situation to be motivated in and behavior by means of which to do something about it. How a given situation will be perceived, however, is already determined by all previous cathexis and counter-cathexis of conditions under which the desires in question could or could not be satisfied, respectively. Therefore we will perceive those things and aspects in a situation that have been instrumental or even just compatible with previous satisfactions of desires, and not perceive those things and aspects that have become incompatible or "traumatic". John, e.g., almost did not see the escort of the girl with whom he flirted, but he did hit upon a girl in the restaurant to flirt with as a substitute. Therefore we may say that he was conscious of the girl, and not so conscious of her escort. If he could perceive or remember her escort without difficulty, then we may say that her escort, or at least various aspects of him, are preconscious to him. His ignorance about him is accidental. If he does not perceive or remember him even when urged by circumstances or by a peeping Tom such as ourselves, her escort, or aspects of him, are unconscious to John. His ignorance about him has a purpose. It will last. If, however, we had unmasked ourselves right in the restaurant, stepped up to John, and asked him: "Do you see her escort?" he would have. In other words, any situation, while it lasts, exposes the ordinary adult practically to everything there is. He will be conscious of some aspects and preconscious of most of the others. The situation may pass, of course, before everything has been registered by us. Thereafter, however, we depend on memories, and they are more hopelessly at the mercy of our previous cathexes and counter-cathexes. When really put to the test, our previous cathexes and counter-cathexes may be unable to "falsify" a situation to any worthwhile degree while it lasts, but they will certainly be free to do so the minute it has passed, and eliminate, i.e. counter-cathect, anything that better not exist. That will become unconscious.

The same would hold for behavior. With an ordinary adult, behavior has become so efficient that practically any part or aspect of it could be made conscious while it is being executed. Remember that all behavior is the result of cathexis, a manifestation of desires or, if you like, even a compound of desires itself, although of "insignificant" desires. In the given situation they have not amounted yet to any intensity to speak of, but their satisfaction would be instrumental to the satisfaction of some other desire that is more intensive and, therefore, does matter (see p. 62). Anything that a person does in order to get to a friend fast, such as take a bus, change to the underground on Harvard Square, get off at Charles Street, turn right at the circle and walk uphill, has been conscious at the time or could have been made conscious if necessary. In fact he would have been able, e.g., to count the steps he had to make in order to get there, had there been a point in so doing. Yet by the time he gets there, he will have forgotten most of it and if he finds that his friend has let him down or been unfaithful, he may even forget before long that he ever went there.

In earlier stages of development behavior is not quite as efficient. In fact, during the first months of life, behavior is either altogether accidental, or it was the satisfaction of a desire in and of itself. Looking, e.g., as long as there were different "things" to look at, moving one's hands, so that they might move indeed and, perhaps, touch something or reach the mouth, producing sounds so that there might be something to hear, all had their ends in themselves, so to speak. Only later would looking be looking for mother, and looking for mother be looking whether food is coming. Preceding that event the baby may produce noises such as a huge scream in order to possibly change the things there are to be seen and bring about the sight of mother. And after mother has come he may move his hands so as to hold the bottle that she has been waving. At this point of development, sucking the bottle is the desire, to which the other desires have become instrumental. Their satisfactions are "insignificant" in the given situation. They have become behavior.

A similar point could be made for perception. All perception originated in stimulation of some sort, and all stimulation is satisfying desires, if not contributing to their very formation. Visual stimulation develops into looking, the kinesthetic and tactile stimulations accompanying the accidental movement of the arms become groping, and auditory stimulation plus kinesthetic stimulation accompanying accidental movements of mouth and tongue develop into active noise making. Looking, groping, noise-making, however, should already be called desires and behavior. In other words, stimulation gets attached to desires and behavior. Stimulation assumes meaning. How? Through the process of cathexis and object-formation. Something seen becomes mother's face, provided that mother's face is a relatively invariant condition of satisfaction of any number of desires. Something felt kinesthetically and by touch becomes an object in a certain distance (so that, e.g., it must be reached for). And something heard becomes one's own voice. As cathexis and object-formation proceeds, the showers of stimulation become ordered and build up the more or less stable and solid world in which we live and of which any particular situation is a specific segment or sample. The world is the system of all objects that an individual has formed in his mind, or the most complex and comprehensive of all objects. If things are that way, however, we must be able to perceive the world, or any sample thereof, in all or most of its complexity no matter what desires are relatively foremost in our minds. We must be able to perceive it "objectively" (see also p. 12). In other words, just as behavior becomes more efficient with development, the world to be perceived becomes more "objective". At last there is rarely an aspect in any concrete situation that we could not, in principle, become conscious of although it may be unconscious to begin with. It is only in retrospect that things change.

Unless, of course, we are under unusually severe conditions of deprivation in some respects. If we have not eaten for very long, the world may become limited once more to anything relevant for getting food, so that we may, indeed, not see the beauty of a landscape or a very rare coloring of the sky. Again, if we have been deprived of human contact for too long, we may see people where there are none or even hear voices.

"Can you not give us something more palpable," the impatient reader may wonder, "something that would permit me to link conscious, preconscious and unconscious up with concepts expanded on in this book?" Well, if I am being cornered, I would say that all cathexes are preconscious, and all counter-cathexes unconscious. All cathexes have once been conscious and can become conscious again. All counter-cathexes have once been cathexes and therefore conscious, but now they can become conscious only with various degrees of difficulty or, more specifically, of anxiety. What becomes conscious, however, depends on all previous cathexes and counter-cathexes. Any given situation will represent a specific "opportunity-profile" in accordance with the individual's cathexes and counter-cathexes of previous situations (see p. 30), and in accordance with the "intensity profile" of his desires at that time. Our conscious experience tells us only that there is something, namely that which we are conscious of, and that may not be all there is. It tells us nothing about the whence and why. What is worse: our conscious experiences at time A tell us nothing definite about our conscious experiences at time B. There is no relationship between two subsequent conscious experiences except that which exists between all those givens and forces that are being experienced, at least in part. In other words: conscious experience or consciousness is an epiphenomenon. It may be among the things that we have to account for in any given case of a person in a given situation, but it does not have value by itself. That does not mean that we can dispense with it. In fact, even the most thorough of all conventional or semi-institutionalised investigations into a particular person's psychological make-up, namely psycho-analytic treatment, relies on that person's conscious experiences and recall of conscious experiences. Outside of so-called transference behavior there is usually nothing else to go by. That is why transference behavior is so important. But conscious experiences and recall of conscious experiences provide only the raw-material. Its underlying organisation must be inferred, and its re-organisation constitutes treatment.

Is not our *thinking* conscious, at least in its more formal appearances? Does consciousness not have a value of its own at least in the realm of pure thought and theory? Well, in the first place the realm of pure thought and theory is not principally different from any other realm of the world such as agriculture or domestic arts, and even the most trivial segment of the world is not bare of thought and theory. Secondly, consciousness again does not necessarily give us the whole story even here. Let me demonstrate this by as simple as dilemma as the following: All rules have exceptions. This statement is a rule. Therefore it has exceptions. Therefore all rules do not have exceptions. Which, apparently, contradicts the original statement. There are implicit assumptions in what "all" means and what a "rule" is that we are not aware of. At least not until we get into trouble.

For those readers who are familiar with the concept of "neutralisation of energy" (Hartmann, Kris, Loewenstein, 1949), a few words should be added. This concept has been introduced to account for the fact that—and these are my own words—there are not only desires in the mind, but also conditions of satisfaction that have been cathected and objects that have been formed. What is more, desires can become instrumental to other desires, the more so, the farther development has proceeded. To an increasing extent it is neither their own intensity nor the degree of satisfaction obtained, but their instrumentality to other desires, that determines whether they will be satisfied in a given situation or not. This is what neutralisation of energy refers to. In fact, we may say that the concepts of increasing control of desires, derivative formation, cathexis, object-formation, and even increasing efficiency of behavior as well as increasing objectivity of perception, all taken seriously, are already covering what neutralisation of energy was meant to cover.

Should we therefore drop the term ? Not necessarily. Since we have allowed for all the concepts mentioned to refer more or less to the same thing, another one such as neutralisation of energy cannot do much harm. Nor would it be terribly detrimental to use "channelisation of energy" to mean the same as neutralisation. We might even call it the growth of the reality principle by which our pursuits of satisfactions and pleasure get sober and more practical (Freud, 1911). We can easily go golfing with as many as eight or nine different clubs, as long as we realise that they are all meant to hit the ball with and that we can use only one at a time.

The Superego

THE SUPEREGO is the system of desires introjected from other people, above all the parents. It differentiates from the Ego to the extent that the growing person's desires begin to conflict with the desires that his parents have for him, and to the extent that the parents have to enforce theirs, which, technically speaking, is punishment. These punishing desires are introjected too and constitute guilt whenever counter-cathected desires are being satisfied. Fear of guilt furthers the maintenance and observance of counter-cathexes.

*　　　*　　　*

The Superego has been defined as the system of those desires that the individual has taken over from other people, first of all the parents (see also p. 5). It comprehends desires such as to eat and drink properly, to keep clean, to speak decently, to treat things with care, to share them with brother and sister, etc. The device by which they are taken over from other people has been described as introjection and identification (see p. 39 ff), and this device or defense mechanism has been defined as the substitution of "existant" external desires for one's own (Freud, 1923).

That, however, is not saying very much. On second thoughts we will have to wonder how such a thing as introjection and identification is possible in the first place. How *can* a child adopt other people's desires and *when* is he able to do so? After all, eating properly, keeping clean, speaking decently, etc. are already highly articulate desires, that we would not encounter at birth. Does that mean that introjection of external desires begins later than that, say, at two or three years of age?

Well, if that were so, we would either have to find reasons for its onset at that or any other particular time of development, or quit altogether trying to account for it by means of our theory. The latter is obviously not what we want. How can we resign after having travelled so far? The former, however, may get us into trouble. After all, it is not just the adoption of external desires that we would have to account for, but the creation of a system of such desires: the Superego.

Now, if Id and Ego begin to form and differentiate from each other through increasing control over desires or formation of derivative desires, through cathexis and object-formation as well as through counter-cathexis, and if all

81

these processes can conceivably start at birth, we would say that Id and Ego begin to differentiate from birth on (see also Hartmann, Kris, Loewenstein, 1946). This is probably the only version of the metaphor, crude as it is, that makes sense. Otherwise we may have to wonder about things such as whether the Id generates the Ego or vice versa, and when? The same, however, would hold for the Superego. Unless we assume that its formation begins at birth, we may have to face the problem of whether the Superego grows out of the Ego or of the Id, or whether Id and Ego have to marry first, before there can be a Superego.

In other words, the adoption of external desires as one's own must, in principle, begin at birth. This would at least be the neatest solution. But is that possible? How can the baby conceivably adopt desires of the parents?

There is a simple answer: The baby cannot possibly satisfy any of his desires *unless* they are, in some respects, the parents' or nurse's desires too. The baby cannot form a desire to suck unless his mother or somebody wants him to suck and therefore offers him the breast or the bottle. The baby cannot form desires such as being touched, looking, listening, etc., if mother does not want him to, i.e. if she does not appear before him, touch him and speak to him. The baby cannot move, make noises, nor even eliminate, unless somebody wants him to.

Wait a moment, one may object. Does not the baby move, make noises, or eliminate anyway? Well, yes, but the baby is also being touched, say, by the blanket and being exposed to light and noise anyway. In fact, he even sucks anyway. That is, whether somebody offers him the breast or the bottle or not, the new-born will begin to move his mouth and tongue, produce saliva and swallow it somehow. But none of any of these will be kept up for long unless there is somebody around who makes the baby's presumable desires—they have not formed yet, but they will—his own. If nobody wants to suckle it, i.e. to let it suck, the baby will die. If nobody wants to let it eliminate, move or make noises, it will die too. That is, only if the baby dies can he be stopped doing these things. In short, if nobody wants the baby to live, the baby will not suck nor be touched, nor look and listen nor move, make noises and eliminate nor, in summary, live for long. We have already indicated (p. 59) that from birth on and even before, the individual is hopelessly dependent upon other people for as little as mere survival. The satisfactions of all of his desires depend on other people's desires. We can specify now that they do so not only in general, but also a very specific way. That is: other people, preferably the parents or mother, must have precisely those desires with respect to the baby—among many others—that the baby is satisfying. The parents' desires for the baby and the baby's desires are one and the same thing. The baby could not possibly distinguish the two from each other at first. What is more: the parents are far ahead of their infant. They have much more control over his desires than he has. Therefore they can desire that he eliminate when he has no idea yet what it is all about. In order to make him satisfy their desire, they might even run to the doctor for a laxative, when all that the baby can make out is some vague, though prolonged, discomfort and his own screams, of which, in parenthesis, he cannot even be sure whether they are his. Also the parents can desire that the infant get the bottle in addition to the breast or that some cereal be added, when the infant has no means yet whatsoever to introduce a little variation in his diet.

This is the way the baby can conceivably adopt desires of the parents. His desires and their part in them are indistinguishable at first. If he wants to suck, we may say that his mouth, his feelings of movement and touch, his sights, his sensations of sound, etc. all "want to suck", and if mother is among his feelings of touch and movement, among his sights, etc., and has been cathected enough to be any kind of an entity at all yet, she would "want to suck" too. That is, he cannot distinguish between himself and the rest of the world. Everything there is, is all one, if we may paraphrase. As the baby gets his desires satisfied while they recur and recur, and as the ceaseless process of cathexis accumulates knowledge of the world including himself, he will gradually be able to make distinctions. He will find one day, although not immediately, that he can, e.g., suck his own fist. That implies that he can substitute for mother's breast or her bottle by his fist. But it also implies that he can suckle himself. There is sucking without mother too. She is not indispensable. Something else is indispensable, though. He must satisfy another desire first; the desire to suckle himself, to "give himself the fist". At which moment it presumably begins to dawn on him that this is what mother must want to do when she does suckle him—a sensible kind of projection (see also p. 87 f)—and what she does not want to do when she is not around. Mother's desire to have him suck and his desire to suck separate in his mind. As a consequence, mother's desire to suckle him can be adopted by him whenever she does not want to do it herself.

Once mother's and the child's desires have separated and adoption or introjection of mother's desires has become possible—not that it was impossible before; rather there was no alternative to introjection; every satisfaction of a desire was an automatic introjection of a corresponding desire of mother's—anyway, once introjection has become possible in that specific sense, the Superego begins to differentiate from the rest of the psyche or personality. Yet there is still a long way to go. The child's desires remain synchronized with the parents' desires for the child under most of their conditions of satisfaction. The child may chew the rattle, the blanket, etc. in addition to his fist, but the feedings still come from mother and even the rattle and the blanket have something to do with her. He may touch and tickle himself or dig a little hole in his pyjama jacket, but the touches and tickles that really matter continue to come from mother when she dresses or changes him, puts the blanket over him or bathes him. The child can produce his own sounds, but if they could not bring about mother too, or even her sounds, which happen to be infinitely more variegated and interesting, his own would not be worth much. When he begins to crawl, mother has to put him places where he can do better than in his bed, such as the play-pen or the entire room, and help him out whenever he gets himself caught or into any kind of trouble.

In other words, his escapades outside the shelter of his parents' desires are short and insignificant at first compared to those that he continues to satisfy in unison with theirs. Their volume increases, however, as control over desires, derivative-formation, cathexis and object-formation proceeds or as the infant develops, and one day the parents find themselves outsmarted for a moment. Mother feeds him porridge with a spoon and suddenly a spoon-load of it is all over her dress. He hit the full spoon, or maybe he just spat it out after it had safely arrived in his mouth. Or he pulls the curtains down, tears a book apart, wants to stay up rather than go to sleep, all in contradiction to what his parents want him to do.

Before long, of course, the parents have enforced their desires. Mother will watch out that he cannot hit her spoon again, or she will let him eat with his own hands all by himself (which may be what he wanted to do when he hit the spoon). Or he will have had the last spoonful for the time being whenever he begins to spit it out. Or the curtains will be lifted, the lower parts of the bookshelves emptied except for his own unbreakable books and, say, some paper that he may tear up. And he may eventually be put to sleep in spite of his screaming and, incidentally, fall asleep within a minute. The desires that the parents have for him are stronger than his own. He will have no opportunity to satisfy those of his desires that they do not want him to.

However, as cathexis and object-formation proceed and his behavior becomes more efficient (see p. 64f) as well as his knowledge of the world more objective (see p. 78 f), it gets increasingly difficult for the parents to prevent mischief. Opportunities for satisfaction of those of his desires that they do not like can be removed no longer. The child can get his own porridge or mud, if necessary, and throw it at mother, should he ever care to. He can step on a chair in order to pull at the lifted curtains or to get a book to tear up after all, and he can climb out of his bed and even leave his room, if he does not want to sleep.

At the same time his desires have become more controlled and, hence, less destructive anyway (see p. 60). He can throw other things such as a ball, and whereas porridge is exhaustible—something may be plastered with porridge at the end, but there is no porridge left for further throwing—the ball stays intact and even bounces back. He can throw something *like* porridge where it is in infinite supply, such as sand or mud on the beach, or snow in February, provided we live far enough North. Also he can pull other things such as a towel from the bar, put it back and pull it again, or he can pull at a swing with all his weight, i.e. while sitting or standing on it, pull one way and then the other and, as a consequence, swing. He can keep a book and look at it again, if he does not tear it up. And if he would really leave his bed at night, he may knock something over, before he finds the light. He may not even reach the light. In fact, he may get lost in the dark and not find his way back to the bed at all. And then what!

Better wait for daytime. More primitive or less controlled desires are likely to be destructive to himself in the long run. They may be fine, or rather better than nothing, in a state of anxiety or anger, but not under more customary circumstances.

Besides the parents' attempts to remove opportunities for satisfaction of those of his desires that they do not like have borne fruit. They have been successful at least in the beginning. That means, however, that counter-cathexis of those desires must have been established already in the child by the time that he could conceivably find out that there is opportunity after all. The very effect of counter-cathexis is that opportunities up to a degree are not even perceived as opportunities. And beyond that degree they arouse anxiety which calls for additional counter-cathexis (see also p. 29 f). If another child should suggest to our boy, for instance, to pull down the curtains, or to tear up a book, or to just throw it out of the window, or burn it in the fireplace, he would be a little terrified. What an intimation!

If he does give in to such temptations, however, and the parents can no longer remove disapproved of opportunities, they will at least resent it. Their desires for their child have, after all, been deprived of satisfaction. As they resent it, or as they are angry about it, they are likely to resort to more primitive and destructive desires themselves. They will shout at him rather than talk to him, and hit him rather than pet him. They may confine him to his room rather than have him all over the house. Or they would rather go out by themselves than have him along. They may not let him have a friend come in and they may refuse to kiss him goodnight. In short: they will *punish* him. They will deprive some other desires of his, if he will not let himself be deprived of a particular one such as tearing up books.

Punishment is destructive to the punished person's desires. Yet there are obviously many different degrees of punishment all the way up to that which means to be, but is not. A mother may beat her child close to death, lock him up in his room for months, let him starve for days or even leave him altogether in retaliation for what she claims he has done to her. On the other hand, a mother may express with barely a grudge that he should not have done it, that he should do something different instead the next time, or she may even just feel a little disappointed and try not to show it. We should also realise that punishment does not come about all of a sudden. It creeps up on the infant from birth on. Even at a time when some of mother's and all of the child's desires are still in automatic unison, mother's desires for the child, or rather for the baby, will not always be satisfied. The baby wakes up at an unusual time, wets himself again ten minutes after he has already done so or vomits all over mother at an unexpected moment. The baby will not be punished literally, but mother may be in a slightly less friendly mood, so to speak. She will tend to take it out on herself rather than on the baby. She will decide that she had done a stupid thing to begin with, say, by feeding him cereals at this time of the day, or by not waiting a little longer before changing him. She may also take it out on her husband. But even the baby is apt to experience a slightly rougher handling, a harsher voice or even an impatient face, provided he can distinguish that already. He may even think that this is better than the usual fun. Later on the child is being punished a little more literally. He must not do such and such, tear up the book, pull at the curtains or throw a spoon. This can only be implemented by making it impossible for him to do so, i.e. by removing the opportunities, yet, what else would it be but punishing, if one has found something enjoyable to do and can find it no more. In fact, every counter-cathexis of a desire that has become impossible to satisfy is punishment in that sense. The only trouble is that the child does not yet know too well what he is being punished for. Still later he does, though, and this punishment is literal punishment. It is punishment even by common sense. It follows upon satisfaction of a desire that has already been counter-cathected by the parents' help.

As a child develops, as his desires form and multiply into derivatives, and as cathexis accumulates an ever increasing knowledge of the world, he will also learn to distinguish between his own and somebody else's desires. He will cathect or learn how to like, among other things, the desires that his parents have for him. Their desires for him have to become some kind of entities in his mind, before he can distinguish them from his own. Cathecting of somebody else's desires, however, or, more precisely, of conditions under which somebody else's desires for oneself can be satisfied is *equivalent* to their adoption or introjection. If he has come to like keeping books intact, leaving curtains alone, or going to bed at the proper time, he has made them his own desires. The parents can stop enforcing them. There will be no more satisfactions of their punishing or destructive desires as a consequence of his own satisfactions, no more admonishing, hitting of the naughty hands, confining him to his room, etc. Their punishing or destructive desires are no longer provoked.

In order to know what would await him if he were disobedient, the child must also have cathected the parents more primitive and destructive desires for him. That means: he must have adopted or introjected them too. In fact, he must have introjected the effects on his parents of all his satisfactions under all kinds of circumstances. He must have introjected the whole gamut of their desires for him ranging from their plain satisfaction to all kinds and degrees of deprivation—due to his misdemeanor—and subsequent enforcements. For what other reason should he be obedient, once he is capable of disobedience at all.

If the punishing or destructive desires of his parents have been introjected too, he will have his own desires for punishment. He himself will want to be punished, whenever he has given in to temptations and violated his parents desires for him. In fact, he will feel guilty *until* he has been punished. The feeling of guilt *is* the feeling of desires to be punished. *Guilt* is the desire to be punished, or any compound of such desires. While he is still being tempted—by an unusually great opportunity to satisfy a counter-cathected desire—he will be anxious anyway. This is what counter-cathexis does wherever it proves in-sufficient. With the introjection of punishment, however, he will also perceive the *consequences* of such an "impossible" satisfaction. He will be sorry, should he follow the temptation. He will feel guilty and have to get his punishment somehow. More primitive and destructive specimens of his introjected desires will have to be satisfied. In other words, he has not only learned how to fear the situation of temptation, but also its implicit consequences.

That is, among all the cathexes and counter-cathexes that determine how a given situation will be perceived (see p. 30, also p. 78f) there will also be the cathexes and counter-cathexes of all the consequences of possible satisfactions. The responses of the environment, above all of the parents, will be perceived too in any given situation. Those of the introjected desires that precipitated zero punishment will continue to accumulate cathexis as they continue to be satisfied. Whereas those of the introjected desires that brought about punishment to any degree when satisfied will be counter-cathected and will accumulate further counter-cathexis wherever necessary. Hence we may say that, in addition to anxiety, the fear of guilt will safeguard the pursuit of satisfactions against failure to obtain them. Anxiety signals an opportunity to satisfy a desire that has become impossible to satisfy. Fear of guilt will be aroused by an opportunity to satisfy a desire that is capable of satisfaction, but *should not* be satisfied; or punishment will follow. Yet the two are not prinicpally different. For one thing, making it impossible to satisfy a desire is a kind of punishment itself, and a crude one. Besides there is just no impossibility to satisfy a desire at first in which the parents had not had a hand. Secondly, all guilt is composed of introjected desires for punishment, and punishment is a deprivation of, or impossibility to satisfy, *some* desires, although not necessarily those, the satisfaction of which precipitated guilt. Fear of guilt, in its most primitive form, *is* anxiety.

To use a more impressive metaphor: The introjected parents will stand by an individual while he scans any given situation. They will be good people as long as he fulfills their desires for him. And they will grow progressively malicious to the extent that he does not. As he develops he will learn better and better how to avoid the latter.

As once before we have been simplifying (see p. 30). Let me briefly show some of the complications involved.

For one thing, the parents need not literally have satisfied all of their more primitive and destructive desires which the child has introjected. We have indi-cated before (p. 83) that the child can form a notion of mother's desire to suckle him only after he has learned how to give himself the best he can by his own means: his fist. This is, in his estimation, the desire that mother is satisfying when she feeds him. Yet, obviously, this is not a very adequate duplicate. He will be able to do much better later on. He will be able, e.g., to nurse a little doll right into the mouth with a bottle, or to really feed himself, for that matter. Now, however, a much more primitive desire is what he perceives mother to satisfy by suckling him, and it is this desire that he adopts. He introjects, so to speak, his own version of her desire. He introjects the relatively most sensible of his projections. Similarly, if, at a later time, mother should slap the child on his hands in a sudden loss of temper, say, because he smeared a piece of chocolate all over the table-cloth, the child may interpret that as an attempt on her part to bruise his (naughty) hands, to squash them, or even to cut them off, desires that he has formed and satisfied himself, not necessarily with human hands, but with plasticine, twigs, insects, or a paper doll. He may even have outgrown these desires. More control may have been achieved over them. They are being satisfied only in more derivative forms, unless the child is anxious or angry over some enduring deprivation. Since mother has been deprived of one of her desires for him, which is certainly not to smear chocolate over the table-cloth, she must have been anxious or angry herself, when she slapped his hands. Doing that is a primitive satisfaction all by itself. But if the child has outgrown primitive forms of such a desire, so has mother. In fact, she has outgrown them probably far more than her child, and a longer time ago. Therefore slapping him will not easily have a more primitive meaning for her than just slapping. Yet it may very well for the child, particularly since he himself will be angry over the slap.

The child can interpret mother's desires only in terms of his own. Such an interpretation will be projection rather than interpretation to the extent that his duplicate is inadequate. All of his own desires have been in unison with some of his mother's desires at first, but with development separation of his desires and hers, or his parents', has been gaining ground. If introjection or secondary unison is to be achieved, that one of his desires on the *substitution continuum* in question that would be most like hers will become hers-within-him. In other words, while satisfying that desire he will be most like her and, as a consequence, expect zero punishment to follow. He will be as well off as can be.

Secondly, the child is not only introjecting his parents' desires for him, but also forcing some of his own on the parents. In fact, once his and his parents' desires have separated at all, there may be struggle over every single re-alignment, and the outcome of each of them will determine the struggles still to come. The parents are overwhelmingly powerful at first and remain powerful forever, but the child's power grows as he develops. He becomes increasingly independent of them, although, of course, his parents are already in him, say, by the time he is in school all on his own for a whole morning and getting forth and back by himself.

Thirdly, the child is not only introjecting his *parents'* desires for him, but also aunt's and uncle's, a maid's, the teacher's and other people's desires. He is introjecting his grandparents' desires for him too, not only directly, but also via his parents who have been children themselves a while ago and introjected *their* parents' desires for them. Very generally speaking one might say that the child introjects the forces or tendencies of the social system of which he is a future member. The first and most influential delegates andi nterpreters of these forces and tendencies are, of course, the parents. Older and/or younger siblings, substitution of one or both of the parents, or even moving to another house, school, city, or country, etc. would all make for further complications of the processes of introjection going on incessantly. Whereby old introjections, like all counter-cathexes, will "attract" new ones. Or more accurately speaking: old introjections will determine how a given situation will be perceived in the first place. Whenever previous introjections did not suffice, additional counter-cathexis, preferably introjection, becomes necessary (see p. 38).

Furthermore, desires that the parents have for their child are likely, on the average, to be a fair sample of their desires in general. Their level of development, as defined by control, derivative-formation, cathexis, and object-formation alike, including all counter-cathexes, will tend to be reflected in those desires that they have for their child. Parents who are engaged in the pursuit of relatively primitive satisfactions anyway and who, under stress of sudden or prolonged deprivation, will tend to resort to still more primitive ones or even renounce satisfactions only in favor of relatively primitive substitutes, such parents are likely to provoke more primitive introjections than parents who developed farther. That would even hold for a child who, for some reason, proceeds faster in his development than his parents did. Think of a very intelligent child of not so intelligent parents, whereby intelligence should refer to something very general to be talked about later (see p. 109f). He may, to be metaphorical again, develop a highly articulate Ego, or highly articulate concepts at least of some aspects of the world, but a relatively primitive Superego. The latter may suffice to stop him from crude offenses, from illegal or criminal acts, but he may, for instance, have very little tact. Beware everybody of having to ask him for favors!

The more highly developed the desires are that the parents have for their children, the more control, derivative-formation, cathexis, and object-formation must have been achieved, and the more "objective", reasonable, and consistent with each other will be these desires. The child will have correspondingly little difficulty adopting them. They will make better and better sense, the more he comes to think of it. And they will even make some sense on their first occurrences. He will have to respect foreign property, e.g., because his own property will be respected in return, say, by his older sister, and not just "because I told you so".

Finally, desires that a parent has for his child will also have to be evaluated in relation to the desires that he pursues at all. The less they amount to in relation to all of them, other things being equal, the more permissive will the parent be, and the freer will the child grow up. However, the extreme, a maximum of freedom or a minimum of imposition of the parent's desires, may well be indifference. If a parent has no specific desires whatsoever for his child, if anything the child desires and does is all right or just as well with the parent, he, the parent, may not care at all. On the other hand, the more the desires that a parent has for his child amount to in relation to all of his desires, other things being equal, the more overbearing will he be. If the child cannot do anything of his own accord, he will become all Superego, so to speak, and be paralyzed in his own actions. An unfortunate combination of these two conditions would be over-protection. The parent is too overbearing in some respects and too indifferent in others. He is overbearing in his desires to control every word, move, sight, etc. of his child, supposedly in order to spare him all deprivations, all pain and hardship, that he can possibly be spared. And he is indifferent as to what the child does once that condition is fulfilled. Anything the child desires to do within those limits is fine with him. The trouble is that such a parent may be able to spare him deprivations now, but not necessarily in the future, say, when the child is in school or grown up. Yet even now he is depriving him of such privileges as learning how to do things all on his own, how to get recognition and acclaim for a performance of something very difficult or even painful, etc.

One may wonder whether there has not been too much emphasis on punishment and too little on reward? I have pointed out that punishment is something relative (see p. 85 f). Zero punishment means that satisfactions continue to come from the parents. Yet punishment of any degree greater than zero still means that satisfactions continue to come from the parents. They may not come as promptly, and there may be some omissions. But even severe punishment will be a condition in which the majority or, at least, a good portion of the child's desires continues to be satisfied without obstructions. Otherwise punishment might not even be effective.

One may also wonder where, in the development of the Superego, the concept of *task* comes in. And is not the acceptance and accomplishment of tasks the noblest and final criterion by which we can judge a person's Superego? May be, yes. But much will depend on what kinds of tasks we have in mind. There are tasks such as to write a paper on mushrooms for a biology course, to finish college well enough to satisfy the family or get into graduate school, to shovel the driveway clear of snow, to do homework for school, to brush one's teeth, tie one's own bootlaces, or eat without help, to keep clean, to treat things with care and share them with brother and sister, etc. In other words, tasks are desires introjected from other people or, if you like, from the social system, provided we realise that it is mainly via other people that social systems communicate their "desires". Tasks are desires that other people have for us. We have accepted those tasks, if we have introjected those desires. They become tasks for us.

That does not mean that we can or will not set our own tasks. Any task that we accept is our own task anyway. But we will find tasks for ourselves under conditions where somebody else's orders are, apparently, no longer involved. Many of us will feel very much like helping a child find his mother who has lost her in a big department store. Or we may feel that to-day is the time to mow the lawn. The weather is just right, and the grass "needs" it. And some of us will not rest until we have entered the last letter correctly in a cross-word puzzle.

Well, nobody else's orders are apparently involved in these desires. Yet desires such as wanting to help, doing what a situation "calls for", or finishing something that has been started, cannot very well spring from nowhere. They must have a history, and somewhere in that history we are likely to find very definite desires of other people or even of the parents. We learned how to treat things with care, e.g., or how to help our younger siblings, whether we wanted to or not at first. We took care of our teddybear's or doll's "needs", feeding or grooming them, dressing and undressing them, putting them to bed, etc. And we learned to finish something, say, our feeding, during the first few months of our lives. We learned that there is an end for everything, be it that the bottle got empty or that we ourselves just did not care for more. And we learned that we could not drag it out indefinitely. Mother would push us a little or put an end to the feeding prematurely. Such introjected desires, however, carry into the future. We have indicated that old introjections will determine how, at a later time, any given situation will be perceived in the first place (see p. 87). The introjected desires have become automatic. They are "in our eyes", whether we notice or not.

One may also wonder where we left the distinction between commandment and prohibition? And is there not a difference? Well, they are two different forms of the same thing, namely the parents' or somebody else's desires for oneself. "Eat properly!" refers to the same thing as "Do not spit or smear food!" "Speak decently!" is another version of "Do not use foul or sloppy language!" And "Share with your brother!" is the same, in principle, as "Do not keep things all for yourself!" The negative version, prohibition, is the earlier and more primitive form of an imposed or introjected desire, and a commandment is a later and more complex form. While the child cannot do yet what the parents want him to do, he can still be prevented from those things that the parents desire him to do the least. This is, in fact, what will amount to punishment. As the child develops, however, the likelihood increases that desires will form on the *substitution continua* in question that come close enough to what the parents want him to do. Cathexis of conditions under which such desires can be satisfied includes cathexis of the parents' desires, and that is equivalent to their introjection. Once they are introjected, however, all more destructive or punishing desires of the parents with which they had to enforce their desires will no longer be provoked. That is, the parents have stopped saying No. The child himself has begun to say Yes to their desires for him.

One may finally wonder how our discourse bears on the concept of conscience. Well, the common sense usage of the term covers a wide range. Its equivalent in our theory may be the entire Superego. It may be a particular aspect of it, such as the fear of guilt. Or it may even refer only to some particular instance of such a fear. Besides it may have metaphysical implications of all degrees. My personal preference would be the first alternative. For our purposes, conscience *is* the Superego, and our purposes are non-metaphysical. Unless one calls theory construction metaphysics.

Quantitative Aspects

LIBIDO is incessantly produced at a quantity given with a given individual. It is the energy that feeds into all motivation and all ongoing cathexis. Libido "makes" all desires grow in intensity until they are reduced through satisfaction, only in order to grow again. The sum of intensity increments by which they grow is equal to C, which is a direct function of the quantity of libido that characterises a person. His overall rate of cathexis is also a direct function of the quantity of libido by which a person operates. At any given moment, however, the amount of ongoing cathexis will vary in an inverse relationship with the amount of overall deprivation, or with the sum of all motive intensitities active in a person. Accumulation of cathexis facilitates ongoing cathexis. The more of a given recurrent condition of satisfaction has already been cathected, the easier and faster will be concomitant cathexis. There will finally be nothing more to cathect. Hence the individual will begin to vary the condition or look for new conditions of satisfaction. The quantity of libido, C, or the rate of cathexis, determine how fast and far Id, Ego, and Superego will differentiate, and how "strong" each of them will become. The quantity of libido by which a person operates can only be reduced by "creeping death" which begins with the beginning of individual life, but shows noticeable effects only at relatively old ages.

*　　　*　　　*

We have maintained before that all desires, once they have become recurrent at all, increase in intensity from zero or close to zero right after they have just been satisfied to finally intolerable heights. Usually, however, they or their substitutes can be satisfied before things are that bad, and can be noticed and, hence, planned for long before they have become even moderately intense again. Usually we can calculate and even manipulate opportunity in a reasonably competent fashion, so that our own desires as well as changes in opportunity will rarely take us altogether by surprise (see p. 16).

So far, so good. The question remains, though: Who does the "pumping"? Who, or what, provides the fuel to man's desires so that they are always on the go? What keeps man motivated to search for and consume satisfactions as long as he is alive? Freud's answer is that "libido" is the energy that does just that, namely keeps the individual motivated in the pursuit of satisfactions or pleasure (Freud, 1905).

But what does that tell us, that we would not know anyway? We might as well ask: "What keeps man alive?" and answer: "Life". Postulating the concept of libido is no more than saying that man does keep motivated, indeed. Unless, of course, this concept has implications. If we postulate, for instance, that a given individual starts out with a given fuel supply and another individual with another, and that this supply changes, grows, decreases, or alternates by certain rules that may be the same for all individuals, or different, the concept of libido would no longer be redundant (although we would have to find out about those rules). Nor would it be, if we postulated that it is of a given quantity with a given individual, and that this quantity does not change at all over certain stretches of time nor, perhaps, even over a lifetime. In fact, this assumption would be the simplest of all possible assumptions about libido.

Since the simplest of a number of equivalent alternatives is always the best, at least in theory construction, this assumption should concern us a little more. It will require some extra reasoning.

If libido is the energy responsible for the incessant intensity increase of all desires after they have been satisfied, i.e. reduced, and if libido is constant for a given individual over a longer period of time or, for that matter, even over a life time, it follows that the sum of intensity increments of all desires that can be distinguished from each other within a given person should add up to a fixed quantity. In other words,

$$\sum_{i=1}^{n} \epsilon_i = C \tag{4}$$

Apparently this formula is analogous to formula (1) (see p. 25), which applied to desires that were assembled on a particular *substitution continuum*. Formula (4) applies to all of a person's desires, or to all *substitution continua* at once on which they may be assembled. In formula (4) ϵ_1 stands for intensity increment of desire 1, say eating, ϵ_2 for that of desire 2, say talking, ϵ_3 for looking, ϵ_4 for walking, ϵ_5 for running, etc. Letter n stands for the number of desires that can be distinguished from each other within a given person at a given state of development. It increases with development. Letter m which is always smaller than n may be taken to indicate the number of those desires that have already been satisfied, of desires in the state of recurrence, such as eating, talking, looking, etc. Desires $m + 1$, $m + 2, \ldots n - 2, n - 1, n$, are desires that have not yet been satisfied, desires in the process of formation, such as graduating from high-school or college, owning a house, marrying a certain person, becoming competent in electronics, etc. We say that they represent something like the "free energy portion" of a person. C, finally, is a constant (Toman, 1957).

Since n increases with development, due to derivative-formation, control of desires, or cathexis, intensity-increments will, on the whole, tend to decrease with development. Which implies, in view of their reciprocal relationship to intensity increments (see pp. 25, 26f) that, e.g. the average intervals between successive satisfactions of a desire or, say, the variability of intervals between successive satisfactions will tend to increase with development. It takes the baby of a few weeks of age about an hour after waking up to fall asleep again. It takes a ten year old some 12 hours, and a twenty year old some 16 hours to be sufficiently desirous or deprived of sleep to go to bed. Similarly, the baby may have been able, in the course of a month, to fall asleep after as little as half an hour, and to stay awake one and a half hours before falling asleep irrevocably, which makes for a range (i.e.

difference between maximum and minimum interval between successive satisfactions) of one hour. The ten year old might, also in the course of a month, have suffered a maximum deprivation of sleep of, say, 15 hours, and a shortest deprivation of 8 hours, which makes for a range of 7 hours. And during the same period of time the twenty year old may have had a maximum of 36 hours without sleep, say, because of a ball that lasted all night, and a shortest interval between the end of one and the beginning of another sleep of, say, 5 hours, which makes for a range of 31 hours. Hence intensity increments of sleep, as estimated by average intervals or ranges of intervals between successive sleeps, i.e. by their reciprocals, seem indeed to decrease with development.

This trend could not be shown as easily with any desire. For one thing, opportunity is a rather variable thing that could complicate the recurrence of satisfactions considerably. Take the desire of talking. It requires somebody to talk to, and all somebodies in question may sometimes be unavailable for talking while, at other times, say, during service in the Navy, a person may be unable to get rid of these somebodies even for a little while. Or take the desire to ski. Well, the enthusiast does it, may be, every weekend in the winter, even takes a whole week off for that purpose, and then does no skiing at all for nine or ten months. Another thing that complicates matters would be the variety of degrees of satisfaction of any given desire. One can sleep two hours or twelve hours and wake up tired or well rested. One can have an exhaustive conversation with a dear person at one time and just a few words at another. In fact, a little browsing through a magazine may sometimes be better for a desire to sleep than just two hours of sleep, and any words exchanged between any two or more persons in the street or on the radio may, when heard by us, satisfy, to some degree, our desire to talk to somebody. Finally, desires can do something for each other. They are all on *substitution continua*, mostly on more than one. Hence we may have to take a look at the entire *substitution continuum* in question while investigating the trend of decreasing intensity increments with a given desire of a given individual. While testing the desire to eat, we may have to consider drinking, chewing or munching candies, gums, or the rear end of pencils, smoking, or even talking, before we can hope to see the trend with a given individual. And we should not even be surprised to find that this *continuum* can do something for as complex a desire as graduating from college. While working very hard for it and seeing the preliminary results drop in only very slowly, a person may take to eating, drinking, and smoking more regularly and frequently than before. A *substitution continuum* may, on empirical inspection, appear to be temporarily regressed because of the effort or energy expenditure that goes into something else.

The crux of the matter is that formula (4) applies fully only in pure theory, where opportunity can be held invariant on the mere whim of the theorist. It characterises the level of a person's motivational development for a given period of time. In very pure theory it would even do so for every moment of a person's life. The great complexity of man compared to all other living beings, however, seems to defeat the formula in practice. The number of desires that can be distinguished within a person becomes unmanageably large even early in development. A child of one year of age has quite a few specific desires of eating already, such as eating porridge, sweet porridge, meat of one kind and another, various vegetables or fruit, of which he may like some and not others, although all of them are good for him, according to mother. He wants to rock in many ways, in his little chair, in bed, while standing, squatting, or even sitting. He wants to touch, hold, and move the pacifier, the rattle, a little rubber bone, a spoon, a cup, a diaper, the bed bars, strings, etc., etc. He even wants to eat, or at least taste, all of those things too. So how can one establish n, leave alone the many ϵ's or C?

Well, the formula can be applied in approximations or by appropriate sampling (Toman, 1957). Let me indicate that in a few examples. Take n first. Suppose two school children are of the same age, of the same social background, and getting along in school about equally well. Something like the number of desires satisfied or pursued outside of school may show us a difference in their n and hence, other things being equal, a difference in development. If one of them does nothing but watch television irrespective of what is on, whereas the other watches television, practices the flute, reads about the animals of South America, builds model planes, and plays chess whenever he can find a partner, the second one is likely, other things being equal, to be getting, or be, further along in his development. Needless to say, consideration of the complexity of desires as rated, say, by the amount of preparation necessary to establish them to a given degree of facility or, may be, by the size of social premiums attached to them, would refine estimates considerably. In fact, the number of interests weighted by the number and complexity of desires that each of them comprehends could tell us something about people's n's regardless of how well matched they are by social background.

It will be more worthwhile, however, to look for intensity increments themselves, and to do so for a smaller and more manageable sample of specific desires 1, 2, 3, . . . $m - 2$, $m - 1$, m, preferably those for which variations and differences of opportunity would matter little, such as sleeping, eating, drinking, perhaps smoking. A person who sleeps more and/or eats and drinks more frequently and regularly and/or smokes more than another person is likely, other things being equal, to operate on a lower level of development. More complex desires could be used as samples too, but the samples would have to be larger in order to make sure that differences and variations of opportunity would cancel. Only if the sum of intensity increments of desires such as, say, watching shows, whether in the theater or on television, reading about people, whether in the newspaper or in novels, being in company, resting (without falling asleep), getting some physical exercise, and making purchases, is markedly different between two people while other things are equal, would we infer a corresponding difference between their levels of development.

If two people have a very different background, even a larger pool of more primitive desires such as sleeping, eating, drinking, smoking, and the like, may fail to represent their developments by our estimates of intensity increments (reciprocals of intervals between successive satisfactions or their ranges). Take a physicist and a tramp. The phycisist may very well satisfy these desires more frequently (in shorter intervals) and regularly (with less variability) than the tramp would and thereby come out with larger intensity increments and a lower level of motivational or psychological development than the tramp, which is absurd. But the "true" intensity increments of these desires are likely to be smaller with the physicist than with the tramp. However, opportunity to satisfy these desires is grossly different for these two people. The physicist has a home, restaurants, and money to his ready avail, whereas the tramp may have air and the earth's ground to walk on, but little else. For that reason our estimates may be off the true values unless we equalise opportunity and throw the poor physicist on a tramp tour for a test.

Formula (4) provides other ways, though, of tackling this kind of problem. That is, we can look for some manageable sample of desires $m + 1$, $m + 2$, . . . $n - 2$, $n - 1$, n, which are desires in the process of formation, desires that have not been consumed yet, or, if you like, the strivings of a person. In fact, one of them, the person's best one, so to speak, the biggest and most difficult thing he strives for and is making progress toward, will tend to be the most indicative of motivational development among any one of them. Difficulty is a difficult thing to appraise, but it has been indicated before that the amount of preparatory work or the significance of the aspired for the social system—which in turn tends to appropriate premiums accordingly—may be fair and handy criteria. Our physicist would presumably be pursuing some difficult goal, one perhaps that neither he nor anybody has reached so far, such as, e.g. a unified field theory, whereas the tramp is engaged in no such pursuit.

It may be necessary to estimate the intensities of these desires-in-the-making, say, by the relative progress a person is making toward the goals of his pursuits. If he is saving money in order to buy a house, the increase of his savings during a given period of time in proportion to his income may indicate the intensity of his desire. If a person is studying for a degree in physics, appraisals may be more difficult, although, perhaps the grading by his teachers give some indication. If a man is courting a girl whom he wants to marry, appraisal of his striving and progress is even more difficult, although not impossible either. We may ask: How much is he willing to do for her or put up with? And how many others are willing to do how much for her? We must realise, though, that intensity of such a desire-in-the-making does not tell enough by itself. A man who wrecks his future life while courting a girl has an intensive desire, but, other things being equal, he must be on a lower level of development than a man who can do other things at the same time. Similarly, that one of two students of physics who has to work harder in order to achieve graduation, so that he will have had no dates and hardly any entertainment, and has been unable to study other subjects at the same time, will be on a lower level of development, provided other things are equal. This does not contradict the notion, however, that the person who can work harder, if necessary, will be of greater maturity or "ego-strength". The person who usually works with ease in a given pursuit can multiply his efforts by more than the person who has always been working close to the limits of his capacity. Whereby these limits are determined by the state of a person's development, and by C.

C, finally, of all ingredients of formula (4), comes closest to representing "libido". The larger and more accurate the sample of intensity increments of desires that are being added, the closer will the empirical value of C approach the true value. Yet this is not really practical, except for purposes of differential diagnosis. The greater the sample of desires from which empirical C's are computed, the more likely will it be that a difference found between any two individuals represents a true difference in their levels of development.

C could, in principle, be established also in a different way. Since n of formula (1) as well as of formula (4) grows with development, since this means no more and no less than derivative-formation, and since derivative-formation is a function of cathexis, n as well as the corresponding decrease of intensity increments and, finally, C are all functions of cathexis. In fact, C can be said to represent the speed with which an individual manages to learn about or to cathect conditions under which desires can be satisfied. It stands for his rate of cathexis. Which, incidentally, could be a hereditary given. Not only that. It would seem only common sense that C should be a constant. If there is anything that could conceivably remain invariant throughout a person's development, it would be something like his capacity to learn in a most general sense. In order to get at C directly, we would have to disentangle this capacity or basic rate of learning from all that the individual in question has learned so far, i.e. from all previous experience. We would have to set up test situations in which the individual can "learn from scratch" only, situations in which, say, rewards follow a certain probability pattern rather than anything "causal", or situations in which some basic sensory learning is required, such as when he has to run around with prismatic glasses that distort or invert his vision. Needless to say, any measure secured that way would only *correspond* to C and permit only differential diagnoses among individuals. It would not be an absolute measure.

If C could be established absolutely, an individual's expected state of development could be computed from his chronological age. What is more: the degree to which counter-cathexis has infiltrated a person's desires and *substitution continua* would show in the difference by which C as computed from empirical intensity increments of his desires would fall short of his "absolute" C. But even C estimated as a function of the rate of learning would lend itself to appraisals of a person's sum-total of counter-cathexis or defensiveness in general. In fact, even less accurate, yet more practical, estimates of a person's rate of learning may do the trick. If we could estimate the knowledge that a person has accumulated in that area of life where he is at his best and divide it by his age, we may, again for comparative purposes only, have a fair enough equivalent of his "true" C. What would complicate such an estimate, however, is the degree to which a person's knowledge in such an area is dependent on very specific talents like those for music, sports, mathematics, painting, etc. The greater some specific talent, the less indicative of his overall rate of cathexis will be the rate of cathexis with which a person operates in that field. A little more about that later (see pp. 112f, 126 ff).

Utilising formula (1), formula (4) would have to be re-written in the following way, if we want to account articulately for the fact that different desires can do different things for each other (see pp. 25 and 93)

$$\sum_{i=1}^{n_p} c_i = \sum_{i=1}^{n_1} \epsilon_i + \sum_{i=1}^{n_2} \epsilon_i + \ldots + \sum_{i=1}^{n_{p-2}} \epsilon_i + \sum_{i=1}^{n_{p-1}} \epsilon_i + \sum_{i=1}^{n_p} \epsilon_i = C \qquad (5)$$

In this formula p would be the number of *substitution continua* on which n desires are assembled, whereby $n = \sum_{i=1}^{p} n_i$. In words: The sum of all sums of intensity increments of desires assembled on all of a person's *substitution continua* equals C. If there were as many *substitution continua* as desires ($p = n$, but also $n_p = n$), all desires would be unrelated to each other. If every desire would show up on every *substitution continuum*, the number of desires that can be distinguished at all would be equal to the product of the number of desires that can be identified on any one *continuum* and the number of *substitution continua* ($n_p p = n$). This would reflect the most intimate inter-relationship of desires possible. Obviously we will not find such a degree of inter-relationship of desires or of "integration" in reality, no matter how far a person has developed. Empirically, however, we can expect that a person with a given n will be the more mature in his motivational development, the greater the number of desires that are represented on more than one *substitution continuum*, and the greater the number of *substitution continua* on which they are represented. Hence both n_p and p, tend to lag more and more behind n with development, whereby n_p will be approximating n/p, and p will be approximating n/n_p, both of course without ever reaching either. Accordingly, testing with a given sample of desires on how many of a given sample of *substitution continua* they appear, will also tell us something about a person's level of motivational development or, more specifically even, of a person's degree of overall object-formation.

There are other relationships that could be investigated by the help of formula (5). How evenly or unevenly do different *substitution continua* contribute to C? Or in other words: What is the variance of all the sub-sums? (of all the c's according to formula (1)). Also: How evenly or unevenly has counter-cathexis infiltrated all *substitution continua*? Alternatively, what is the variance of "decimation" of the sub-sums, i.e. of the difference between their "true" values (given, say, by the rate of cathexis as estimated by experience-free learning tests and multiplied by chronological age of the person in question) and their estimates as computed from intensity increments of empirical samples of a person's desires? Complicated as all these formulations may sound, that which constitutes clinical appraisal of persons in the absence of gross symptomatology of any kind is even more complicated. What may matter more: in clinical appraisals we are doing something similar to what our formulae could do for us in theory. All clinical appraisals go somewhat along the lines indicated, although more tacitly and implicitly so.

We have shown what it would mean, in principle, to assume libido as of a constant quantity throughout longer periods of time or even lifetimes. It means that the intensity increments with which all our desires grow incessantly from zero or close to zero to that intensity at which action is usually taken and, sometimes, all the way up to that intensity at which some kind of action must be taken by all and any means, well, it means that the intensity increments of all our desires add up to a given quantity C. It also means that the process of cathexis is going on incessantly and at a rate that is constant over longer stretches of time or even a lifetime. The rate of cathexis is a direct function of C. It is given with an individual. In fact, it might be *the* hereditary given.

Derivative-formation has been said to be a function of cathexis (see p. 9). Therefore it is a ceaseless process too, as has also been pointed out before (see p. 26). A person's desires multiply steadily as he develops. That would imply however, that the intensity increments of his desires become smaller as he develops. Libido feeds into more and more different desires and, since it is assumed constant with a given person, "dissipates". That means no more and no less than that, as a person develops, it will take desires increasingly longer, on the average, to reach a given intensity. The appetite of an adult, e.g., would tend to be less intense than that of an adolescent after a given period of starvation. The adult would have to starve longer in order to get as intensely hungry as the adolescent. The intervals between successive satisfactions of any one of a person's desires will tend, on the whole, to increase with development and so will the variability of these intervals. All provided that neither changes of opportunity nor substitute desires nor the variability of degrees of satisfaction complicate matters.

Cathexis is cumulative (see p. 9 ff). All ongoing cathexis of conditions under which desires can be satisfied adds something to cathexes already established. It adds to our knowledge of the world which, parenthetically, includes ourselves. And all knowledge of the world is itself the product of cathexis. This is why we can cathect only so much at a time (not more than our rate of cathexis permits) and nevertheless cathect more and more, as we develop. Our libido supply does not grow any less, as we "spend" it, but spending it has lasting effects. Not only that! These lasting effects—knowledge—facilitate future spending, as we shall see in greater detail a little later.

But is it not non sensical after all to claim that libido is constant? What about puberty? Does libido not increase in puberty? Well, not necessarily. A whole chapter will be devoted to puberty later on, but let me indicate that the inflation of some of a person's interests such as in other people or himself may well be accompanied by a deflation of others, such as the study of mathematics, botany or a foreign language. The decrease of intensity increments of desires in one area of the world may be slowed down, while those of another decrease more rapidly over a certain stretch of development. Cathexis proceeds at the same rate, but one type of condition becomes more frequent and extensive than the other, so that more knowledge can accumulate indeed. Why they become, or why they are even made, more frequent and extensive is another story (see chapter on Puberty and Adolescence). At any rate, libido will be spent in different ways, not necessarily in a different quantity.

But then, do we not feel quite invigorated at times and very low at others? If you have in mind that therefore libido has increased or decreased, you are mistaken. Libido is not what we feel. It has something to do with it, but the relationship is not as simple as that. Satisfactions of desires will generally tend to "refresh" us and deprivations beyond a certain point of intensity (at which anxiety is triggered off) or for good (so that the establishment of counter-cathexis is a must) will make us feel depressed. Complex inter-relationships of things within the world that we have made ours through cathexis will determine the prospects and arrivals of such satisfactions, deprivations, and losses. Opportunity to satisfy desires is a very complex thing in itself, different for different desires at any one moment and always subject to change. Suppose we are bored by and tired of a meeting in which we have to participate, and all of a sudden a beautiful girl and a handsome young man enter the meeting room. In such circumstances we may find ourselves quite interested again. The same may happen if some kind man has thought of providing some refreshments. These instances imply, however, that opportunity has changed so that some desire, for instance that of hunger, or of inspecting new faces rather than the stiff old crowd of the meeting, is suddenly being satisfied. The intensities of these desires decrease, since they have been satisfied, and there is more room for other pursuits, including the matters of the meeting. Libido, the energy that feeds into all this, could conceivably remain unchanged in quantity. The change of opportunity may be enough to account for our changed feelings. In fact, man would be a rather unstable and shaky creature, if his environment could do such things to his "fuel".

"You said, or implied at least," one may wonder, "that libido feeds into intensity increments of desires and into cathexis. How much, then, goes into one and how much into the other?" The reply will sound absurd for a moment, but on the basis of what has been said so far one might guess it anyway. All libido feeds into intensity increments of desires, and all of it feeds into ongoing cathexis. In other words: the sum of intensity increments of a person's desires and the rate of ongoing cathexis are different aspects of the same thing. The rate of cathexis with which an individual operates from birth onwards, determines the quantity, other things being equal, to which intensity increments of all his desires will add up at any given period of development. Derivative-formation is a function of cathexis that has accumulated, and the number of desires that can be distinguished in a person is a function of derivative-formation. Intensity increments will tend, on the average, to be smaller, the farther derivative-formation has proceeded, or the more cathexis has accumulated. But they will continue to add up to C, just as cathexis will continue to occur at the given rate.

These relationships hold on the whole and in the long run. They can be utilised in characterising a person's motivational development for a given period of time, say, for the past year, or for a month. But would they hold also for every moment of life, as has been suggested passingly before (p. 94, small print). We have also spoken of feelings of vigor and depression which refer, after all, to more momentary states of motivation (see p. 98). Have we tacitly shifted our ground?

We must remember that we are not only functioning on a given level of motivation, but that we are also very concretely motivated at any given moment of life. If a person were, and had always been, living in a monotonous field of opportunity in which nothing would change except by his own actions and satisfactions, and all that he has ever had would be accessible with equal ease, we might find that the sum of intensities that this person's desires had accrued at a given moment would add up to a given constant quantity too. Let us call it K. In other words, such a person would, on the whole, stay about equally motivated, even though the desires that are foremost in intensity would change all the time. They would be satisfied, i.e. reduced in intensity, and enter the race again at the rear end. Should one desire become unusually intense, it would be at the expense of others. The others could be tolerated only up to intensities smaller than usual.

However, we are not only motivated, but are also satisfying desires, at any given moment of life. Yet we are doing so to very different degrees at different times and occasions. Sometimes we are working very hard and at other times we have things taking place with very little effort on our part. Driving to a distant destination at top speed and through heavy traffic might be an example of the first; and being driven by a chauffeur to a destination not too distant, with no hurry, through light traffic and even through a beautiful countryside, an example of the second. In one case we are probably intensely motivated, at least one desire, the desire to get there, is extremely intense, while in the other we are mildly motivated in various ways and presumably enjoying the trip a lot.

If, however, a person were, and had always been, living in a monotonous field of opportunity in which he would stay about equally motivated at all times so that his motive intensities would add up to K, he would also be consuming satisfactions at a steady rate. One implies the other. Degrees of satisfaction show in the decreases of intensity of the respective desires. In fact, they could be defined that way. Hence we should rather say: Only if satisfactions are being consumed at a steady rate, can motive intensities add up to a constant quantity, K, in the first place. That, precisely, is the characteristic of such a monotonous field of opportunity. All and any kinds of satisfactions are available at the whim of the person who lives in such a field. His world is a storehouse of everything ranging from the most beautiful girl or the most handsome and attractive man all the way down to single cigarettes, candies, or the inexpensive light spectacles of a pinball-machine. A simple glance or nod of the head would bring them all.

In reality, however, man is exposed to an extremely variable field of opportunity. If he happens to be a plane-wrecked pilot in the desert, his K will mount to intolerable heights due to the continued deprivations of quite a few of his desires while he goes unrescued. If he happens to be a lazy oriental prince who can have everything that he wants to have, his K may have been simmering in the very lowlands of human motivation. And any given person may be in situations sometimes close to that of the plane-wrecked pilot, and sometimes close to that of the lazy prince. In other words, K, which reflects something like the overall degree of opportunity to satisfy one's desires, is variable. Yet all empirical values of K would tend to scatter around a mean with a given person. It is this mean or average value of K which an individual will tend to maintain over longer stretches of time. He, and everybody, will tend to behave and satisfy desires in such a way as to keep a balance between his strenuous and easy times, one that suits him personally, and with a range that suits him likewise. That is, he will do so to the extent that he has a choice, to the extent that he is not thrown into extreme situations such as jail or combat on one hand or the sick-bed where he may have to take it very easy on the other.

The greater a person's K at any given time, the more "hard-up" for something he is, the more strenuous is his life at that time, and the less satisfaction or, generally speaking, the less consummation of pleasure can be going on at the same time. Increase of a person's K means less, and decrease means more, simultaneous satisfaction by definition. Since cathexis of conditions under which desires can be satisfied accompanies all satisfactions or, as we may also say, all consummation of pleasure, it is plausible that there should be more overall satisfaction and hence more comcomitant cathexis going on, the smaller K, and vice versa. In other words, the ongoing process of cathexis will vary in an inverse relationship with K.

But have we not said that C, the quantity to which intensity increments of all of a person's desires add up, is a constant? What is more: have we not even maintained that cathexis is a direct function of C? Whereas now we say it is an inverse function of variable K (which, obviously, is a relative of C). Is there not a contradiction?

The *mean value* of K which an individual would try to maintain should stay the same over longer stretches of time, possibly throughout life. That is, provided he has a choice. Hence the average rate of concomitant cathexis will stay the same too. In fact, his rate of cathexis will determine K and the variance of K that he can tolerate at any given moment. This, however, might need a little further inspection.

Suppose a person satisfies a desire recurrently under a recurrent condition that does not change. Its "objective" diffculty is the same. Every time it involves the same degree of overall deprivation as measured, say, by the time that an individual has to wait before satisfaction is possible, or by the number of, and the lack of control over, desires that are instrumental and would have to be satisfied first. Suppose a person has to always wait five hours for his next meal. Or suppose that he always has to prepare the meal himself.

Since intensity increments of all recurrent desires tend to decrease slowly with development (see pp. 93, 97 f), the desire to eat will not mount to the same intensity in those five hours of waiting as it used to, say, a year ago. The meal will be consumed while the intensity is still short of its corresponding height a year ago. Hence that portion of K that is occupied by the desire to eat after five hours of deprivation has become smaller. If other things are equal, i.e. if the rest of K is unchanged in quantity compared to a year ago, K as a whole will be smaller than a year ago by the amount that the desire to eat is smaller after five hours of deprivation. If K is smaller, however, ongoing cathexis will be correspondingly larger. That would mean that such a person, while still waiting for his meal, could absorb more while reading, or could do whatever he cares to with greater ease and learn or remember more about it than he could a year ago. That would imply, for instance, that he could prepare his own meal, a certain dish, say, potatoes, a cube-steak, and salad, with greater facility. There is more ongoing cathexis than a year ago. Therefore the instrumental desires involved, boiling (the potatoes), frying (the steak), washing and mixing (the salad), but also securing the food to begin with, etc., could all be controlled better.

If K is smaller than a year ago due to the smaller portion that is consumed by the desire to eat, the situation could become more difficult "objectively" and still be mastered. If our friend had to wait six hours for his meal, the portion of K that is occupied by the desire to eat at once may still be below, or just equal to, the intensity to which the desire mounted within five hours a year ago. Or he may be able to prepare a more complicated meal himself at the usual eating time, such as potato pancakes, onion steak, and a better salad, mixed with vinegar, oil, and blue cheese in a specific ratio. He can easily tolerate a delay that may be due to the preparation of the pancakes, which requires grinding the raw potatoes, I understand, or due to the onion steak which needs more careful frying or broiling. And while doing either, waiting or preparing his meal, he will remember better just what he did and learn more for the future. May I be forgiven for being so schematic.

Since the decrease of intensity increments of recurrent desires is a function of the process of cathexis (see p. 93), they will decrease the faster with a given person in a given period of time, the greater the average rate of cathexis on which he is operating. The rate of cathexis will determine how much the portion of K that goes into the desire of eating has been reduced during a given period of development when satisfied under ordinary conditions. It will also determine by how much these ordinary conditions can be exceeded in difficulty and still be mastered. The smaller the portion of K that goes into the maintenance of a given desire, the relatively larger can it grow under extreme conditions of deprivation or difficulty.

The portion of K that goes into a desire just before it is being satisfied under a given recurrent condition that does not change is an exponential function of the number of recurrences of that condition, perhaps something like this:

$$y = Ke^{-ax^2} \tag{6}$$

In formula (6) K is the sum total of motive intensities that a person can tolerate on the average; e is the basis of the natural logarithm; a is a constant determined by something such as a person's talent to learn under the specific conditions in question, or his particular "sub-rate" of cathexis. (See also p. 126 ff.) Since the sub-rate of cathexis in a particular field of the world will not generally be too different from the overall rate of cathexis by which a person operates, and since K itself is a function of his rate of cathexis, a may often be taken as 1 without too great a risk. As the values of x, or the number of recurrences of the condition in question, get very large, y will approximate zero.

The analogous formula for the amount of concomitant cathexis as a function of the number of recurrences of the condition in question would be something like formula (7)

$$y = B(1 - e^{-\beta x^2}) \tag{7}$$

whereby B would be the maximal amount of ongoing cathexis that a person is capable of (which, in turn, is a direct function of C), and β something like a of formula (6), namely a constant determined by a person's particular "sub-rate" of cathexis in the field of the desire in question (see also p. 126 ff). For practical purposes β may often be taken as 1, like a. As the values of x, or the number of recurrences of the condition in question get very large, y will approximate B. Hence the amount of ongoing cathexis will be greatest when, according to formula (6), the portion of K consumed by the desire in question is close to zero, or when the available K supply would be consumed the least. Many or most of the *data* that constitute a condition have been cathected already. The "jigsaw puzzle" of accumulation of cathexis or object-formation approaches completion. New aspects of the recurrent condition in question, or new conditions altogether, new "jigsaw puzzles" to fill, may have to be searched for soon. Otherwise there would be nothing to cathect. The individual would go "hungry".

The degree to which a given recurrent condition can be delayed or made more difficult and still be handled by an individual is determined by something like formula (8)

$$y = K(1 - e^{-ax^2}) \qquad (8)$$

whereby K and a have the same meanings as in formula (6).

What has been shown to hold for a given recurrent desire, will hold for any other, and for any number of them. If conditions under which a person's recurrent desires could be satisfied would always stay "objectively" the same, K would simply decrease with development. That, however, would have a peculiar consequence. With K decreasing, the amount of concomitant cathexis will increase. Since cathexis is cumulative, the individual will approach increasingly faster a state of affairs in which all that can be cathected of these invariable recurrent conditions has already been cathected. One day there is nothing left to learn about or cathect, unless new aspects can be found among these conditions that have not yet been considered, or new conditions altogether. If this is impossible, the situation will soon deteriorate to one of growing deprivation and necessitate counter-cathexis. Just imagine that our friend will always eat after five hours of abstinence, prepare the meal himself, and the meal is potatoes, cube steak, and the same salad for keeps. He will be bored stiff and end up in utter despair The only way in which an individual can, and does, avoid the plight of boredom, and worse, is to search all the time for new and more difficult conditions—although not too new or too difficult, at least not all of a sudden—under which his desires can be satisfied, or to embark on increasingly greater and far-reaching tasks (desires $m + 1$, $m + 2$, ... $n - 2$, $n - 1$, n, in formula (4), p. 93). Otherwise K will decline. Thus the concept of K—as well as that of libido, or C, or our formulas (4) and (5) for that matter—show how man's ceaseless travel to ever new lands of experience and endeavor does not have to be a theoretical postulate itself, produced from nowhere or, at best, from plain description. It derives by necessity from metaphysically uninvolved technical assumptions that we made in the beginning and that have carried us all along.

But is not K or the sum of motive intensities that, for example, a three months old child can tolerate incomparably smaller than that of an adult or even of the same person twenty years later? Is it not the growth of K which reflects the psychological growth of a person? Can an adult not go without sleep, food, company, and what not for forty or fifty hours, whereas a three months old cannot spare anything he has begun to entertain at all for more than a very few

H

hours ? Would that not make the portion of K that goes into those desires many times larger with the adult ? And would not K have to be larger in order to do that ?

If you compute it that way, you might as well include all those many desires maintained by the adult's K that the child does not even show yet to any degree. K would come out even larger with the adult. That is one approach, and a good one for purposes of differential psychology. That one of two persons who comes out with a larger average or maximal K than someone else would, in all likelihood, be the more mature. He has developed farther and must either be older or operate by a higher rate of cathexis. In fact, that is what formula (4) and the assumption of a constant C, libido, or rate of cathexis, would lead us to do in practice (see pp. 93, 94 ff, small print).

What the critic underestimates, however, is how rapidly desires grow to the intensity at which they are usually satisfied, and how soon thereafter they are already intolerably intense, with the infant. An hour after waking up he may ordinarily fall asleep again, and after another hour almost nothing can keep him awake for another minute. If we let him wait an hour beyond his usual feeding time, he may be in a panic; so soon will the limits of his capacity to tolerate deprivation be reached and surpassed. Whereas with the adult the desire to sleep reaches the same intensity, that one at which he usually goes to sleep, after some sixteen hours, or that one at which he can no longer stay awake under any conditions, after fifty, sixty, or even seventy hours only. Likewise for eating and other desires. In fact that intensity which leads to the same effect whether a given person is still an infant or already an adult, namely action or, in our terms, satisfaction, can be taken to be the *same* intensity, although that intensity is reached with different speeds at different times of development. That would be another approach to the matter of K, and it is ours too. It is by this approach that K could indeed come out to be of a given average quantity with a given person. As a matter of fact, that intensity of a desire that can maximally be tolerated would be as good an estimate of K as any one measure can provide. It is that intensity at which practically all of K is being consumed by the desire and little or nothing is left for others. Since this is an impossible state of affairs, the individual will be on the verge of temporary regression, i.e. of satisfying these other desires or even the heavily deprived one by any means, no matter how primitive and destructive (see also p. 58). This effect will tend to be the same, in principle, whether the person is still an infant or a full-fledged adult or, in other words, whether it takes him a little while or the longest time with a given desire to reach that point. Compared to another person of a comparable background and age, however, it may take him longer or shorter to get to that point. This would indicate a difference of their K's, other things being equal, and by inference also a difference of their rates of cathexis on which they have operated throughout their development.

Another thing that the critic may underestimate is how little cathexis has as yet accumulated in a child of three months old. Sucking is still a fairly big job with him. Very many of the conditions under which it occurs are still unknown to him, or uncathected. He could not do a thing, if adults would not carefully assist him. Not even his own fists come to him when wanted as a substitute. And sucking is by far the most highly developed of all *substitution continua*, or of all he can do. If he wanted to see more light, he would not have the slightest notion of how to go about it himself, and if he wanted to hear a human voice, he would still have to struggle hard to produce his own little burps and grunts just then. Whereas the adult goes to the refrigerator, dining room, or restaurant for food and turns a switch in order to have more light or hear a human voice. What is more, he knows which switch brings which. In fact, he knows many different switches and operations that make all kinds of things available. His bigger jobs begin when he makes up a food budget for his family or for the hotel of which he happens to be the manager, when he designs a house for himself, that will have more light, or when he studies, or even conducts a choir performance. Although an adult could go without sleep, food, companionship, for many hours, he does not, if he can help it. He holds out for as easy and well-regulated a life in those matters as he can get. He does so in order to be free for other and greater affairs.

Hence C, or the quantity of libido given with an individual, or his inherited rate of cathexis, seem indeed to determine K and its variance, at least its ideal mean values, those under which the individual would thrive best. If the situations he encounters on his pursuits of satisfaction or pleasure are chronically too difficult, his K will be chronically too high, and concomitant cathexis too low. If a child is sent to a school where he can keep up with the other children only through very hard work, he is likely to fail before long. Any small burden of additional work which the other children can master with ease may throw him off balance, since he has already been working close to the limits of his capacity. The opposite case, however, would not be any better. If a child is in a school where all the other children cannot possibly keep up with him, he will be bored, look for additional things to do, including those that the school might not permit (because they amount to mischief) and finally be advised to leave for something better or different. We should also be aware, though, that certain things require higher K's in order to be learned at all. Nobody can hope to satisfy a desire such as playing the piano well unless he goes through the hardships of practice first.

One may wonder whether K, in its variations around a mean value, can ever be zero so that there is nothing but satisfaction of a desire and, therefore, maximum concomitant cathexis. Well, we may say that there are conditions that come at least close to it. One is sexual or, more specifically, genital excitement and orgasm. Voluntary effort is minimal at last, K close to zero, and concomitant cathexis maximal. The partner and even oneself will be learned about in all of a person's aspects including the most primitive and primeval. If consumed with abandon, i.e. without defensive maneuvers or reservations to speak of, this experience will be the strongest of all ties between two people, and the partner will become the dearest of all persons before long, if he or she was not already. Another instance of maximal satisfaction may be a superb performance of a symphony or a great play, but also something such as skiing at the height of one's skill and under conditions of powder snow, huge sun-flooded slopes, a blue, blue sky, thinnish air and, if you like, nobody but God and his angels as observers. May be, also crowds of people instead who are cheering while the hero is racing down a giant slalom for fun. Cathexis is maximal. The hero "takes it in" avidly. He may learn about creation's innermost secrets, about his own greatness, about fragile man's unique position in the infinite universe or about the feminine caprice of a ski slope. Still another one is sleep which can be consumed only if it is without effort. Otherwise it will not be sleep, but dreaming or being awake. Satisfaction is maximal. Hence cathexis must be maximal too. Cathexis of what, however? There is nothing psychological going on in real sleep. So what is being cathected?

Everything that has begun to be cathected during the day. Cathexis should not be viewed as a momentary process. The exposure to the *data* that will or will not be cathected may be momentary. We may see an interesting face at the railroad station. Or we may get a telegram: "Coming to-morrow evening. Bob." And Bob may be a dear friend of ours. Cathexis goes on beyond those moments of seeing a face or reading a telegram. That night, while already in bed, the interesting face may come to our mind once more. We may wonder about the peculiar expression that we seemed to see on it and about the features that struck us as familiar, now that we think of it. Or we may wonder what Bob will look like, now that we have not seen him for a number of years, and we may think of a few of our times together with him, of discussions, of that date with the Robinson girls and that stunt we pulled in class on poor old Smith, the Zoology teacher. What stunt? Nothing much. Just putting six white mice in the drawer of his desk which Bob had opened with one of his skeleton keys. He was a great burglar. Could get in anywhere. We may also think of what we should do in order to make ends meet tomorrow. Soon after which we fall asleep.

Well, if both events have continued to work in us somehow—and why or how else could they have recurred at night?—it is conceivable that work on them, cathexis or counter-cathexis or any complicated combination of the two, in accordance with all pertinent previous cathexes and counter-cathexes, goes on in sleep. In fact, there is evidence that this does, indeed, happen. "Sleep on it!" is the proverbial advice suggesting that we will do better the next morning with whatever problem we are trying to tackle. Usually we *do* "do better". Therefore something relevant to that problem must have gone on during sleep. But there is also physiological evidence suggesting that memory ground work is not over until a few seconds after exposure to an event and that the accumulated memory work of five and even ten hours is still unstable enough to permit retroactive amnesia under certain severely traumatic circumstances such as a concussion of the brain.

To come back to our examples: If we have attended a very exciting party that night from which we come home rather late and exhausted, the interesting face encountered at the railroad station may not come to our minds any longer. In fact, the event may be gone for practical purposes. We may forget even our friend's arrival and remember it with a start only the next afternoon at work and by a time when it may already be too late for certain preparations.

At any rate, sleep can be viewed as another of those satisfactions during which K is at a minimum and ongoing cathexis at a maximum. Ongoing cathexis, however, works on nothing new, but on all the cathexes begun and developed to different degrees during the day. Freud has described it as the withdrawal of cathexis from the world to oneself (Freud, 1915 b), a metaphor which must be taken with a grain of salt. It does not mean that the pseudopodia of libido are drawn in, if for no other reason than that libido does not have pseudopodia. In sleep everything has been arranged by external measures (dark, quiet, comfortably warm room, lying position, blankets to wrap the sleeper, soft mattress, etc.) and by physiological devices (increase of overall stimulus-threshold, tonus-, circulation-, respiration-, and cortical activity-changes, all controlled by certain centers in the brain) in such a way that K can indeed be close to zero much of the time. It mounts to noticeable quantities only if severer disturbances occur, say, noises, a cold draft or heat coming from a house that is aflame, and it will either be used to restore the original condition, sleep with zero K, or shake the sleeper out of it completely so that he can act, if necessary. I would even go as far as to suspect that other desires do not increase during sleep or, for that matter, during any kind of maximal satisfaction, although it would show most clearly with sleep. The others do not usually last long enough to make too much of a difference. Even a heavy smoker who takes to a cigarette every half hour will not smoke for some eight hours during sleep. Some addict-like may have to get up once during their sleep and smoke a cigarette, but even so they can abstain at least for some four or five hours. Also we do not tend to have our last meal just before falling asleep and breakfast the minute we wake up some eight hours later. Frequently these two meals are separated by something close to the average intervals between any two meals during daytime plus the time of sleep. Just to mention a few examples.

A temporary arrest of motive intensities would add to the complications surrounding formula (4) (p. 93 ff). However, the formula is filled in by estimates of *averages* of intensity increments. To rule the complication out for practical purposes, it may be enough to make sure that sleep has been either extrapolated or included uniformly.

One may also wonder whether K, in its variations around the mean, can ever be maximum so that concomitant cathexis is zero. Well, if concomitant cathexis is zero, we would have no recollection of the events in question. Hence we may ask: "Are there such events in which we must have been maximally motivated? Otherwise we could not have survived? Yet we have very little or no recollection of how we did it. Are there such events?

An accident involving ourselves, or barely escaping such an accident, is often of that nature. We or the person in question may stagger out of the battered car unhurt, as far as he can tell and not remember what happened nor sometimes what he saw during the last few minutes. He may not even know where he is for a moment. Yet he must have behaved reasonably. Things could be much worse. Or suppose we would find ourselves surrounded all of a sudden from head to toe by icecold water. We will probably make a desperate effort to get out of it and if we succeed at all, we are likely to remember little or nothing of how we did it. Only in retrospect will we recall that we were walking across a rumpled meadow at night for whatever reason and finding a little lane at last which must have been the six-foot deep irrigation canal from which we have just crawled out soaking wet. All of which are cases of danger, and the state we are in is anxiety at its best or panic, which, incidentally, has not sneaked up on us like a disease, but hit us like a bomb. However, we would be in a similar state, if we were the plane-wrecked pilot in the desert and remained unrescued as time goes by (see p. 17). At last K or our hunger for everything, for water and food among the first, would be intolerable. We would be in panic whether we act it or not and remember little, if anything, about our last hours before falling altogether unconscious, provided we live to test our memory. The baby who has been starved too long will more inevitably be in a state of panic. As has been indicated (see p. 16), he may be unable to "recognise" the bottle even when it is put right into his mouth. He may be unable to cathect anything for the time being which, by the way, would include even the utilisation of cathexis already established. Could he utilise it, it would be in the course of some satisfactions, and once they are possible, ongoing cathexis is too.

The greater the deprivation of desires, the greater K and the smaller the amount of concomitant cathexis. Anxiety prevails when deprivation has exceeded a certain point. One might even say that this deprivation beyond a certain point *is* anxiety (see p. 22). It is evident then that, what holds for deprivation in general will hold for anxiety as well. The farther anxiety has mounted, the smaller will be concomitant cathexis. Ultimate anxiety or panic would be equivalent to zero concomitant cathexis. The turmoil of panic shuts off all intake of *data*. It even stops all latent work on those just taken in—which tends to make them crumble, which, in turn, creates retro-active amnesia.

Can this amount of ongoing cathexis be measured? If not, why all this talk about its relationship to K? Well, it can be measured, although not directly or absolutely. It can be measured or appraised comparatively by the amount of knowledge that different people have acquired of the same event. Of two students attending a given lecture under comparable circumstances the one who knows and can recall more about the lecture has cathected more. Hence we can assume that he has operated on a relatively smaller K than the other person during the lecture. If both of them have the same rate of cathexis, the difference in retention may be due to a difference in familiarity with the subject-matter. The person who has retained more of the lecture has possibly known more to begin with. Or it may be that the other person is in a state of deprivation, perhaps hungry or in the process of running out of money these days. If their rates of cathexis are different—as some estimates outlined above (see p. 94 ff) might suggest—more complicated pro-ratings might be necessary, but comparison would not be impossible either.

Is that not very far-fetched? Well, I think we tend to make such appraisals now and again while dealing with people in everyday life. A teacher, e.g., may notice that a student does not comprehend very well, either during a given lecture or even during the semester, judging from his cooperation in class or from his work on various tests. If he has seen that student do better before, he knows that he *can* do better or, in our language, that his rate of learning or cathexis is not represented by what he shows now. Hence the cause must be something else. And one of the questions that we may find such a teacher asking his student, provided he cares to at all, is: "What's the matter with you? Something wrong?" Or a parent may ask that very same question of his child. And if parent or teacher were talking in our jargon they might ask: "Have you suffered a loss? Are you in a state of greater deprivation than before?" Or they might ask anyway: "Can I do something for you?"

I do not want to be misunderstood. A sad face, unwillingness to eat, sickliness, truancy, etc., can be very telling indeed. In fact, there are many qualitative entities such as phobias, obsessions, conversions, paranoic delusions, compulsive promiscuities, that we better not overlook. The point is that, in the absence of all of these, there are still things we can tell.

Let me give a few more examples of appraisals of ongoing cathexis. Of two people who attend a party the one who recalls more people and more about the swarm of little conversations and doings is likely to have been more at ease, on the whole, than the other. Of two people who run around in the city the one who remembers much about the city's lay-out, sights, monuments, buildings, appearance of people in the streets, etc., is likely to be the tourist, whereas the person who remembers little about the city except how to get to some twenty drug-stores is more likely to be a hard-working (i.e. highly motivated) salesman. Of two people who have been in the same army unit for the same length of time, the one who remembers more about all of it is likely, other things being equal, to have had a better time (less overall deprivation) than the other. Of two mathematicians the one who does distinguishably better than the other, say, as measured by the quality and/or number of his scientific contributions, is likely to be the better mathematician. Which implies: he is likely, other things being equal, to operate at a slightly higher rate of cathexis in this particular area of the world or, if their initial talents have been tested to be the same, he has had an easier time on the whole than the other. In fact, that may hold even for something more comprehensive, psychologically speaking, such as intelligence. The tests by which it is commonly measured are always also tests of knowledge and to the extent that they are, they also measure how much has been cathected or also, at what rate cathexis has been operating with different individuals, provided we can assume that they have all had comparable opportunities. This is indeed what intelligence tests assume by implication. They are made up of items that are not experience-free, but supposedly free of all those types of experience that a sizeable portion of the population in question might have missed. They purport to measure the intelligence with which any given person has acquired whatever knowledge he has, and not his knowledge alone. Intelligence, however, can be viewed as a function of a person's basic capacity to acquire information or knowledge, to gain control over conditions under which desires can be satisfied, to learn or to cathect. It is a function of the rate of cathexis with which a person operates. Hence even something as popular and widely used in schools and clinics as are intelligence tests can, under certain conditions, help us estimate ongoing cathexis.

How do the Id, the Ego and the Superego share in K or in libido for that matter ? Well, K as well as libido or the rate of cathexis cut across all three subsystems. The rate of cathexis determines how quickly primitive desires develop into more complex derivative desires, or how quickly the Ego forms. But it also determines, other things being equal, how unconscious the unconscious portion of the Id, or the Id proper, will be. This derives from the following: All counter-cathexis is a kind of substitution of desires. It will be the easier to substitute for a given loss, the larger the *substitution continuum* in question. The *substitution continuum* in question will be the larger, the greater the number of derivative desires that have formed in a given time or the faster they form in general. And they will form the faster in general, other things being equal, the greater the rate of cathexis by which the individual operates. Hence counter-cathexis will be the easier to establish, closer "relatives" of the counter-cathected desires will continue to be satisfied and, hence, the unconscious desires will be less unconscious, other things being equal, the higher a person's rate of cathexis. That would mean, for instance, that an intelligent person can become conscious of given unconscious desires more easily than an unintelligent person, an inference well born out by clinical evidence. To mention just one: psychotherapy and psychoanalysis—in both of which unconscious desires are made conscious, among other things—are more effective with intelligent than with unintelligent people.

What holds for Id and Ego, holds for the Superego as well. We still remember that it is the system of introjected desires, whereby introjection is no more and no less than the cathexis of other people's desires for oneself. Cathexis of other people's desires, in turn, is substitution of whatever desires are in conflict with their desires by optimal duplicates of one's own. Introjected desires are those of our own desires that come closest to the desire that other people have for us (see also p. 87f). Hence the Superego is, in a sense, made up of our own desires too. Consequently the rate of cathexis determines Superego-formation too, provided all other circumstances are comparable. It will develop the farther in a given time, the greater the rate of cathexis.

What holds for rate of cathexis, holds for the other indicator of libido, the sum of intensity increments of desires, as well. Libido feeds into the intensity increments of all desires assembled on all of a person's *substitution continua*, and there are primitive (hence counter-cathected to various degrees), complex, and introjected desires on all *substitution continua*. Take the *continuum* "sucking" as an example. There is sucking mother's breast, a heavily counter-cathected desire, eating voraciously, kissing people by force or drinking from a puddle in the street, as examples of desires not so heavily counter-cathected, yet primitive and aggressive enough; there is eating efficiently with knife and fork, smoking or drinking, as examples of complex derivative desires, and there is eating with grace, drinking just so much and no more, holding back on food too, etc., all desires that have been introjected more evidently than the others from other people, first of all from the parents. Apparently all three sub-systems of the psyche, Id, Ego and Superego, are represented on this *substitution continuum*, and they are on all others too. There are none with which other people or the parents would not have had some say.

Therefore, if libido feeds into the intensity increments of all of a person's desires, it also feeds into Id, Ego and Superego. Special circumstances determine how much of it goes into each of the three. The relationship between Id and Ego would be determined by the overall amount of control or cathexis that has been established, whereas the relationship between the Ego and the Superego will depend on the amount of introjection a person had to achieve. The smaller the amount of cathexis established on all of a person's *substitution continua*, the less libido has fed, and is currently feeding, into the Ego, hence the "weaker" the Ego, and the "stronger" the Id. The greater the amount of introjection that has infiltrated all of a person's *substitution continua*, the less libido has fed, and is currently feeding, into the Ego, the "weaker" the Ego, and the "stronger" the Superego. Libido (or C of formula (4), p. 93) will be distributed differently according to circumstances, and these circumstances, might even change in the course of development. But its amount is given with a given individual. Hence a man cannot have a strong Id, a strong Ego *and* a strong Superego, unless we mean that he operates on a high rate of cathexis or on a large amount of libido and has been exposed to circumstances that permit an optimally even distribution. He has enough wildness and craziness left in him which, however, he can hold under any number of degrees of control. And he has a strong concern for other people wherever it would matter. Few of the desires assembled on any one of his *substitution continua* have dropped out altogether. A large gamut of desires, ranging from rather primitive and aggressive ones to late and complex derivatives, are acted upon and satisfied with many different degrees of regard for the desires of other people, but seldom without such a regard. He is always acting also by his introjections without ever being debilitated by them. Such a person can put up a fight in sports or elsewhere with great abandon, but also act with the utmost of control and efficiency in very complicated endeavours, and never hurt anyone seriously. Yet he would not be afraid to hurt people up to a degree wherever it might be in the interest of larger communities of people or even of those hurt. Such a superman of a healthy person is passionate, efficient, disciplined and moral. In terms of K we can say that he would be able to tolerate the largest variations. He can work hard and have concomitant cathexis at a minimum, and he can enjoy happy, lazy times, times of very low K's, as well.

Let us look at other variants for a moment. A person with a strong Id in relation to Ego and Superego will tend to be impulsive, uncontrolled and inconsiderate all the way up to being a psychopath or delinquent. A person with a strong Superego in relation to Id and Ego will be overscrupulous to the point of incapacity to act. A person with a strong Ego, but a weak Id and Superego will be a cold, efficient calculator. And a person with a strong Id and a strong Superego, but a weak Ego, will be thrown forth and back between these two power-systems. The Ego will mainly function by means of counter-cathexis. It will be barely able to prevent the worst of clashes. The person will be neurotic or worse.

We seem to imply that the overall determinant of a person's psychological development is the rate of cathexis or the quantity to which the intensity increments of all his desires add up, one being, on the whole, a direct function of the other. But what about an aggressive person, or a very passive person? Do these characteristics not refer to additional determinants that would have to be considered besides the rate of cathexis?

Not necessarily. It may be convenient to treat something like vitality independently of rate of cathexis. Yet in principle, vitality, aggressiveness or passivity can be derived from a person's rate of cathexis and the overall degrees of opportunity that he lives in. If that opportunity is the same for two people, passivity is a function of cathexis. The person who operates on a lower rate of cathexis will tend to take longer than another one before getting so bored with given circumstances that he would search for or create new ones. A higher rate of cathexis will, on the whole, impress us as less passivity or a higher degree of activity, and vitality has a similar explanation. The greater the overall rate of cathexis, the greater the push for new conditions under which desires can be satisfied and the greater vitality, provided opportunity is equal. This relationship may be complicated by specific talents which, in our terms, result from a higher rate of cathexis in the area of talent than in other areas of a given person's world. Somebody may have a great talent for painting or chemistry, but operate on not so high a rate of cathexis in all other areas. Hence he might not impress us as particularly vital or active except in the area of his talent. However, since man lives in social systems and since these need many different kinds of people and talents and tend to create specific opportunities for specific people and talents, such a person may appear rather vital and active after all. We are likely to get to see him at his best, working under conditions he likes a lot and also enjoying other things that hinge on it, such as making a livelihood, having a family, vacations, etc. That is, provided the social system is also functioning at its best. This picture may change rapidly in an emergency, war, famine, etc., when painters or even chemists may temporarily be of little use unless they switch to something else. They will seem to "lose" vitality, as anybody will whose opportunities are radically reduced. Whereas the person who has developed manual skills or brute muscular strength may not only impress us as more vital, but even be it. His life expectancy will be greater while the crisis lasts, and vitality is life expectancy by definition. Aggressiveness, finally, depends on the rate of cathexis too. A person who operates on a lower rate of cathexis is likely, other things being equal, to run out of his wits sooner than another person when a situation gets more difficult than usual. If he tends to solve protracted deprivations by attempts at satisfactions of more primitive and destructive desires rather than by renunciation, whereas another person can still wait, he will impress us as aggressive. So might anybody, for that matter, whose opportunities have just been reduced radically enough.

One may wonder at the end, whether libido can really and feasibly be assumed to be a constant with a given individual? I have already pointed out that this is, if nothing else, the simplest assumption about libido, and shown that it is not an impossible assumption in principle. But it could well be that it changes with development in some lawful way. It may increase, decrease or do either in cycles. My thesis is, however, that the simpler assumption is the better one by its very simplicity, as long as it has not proven untenable. I have myself tested it in a number of ways, none of which did any harm to this simplest assumption or to formulas (4) and (5), although they were intended to do harm, if they could at all (Toman, 1954a, 1956, 1957). But even if libido, or C, would change in quantity with a given individual, formulas (4) and (5) and the relationships implied would probably hold up.

The crux of our assumption is, apparently, that intensity increments and, in a sense, even intensities of desires are additive and that only a certain amount of overall motivation or disequilibrium, no more, can be tolerated at a given state of development, or even throughout it, as we believe. If they are additive and cannot surpass a certain sum, however, they *must* be interrelated. Hence our assumption—i.e. Freud's assumption with my articulation—is a truly holistic one. In fact, it is the simplest of all holistic assumptions about the mind.

But why should libido be constant or change in a lawful way at all? Why could its quantity not be utterly unpredictable from moment to moment? It could. Yet with such an assumption we would be nowhere. Coming to think of it, this would not even be an assumption, but defeatism. Besides man's mind simply does not appear to go like a butterfly, not even to the most romantic or existentialistic of man's observers. Even for them there is something regular about it.

Is the mind, the psyche or personality, not much more complicated than I have outlined ? It is. Yet in order to make any sense at all we had to simplify. We had to ignore, e.g., how much goes on in a person simultaneously with a given state of deprivation of a particular desire or a number of them. Some desires are always being satisfied, and they may have some specific satisfaction value for the deprived desire. Besides all of a person's desires are entangled in a network of instrumentality that may often be inextricable for an observer. Yet it guides the person in question and imbues apparant satisfaction values to desires that they might not have otherwise. We have also ignored, how intricately man manages to regulate the dynamic balances of his pursuits and overcomes dejection temporarily by anticipation and cognitive rearrangements. While still in the midst of school, a child longing for his vacation can work on schedules of things he plans to do at the resort and even make provisions for them, write to a friend living there, build a boat to take along, etc. However, the commentator can believe me that the psyche is complicated enough even with our simple assumption. The assumptions themselves are not even too simple when it comes to practice and implementation. The second part of this book, The Theory at Work, will show how complicated things remain in life and psychological development after all, but also, I hope, what psychoanalytic theory can do to help us see some aspects of the order it abides by.

How does ageing and death figure in this ? Development is a function of the ceaseless process of cathexis—and counter-cathexis wherever necessary—or of the incessant accumulation of information and knowledge of the world. When does this process show its first signs of reversal ? When does ageing and final death begin to catch up with us ?

From the very beginning of all individual life. While we have barely begun to drink the world and to organise it for our own designs, we are already dying, although in infinitesimal steps. Cortical neurons, e.g., are supposedly perishing all the time, and they are irreplaceable. Yet the losses amount to very little at first. They do not show at all for quite a while in development. Once they do, however, we would expect them, among other things, to do so in the rate of cathexis which, after all, must have something to do with neurons and neural activity. Hence the question arises: When could the steady rate of cathexis on which an average human being operates conceivably show a decline for the first time ?

I can think of a few alternative answers. One would be to take the supposed end of the "growth of intelligence" as measured by conventional intelligence tests as the earliest indicator. This would be in the teens. Another possibility may be the twenties from when on it gets increasingly difficult to embark on the training of an altogether new talent or on a radically new profession. If a person does, he is easily overtaken by younger competitors. Still another alternative would be the late fifties or early sixties when most people except a few chosen ones begin to prepare for retirement. Until then, however, a person may still be "growing" in the area or some sub-area of his work while already becoming rigid and stagnant in others. Thereafter he may decline even in his most special area of work.

For various reasons my private sympathy is with the last alternative. Until then we may be observing the by-products of the accumulation of cathexis rather than the decay of the rate of cathexis itself. The accumulation of cathexis creates order in a person's concepts of the world and order of one kind is always in opposition, no matter how small, to other or new orders. A new area of the world cannot be cathected so easily in later life because most, if not all, elements of that new area are likely to be members of established orders already. A language learned in later life, say, in the country of that language, would be an example. Up to about sixteen years of age an intelligent person can adopt a new language and learn to speak it as well as his mother tongue. Later on he cannot do so well any more. He keeps an accent, retains idioms of his first language which come into conflict with those to be newly acquired and stays generally less versatile in his new language than he would have been in his old except, may be, for areas that he has learned about only in his new language. It looks as if, after sixteen, he has heard and said too much already in his first language as to be able to keep it out of his second altogether. The fifty year old is handicapped for the same reason when he wants to learn a new language. He has heard and said so very much already in his first language, that every single word and phrase of his new language is heavily obstructed by the old ways of saying things. He will acquire the new language only rather imperfectly. In either case, however, this need not be due to a real decline in his rate of cathexis. It could be a matter of conflicting orders.

There is another evidence, however, that would speak against my preference. If we can trust biographical, auto-biographical and historical evidence, we learn that most of the great new ideas in the more complicated fields of human endeavor such as the sciences, but sometimes even in more extensive and agglutinative fields such as history or literature (where new ideas may not always have such far-reaching consequences), anyway, most of the great new ideas were conceived by their authors before they were thirty years old. It may have taken up to a decade and more to spell out and prove them to everybody's satisfaction, but this was more often a matter of bare labor than anything else. Yet even here we may be dealing with a property of the orders of *data* rather than a decline of the rate of cathexis. A certain amount of knowledge is necessary to enable a person to play with it, but as he continues to accumulate knowledge, he may one day know too much to be able or even dare to play any longer.

Primal Desires

PRIMAL desires must be those of all desires the satisfaction of which is most immediately instrumental to, and indispensable for, survival of man as an individual and as a species. They are oral stimulation and manipulation (culminating in swallowing), stimulation and manipulation of the trunk and the extremities (culminating in the act of elimination, but also in highly diversified manipulation proper) and genital stimulation and manipulation (culminating in orgasm). They can form only in that sequence. Libido may feed into these three primal desires and all their derivatives, or into these three basic *substitution continua*, in different proportions. The rates of cathexis by which the basic *substitution continua* or drive-systems operate may contribute in different ways to the overall rate of cathexis by which the person as a whole operates. Different general interests and different types of relationship to other people and the world in general may result.

*　　　*　　　*

What desires are there? What are man's basic or primal desires? Or what are the *substitution continua* on which all of man's desires are assembled so that none is left without a "home"? Are they not practically infinite in number? And is that why you preferred the general and non-committal treatment all along?

True, I have done that. This does not mean, though, that they cannot be treated qualitatively too. In fact, I have even done that too, implicitly. But let us look at the matter closer. Or, rather, let us summon God once more and let him pose the question: "What primal desires should I give man?"

If we were being insolent, we would ask him back: "For what purpose? What do you want man to do?" But we know it anyway. If man was created to live, he must live *on*, and in order to do that he must eat and eliminate. This is what every animal does as well. In fact, there is no living being, no matter how primitive, that could do without either. But in order to live on, he must also come into being in the first place. Which means that procreation is an indispensable condition of man's very existence—excluding Adam and Eve from our considerations—and will be for centuries to come. In order to live on, man must create offspring. Hence the primal desires that God should give man, were He to follow our advice, would have to guarantee that man eats, eliminates and re-

116

produces. There are other things, of course. Man has to be able to absorb carbohydrates, proteins and fats, to keep his water and temperature-household balanced, etc. But these things do not by themselves require behavior in a psychological sense, nor the formation of desires, nor cathexis nor consciousness. Even breathing and sleeping could be included for that matter. Both of them function automatically and unconsciously. Sleep, in fact, cannot even be consumed any other way and breathing goes on during sleep.

As it is, however, God must have anticipated our advice long ago. We would not otherwise be here and do all this reasoning. He must have equipped man with foolproof devices that ensure from birth on that he eats, and there are such devices. One is the sucking reflex. Whenever something stimulates the new born's lips, he will tend to surround it with his lips and suck it in. If he can get it or something of it into his mouth so that it stimulates its inside, by touch, temperature and taste, another reflex will rush to act on that stimulus: the swallowing reflex.

Similar devices have been installed in elimination so that it functions from birth on. The sphincters are automatically released and the wastes automatically expelled whenever intestinal or bladder pressure reaches a certain intensity. There is a close to foolproof device even for procreation, although the individual has a long way to go for that final "purpose". But let us look at the other two first.

We have learned that the ongoing process of cathexis varies in an inverse relationship with K (see p. 101 ff) which, in turn, is a function of the difficulty of the situation under which satisfaction of a desire can be obtained. If the reader did not skip pp. 102–103, he will also know that the first recurrences of a condition under which a desire can be satisfied consume a lot of K and are accompanied by very little ongoing cathexis. In fact, the very first occurrence of such a condition would be the most difficult of all. It would require all of K and be accompanied by no cathexis. The individual would learn or cathect nothing. Hence the first recurrence of the condition would be like its first occurrence. In other words, the individual would be in just as difficult a spot as he had been the first time and just as flabbergasted. In fact, he would never get acquainted with the condition.

Such a state of affairs is quite unlikely in later life. Almost nothing can be that radically new for an adult. Accidents or other sudden great dangers would be examples, but even then there is often some concomitant cathexis so that we do, e.g., recall a little of what happened and what we did. With the newborn, however, this is different. His first feeding is an extremely new and difficult situation, so difficult, in fact, that no concomitant cathexis may occur unless there are inherited facilitations that make the first feeding a little short of maximally difficult. If the behavior necessary in order to achieve the intake of food is pre-established to some extent and automatically responsive to certain stimulations, there will be concomitant cathexis, no matter how small. Since cathexis is facilitating future satisfaction in general (see also pp. 98, 102f), the second feeding will already be a trifle easier and the amount of concomitant cathexis a trifle larger than the first time. Hence, if there are inherited facilitations of sucking to begin with—and we have already said there are—the newborn is safe. He can board the ship that can bring him slowly, but steadily, to all the pleasures of the world. If there were no such facilitations, he could never even get aboard.

Any other radically new situation would place the infant in a similar position as the first feeding might have, had it not been for the inherited facilitations. Being wrapped in diapers, dressed or carried, being bathed, moving any part of the body, seeing daylight, hearing noises, etc., would all be frighteningly new unless they also have inbuilt devices that make things a little less than maximally difficult to have or unless they simply are not quite so radically new. Both "unless's" may be true, but if we could demonstrate one, say the latter, we would not have to worry about the first. In order to demonstrate the latter, however, we would have to show that there is no situation which the infant can be exposed to that would not have some resemblance to the first feedings and its roundabouts. If they do have a resemblence, they are not radically new, hence K would not have to be maximal and some concomitant cathexis *could* occur. Do they have that resemblance ?

Let us inspect the examples chosen. Being wrapped in diapers, dressed or even carried, is a special kind of being touched, and sucking is a kind of touch too, first of the lips and then of the mouth's inside. Being bathed is being touched by warm fluids, and sucking is being touched by warm fluids too. Moving any part of the body is like moving a particular part of it, namely the mouth, and the mouth, lips, tongue, jaw, is being moved during sucking. Seeing daylight is a special kind of visual stimulation, and there is visual stimulation, with sucking. The infant opens his eyes occasionally and that implies visual stimulation, no matter how little he can do with it at first. It takes longer for visual and auditory stimulation than for others to "become" desires, the desires of seeing and hearing. Sucking, which involves being touched and moving (lips, tongue, jaw), becomes an identifiable desire long before seeing and hearing does.

The point is that feeding, with what it intrinsically involves as well as with its accidentals, is the prototype of all possible other situations, and eating or sucking, the desire that emerges first of all, is the prototype of, and link to, all other desires that may ever form. Nothing is entirely different from sucking and all it involves, although I would not want to delude myself or anybody else. Preparing a speech for an election or devising a bridge that is to go across the Mississippi River is very very remote from early primitive sucking. Yet preparing a speech, among many other things, is doing something with your mouth, namely speaking —perhaps tacitly while also writing it—and so is sucking. And devising a bridge, among many other things, is *doing* something, and so is sucking. The mouth is the first "doer" of all, chronologically speaking. Devising a bridge may concretely be drawing the plans for it, and that is a "doing by hand", among other things. However, we shall see that the hands can be brought under control by the infant only to the extent that they become able to reach and touch the mouth and duplicate what the mouth does, awkwardly at first, but gaining competency and efficiency and finally out-distancing the mouth in either. Just as the mouth can hold things, e.g., so can the hands, and they even have a greater reach. Anything new will have to be brought to the mouth for inspection, for the "test of existence", so to speak. Is what I hold and feel, really, that is orally, what I think it is ? Only gradually will the hands be able to judge by themselves. Finally even the eyes can take care of many things. They can inspect what the hands would feel if they were at the focus of our glances. In other words the "psychological mouth" expands to include the hands—they are the mouth's "extensions" —and the eyes—they are the radars of the hands. It finds even its own way of control over them: through words. Hence there are no radically and altogether new situations, once sucking has begun to get established as a desire. Even if gravity would all of a sudden stop and leave us afloat we have already had similar experiences. We could hardly have had any feeding without being lifted, carried or put down again, i.e. without "floating" somehow from one place to another.

In addition, however, there are hereditary facilitations. The grasping reflex, which makes for a kind of closing of the hand whenever the palm is touched, the movement of all five fingers or toes at once, the co-ordination of the eyes so that they move jointly and can eventually focus on something, would be a few examples. They are the other type of insurances set up by Nature or God that development or, more specifically, cathexis of conditions under which desires can be satisfied will take place indeed.

If, after sucking, no situation is radically and altogether new, elimination should not be either. It has been functioning by reflex action since birth, but it has not come to the infant's notice yet. The infant may have had sensations of being wet or "full" somewhere in the lower region. The lower region of what, however ? He has not learned about or cathected his own body yet to any noticeable degree. His lower region is not too different from the ceiling of his room or from sounds that he will later on identify as his mother's voice. His lower region is not "his" yet, nor is elimination.

So when will something like elimination become "his" ? Well, first of all the infant has to learn that he happens to produce excrements. After that he will have to learn how to do or not to do so by intention. In order to learn that he does produce excrements, however, he would have to get hold of them. In order to do that, he would have to get them in his hands, and in order to find out what it is that he is holding in his hands he would have to bring them, if you pardon me, to his mouth. Yes, he would *have* to. This is his final test of existence of anything during his early life. In other words, the infant's mouth would have to "expand" to his hands and the hands would have to get hold of his excrements and bring them to his mouth before they can possibly become an entity for him.

I

If he does not take them to his mouth or if he does not even touch them, counter-cathexis of some degree has already become effective. At any rate, we may say that excrements become the potential or actual object of sucking, something comparable to food or something like food. Thereby they assume psychological existence.

Once the infant has come that far, perhaps even sooner, he will also learn about how he has been managing to produce excrements all this time, and again the mouth will furnish the most sensible idea of how something can possibly be produced: the idea of spitting. Whatever goes on in that mysterious tail-end of his can only be something like spitting. How else could it bring "this stuff" into being? There is a difference, though. Whatever the mouth can spit out it has also taken in not too long ago (except saliva). What the tail-end spits out, however, has not been taken in at all. Or has it? But how? No, it is a much more personal production than that. It is the child's *own creation*. He makes something out of nothing. There may be suspicions, though, that the excrements are "put in" per anum just like food is put into the mouth. It will also dawn on him before long that this is, done properly, the perfectly acceptable spitting out of what the mouth has taken in, while oral spitting is no longer all right.

Since the hands must have been cathected so that they can, in principle, bring excrements to the mouth and since it takes time for the mouth to "expand" that far and thoroughly, but also since the desire of spitting comes necessarily later than the desire of sucking, and since spitting has to be reasonably under control in order to be able to furnish the idea for other kinds of spitting, elimination *can* enter the picture only considerably later than sucking. It will become a desire to be sure, and control over conditions under which it can be satisfied will be formed. Either is inevitable, provided the infant goes on living at all and is only mildly in the possession of his senses. But it will come with a good delay, compared to sucking.

What holds for defecation in particular, holds for urination as well, although formation of the desire and final mastery of the conditions under which it can be satisfied would come still later. For one thing, urine escapes more readily than do the excrements all attempts to handle it and bring it to the mouth. Urine is a more ephemeral object at first. In fact, only if it is in a container of some kind, will it last any length of time, whereas excrements could do so without one. Hence urine will take longer to become an object or an entity for the child. There are other considerations too. For one thing, urination occurs more frequently than defecation. At a time when control has been achieved over either, urination can be engaged in even more frequently and, sometimes with very little to urinate. Defecation, for physiological reasons beyond our concern, requires enough accumulation of matter in due time before it can take place at all. Urination is likely to occur under more different conditions and with a larger variety of intervals in between than defecation. There is more to control. Hence it should take longer to achieve a given degree of control in practice.

Another consideration is the desires of parents. For obvious reasons the parents would tend to be more anxious to control the child's defecation than his urination. Here the ephemeral character of urine is its very advantage. Much less can happen to clothes, furniture, other people, etc., if the child wets himself. An accident in defecation would usually be a little more inconvenient. All of these may be responsible for urination taking even longer than defecation to get under control.

We have seen how intake of food and elimination manage inevitably to become desires. What about procreation which, as indicated (p. 117), has a long way to go? What inbuilt device is there to begin with and in what way will previous cathexis or experience be helpful in assuring its occurrence and "cathectability"?

For one thing, genitals, i.e. the immediate organs of procreation, are particularly sensitive to stimulation, to touch, pressure, temperature and friction. But do they get stimulated? Well, in order to guarantee that they do, they should be automatically, if not anatomically, linked with other indispensibles of man's survival. Knowing what we have just discussed they should be linked with the intake of food or elimination or both. As it is, i.e. as God has anticipated what we would advise him to do, the genitals are also the organs of urination. If urination recurs regularly and needs somebody's attendance every time, the genitals will get it too. They will be wiped, bathed, wrapped, and that *is* stimulation by touch.

How sensitive to such stimulation will they have to be? Well, sensitive enough so that they will finally outdo any other stimulation. Their stimulation must win over all other modalities of stimulation such as taste and smell, sound and sight and kinesthesis. But it must also win over all stimulations of its own modality, touch. It must be more sensitive than any other part of the body's surface. Otherwise man may eventually decide to eat or drink, to take hikes, read, pray or do anything, for that matter, rather than to obtain genital stimulation.

If that is so, however, and if we want to keep man alive until he is physically mature and capable of procreation, we will have to arrange for a sufficient delay of the formation of genital desires. If they have to be linked up with an indispensable of man's individual survival, it should be the latest that goes under control: urination. And it is. If it were linked with eating instead, things might never get to the point of procreation. Such an infant could conceivably stimulate his genitals rather than eat. Whereas he has no such alterative if it is linked with urination. He cannot control urination at first. Hence he cannot control genital stimulation either and his parents usually do not help him out on that of their own accord.

Could we not assume that genital sensitivity is a matter of maturation? It simply springs into being at a certain point of development? What kind of an assumption is that? Forgive me the undertone, but have we not dealt with such things when talking about the Superego (see p. 81ff)? Besides, maturation is, at best, one rail of the railroad track to maturity and adulthood. The other would be the accumulation of cathexis or, more colloquially speaking, the growth of experience. At worst, the two would be equivalent and perhaps the worst assumption is not the worst at all. Let us remember that it is principally impossible to demonstrate maturation without demonstrating experience too. In all tests of supposed absence of some specified experiences—such as found, e.g., with babies of certain cultures who live in swaddles for a year or so and learn how to crawl, sit and stand within a few days or even hours; which should prove maturation—experience was not really absent. Such a swaddle baby can, e.g., exert a hundred different types and degrees of pressure against a swaddle. In fact, the swaddle usually is not even as tight as to forbid all movement, even the slightest. Besides he is not in the swaddle all the time. There are interruptions due to cleanings, whether of the baby or of the swaddle. All of these conditions would make for experience. Finally there is even very concrete evidence. Sensitivity to genital stimulation can be demonstrated as existent with an infant soon after birth.

Is it not the peculiar physiological mechanism of orgasm that makes for the difference between genital stimulation and all others ? Well, orgasm is a part of the sensitivity to genital stimulation. All auto-erotic or heterosexual efforts steer in the direction of maximal stimulation and maximal satisfaction, which is orgasm. But eating and elimination have their "orgasms" too. Sucking, munching, chewing and the like, would not be complete unless they are followed by swallowing. The climax of oral stimulation can only be reached while something enters the oesophagus. That is why some of the ancient Romans took to peacock feathers and vomiting—so that they could eat again—rather than to chewing or sipping all their delicacies, but spitting them out before they could get down their throats. If it were not so, the infant's intake of food would be jeopardised. He might suck and munch, but forget to swallow. The same would hold for elimination. Once he has a choice at all in elimination, once he can decide whether he will do it or hold back, a premium for doing it indeed must already have been installed. Otherwise he may forget. The maximum of stimulation or atisfaction must be obtained while the excrements and urine pass the sphincters and get into the open. Otherwise there might be trouble that could affect as much as the survival of mankind.

There is a difference, though. Reflexes guarantee that the infant swallows and eliminates before he has a choice. Once he can choose, however, he will judge for himself, so to speak, how much more satisfying it is to carry through with eating and eliminating than to stop half-way. With genital stimulation, on the other hand, the climax that would be comparable to the moment of swallowing or eliminating does not come about for a long time. Genital orgasm is dormant at first. All genital stimulation experienced up to the time at which control over urination is achieved tends definitely to stay short of orgasm. At that time, however, i.e. when urination and all manipulation involved is up to the child, genital stimulation *could* be carried on until something like an infantile orgasm is reached.

Yet by that time another thing has happened too. There have been, say, some five thousand moderate genital stimulations in connection with urination until then and generally none of them was kept up sufficiently long to lead to orgasm. They may have led to erections and their female equivalents, and erection, for one thing, increases genital stimulation, if by nothing else than swelling the area of stimulation. Every infant got started in the right direction, so to speak, but was halted each time after a while. Sometimes this would happen sooner and sometimes later. Whenever it would happen sooner than previous times, he would want it to last longer, and if it does not or cannot be brought about, counter-cathexis would become necessary. Thus the continuation of genital stimulation to the point of orgasm gets counter-cathected before orgasm is ever reached. Counter-cathexis is usually well established by the time the infant does gain control over urination and could conceivably carry genital self-stimulation or masturbation to the point of orgasm. Therefore the child tends to stop "playing with himself" after a while whenever he got started, or does not start to begin with. This is even more true for girls who, by their very anatomy, receive still less genital stimulation from the parents in connection with urination and otherwise than do the boys. Hence counter-cathexis would generally be stronger or more pervasive.

This should not imply that there is a little boy or girl anywhere on our planet who would not try genital self-stimulation to some degree or, if counter-cathexis is too strong, substitute urination, say, in the form of short continence, nightly bedwetting or simply of some kind of special or secret indulgence in urination *per se*, sometimes also in further substitutes such as being naked, looking instead of touching, naming, talking about or alluding to the forbidden, etc. The discovery of the existence of two sexes in this world of people—and of animals and flowers as well for that matter—will even tend to give a new twist to whatever satisfaction the counter-cathexis established permits. New opportunities dawn and will become checked by new dangers or threats, as we shall see (p. 165ff). But it must not take us by surprise that the desire for genital stimulation, once it has formed, remains more or less arrested due to early counter-cathexis. Its full development and the "accident", psychologically speaking, of procreation can be delayed indeed. Which should not mean that procreation is only or always an accident. Nearly everybody develops also *desires* for children. But even an imbecile who is unable to form such a desire can nevertheless *have* a child, sometimes much to the surprise of somebody.

How can a person, on the basis of what has been discussed, ever get the idea of turning to another person, and to one of the other sex, for genital stimulation? And would you not have to account for that, if you want to account for procreation? Well, we do want to account for procreation, but no extra account for a person's turn to a partner is necessary. As a child he has already had a partner.

In fact, he had genital stimulation by the help of a partner long before he could manage such a thing himself. He had his mother or somebody to take care of him, and if he has ever been changed or bathed, he has had his genital stimulation. Therefore, when he does make his very special and articulated advance toward mother around the age of four years, he is doing nothing new. It would be more surprising, if he would *not* make such advances to mother. After all, she led him on to it. She led him to believe that genital stimulation by her is possible. There is a long way to go, of course, and many people other than mother intervene before he settles down with a girl for good. A girl, on the other hand, has an even longer way to go. For one thing, she is tied to mother for genital stimulation and anything at all as much as the little boy is, and has to give her up in favor of father if she wants to have a person of the other sex. Her way is longer by at least that switch. There will be more about this later (see p. 170ff).

If, after the desire of sucking has formed, no situation is radically and altogether new, genital stimulation or even procreation should not be either. That is, in some respects, no matter how minor, genital stimulation including heterosexual intercourse should be like what the mouth can do and experience even in early life. In fact, one's genitals will have to "reach the mouth" somehow in order to begin their psychological existence in the first place. The mouth would have to find them, just as it found the infant's hands and feet. If that is not possible, the hands would have to bring them to the mouth. If that is not possible either, the hands and their "radars", the eyes, will have to experience and judge for themselves. The hands will have to touch, hold or manipulate the genitals as otherwise, human anatomy permitting, the mouth might. The genitals will become "objects of the mouth" by mediation.

On the other hand, genitals can be touched as the mouth could and can be, and they will even respond to that themselves somewhat like the mouth does. The male genital can move, passively as well as actively through erection or through movements of the pelvis. The corresponding skills of the mouth: movement of the lips, the jaws, the tongue and the head as a whole. The female genital cannot move quite so well, whether passively or actively, but it can, in principle, although not necessarily—we hope—in early life, take in and hold, which the mouth can do too. The male genital can behave and experience like an active mouth, and the female like a not so active mouth. In fact, before a grown-up couple gets as far as sexual intercourse, they are likely to exercise quite specifically in kissing what they will or might do genitally. The girl opens her mouth under the man's lips and permits his tongue to enter and meet hers which she keeps somewhat in the background. If a girl does not, but reaches out for his mouth instead, this could easily be held against her as unfeminine.

What is the upshot of all this? Well, it looks as if we can distinguish three primal desires, hence three basic *substitution continua* or drive-systems, one related to the intake of food, one to elimination, and one to procreation. *Oral manipulation and stimulation* would be one basic *substitution continuum*. It includes such desires as sucking, biting, chewing, spitting, babbling, talking and all kinds of derivatives thereof. Its climax or "orgasm" would be swallowing. *Manipulation and stimulation of the trunk and its extremities*, arms and hands, legs and feet, would be another basic *substitution continuum*, whereby the trunk can do the most impressive and climactic: produce excrements and urine; while the hands become the most sensitive and diversely efficient part of the body. They mediate between these and other stimulations. They "handle" them. They do manipulation proper, so to speak, although the legs and even the mouth can help, the legs by locomotion and the mouth by sound, words and speaking. Desires such as smearing, painting, writing, cooking, digging, cutting, hitting, constructing, etc., would be examples. They all require something to do it with, e.g. paint, ink, food, dirt and the like. *Manipulation and stimulation of* a special part of the body, *the genitals*, would be the third (see Freud, 1905; also p. 165ff).

It has been pointed out, however, that any desire, even the most primitive, say sucking, is actually an assembly of several desires (see p. 30f). It belongs to a number of *substitution continua* such as taste, smell, touch, the feeling of temperature and of a food's or object's consistency. In that case, however, *substitution continua* would be areas of stimulation. Hence the following *substitution continua* should be distinguished: touch (including temperature and pressure), taste, smell, kinesthesis (stimulation caused by one's own movements), sound and sight (see p. 121, also p. 78). This distinction, however, may not be too practical by itself. After all, kinesthesis may come from movement of the head or mouth, of arms, legs, sphincters or genitals. Touch is very different with different parts of the body. The mouth, the fingertips, or the genitals are highly sensitive, whereas the skin on the back is rather immune. Hence some areas of kinesthesis or touch might be more basic than others. True, stimulation is the end of all desires. Yet it is almost never just one kind of modality of stimulation. Besides, different kinds and modalities of stimulation require very different degrees of effort. Instrumental desires of very different complexities must be arranged in various ways in order to bring them about. Any kind of food, e.g., is usually easy to obtain, whereas a fancy dish in a ritzy restaurant right by the ocean is not so easy to get at all. Similarly, genital stimulation by masturbation requires another effort than genital stimulation coming from the dearly beloved and very beautiful girl or handsome competent man whom one may want to marry in the first place.

This brings us to still another issue, namely people. Do not our relationships to people form a *substitution continuum* all of its own, and independently of the basic *substitution continua* mentioned? Well, anything that we can possibly do and experience in relationships to other people will be oral, bodily or genital manipulation and stimulation. Not only that. There is no manipulation and stimulation that would *not* be related to other people, whether acutely or by means of "memories", i.e. previous cathexes. People would form a *substitution continuum* in a person's psyche, but we would still have to know in what

proportions the basic *substitution continua* are participating. A person who wants
and gets mainly oral satisfaction from other people has a very different relationship to them than a person who uses, above all, manipulation proper, and still
different from a person who wants and gets genital satisfaction from at least one
other person and needs neither oral nor manipulatory satisfaction too badly.
The first one will cling to other people and feel he never gets enough, whether
he just pesters them or tries to hurl them around in would-be grandiosity. The
second will devise and plot things, will bribe, subdue and punish people all the
time without ever consuming any of them for what they are: people. What is the
worst: he cannot court for nor consume heterosexual relationships, although a
part of his plots may be to have many affairs and leave broken hearts wherever
he goes. Or he will stay away from people altogether and turn to "things"
instead. The third one does not want so insatiably much from other people,
does not have to manipulate them so desperately or stay away from them altogether, and *can* court (or wait for) and consume heterosexual relationships.

We have indicated a while ago that specific talents which, in our terms, are
defined as specific rates of cathexis in specific areas of manipulation and stimulation may complicate our appraisal of the overall rate of cathexis by which a
person operates (see pp. 96, 112f). In fact, the readers who have not left out
pp. 93–97 will remember that the sub-sums of intensity increments of desires
assembled on all of a person's *substitution continua* add up to C. To use a metaphor: Libido feeds into all of a person's drive systems or *substitution continua*. If
we distinguish three basic or primal *substitution continua* or drive systems, the
oral, the bodily and the genital, we would have to expect that libido feeds into all
three. Inversely, the "fuel" supply of all three would add up to that quantity of
fuel or libido which, we say, a person operates on. In terms of cathexis: the three
primal *substitution continua* may operate at different rates of cathexis. Their mean
value is the person's overall rate of cathexis. This overall rate of cathexis, in turn,
is a direct function of the quantity of libido by which a person keeps going.

Consequently, we may expect a different variance of the rates of cathexis of
the three primal *substitution continua* around the overall rate of cathexis with
different people. Some may cathect easily and rapidly in the area of oral manipulation and stimulation, and not so well in the others. They will learn easily and
fast as long as they do not have to do very much themselves. Their talents may
lie in the world of foods, of words or even of contemplation and thought. They
may become gourmets of anything edible or of literature, connoisseurs of art
fashion, interior design and the like, nature lovers, quiz heroes, eclectic philosophers or even mystics. With some additional talent in manipulation proper they
may turn cooks, orators, critics, art dealers, designers of fashion or interior
decoration, geographers, actors, perhaps systematic philosophers or even
logicians.

Others may have greater talents in the area of manipulation proper. They can
cathect easily and rapidly, as long as they can handle, or even create themselves,

the things to be cathected or as long as they can be "doers". They would tend to become painters, sculptors, plumbers, mechanics, engineers, farmers, surgeons, chemists and physicists, administrators, career soldiers, drivers, pilots, manufacturers, etc.

Still others may have great talent in the area of genital manipulation and stimulation. They may make excellent lovers. If they are female and hit upon the right male, they may be well taken care of even if they have no talent to speak of in either of the other primal drive systems. If they are male and hit upon the right female—a woman who needs to be very rich—they may also be all right. However, if they are not that lucky and do not have some, at least moderate, talents besides, they may end up in prostitution or worse. That is to say that a person can usually hope to find enough, and good enough, conditions under which to satisfy genital desires only if he or she has some other talents too. For one thing: other people will be very meagre psychological entities, very shaky and unstable objects, if they have not been cathected from earliest childhood on and via mouth and via body first. If a child does not learn that mother exists while being nursed and taken care of by her nor while roaming the house on his first excursions, she cannot be much of an entity by the time the child learns that mother is a woman. Somewhat the same would hold for father. Hence other people in general cannot become much of an entity either. They are carriers of one or the other kind of sex-organ, so to speak, and little or nothing more.

The point is that different people, even when they happen to have the same overall libido supply or rate of cathexis, may still operate differently throughout their lives depending on how the libido supply is divided or what the different rates of cathexis within the primal *substitution continua* are that contribute to the overall rate of cathexis. These sub-rates of cathexis may be given with a person just as is his "true" overall rate of cathexis (see also p. 96), the quantity of libido on which he operates, or his C. Not only that. The primal *substitution continua* comprehend further subdivisions and even these could be hereditary and invariant. Oral manipulation and stimulation may be eating or talking, but also "adjacent" kinds of stimulation such as listening to talk, even to music, or watching the ongoings, also plays in the theater. The rate by which a person cathects food need not be the same as that by which he cathects talking or music. Developing at such different sub-sub-rates of cathexis, one person may, at a given age, have become an excellent listener and talker, but be disinterested in eating beyond getting his belly stuffed, whereas another person may have developed the fanciest pre-occupation with the world's dishes and be a poor talker, a poor listener and even a hater of music. Yet in general and on the average these sub-sub-rates of cathexis that determine the sub-rates by which a person's primal *substitution continuum* operates are not too different from each other. Very specific and pronounced talents are rare. Different areas and modes of stimulation within a drive system may have different rates of cathexis—

rates of cathexis are also stimulation-specific (see p. 78)—but, as has been indicated, there is no stimulation whatsoever that would occur in isolation. Several modes and kinds of stimulation are usually cooperating in order to produce something as simple as eating or vocal noises. Although we might be able to distinguish different sub-sub-rates of cathexis within a person's primal *substitution continuum*, they are likely to merge in their effects and produce something like a sub-rate of cathexis that will be more reliable and significant. We must realise, in fact, that everybody has every talent there is, although very different degrees of them. Everybody except a complete idiot operates on some rate of cathexis in all three primal *substitution continua*. What is more: as development goes on, the three basic *substitution continua* or drive systems tend to mingle with each other more and more. They are like three nationalities that fill a city and, after a few generations, are usually heavily intertwined. Hence even the basic sub-rates are likely to submerge more and more in an overall rate of cathexis by which a person—or in our metaphor: by which the city—operates. That overall rate will be an even more reliable and significant measure of a person, provided we can get it.

Even then, however, the sub-rates of cathexis could probably still be recognised. Something like the relationship between the amount of stimulation that a person desires and the amount of effort, work, or manipulation that he is willing to invest, may tell us something about a person's oral rate of cathexis in relation to that of manipulation proper. And the degree to which stimulation and manipulation involves other people, especially those of the opposite sex, will give us an idea of a person's "genital rate of cathexis" in relation to the other two. Always provided that other things, especially opportunities, are equal.

But can something like the sub-rates of cathexis conceivably stay the same throughout development, as we seem to assume? Well, we might proceed as once before (see p. 113f) and show at least that it is not an impossible assumption.

According to formula (1) the quantity to which the intensity increments of all desires add up is a constant with a given individual (see p. 25f). Since n, the number of desires that can be distinguished on a given *substitution continuum*, say eating, increases with development, the intensity increments of desires that can be distinguished on that *continuum* with an adult cannot add up to more than the intensity increments of those few desires did that could be distinguished on that *continuum* in early life. We have shown (see p. 26f) that intensity increments of desires can be inferred, among other ways, from the average intervals between successive satisfactions. If an infant of two months of age is being fed a quarter of an hour after he has woken up and falls asleep with the end of the feeding, and if we assume that in sleep intensities of desires other than sleep remain arrested (see p. 106f), we might say that the average interval between successive feedings (counting from the end of one to the onset of the next and ignoring sleep) is a quarter of an hour. Hence the intensity increment per hour would be $1/0.25$, or 4, and if the infant is only drinking mother's milk so that, to the best of our knowledge, no other desires can be distinguished with him on the *continuum* "oral stimulation", c would be equal to 4.

Now, take him as an adult, determine the intensity increments of his desires to eat and drink and see whether they could conceivably add up to no more than that quantity. Let us assume that, as an adult, he tends to eat in average intervals of four hours—again counting from the end of one to the onset of the next satisfaction of the desire and not counting sleep, as before—and he may drink with meals and three times a day extra, which may amount to an average interval between successive drinks of two hours. The intensity increments of these two desires would be 0.25 and 0.50, adding up to 0.75, which, obviously, is still far from 4, the value of c. The *substitution continuum* "oral stimulation" requires additional desires in order to be "full" or in balance, something at least similar to eating and drinking.

So the individual in question may chew gums or smoke cigarettes. He may chew for half an hour every hour and thus earn an increment for chewing gum of 1 and he may smoke a cigarette in average intervals of an hour and earn an increment of 1 again for smoking. This would boost the sum of intensity increments to 2.75, which is still short of 4, but getting close.

The difference from c, i.e. 4 minus 2.75, will have to be "filled" by still other desires and the most available of all desires that we can easily identify on that *continuum* would be talking. It is oral stimulation to be sure, although not a terribly satisfying one by itself. However, it also produces sounds, hence makes for auditory stimulation too, and it even carries meaning. It permits articulate communication with other people. Let us assume that our subject is a very sociable and busy person, perhaps some kind of a salesman. He has an average period between successive conversations of an hour, hence an intensity increment per hour of 1. If he also smokes and chews gum as indicated, his sum of intensity increments may be boosted to 3.75. Which leaves him still 0·25 short of the balance. Well, for the rest he may kiss his beloved passionately every evening or read, which is a kind of mild, tacit, inconspicuous talking along with the printed word.

What about somebody who chews gum, talks or smokes incessantly? Does that not overthrow our calculations? Well, for one thing, these desires are not really satisfied incessantly. We usually just say so. But if they were with a particular person, we would either find that he could not wait for a minute even when he was a baby (perhaps $c = 20$), or that he is under some extreme stress or in a state of considerable (partial) regression. At any rate, it is obvious that neither smoking nor chewing gum, nor talking, can be very satisfactory to such a person at all. Otherwise he would not only be able, but even wish to refrain from it for a while and do so the longer, the greater the satisfaction was. This relationship would hold by definition.

Yet I do not want to give the impression that all such calculations should be carried out in earnest. If somebody smokes incessantly, we know without computing that he is not getting *some*thing and if he cannot stop talking even for a short while, there must be something seriously wrong. Besides he will certainly come in conflict with others that way. A few glances or questions may give us a better idea of a person's plight than such clumsy computations. In lack of gross enough clinical symptomatology, however, we may obtain some help from them. In fact, we are probably resorting to such computations and calculations more often than we think, although implicitly.

If I understand you correctly, one may wonder, and if you treat eating as a *substitution continuum*, eating anything at all would be among the most primitive of the derivative desires of that *continuum*, and something like eating roast beef, asparagus, apple pie, marron glacé, etc., would be among the later and latest derivatives. Now, if you consider that a man and not even a great gourmand, would have some hundred dishes in his mind which he likes, hence hundred derivative desires or "appetites" and if you consider that they all grow by certain intensity increments all the time, would not that exceed the sum of 4 that you have computed ? Well, not really. Assume that he has roast beef every other day, which makes for an average interval of two times 16 waking hours or 32 hours, and for an increment of 1/32 or 0·03. Asparagus he may have once a week, which makes, by the same device, for an increment of 0·01, and marron glacé may come every other month, which makes for an increment per hour of as little as 0·001. Well, if we want to split up meals and drinks into their ingredients for our calculations, we will find that, again, our barrel of size 4 does not burst.

Summary and Forecast

THE INDIVIDUAL is always in the state of some deprivation. This is an intrinsic condition of being alive. The intensities of his desires are incessantly building up until they are reduced through satisfaction, only in order to build up again. However, the individual is also always satisfying desires, and as he does so, he cathects conditions of satisfaction. Whenever he fails for good to obtain satisfaction, counter-cathexis—i.e. cathexis of substitute conditions—will occur. Both cathexis and counter-cathexis are cumulative processes. Every situation will be perceived in terms of all relevant previous cathexes and counter-cathexes. They determine a situation's opportunity profile. The optimum of satisfaction calculated in view of the acute drive intensity profile determines a person's course of action. This calculation will function the better, the more cathexis has already accumulated, and the less pervasive is counter-cathexis. Yet even so it is largely preconscious and unconscious.

The fuel on which an individual operates psychologically is libido. It is incessantly produced at a quantity given with a given individual. It determines how rapidly desires grow in intensity in the course of time, and how much overall deprivation can be tolerated at a given time of development. It determines how much cathexis, how much knowledge of the world and oneself, will have accumulated at a given time of development. And it determines the rate of ongoing cathexis by which an individual operates at any time of development. It feeds into three basic *substitution continua*: oral, bodily (anal), and genital. It also feeds into the sub-systems of the psyche, into Id, Ego and Superego. It may do either in different proportions even with otherwise equivalent individuals.

This summary, however, is only the most general and perhaps meaningless, skeleton of our conceptual introduction. Although the Theory at Work is a much freer and probably more amusing enterprise, I do not think that the conceptual introduction should have been omitted. It should not even by readers who knew all about psychoanalytic theory to begin with. I understand that they must have felt a little confused at first, but if they kept at it, they may well be in a better conceptual position than they were before.

The Theory at Work will show what psychoanalytic theory has to contribute to the psychology of human development. The first five chapters could even be called the psychoanalytic theory of development, including major implications. However, it is not strictly a theory. It is more of a description, for my money.

131

The subsequent chapters deal with various broader issues of psychology, among which are some controversial ones. Again I will attempt to show that psychoanalytic theory has something to offer; in fact, more to offer than any other theory conceivably pertinent to these issues; although not necessarily more than what a genius of a novelist or, perhaps, a painter may have to offer to some of them by their works of art; nor more than what a family may contribute by as little as achieving happiness of some kind for themselves on a difficult planet such as ours. None of them, however, is likely to be quite as articulate as our theory.

PART II

THE THEORY AT WORK

The First Year of Life

THE PSYCHOLOGICAL life of an infant begins long before birth. There is movement, and there is some sensitivity to stimulation. The fetus reacts to pressure, vibration, and even sound. He moves in response to all of them. Consequently there is also kinesthetic stimulation, and even movement in response to kinesthetic stimulation. Yet compared to what he shows even on the very day of his birth, we may say that he feels and does very little. He is quite well protected in a physical sense. If the sleeping infant has been seen as heavenly happy, the fetus might be considered twice as happy. And if the sleeping infant is asleep by definition and his conscious psychological life grossly reduced to the best of our knowledge, this will be even more true of the fetus. He is very, very much asleep, we might say, and his psychological life is still poorer. He does not even have to breathe or eat in order to stay alive. He is being fed intravenously.

However, this side of a fetus' psychological life is not so important. What is important is how the parents are getting ready for the big event of birth. They have either wanted a child or not. If they have not wanted it originally, they may come to like the idea as time goes on, or they may dislike it more than ever. And even if they liked it from the very beginning and planned the whole event, there are many different ways of doing so. The coming infant may be the first or the nth of those parents' children. The parents themselves may be young or old, madly or mildly in love with each other, dissatisfied with some of each other's aspects and hence ambivalent to various degrees, or outright hateful. In fact, the father may have run away with another woman by the time the child arrives, or the mother-to-be may have gone back to her family. Even if the parents are in love with each other, that may mean many different things. The husband who was the younger of two brothers in his own family is likely to choose, and find satisfaction with, his wife in different ways depending on whether she is an only child, the older of two girls or the older sister of a brother, etc. Also he may be the son of a domineering, aggressive, and much older father and a young, soft, loving mother, of parents who are companions above everything and even look and act very much alike, or of a young, though harsh and cold, mother and a pleasant, rich, but weak and dependent, father.

Whatever the background of the parents and whatever their relationship to each other, it will be reflected in their desires and wishes for the child. They will either want or not want a child at this particular time, will wish for a girl or a boy to different degrees, and have many more and specific desires for the infant beyond that. Birth will tell them whether their wishes for the child's sex have been fulfilled, and all other wishes will gradually get opportunities to be, or not to be, satisfied. We remember (see p. 82f), that the child cannot possibly satisfy any of his desires, whether at all or in the long run, without the parents' assistance. That means that the parents must have precisely those wishes for him that are to develop in the child. They must want to suckle him, if he is ever to suck or eat. Moreover he has other needs for them to fulfill such as keeping him warm, clean, asleep, touching and carrying him, talking to him so that there is something for him to hear, and giving him something to see, no matter how little he can yet attend. The suckling or nursing, however, is the most important of all. It can be missed the least, and it requires the provision, the giving of, food, preferably from mother's breast.

This could already be the first stumbling block for the infant. The young mother may, for some reason, refuse to breast-feed the baby. Perhaps she thinks that her beauty will suffer, or she thinks that her husband and all kinds of people could think so. On the other hand, she may be willing, even anxious, to breast-feed the baby, but have little or no milk supply. Hence she cannot. Not infrequently in such cases she does not really want to either, although she would not dream of admitting to it. She wants to, because she feels she should want to. If it were not for that, she would just as well refrain from feeding the baby "with her own body". She has fed him long enough, namely during pregnancy. She does not want to get all emaciated. She cannot let the baby feed on her very substance. Where she got that idea is, of course, a separate story.

However, absence of a milk supply or the unwillingness to breast-feed in spite of a supply is not really the stumbling block. A bottle with human milk may do a fairly good job too, and cow- or goat-milk has most often in such cases had to be enough. The bottle may even do an excellent job, provided that mother duplicates the breast-feeding situation as closely as possible. She can hold the infant in her arms while sitting comfortably herself. She can hold the bottle attentively for him, can let him play with it as much as he wants to without getting impatient herself and, perhaps, switch him to her other arm after a while. She can maximise concurrent stimulation and watch out for him so that she can introduce variation as soon as he asks for it.

But will she? If her beauty is so important, if she does not want to look as if she had nursed babies, or if she does not want to "give substance from her own body", she may do or not do other things to her baby as well. She may want to get the feeding-time over quickly. She may be angry if the baby does not drink right away, or put an end to the feed although he wants to have some more after a little play. She may leave him in the crib and just hold the bottle down to him, and she could even install a gadget so that the bottle will hang into his mouth by itself. Finally she may hand him over to a nurse altogether who, if she looks after him long enough, is likely to become the infant's psychological mother instead.

It is in that sense that feeding the baby could already be a stumbling block. Not the feeding itself would make the difference, but all of mother's wishes and desires with respect to the baby. They have preceded the event of birth and will be active even when the baby has grown up and begun to go to school. They will manifest themselves in the form of attitudes which, by the way, are desires themselves, although controlled and counter-cathected to various degrees and, hence, guiding behavior only "from a distance". The earliest occasions at which these attitudes can come to the infant's notice are the feedings. If he keeps being cut short, he may one day interpret this as the behavior of an ungiving world. Somebody in that world, and obviously somebody important, does not want to suckle him. And if he keeps being handled more roughly, whenever he plays a little too long or bites a little too hard, or if a little period of looking at something —mother's face—and listening to lovely sounds—her voice—is dropped because of that, he will come to think that the world "retaliates".

If the infant is to survive at all, somebody must feed him regularly, and as long as the ceaseless process of cathexis has not accumulated much of a "world" yet, everything may still look good even when it is not. An infant who grows up in an orphanage and shares three alternating nurses with ten other babies may initially want no more than he gets. It is only after some weeks of life that he could, for the first time, need more stimulation or fun than the orphanage's set-up is likely to furnish. He is awake a little longer, and sucking has become easier. He could feel around for touches, sounds, and even sights in addition. He could engage himself in a little pull-and-push game with his mouth. But the nurse is in a hurry. May be one of them is not, but the other two are. That, however, is as bad as if all three were, at least as long as he cannot distinguish them from each other. And that he cannot.

While sucking itself is still so difficult and ongoing cathexis so small that the infant can only attend to the most elementary aspects of feedings, he is safe, provided that the environment lets him live at all. Other stimulations such as those of touch of the body surface, sound, sight, and kinesthesis resulting from passive or active, though accidental, movements, are more or less irrelevant. They happen; the infant cannot possibly feed without exposure to all these other stimulations. But variations in kind as well as in extent make little difference. In fact, even scent and taste of the liquid offered during the first feedings can hardly be distinguished. One tastes and smells like the other, as long as it is not acid or really bitter. Touch (which includes temperature) is about the only stimulation that the infant can distinguish and handle by his mouth, whereby even "handling" is something very limited, namely either holding and swallowing it, or spitting it out. At that stage of development it obviously cannot matter too much how the mother or nurse feeds him, as long as they do so at all, nor what else they do to him for his entertainment.

By the *end of the fourth month*, however, the infant has gone a long way, and prevalence of optimal versus all other conditions would, indeed, make a difference.

Let us look at *sucking*. It has spread out into a number of derivative desires, all of which are being satisfied recurrently at various intervals. The infant drinks, eats semi-solid food, takes it from the bottle, provided the nipple has an extra large hole, or from a spoon, sucks the pacifier, bites at a rattle, sucks and bites his own fists, etc. He has even begun to expect different kinds of meals at different times of the day, and ever since he started skipping one of the night feedings and delaying another one until six or seven o'clock in the morning, the day has taken a little shape for him. But then he also babbles, coos, screams, whines, and the like, for something to listen to, or in order to bring about certain effects, such as the appearance of mother, or even a very specific twist in her top part, the face, namely a smile.

Oral stimulation is the most highly developed. The infant has learned to control and manipulate it best of all modes and kinds of stimulation. Compared to those he has brought the largest number of distinguishable conditions of satisfaction under his control. But other kinds and modes of stimulation have developed too. Take *touch*. The infant's body surface has been touched many many times, and he has learned to distinguish some touches from others. Being held one way is enjoyable and being held another way is not so enjoyable. A bath is wonderful except when water is poured over head and face; that is terrifying. If one gets cold, one has to scream (so that somebody will come and wrap one up again). If one does something strange and remote (elimination), it gets warm somewhere, but then it cools off and one has to scream again. Take *sound*. The infant has been hearing things for a while, a bell, a rattle, bangs of things thrown to the floor, noises (people talking, walking, or doing something), and even peculiar burps, babbles, and coos that would finally come almost any time he wanted to. Easy enough for us to see why: they were his own. Take *sight*. He has been seeing things in his room, in other rooms, and seeing things while being moved himself. There are the colorful walls, the blue sky in the window, daylight, electric light, dawn, darkness, and real blackouts. There is something relatively steady of a fair color (mother's face), something unsteady of the same kind (her hands), and either of them could of late be looked at and pursued by sight as they moved.

All these stimulations, those of touch, of sound, and of sight, have neither recurred nor been varied frequently and thoroughly enough so as to permit the formation of objects. Not even mother is as yet pieced together in the infant's mind. The face is not an integral part of being fed or carried, and the voice could come from her hands or even from the corner of the room, if it were not for these peculiar movements of that hole at the bottom of the face (her mouth). Perhaps the baby can almost see what sort of thing that is, but he is not sure.

There is still another stimulation that would work as a valuable machine of object-formation, were it only under better control. It is *kinesthesis*, stimulation brought about by movement. The mouth, we said, is the sole part of the body that can really move at the infant's discretion. Of late, however, the hands have begun to do likewise. They have begun to reach the mouth more regularly whenever intended. They can be touched and sucked by the mouth, and they succeed even in touching and "sucking", i.e. holding, things themselves. What is more: they can bring them to the mouth on rare occasions This includes something as restless and uncontrollable as the feet. They may get dragged into the mouth too. In fact, the eyes are even beginning to establish the very first steps of visual control. All of this, however, is still quite shaky. Only in the fifth or sixth month of the first year of life will the child really gain control over the hands and, to some extent, over the rest of the body; enough at least, so that he can bring himself into all kinds of positions and even move from place to place. Not that he could not do a little bit of sitting even now, i.e. in the first four months, and not that he would not lately end up in all kinds of places within his crib. But he would either fall over as soon as he was no longer supported, or be uncovered, hopelessly caught and, inevitably, end up screaming for help. He also can turn from his belly to his back, although not necessarily yet from his back to his belly. However, all in all, he is still mainly a "*lier*" and a passive "*floater*", if we consider that he is being handled and carried a lot and must experience it somehow.

It is not too difficult to see where a neglectful or antagonistic mother or an indifferent nurse could thwart the infant. Most of these things require some attendance and assistance. The most gratifying of them are even most immediately contingent upon the adult's cooperation. Hence if the adult, say mother, is not available during the infant's waking life, the periods of which, incidentally, happen to increase with age, if she does not want to see what the infant wants, or if she leaves him in solitary confinement much of the time and lets him "scream his discomforts out", he is likely to counter-cathect, or not even develop in the first place, certain derivative desires. He will stop moving around, if it gets him into desperate troubles, will not eat too well, but cling to his pacifier or anything that he can consume "auto-erotically", and decline to attend to the sounds of the world except those that he can produce himself. Even much later he will still look with blank eyes and a drab face at the adults who supposedly take care of him. Impoverishment of his psychological life can already begin in the first few months of an infant's life, if conditions are accordingly, and whatever has been missed at any stage of development is not easy and, if too much time has elapsed meanwhile, even impossible to catch up with. Abandoned children who grow up in orphanages are usually the worst off for this reason. The earlier they can be adopted into another family, the better for them as well as for the adopting families. Both parties will have more fun with each other. Four to six weeks of age, to name a time, is by no means too early. After three months some irreparable damage may already have occurred, unless the orphanage is very well financed, staffed, and run, or unless the infant is a particularly attractive and alert one, so that he can win even the most indifferent of his routine nurses over to his side.

The *first four months* of life could be called the early oral phase and summarised in the following manner:

The *primal desire*, i.e. the best controlled desire, the desire from which the largest number of derivative desires have formed or, in other words, the desire that can be satisfied under the relatively largest number of different conditions (see p. 6ff), is sucking. Other desires are touching, moving, listening, and looking. However, these areas of stimulation cannot be manipulated by the infant to any great extent. He depends to a high degree on the provisions made by the outside world. He appears to be relatively passive in these areas, although, in principle, he is as active as he will ever be. But very little cathexis has accumulated so far that would, in turn, be facilitating further cathexis. He has to work much harder to achieve specific effects.

Object-formation has not proceeded very far. The feeding breast or the bottle and the infant's own mouth have been cathected sufficiently. They form objects of some kind. But any objects or contexts beyond that, such as the infant himself or his mother, are largely non-existent yet. The infant's objects are prepersonal. The mouth *is* himself, so to speak, and the bottle or breast *is* the other person. There is practically no distinction between himself and the outside world. The sound of steps heard upon screaming is as much a part of himself as are his own legs, and, inversely, his hands may be as alien to him under certain conditions as might be the sight of his mother. Yet a rudimentary distinction is already possible. "Outside" is anything touching, or inside of, his mouth, and he himself is the mouth. Everything else may still be undistinguishable as to where it belongs.

Counter-cathexis is more difficult to establish, the earlier it becomes necessary (see p. 28ff). Losses are hard to make up for by substitution. However, objects have not assumed specificity and individuality yet to any remarkable degree. They can be replaced without much trouble for the infant. One bottle is not too different from another. In fact, mother's breast is not too different from another mother's breast, although such exchanges are unpopular these days. One kind of touch, sound, sight, etc., is not terribly different from the other, even though variation of stimulation is getting to be appreciated by the infant. Little of what there is can be done without, provided the child is to live. Under favorable circumstances there may be no radical losses and hence no counter-cathexes to speak of (although, in a broader sense, all cathexis involves some kind of counter-cathexis; see p. 44f). Under unfavorable circumstances there may be no radical losses either, but little losses could be taking place all the time. Counter-cathexis will accumulate inconspicuously. These two types of babies are often hard to distinguish by the naked eye. A little later, however, when person-objects are being formed, one will do well, and the other very poorly. The predominant defense mechanism that can be distinguished in the first four months of life is repression.

The *primal fear*, if there is one, may be something like disintegration of everything there is. The whole world may fall apart. It may drown in total panic. That is, there is a question whether it should not be called primal anxiety rather than fear (see also p. 16ff).

Frustration tolerance, which could be defined as the degree of deprivation of desires that a person can tolerate, or as a function of the decline with development of the intensity increments by which a given sample of a person's desires grows (see also pp. 25ff and 93ff, esp. p. 95), has increased. The infant can wait a little longer than he could at birth for the satisfaction of his desires. Eating may be delayed by a quarter of an hour, and he may not be very unhappy yet. Appearance of mother may be screamed for, but the screaming is not desperate as long as she does not keep him waiting for too long. He may even interrupt screaming and entertain himself for a while with something else before resuming his call for help. Deprivation of sleep can be tolerated for an average time of two hours and for a maximum of three hours and more, before the infant will inevitably fall asleep again, whereas soon after birth the average waking interval between successive sleeps is less than an hour, and the infant will not last much longer under almost any circumstances. Incidentally, sleep is perhaps as good an indicator of frustration tolerance as any other single desire. It operates more than any other by self-demand, i.e. independently of variations of opportunity, and it requires no learning or cathexis before it can function. In fact, it is the matrix of all cathexis, the condition under which all cathexis that has occurred during the previous waking period thrives best (see p. 106f).

At about the beginning of the *fifth month* of life we encounter a few innovations. Not that they come overnight. Nor has there been a single day in the infant's life without some kind of innovations. The ones that come to our attention at this point of development, however, are more far-reaching. The infant begins to suck harder, move his jaw forcefully, press the gums at each other, and cut his first teeth. In short: he begins to *bite*. Furthermore his hands reach his mouth with increasingly greater accuracy and speed whenever desired. They become an expansion of the mouth. They cannot only travel to the mouth by themselves, but even bring things that they happen to grab. They can reach farther than the mouth can. They and their doings can even be watched. Not only that; something that is being seen in a distance can be reached and brought to the mouth for "supreme court" inspection. In other words, the hands become objects (see also p. 12). In addition, an event begins to draw near or has perhaps already occurred that can be called the first radical loss in the infant's life: the end of mother's milk supply, or *weaning*. Not that this event comes all of a sudden. For a while there may still be two and then one breast-feeding per day. The other feedings will be from the bottle, and even semi-solids are usually offered by that time. But one day the infant has had his last breast-feeding and no more thereafter, no more, in fact, for the rest of his life. That is the loss that does require counter-cathexis in its more articulate and drastic sense. The infant may have cut down on breast-feeding of his own accord. He may have grown tired of it and reduced himself to two and one per day in order to get other foods and more variety. He may have been satisfied at last with one breast-feeding per week. What he can and will not do of his own accord, though, is to give it up altogether and forever. That aspect is imposed on him by mother or by her physiology, and that is what requires articulate counter-cathexis.

What about a bottle-fed baby? Well, he was weaned from mother's breast in the first weeks of life, that is at a time when he had not learned yet to distinguish breast and bottle from each other. He may even never have been given the breast. Is that not much better? Does that not save him a later trauma? It does certainly, but earlier or exclusive bottle feeding is not *a priori* a-traumatic. By considerations outlined (see p. 136ff), it may be more traumatic, although less conspicuously so. The infant of six months who is slowly weaned loses something, but he has at least had it. The infant weaned at birth or soon thereafter has been missing some aspects of life for six months already by the time he reaches that age. One might as well ask: "Is it better to live this troublesome, difficult life, or not to live at all, better perhaps to die soon after birth or never be born at all?" The latter is obviously the least traumatic. Yet, is it really? Is not the most hideous life still better than no life at all?

Finally there is an innovation of perhaps the greatest significance of all. It has been prepared for all along. But now it reaches a first close. *Mother becomes a person.* She assumes specificity and individuality. Something like the following has been established in the infant's mind: "The bottle that feeds me, the hands that give it to me, the mouth that moves with the sounds I can hear, and that stretches at times in such a lovely way (he means her smile), the whole patch of fair skin with two sparkling dots in it (the face with the eyes), the touches, lifts and cuddlings, that I get, the things I feel when I rub up to her with my face or if I throw my hands at her, the gentle bangs I hear (her steps when she is coming), etc., etc., do all belong together." Yes, they do. They pertain to "mother". In fact, they constitute mother for him. "She is that which I have seen and heard, felt, smelled, tasted and even sucked most frequently of all things I have been in touch with." Yes, she is the most instrumental, the most variegated and yet the most invariant of all the conditions under which the infant has ever satisfied his desires. With her there are new things to learn just about every day: another dress, a new song she recites, a new drink she fixes, a new place she takes him to in the baby carriage. But she also contains the earliest aspects of anything he has ever learned: sucking, being held, being kept warm, etc.

If object-formation has proceeded that far, if mother assumes specificity and individuality in the infant's mind, she can be exchanged for another mother only with the greatest difficulty. Mother has become irreplaceable. Her loss is the severest thing that can happen to the child even when somebody very much like her takes her place right away. A few months ago that may still have worked. Now, however, there will be a period of prolonged and severe anxiety, before counter-cathexis of all the conditions in which mother took part have been "forgotten". In other words: There will be a pronounced period of mourning which can end only after every aspect of mother has been repressed.

This does not mean that a loss of mother at a later time of development may not take longer to be counter-cathected. Object-formation has proceeded still farther. Mother has accumulated more cathexis. Hence her loss is even more of a loss. However, the child is also in a better position to make up for it. Other parts of the world have accumulated more cathexis too. Father has also become more of an object, or a more stable and reliable one, and other women have entered the child's horizon. There are aunts and grandmothers who may have become very dear to him too. Mother is the most important among a number of relatively important people, whereas in the first year of life, mother is the most important person, period. There is no other person to speak of in the infant's mind. This is in line with the general trend of all cathexis and object-formation as well to accumulate or proceed very slowly at first, but with increasing ease and speed as the condition in question continues to recur (see p. 101ff). At first a recurrent condition, or person must be as regular and invariant as can be in order to get cathected at all. Later on variation is possible and still later it is even actively sought. A given person will be welcome and cathected under new conditions, and new persons will be welcome under given as well as new conditions. A week's separation from mother during the second half year of life may already be equivalent to a loss of mother, whereas at the age of five or six years it could be an easily manageable experience, perhaps even a new and interesting aspect of mother.

There is an intimate relationship between object formation as it affects oneself and object-formation as it affects the other person (see also p. 11f). While the infant was no more than a mouth, psychologically speaking, he was not a person for himself, nor was there another person. Ever since birth, of course, cathexis has been operating towards amelioration of such a "deplorable" condition. Only with the recruitment of his own hands accomplished, however, has he really begun to do the trick. Only if he learns that he can do things to his hands and his hands can do things to him (to his mouth), for which he depended entirely on mother before, can he conceive of the possibility that he is somebody too, somebody like mother. And only when he knows that, can he conceive of mother as being somebody like him. He can suck his own hand, e.g., as he has sucked mother's breast or her bottle. And he can give himself his own hands as mother has given him the breast and the bottle. He is sucking as well as suckling himself and thereby learning what mother's breast or the bottle may feel or desire when he sucks from them and learning what mother must feel or desire when she suckles him (see also p. 82f). The first could be called projection of his desire on mother and the second introjection of mother's desire. The two go hand in hand. They become possible because the infant has begun to distinguish between himself and the rest of the world.

This coincidence is also what may teach the infant not to bite too hard on mother's breast, the bottle, and a few other things. He bites his own hands, does not like it, i.e. deprives his desire of staying physically painfree (see also p. 21f), and counter-cathects biting under such, or certain, conditions. If he does not and, consequently, cannot let go of biting mother's breast, mother may even wean him because of it. Perhaps a double precaution, installed by God or Nature in order to assure that weaning comes about.

There are other characteristics to be mentioned. Now the infant learns to turn from his back to his belly, to crawl, sit up, stand with support and do so even without support. By the end of the first year of life he is on the verge of walking all by himself. His hands can hold and move things while he lies or sits. They can even hold two things at once, bring them together and "work" with one on the other or on something else. He can give a thing from his hand to his mouth, from his mouth to his hand, from one hand to the other and even to another person's hand. From the latter, however, it must come back right away. Otherwise it is gone and forgotten.

Sight has begun to co-control from a bird's eye view anything the infant can do of his own and even those aspects of his environment that are beyond his immediate reach. He cannot reach for and touch all things there are, but he can follow some of them with his eyes as they move. He can pursue people, cars, dogs and the like whether they come to greet him or not. He recognises what mother is bringing or going to do. He looks for things that have disappeared. He tries to recreate them for his sight and, if possible, for his touch and mouth too, say, by crawling after them or pulling down a cloth, by grabbing and even sucking them.

Hearing has differentiated considerably. Somehow he recognises noises of doors, steps, bells, the telephone, rattles, etc. What is more, he recognises voices and, gradually, even some of the things they say. "There is the milk for our baby", "We must change him", "Where is the teddy bear?" and the like may provoke distinguishable responses in him. He may struggle to get up and even say "meeh" (milk) himself. He may wriggle away and perhaps say something like "No" to the suggestion that he should be changed. And he may point in some direction in reply to the question about the teddy bear. He can be fooled, though. Just tell him: "There is the silk for our lady", and he may struggle to get up and even say "meeh" (milk) just the same. He also produces his own sounds, among which there are just about all that the alphabet contains and a few gargles, hisses and grunts in addition. Simple combinations such as "da", eh"", "boo", "bye-bye", "Mama", "Papa" and a few more have also made their way into his repertoire. They even have some kind of meaning, although not one as precise as words of his second year of life will.

The *last two thirds of the first year* of life could be called the late oral phase.

The mouth is still king among the infant's achievements, although the hands have begun to severely contest it. Since oral manipulation can be either more gentle or more destructive, i.e. either sucking or biting, and since it is up to the infant to some extent which one will be chosen, this phase has also been called the oral-sadistic or oral-aggressive. Not that the infant's ways of satisfying desires were undestructive during the first months of life. On the contrary, they were even more primitive and destructive. But there was no alternative. If the infant were not so weak nor his behavior so inefficient (see also p. 64f), he might almost inevitably eat up mother, if she keeps him waiting just a little too long, or may do so even for the mere fun of it. Or he could knock or kick her off the ground or tear at her with mouth and hands so that she may, perhaps, come apart. It should be understood, however, that the change does not come overnight. The growing infant is always in transition. The incessant process of cathexis tends to make the satisfactions of all desires less primitive and destructive all the time and also to increase the range of alternatives, so that more as well as less destructive forms of satisfaction appear side by side. The infant has become ambivalent, so to speak, whereas before he was pre-ambivalent (see Abraham 1924, Fenichel 1945, esp. part 1; also pp. 65, 288f).

The *primal desires* of the first year are sucking, biting and swallowing. In addition we find touching by hand and moving the hands, locomotion (with first attempts to maintain upright posture; while a "lier" in the first months he is now a "getter-up"), looking, listening and "babbling" (creating one's own sounds). They all are under the infant's control to a much greater extent than they were at the end of the first four months of life. Consequently, the infant will appear considerably more active.

Object-formation has resulted in the creation of at least two persons: mother and himself. He himself is that which possesses hands and even legs, that which moves with him as he moves, that which feels, hears and sees. He himself is that which is within him. Everything else is the outside world which is thereby distinguished from himself. Its most prominent part is mother who has become an object by a similar device. She is that which treats and carries him, speaks to him, bears this—now unmistakable—face and even looks at him, looks right into his eyes. Mother can be replaced only with great difficulty. Even immediate substitution of another "mother" cannot prevent the experience of loss or trauma. All other objects are insignificant compared to her.

Counter-cathexis has become easier since *substitution continua* have expanded. It takes less than in the first months to make up for a given loss. Yet counter-cathexis has also become more difficult, since objects have assumed more specificity and individuality. The loss of an object is more of a loss, the farther it has been established in the infant's mind, and some are already farther established than others. This implies also that the losses which an infant can experience have a wider range than before. Most infants tend to counter-cathect biting and swallowing under some conditions and drinking from mother's breast under all conditions, although other aspects of mother remain intact and are being developed all the time. The severest loss that can happen to him is the loss of mother. The predominant defense mechanisms other than repression that can be distinguished in the latter part of the first year of life are introjection and projection. This is no surprise, since the distinction between himself and the world has improved radically. This distinction, however, must have been made before projection or introjection became possible (see also pp. 83, 87 f).

The *primal fear*—which, in parenthesis, is the most primitive, yet distinguishable, of the infant's desires projected into the outside world and, consequently, the most primitive desire perceived in the outside world and introjected (see also p. 87), or, in short, the most primitive desire on the staff of the Superego— is that of being chewed up, devoured, swallowed or incorporated. The major desires are sucking, biting and swallowing, which are on the same *substitution continuum*. This *substitution continuum* or drive system must, therefore, comprehend the largest number of derivative desires among all *substitution continua* established (see also pp. 140, 6 ff). Hence primitivity and destructiveness on this *substitution continuum* is likely to be paired with the relatively greatest efficiency of behavior or with availability of the relatively largest number of instrumental desires (see also pp. 62 f, 77 f). As a consequence it will also contain the desires creating the greatest amount of conflict with other people (see also pp. 58 f, 66 f), therefore the most heavily counter-cathected desires and, therefore, the most likely candidates for projection and subsequent introjection. Counter-cathected desires that are being satisfied, or even merely attempted to be satisfied, will arouse guilt. That is, the believed or projected consequences of "disobedience" have been introjected and will appear as desires for punishment (see also p. 86 f), and the most primitive punishment he can wish for will be modelled after the most primitive desire that he can satisfy himself.

If the infant is so mad because of his mother's prolonged absence and his own hunger that he could eat her up, partly in order to satisfy as radically as already necessary his desire for food, partly in order to never let her do that to him again, he would be attempting something heavily counter-cathected. At least for the past few months he must have seen that he was never really able to do that, and this alone would make for counter-cathexis. In addition he has found that even little things like doing a bit of biting or spitting would entail "retaliations" such as withdrawal of the breast or termination of feeding. How much more retaliation must there be for a wish to eat up mother. She or somebody is going to eat him up in return. After all, mother and perhaps even another adult have eaten from the same spoon as he has, have kissed him, have even nibbled at him. That is not far from her taking his hand into her mouth which, by the way, he may have wanted to poke into it himself. If that can happen, however, then he as a whole could be taken into her mouth as well.

If the infant's mother should be absent for good—because of death, divorce or something—he would at last have to resort to the only interpretation that stands up, namely that he has swallowed her. That would be his way of cathecting her "wish to disappear", and this cathexis amounts to the introjection of that wish (see p. 86 f). If he has swallowed her, he has brought the event about himself. Only if what he got is what he wanted is he in control and can he have peace. Then, however, he will have no peace. He will be haunted by strong desires of punishment for such a horrible deed. He as well as the swallowed object or all of the world will be swallowed in turn. The end of everything is near. There is no hope but that for a gloomy, gloomy end. In other words: depression prevails (see Freud, 1916a; also p. 456 ff).

Frustration tolerance—or Ego-strength, if you like—has increased considerably. The infant is able to tolerate greater degrees of deprivation as well as greater variabilities of degrees than half a year ago. He may keep himself, or be, entertained for half an hour beyond the time a feeding is due. He can stand being awake and yet by himself for as much as an hour, if only he sees or hears mother or has enough toys to play with. And he will stay awake for an average interval of four or five hours and tolerate a maximal deprivation of sleep up to seven hours before falling asleep under almost any circumstances. Of course, he can fill his waking times by many more things than eight months ago. He has a kind of a repertoire of amusements that he can engage in by himself (wriggling, groping, babbling, chewing, clapping, etc.) and even one that will make him forget his hunger temporarily (sucking a toy, a pacifier, his fists, his feet, even an empty bottle that they may have left in his crib).

Early Childhood

THE SECOND AND THIRD YEAR OF LIFE

AT THE beginning of the second year of life the child begins to walk. He has managed to stand with and even without support which, incidentally, liberates his hands for new tactile adventures. Now, however, he dares to set one foot before the other, maybe at first while holding or pushing something that can support him, say a chair or a carriage, later on all by himself, still later even while holding portable things in his hands. He can go to interesting places that formerly he was able to explore only by sight or with the help of a parent. He can pick up interesting things, carry them and deliver them to new places.

We might say that after having "expanded" his mouth to include his hands in the late oral phase, he now expands his "mouth-hand personality" to include the rest of his body, his feet and the spaces they cover. He was a "crawler and getter-up", but now he has become an "upright-getter-around" and along with it gravity as well as the three dimensions of his environment, the distances, corners, niches, holes and all kinds of primitive spatial relations (before, behind, above, below, beside, standing, hanging) come to his notice. That is, they are being cathected. Now he gets to know why the left side of a sofa cannot be seen when one comes from the right, why the white big board in the wall of the room is sometimes dark—it is the closet door and sometimes is open; the dark is the inside of the closet—why a box or a cup might sometimes lose its content—when it is held upside down—why things disappear when one drops them, and where they go—to the floor—etc.

The experiences with distances bear on something like the sizes of objects. In his third year an observant child may comment about his approaching father: "If Daddy is far away, he is small. If he is close, he is big." A rather sophisticated statement. Yet he must have made such observations all along, even if he could not put it so well before. While running around in his home and perhaps in its immediate vicinity, say, in the garden, while covering distances of a yard or two, or of five or ten, he must have noticed, among other things, the growing and shrinking of objects.

The experiences of these changes of the apparent sizes of objects bear on something achieved in the second year of life that even the highest animal can never quite make: the recognition of (two-dimensional) pictures and (three-

148

dimensional) images. At the beginning of the second year he appears to notice only the board qualities of a picture, its stiffness and, perhaps, its ability to cover something else, and maybe its colors. He prefers bright colors to dull ones or none and perhaps a number of them already to just one or two. Gradually, however, he begins to recognise a mouth on the picture, then a hand, may be eyes, even a face and one day he calls it a doll or a baby. And a plastic soldier that was no more than a stone before, suddenly becomes a Daddy. The picture or image may be small as well as large. In fact, he will want to see some very small ones also, although his preference is for large, even as large as a poster.

The liberation of his hands that goes with walking furthers the liberation of his mouth. While in his first year the mouth was the supreme court of inspection, the hands turn out to be as lucrative as the mouth or even more. For one thing, what the hands do can also be seen, while the mouth operates in the dark. But hands, at least two of them together, can also handle larger objects than the mouth can. And after they have manipulated an object, say a lump of food, excessively, it may be smeared to pieces, but the pieces are still there. The object is already too dissipated to be handled further, but it can still be seen. It is all over the wall. Whereas what the mouth has manipulated to pieces tends to disappear altogether. It lands in the belly. Anyway, the mouth gets relieved, gets liberated to do something else, and short of eating it can always produce sounds. It can babble, talk, imitate noises, sounds, the parents' sounds and even words.

At the end of the first year he might already have had some small vocabulary. "Meeh" may have stood for milk. Yet it meant something more situational and global, something like "Now the milk is coming". A bottle of milk seen on a picture, milk in a wax container, milk that was just being heated on the gas was not "meeh". He may have said "Mum"—which stood for Mama or Mother, the parents claim—but again it would not mean mother in the adult sense, mother whether she drives a car or is in her gown, whether you see only her face or whether she is singing, whether you have just a snapshot of her to look at, or merely her signature. Rather it meant "Mother is going to feed me". Mother has been so universally instrumental to anything the child could have from the world that she may already represent a number of different situations, yet not too large a number and, what is more, global situations only. They even had to involve himself rather directly. Mother who played with the infant's older sibling is not "Mum". And if she fed him food he did not like, or familiar food in an unfamiliar situation, say in a railroad station, she might not be "Mum" either.

In the second year of life, however, his words come closer to adult words. They begin to mean objects or aspects of objects more "objectively". Mother may be called and understood to be "Mum" or "Mama" whether she turns to him or does not and whether she is in his room or in the kitchen. He may recognise an absent toy by its name mentioned by mother and bring it. Or he may name it in the hope of getting it. And he may say "doll" to a picture of a doll. He understands much more than he can say—which is not unique for the second year; it holds for all stages of youth, and even for fields other than language—but there are some things he can say quite well at the end of his second year. "Mummy come", e.g., which means "Mother is coming". "Daddy beard vvvvv", which means "Father shaves his beard (electrically)". "Mummy socks high up", which is to say that mother's socks or stockings are high up there. "Car gone", "Tommy (wants) no milk", "Panties wet", would be some examples. While formerly one word was all he uttered at a time and it referred at once to an object, an activity or quality, and himself, noun and verb or adjective have separated, and he can speak the "sentences" as if he were someone else.

Yet all of this may look peripheral compared to his unceasing attempts to touch and handle with his liberated hands whatever can be touched and handled. He gets around erectly, but wherever he goes there are things to be explored by manipulation. Some are more gratifying than others. A big board such as the closet door can be pushed, but then there is a click—the handle has locked the door—and this is the end of it. A picture can be looked at, but if you also try to do things with it, it will either give way and get torn (which finishes the picture) or it will not yield (since it is made of cardboard or wood). But then it is only half the fun. Sand on the beach, however, is perfect. Easy to handle, easy to destroy, yet infinite in supply. Mud or dirt are even better. And plasticine would be the urban substitute for it. By no means an infinite one. But if it has been scattered all over the table, mother will scrape it together again, and the pulling, pounding, pressing and squeezing can begin all over. Water is another fine substance, although a little too elusive. It requires a container in the first place, a pail or something, and before you know it, there is nothing left of it. Except when you are right by a big body of warm enough water. Then it is inexhaustible too, and it can be thrown, whipped and splashed around. Stones and pebbles or their substitutes provided by the toy industry, namely blocks, are another wonderful thing. When they are in a box, they can be dumped, and when they are on the floor, they can be pushed, shoved or even kicked in all directions. They can even be re-assembled in the box, at least a few of them, and they can be put side by side of each other, maybe one on top of the other. But there must be more gratifying ways, say, screaming until somebody, a parent or sibling, fills the box again, puts it on the table and, thereby, gives him yet another chance to dump the whole thing on the floor. What might even be better than blocks for that purpose, i.e. for the noise and the wonderful mess, is marbles. They really go places all by themselves!

We could say that a desire to manipulate by hand, to manipulate to the point of destruction, joins the desires already in existence, such as sucking, biting, touching, looking, listening, crawling, walking, babbling, etc. Not that it had not existed before. Its formation began when the mouth succeeded in finding the hands and they, in turn, learned how to make their way to it whenever intended, even how to bring objects along. Now, however, manipulation by hand has spread out into a number of distinguishable recurrent derivatives: manipulating solid, semisolid and fluid foods, also any specialty thereof, manipulating inedible objects of the same three consistencies, but also grasping, carrying, dropping, throwing, pounding, pressing, squeezing, pulling or simply smearing any of these objects (see also p. 124 f). The hands can really do something to their objects. They can manipulate them to pieces. They can do so until there is nothing left to do. In fact, only then will the child ordinarily stop the game. That is why it often becomes difficult for parents to tear their child away from an infinite supply of sand, dirt, pebbles or water. The same would hold for more complex toys such as a doll or a car. If they are not sturdy, they will give way, the wheels may come off or the cotton of the inside may come out, and that is precisely what the child is after. The same would even hold for drawing provided he cares for and is able to do such a delicate thing already. He will tend to scribble all over the board or paper and stop only when the board or paper is "destroyed", i.e. when there is no more room to draw on.

The child is destructive in his manipulations because he can do no better. Cathexis of conditions under which he satisfies his desires of "manual manipulation" has not progressed far enough for him to act differently. Yet we would assume that his desires of manual manipulations in the first year of life were still more primitive and destructive. They did not necessarily appear that way, though, because behavior had not become sufficiently efficient to implement them (see p. 64). It will take some time before the incessant process of cathexis has built up enough knowledge of the world and enough skill (which is knowledge of himself and of what he can do), so that alternatives to the most primitive and destructive manipulations become possible and apparent. Once this is the case, however, once he can decide whether to dump the box of blocks or to take them out one by one, whether to leave the sand mountain alone that another child has built or tread right into it, his parents' desires for him will come to his support. They will help him choose and pursue the right thing and counter-cathect the wrong. He will feel increasingly guilty over "bad choices", the more choice he has (see also pp. 67, 86 ff).

This should not be understood to mean that alternatives of satisfaction crop up overnight and do not exist before. The ten-month-old has already some choice among alternatives of manual manipulation. He can either move or not move his hand to his mouth and do so with his left or his right one. He can take a mouthful of porridge in his hands or leave it in his mouth. And once it is in his hands he can either put it back into his mouth or smear it over his belly, perhaps wallow in it, if there is enough. Even at that time mother will already assist him on one course and resist the other. It does mean, however, that clearly and predominantly constructive manipulations come later. Only in the third year of life will manipulation proper, more frequently than not, end short of destruction. Only then will a "piece of work" emerge for the first time that is more complex, at least in some respects, than what the child started out with.

L

There is still another area that has steadily accumulated cathesis and is showing observable results. Elimination has become a focus of interest. Not only because the child has expanded his "mouth-hand personality" to include the rest of the body, and because the trunk can do the most impressive thing of all: produce something out of nothing, or in other words: create an object that is really and truly his own (see also p. 120 f); but also because the parents inevitably pay a lot of attention to it. After all, the child is running around now. If his diapers are filled and he is not attended to soon, his play pants or the carpet, the floor, the furniture, etc., may suffer. Also there is some smell that should not stay about for long. It may not even be too good for the child himself. He may feel uncomfortable or cold after a while or he may develop an itching sore. Besides there are even more powerful counter-cathexes which the parents have adopted while children themselves. "It just is not done. It is dirty. No nice child would do a thing like that," are some of the slogans taken over from their parents and passed on to the child, although their origin may have been repressed.

If toilet training has not begun yet as a formal affair, and the chances are small at the onset of the second year, the child will have to be changed and cleaned some six times a day. That is probably more often than he is being fed, also more often than he is being put to bed, taken out of it and dressed or bathed. And it does take time. Most parents will concede that. What is more, he is expected to produce a bowel movement in somewhat regular intervals and if he does not, the parents get all excited. They did so before. Only now he notices it more clearly. So he would come to think that the whole thing must be quite important to them too.

What heightens that importance is the fact that he hardly gets to see what he produces, let alone to touch or even taste it (see p. 119 f). They take it away from him almost as soon as it comes. He can experience hardly any of the aspects of his dear, but so strongly forbidden, product. Even the smell is stopped quickly. They open the window and out it goes. Although the smell is one thing they cannot deprive him of altogether. He might even get more of it again when he learns how to use the pot or toilet seat, when he can sit on it, so to speak and even conceal for a while whether it has or has not come yet. And much later, already as an adult, he may still take the liberty of tacitly indulging in the smells he can produce. Anyway, the child has such regular contacts with his elimination and yet is restricted to such an extent by his parents, that it is difficult to see how elimination can but assume considerable psychological significance. This may be especially obvious to his parents as soon as they have embarked more seriously on toilet-training him. "Has he?" "Hasn't he?" (wet the bed, soiled his pants, had a bowel movement, had trouble with it, had diarrhea, etc.) is one of their very frequent concerns. Although once he is trained they tend to forget the struggles they had with him almost as radically as the child does himself. As a matter of fact, they might think I am harping on this issue unduly. Which is their privilege, if they have outgrown that age and are not really reading this book.

Counter-cathexis of manipulation and other kinds of fuller experiences of excrements is facilitated by the host of substitutes that the world provides. As a matter of fact, all the desires mentioned above, manipulating mud, sand, water, blocks, marbles, plasticine, etc. all drain (i.e. reduce to some extent the intensity of) the desire to manipulate excrements. They are not only not forbidden, but even encouraged within relatively wide limits. There is rich derivative-formation that may later on develop into more serious painting or sculpturing, into gardening, cooking, building construction, engineering and the like, in other words into any kind of "work". This is in contrast to what happens to early desires for genital stimulation and manipulation. Normally there are not too many substitutes for it and we have seen already that counter-cathexis tends to begin before the infant or child has even a choice. Urination involves genital manipulation and stimulation, but it will tend to stay well within the narrow limits established by counter-cathexes. Urination can be maximised, say by holding back for a very long time or by drinking lots of water, wetting under inappropriate circumstances, say in company or in bed, or merely playing with any kind of water rather than urine, or with the garden hose, the kitchen faucet. These are all some kind of substitutes, but they are not very strong, at least when compared to what masturbation or extensive genital stimulation by another person might yield. Of course, counter-cathexis and new anxiety wherever counter-cathexis is insufficient would be acting against it.

As for relations to the parents, the child in his second year elaborates on the cathexes of his mother. He is no longer quite as dependent upon her help as he was. Nor does he have to summon her all the time by screaming. He can also go after her. He can look her up in the kitchen. Now he sees more of how tall she is, and how powerful even outside his play-pen. If a curtain yields to his pull, comes down on him and covers him up, so that there is no getting up or out, so that screaming is once more the only thing left, there she comes and undoes him immediately. He has begun to take his meals in his own little chair and he can watch from it what mother does while she prepares his meal. He can go for walks with her. Her hand offers infinite support. One might dangle from it all of a sudden while trotting by her side, but one does not fall. And she may wheel one to all kinds of places and pleasures too distant to "ever" be reached by his own efforts. He gets toys from her, also those he has just fumbled or lost, although occasionally she also takes them away from him. And he can get her to change him, later on even to put him on a pot or toilet seat. Not only that. He can also refuse to be changed or set on the pot. Mother may want to go on a shopping trip with him, and in order to have no trouble then, he should be taken care of right here and now. Yet "why now ?" the little one may ask, although in not quite so many words. "I have no desire to move my bowels," he may imply by his fuss. But half an hour later the desire could be "there" and then there is no holding him back. That's why mother wanted to have him changed or clean to begin with. It is fair to say that in his elimination expulsion of excrements predominates over retention and control. Once the desire to expel has reached a certain intensity, satisfaction is sought with little or no delay. This will be different in the third year of life.

At any rate, mother is not only instrumental to many new modes of satisfactions of desires, but also an obstacle to others. There are short-lived, but fierce, struggles over who gets his will. Short-lived, because the child can easily be outsmarted or distracted. He will not even realise yet how right mother was in the first place. He does not understand too much of what she tells him. He could not possibly grasp her comment "I told you so half an hour ago". What is that: half an hour ago? he might ask in return, if only he could formulate it. And what is it that you told me? He does understand her physical language, though. If she puts him in his eating chair, he understands that this is what she wants. He may notice the intention and struggle against it while "flying" through the air, that is for a few seconds, but then he finds himself surrounded by a table board, grasps a rubber doll that mother has put there, sees a spoonful of jelly coming to him and may already have forgotten what he was struggling against. If he does not, if he hits the spoon or spits the jelly out, another distraction such as light on, light off, light on, light off, while being fed, or a little song chipped in for free by mother may make him obey. What he really did not want was any old feeding. But as soon as there is a little circus too, things are different. "Why did you not tell me so," he might imply. But, of course, if mother had tried to, he would not have understood.

The same holds for elimination. Yet while he has developed his own desires of eating and has come to know mother's desires where they differ from his, he does not know too much about, i.e. he has not progressed too far with his cathexes of, elimination and he knows little about mother's desires in that respect. He would want to eliminate on the whim and play with his product. She wants him to eliminate at certain times, hold back one time, speed up at another and she takes the thing away from him. What is worse: She wants him to give it to her all by himself. Which means, her desire should become his. He should identify with her on that matter. The power struggles over feeding may have come under some kind of control by now, but those of elimination are too new yet. They will flare up again and again, especially over this issue. Hence mother may well be viewed by the child as powerful and fierce, at least if he does not make her the presents she has in mind. She may not only appear as an ever-new gratifier of desires, but also as an omnipotent manipulator whom one has yet to learn how to out-manipulate. She can become quite adamant and threatening, even if the really grim aspects of her are largely the child's projections (see p. 87 f).

Where is father in all this? Well, while he was an easily dispensable person as far as the child was concerned, indispensable only to the extent that say, his disappearance for good would reflect on mother's comfort and well-being, and while the child, in his first year of life, could not even manage to cathect more than one person to any memorable degree, he is ready now for other people and also more likely to come in contact with them. After all, he is crawling and running around in the house now and he is more ready to go on trips. Inevitably he gets in contact and, maybe, into conflict with the guests of the house, and he experiences other adults, children, dogs, cats, cars and so on. Father is not around as much as mother is, but under ordinary circumstances he is around more regularly and for longer periods of time than all other people except mother or the child's siblings, if there are any. Siblings, however, are—or should be—under the spell of the parents. Although they may be more available, they would tend to matter less at first. Since father may also have to take care of the child on some of the most frequent occasions, feeding, changing, dressing or undressing, him, leading him by the hand, carrying him, putting him to bed, etc., he will be cathected for his cooperation. He will become a secondary mother, so to speak. Which does not imply that he turns female in the child's eyes. Rather he is neither male nor female, just like mother is not, and he, the child, does not know about his own sex either. At least he knows very, very little about it. He may say: "Boy" in reply to the question: "Are you a boy or a girl?" But if mother asks him: "Is mother a boy or a girl?" he may also say: "Boy".

If father becomes a kind of a second mother, he will be a gratifier as well as an obstructor, just like mother. He will be an omnipotent manipulator too. In fact, the power aspects, the degrees to which parents can control him and the supplies of food and toys, the degree to which they dispose of things and either give them to him or withhold them, take them away for good or for the moment, will come more and more to his notice. He will try to manipulate his parents in turn. He will try to handle them like some toy or animal that he can already master, and to extract the kind of satisfactions from them that a toy can give. These satisfactions have, of course, been derived themselves from actual satisfactions that the parents provided in the first place. Just about everything that he can do to a toy he has seen his parents do to him in some form, whether it be holding or carrying, depositing, lifting, stroking, feeding, putting "to bed", but even poking or throwing (the parents would, e.g. touch or tickle him caressingly, perhaps even slap him gently when just a tiny bit angry at him, and throw and catch him for his giggles of delight over these defiances of gravity). Later on, in his third year, he will even try to play one parent against the other, to get from one what the other refuses to give him.

Manipulation of the parents and cathexes of their power aspects is by no means a new thing. There have been conflicts between the parents', especially mother's, desires and his own in his first year of life. The infant had to learn, e.g. how to forget about biting while being nursed. But he could accept one kind of food and reject another, insist on feeding before being changed, take things into the mouth that mother would not let him, such as soap or a fork that he grabbed by accident. However, his own powers were oral, and whatever omnipotence he recognised in his parents was in terms of oral manipulation and stimulation.

The conflicts are more or less limited to that and not so likely to make an impression on the parents. His desires may be wild and destructive, but what can he do? His behavior is still quite inefficient. In fact, that holds even for the second year of life. The power struggles do not amount to very much as far as the parents are concerned, no matter how high-flying and primitive the child's goals may be. Only in the third year, when the issues have already been mitigated and cut down in size and the child's behavior has gained enough efficiency to implement desires, will the parents really get into tangles, fights and ambushes. The third is the year of *apparent* spite and obstinacy. The child's *imagined* power is greatest when he first discovers he has any and it is his. It declines ever after. The child's *effective* power increases steadily and is strong and reasonable enough at the age of three to create some real, though rarely serious, troubles for the parents.

The *second year* of life could be called the early manipulatory phase, also the early anal phase due to the importance which elimination begins to assume. Since manipulation proper (see p. 125) is still rather primitive—it tends to end only when there is little more but the pieces left of the object, i.e. when it has been destroyed—it has been called the early anal-sadistic or anal-aggressive phase. Yet again, as once before (see p. 145), we will find that the child has few alternatives to his primitive maneuvering of things. Although his modes of satisfaction are primitive and aggressive, his behavior is not efficient enough yet for him to do much harm. Counter-cathexis, if seriously requested, would involve a ban on just about all manipulation. Hence there will be little effective control, but also few incidents of guilt over too little control. The infant is generally more destructive than he will be in his third year, but he is likely to feel much less guilty even so. Smaller "offenses" against the parents' desires for him will arouse more severe guilt feelings, more imperative desires for punishment, at three than they do at two.

Besides all desires surviving from previous periods of development the *primal desires* of the second year are manual manipulation and elimination, but also walking and running around. In addition seeing has been developed to the point of substitute gratifications through pictures and images of objects which, like many a new thing, unfolds its own advantages such as easy availabilty and storability. Hearing has been developed to the point of distinguishing the parents' and other people's words, and babbling to the point of using names of things and people as well as verbs and adjectives in order to say something, to speak in very simple, yet recognisable sentences.

Object-formation has proceeded further with mother and himself, but father has also been recruited, psychologically, and other persons such as siblings, grandparents, aunts and uncles, begin to play a part in what constitutes his world. Besides them the immediate surroundings, the house or apartment, but also the garden or a regularly frequented play-ground, the car, the neighborhood's animals, toys and the like, emerge in his mind. They are being cathected too. Primitive power aspects of the parents are predominant. They are conceived in terms of his own primitive powers or understood to the extent that he can provide his own simple analogues of their desires (see also p. 87 f). His own powers—to handle things, to run around, to produce something—are primitive too, although not quite as primitive as they were in his first year of life.

Counter-cathexis has been facilitated further. All *substitution continua* have gone on expanding. There is more than at the end of the first year of life that can substitute for given losses. On the other hand, the amount of cathexis that constitutes an object in the child's mind has generally increased. If it gets lost, through death, destruction, or plain disappearance, there will be more to counter-cathect. "Mourning" (see p. 37) will be more articulate. The child will feel the loss more clearly. However, even the most complex and gratifying, i.e. the most important, object in the child's mind, mother, is no longer the only parent nor the only adult that matters. Although her loss would generally be the severest trauma he can suffer, the effects would not be quite so detrimental as they are in the first year. The child can accept a substitute mother somewhat more easily. After all, he has had substitute mothers already, say Grandmother, and aunt, or father, for that matter, all of whom took care of him for certain periods of time.

In addition to all counter-cathexes established so far (such as those of breast-feeding, biting, and others), manipulation of excrements is the most universally counter-cathected in the second year of life. As a matter of fact, there is no society without some provisions to get rid of human wastes quickly and neatly. Even if mother just holds the child off their common bed in order not to get wet or soiled herself, she is depriving him of his products and imposing counter-cathexis on him. Elimination itself, on the other hand, has not been counter-cathected far enough so as to give the child control. He still eliminates more or less when, where, and how, he pleases.

Among the defense mechanisms that can be distinguished in addition to those already "in existence" are reaction-formation and sublimation. *Substitution continua* have expanded far enough to permit the former, and the latter can even be viewed as an equivalent, or perhaps a more conspicuous form, of derivative-formation in general (see also pp. 75 ff, 8 ff). Identifications focus on the parents' primitive manipulation- and power-aspects.

The *primal fear*—which is always related to the most primitive of one's own desires (see p. 146)—is that of being manipulated to pieces, that is of being destroyed, smashed, crushed, or severely mutilated. While the worst thing that could happen in the one-year-old's imagination was to be incorporated, devoured, dissolved, to disappear in substance, his substance is now being preserved. That is an advancement, if a small one. These feared mutilations would include elimination. Excrements might be ripped out by force (as in enemas), the trunk may be disemboweled or, generally, one might be attacked and mutilated from the rear.

How do we know about all this ? After all, the child can hardly talk. Yes, but he can play-act and tell us that way, what is on his mind. And one of the things he might do to a doll is to rip it apart and finally to hundred pieces. If he is not supposed to, but has the desire, projection will be a possible compromise, at least for the time being. He will be ripped apart like that, if he does not give up on his bad intentions. This is how he may perceive the situation and play-act it in turn. One doll has been bad, he pretends. He or she has broken something and another doll may rip him or her apart for it.

If, however, we can wait a little longer, say until the child can speak up for himself, we may get his story also in words. He may be afraid of people, at least of some and under certain circumstances (e.g. of a huge man in a dark corridor) and, if asked what he is afraid of, tell us: "They (or he) will eat you up." Later also: "They'll kill you." or: "They'll cut you up." Whereby we can be reasonably sure of one thing: Now, that the child is able to speak about them, he is in the process of handling them and may even have done so already. What he can name and speak about is under some kind of control. The reverse may be true as well. Because he has handled those fears (through successful counter-cathexis of all those desires that may precipitate punishment of the sort expressed in his fears), i.e. because they no longer loom as large as before, he is able to talk about them. Fairy tales and some comic strips even formulate these things for him. Ogres or very wicked and cruel killers populate them richly, although eventually they are defeated by the good little boy or girl and the help of a good mother, father or sibling, say a fairy, God or goblins and midgets, respectively. And what do ogres do? They eat little children. And what are bad giants or human monsters after? They slaughter everybody in the country, or little children, grandmothers or animals. They also destroy cities, wreck bridges and barns, blow up trains, etc. Transformation into a frog, an ugly beast or a rock has also connotations of temporary destruction with preservation of the substance, although it also plays on being a good child, a happy prince, full of desires that parents like, i.e. full of their desires for oneself, at one time and a bad one, that abounds with the most evil mischief, just like a beast, at another.

These primitive fears and desires prevail even in some of the metaphors of our adult language. A businessman may "eat up" his competitor, until there is nothing left of him. Economically that is called a merger. Or he may "break his neck" or "kill him". Implying that he ran him out of business. Or a person may "blow up" from impotent rage, "stew" in the enemy's pots, end up as a "nervous wreck". He may also "scare the shit" out of another person, if you forgive me the expression.

Frustration tolerance has increased further. It takes still longer for the child's desires to reach given intensities, say those at which they are ordinarily satisfied (see also p. 93 ff). Now he can be alone even without the sound or sight of a parent for as long as an hour, although he might not have too many chances of that extent. There is too much mischief he can do now. Mother will even look after him, if he gets too quiet. After all, she may find him trying to light his bed with matches that he has found somewhere. Or he may be drinking father's ink.

The two-year-old may forego a meal for as long as an hour or more if properly entertained or busy. And he may stay awake for an average of five or six hours in a row and tolerate a maximal deprivation of sleep up to eight or nine hours before falling asleep under almost any circumstances. Of course he can fill his waking times by still more different things than he could at one year. What is more, some of his desires such as those for verbal communication, walking, manual manipulation, or even elimination, have become instrumental to a number of other desires such as getting special foods, e.g. candies, or going on a ride, being permitted to fuss around with mother, or to have her fuss around with oneself, being petted, praised, etc.

The *third year* of life elaborates and refines what has been achieved (i.e. cathected and counter-cathected) during the second year. We can be briefer now.

Object-representations develop into a realm all of their own. The child begins to love picture books with stories, he wants to know everything about them and he likes to look at and point out all the details he sees on the pictures. This takes a parent or adult, of course, to keep him company and assistance. But by the end of the third year we may even find him studying his books all by himself, sometimes for half an hour and longer.

His language reaches a state of preliminary perfection by the end of the third year. Now he speaks in "real" sentences, even in parataxes and hypotaxes such as: "Ellen takes the doll and Bobby takes the teddy-bear." Or: "If Ellen falls, she hurts herself and cries." Even something as highly conceptual as this: "The horsie must make a noise, so that one knows that it is a horsie." He listens attentively to what the adults have to say, but also registers events of his own accord. He can relate a story told to him as well as one about what he experienced himself. "Daddy and Mummy and Ellen and Bobby went to Lake Mooseheart. Mummy and Daddy sat down. Ellen made sandcakes. Bobby played in the water. Bobby made splash, splash, splash." As a matter of fact, he may already have begun to speak of himself as "I" and "me" rather than by his name, by the third person, or by "you"—as he hears his parents address him—and of possessions as "mine" and "his" and "hers". If he does not yet, he will soon.

His manual manipulation has been refined considerably. While materials such as sand, mud or snow, are still fascinating, he has become more obviously constructive. He makes mountains and cakes, a road, a tunnel or a big snowball. He "preserves" substances even where the supply is infinite, and where it is not, such as at home and with clay, he can hold it together. He had been collecting things already in his second year, but he tended to forget in the process what it was that he had just been collecting, placed things irretrievably or just lost them. Objects were short-lived and an important aspect of them, ownership, whom do they belong to, was still very weak. Now, however, they have become more stable, they have places and even times (he may know that he put the ball into the toy chest a moment ago, or just before they left the house) and they do belong, indeed. They are his and he does not want to part with them except on his own terms.

He has become persistent enough, e.g., to put a whole lot of pearls on a string or all the red marbles of a Chinese Checkers game in the corner of the board. And he may build a tower of blocks and fail to get tired not only of putting one forever on top of the other, but also of starting all over again, once the structure has collapsed. He even has effective number concepts of one, two, three and "(very) many", although he may rattle off the names of numbers up to ten and farther. But he cannot really count beyond three, on the average.

In drawing he has outgrown the scribble stage. He no longer "fills" or "destroys" the white paper (leaving no more room for further scribbling). He has begun to draw *something*, a ball or a stick, a little girl consisting of a circle (the face) and two lines (the legs). Later on he may add eyes and ears, even arms, although in strange positions as far as the trained eye of the adult is concerned. The arms may come out above the ears, e.g., and the eyes may even be outside the face, although in the vicinity of it. He produces what he "knows" rather than what he "sees". By the end of the third year he is likely to be able to draw a small number of different objects in addition, such as a mouse, a snake and a kind of a simple polygon which he calls a house. And he tends to add some details: ears and a tail to the mouse, a mouth with a split tongue for the snake and, say, a chimney for the house. Also he prefers colors and crayons to lead pencils. Yet the use of colors is still highly arbitrary, at least as judged by adult standards. Artists, however, may sometimes find interesting or even daring and, at any rate, plausible aspects in his color combinations.

Elimination has generally been mastered by the end of the third year. While expulsion of excrements characterised the process in the second year, it is the control of elimination, retention and deliberation over whether one should or should not eliminate, whether one should give it to the parents or retain it, that dominates now. Even urination, which lags somewhat behind defecation (see p. 120 f) is almost under control. Only bed-wetting is often kept as a last reserve in the struggles with the parents. It is used for barter. In fact, "presents" and "gifts" and their exchanges have become generally important. If he has not wet the bed, mother must give him something, a toy, a spoonful of honey or permission to help her wash the dishes. Or, as a bribe, he may put his scattered toys away in a jiffy. But then mother must take him on her trip to town, buy him a lolly-pop or take him to his cousin Tommy who has that vast amount of toys and a rocking horse like he has never seen one. If he is to let go of a toy-tractor in the "Five-and-Ten", then he must not be forced to play with little Susan from across the street, and he will get ready for bed, if mother lets him light one match, etc.

Occasionally these power struggles with the parents may flare up to greater dramas than ever before. It has been pointed out already (see p. 155 f) that apparent spite and obstinacy increases in the third year. In contrast to what he can do or ordinarily does, his excesses are much more conspicuous than in the second year period, when he behaved primitively. He might not move his bowels for three days in a row while having been quite regular all along. Or he may have an accident, a real bad one, in the house of a former schoolmate of mother's. And mother went to see her in order to show off her bright and pretty little son. But things go well on the whole. He cooperates with his parents' desires in that matter—their desires are an important part of the control he has gained over elimination—and he needs little help. As a matter of fact, some children may already do it all by themselves, including the wiping.

He cooperates with his parents' desires on most matters. The power struggles with them are mitigated whether they concern elimination, eating, playing, getting dressed for a walk, taking a nap or being put to bed for the night which, in a way, means separation from the parents, the living room, and all its fun. Yet the child's effective power has increased considerably. For one thing, he understands the parents' language and can say himself just about anything of concern. The parents' imagined powers, on the other hand, have shrunk to more realistic dimensions. This leaves them still very powerful, indeed, but he is on the same platform more often than he was in his second year.

The number of people who have come to his notice have increased further. Mother is still the most important and father the second-most, but there are also aunts and uncles, grandparents, neighbors, friends, etc. The child may be able to recognise by name, or remember the names of, some ten adults. He may know as many children by name and a few dogs or cats in addition. Besides he knows and loves all kinds of animals, elephants, monkeys, giraffes, bears, lions, kangaroos, ducks, etc., whether they are in the zoo, in picture books or in his toy box. He will easily make sex-distinctions among children and adults as well as on pictures. His distinctions, however, will tend to be based on such things as long hair and short hair, dresses or pants, a beard or no beard, perhaps also the voice. Something as obvious as women's breasts are rarely mentioned. After all, little girls do not have them. And primal anatomical sex-differences may have been observed already, but they still tend to be quickly forgotten, i.e. repressed or counter-cathected. Such strange sights do not quite make sense. Or they better hadn't, because who knows what they entail? Only in the Oedipal stage of development, in his fourth, fifth and sixth years of life, will the child come to grips with the "facts" of the sexes and their differences. For the time being distinctions are made only in a cursory and *ad hoc* manner, if at all. The sex of a person does not matter much. Even his own sex is not at issue. He would not be too surprised if sexes could change in time or even at will.

The three-year old can enjoy the company of his contemporaries better than before. He even seeks it. He can play with children of his age for a while as long as they stick to teddy-bears, tricycles, rocking horses, balls, etc., and as long as there are enough toys, or at least two of those in question, and sufficient room for "parallel" play, that is as long as they can both do the same things without getting into each other's interests. There may be simple barters, although possessions have become extremely valuable, especially under such a challenge. As a matter of fact, after half an hour or so they are bound to slip into fights over who owns what and gets what when, and an adult, a parent or the nursery school teacher, will have to intervene. Otherwise they may well pound or scratch each other, pull the other's hair or kick him. Even attacks at the other child's property, as a substitute for direct attack, may occur, although they would be more noticeable in subsequent years.

His physical and geographical environment has spread too. He knows his way around in the neighborhood, in a close-by food store or on the golf course three blocks away. He recognises and even anticipates landmarks on some of the family's more frequent trips, say a Shell sign or a big dog on a poster jumping for his dogfood ration. He knows more about distances. He may claim that Jimmie's house is farther away than Dick's, and this may be perfectly true. But he may also claim that the distance is ten miles, while in reality it is only two hundred feet. Something similar would hold for money. He may claim that a lolly-pop costs a nickel, but also that a pound of bananas costs eighteen dollars. A car may also cost "eighteen dollars, perhaps more" or as much as "hundred lolly-pops".

His concept of time has improved too. He is still "drifting" compared to the ambitious and complicated pursuits of an adult, but it is no longer from minute to minute that he appears to do so. He lives by some kind of clock and he knows something about it. He may say: "Today Bobby (or I) has (have) not wet the bed," and thereby refer to the past night. Or he may claim: "Today we shall visit Dickie." He means: this afternoon, after lunch or after the nap. As a matter of fact, he may not even be able to sleep because of the anticipation. "Yesterday Jimmie and Carol were here", means that Jimmie and Carol were here, yes, they are here no longer, but that was not yesterday. His concept of yesterday may include the day before yesterday, last week and even "any time before today or now" in addition to yesterday. His comment may indicate that once upon a time Jimmie and Carol were here. "To-morrow we'll go to the circus," may mean next week, to-morrow, or even this coming afternoon. By the end of his third year, however, he may already distinguish between to-morrow and any time beyond to-morrow as well as between yesterday and any time before that. He may even have some notion of what an hour is, but it will be a rubber concept referring sometimes to half a day and other times to a few minutes.

All of this should not be confused with the child's *sense* of time which is intimately linked to the intensities of his desires and can be identified in its most primitive forms soon after birth. The infant, e.g., wakes up to his feeding. He gets restless, because it is time to eat, just as it becomes time for a smoker to have another cigarette or for a person who has been awake long enough to go to bed.

A person's sense of time is his sense for the intensities of his desires while they go unsatisfied (see Toman, 1956, also p. 16). It can be traced no sooner than desires have formed, although it will get increasingly refined and complicated as the individual develops.

The child of three has also become quite busy with role playing. He acts his father or mother, occasionally also another child, plays cooking, or hammering, riding in the car, cleaning the floor, eating, feeding a teddy-bear, repairing the house, dressing and undressing a doll, ironing, etc. One may wonder whether these games of identification are not something new altogether. No. It has been pointed out already (p. 83, also p. 40 ff) that the earliest distinguishable forms of introjection, such as giving oneself the fist like mother gives one the bottle or babbling the way she talks or sucking one's fist like she sucks one's face (he means her kisses), are identifications, although by very primitive means. The mouth or, maybe, hands and mouth together are the instruments, by which the infant can adopt mother's desires for him during his first year of life. Now, that he is running around upright, moving in the same places as his mother or his parents do, and capable of handling things much more articulately—he can even sit down with a book and "read", turn the water on and off in the bathtub, "use" the telephone, open and close the refrigerator—now he is in a much better position to introject the parents' desires. This is why the parents and friends come to notice his endeavors more clearly. They are articulate enough even for the naked eye, while before one had to look closer and even make some inferences in order to make out ongoing introjections.

Summarising the third year, we could say that, in addition to the desires formed in previous years, the *primal desires* are manual manipulation which leads no longer to the destruction of the object, and control of elimination. His *object-formations* have included further developments of the objects of his second year and new developments of a few others. Their and especially his parents' power aspects as well as his own have become refined and more realistic. The parents are not only antagonistic, but also protective, it turns out. And sometimes they can be played against each other. *Counter-cathexes* include the manipulation of substances other than excrements that are too messy, dirty or smelly to play with, the primitive indulgence in expulsion, and the parents' more primitive or destructive ways of asserting their power, which have been provoked by the child less and less frequently. Identifications focus on their subtler and more articulate manipulations. The *primal fears* are those of being manipulated, although no longer destroyed, or mutilated, although not too severely, perhaps even disemboweled or killed, but in milder fashions than was feared in the second year of life. One might lose only parts of the inside, or one might be shot, which would not look too differently from being unconscious or asleep.

Frustration tolerance has increased further. The child can be alone an hour and longer even under somewhat unfamiliar circumstances, say, in a room of friends of his parents, provided there are enough toys to entertain (or distract) him, and enough things to do. What is more, the parents would let him be alone. They have sufficient reason to trust him already. With a familiar substitute he can spend up to a whole day without noticeably missing his parents too badly. This better not happen too often, though. He can go without a meal, sometimes up to two hours beyond the regular feeding time. He may stay awake for an average of some six hours and tolerate a maximum deprivation of sleep up to eleven hours. That is, he may occasionally skip his nap without too much fuss.

The networks of instrumentality have grown even further. While a stick was something to hold and, say, pound with at two, it has become a means of reaching something otherwise beyond reach, a means for drawing in sand or snow, an arrow that can be thrown or sometimes even shot from a bow, and a boat that can swim in water. Mucilage is no longer a nice substance for smearing, but it can glue things together, make an icing on a clay cake, and perhaps even glue a napkin on a doll. An (old) newspaper can be read, stepped on, used for wrapping a ball, cutting holes with a plastic scissors, making cornflakes (by tearing it to little pieces), or serving as a blanket for a doll. A thread can imitate a snake, bind two things together, be wrapped around the finger and make it pale or blue (by blocking the blood supply) and even carry a chain of pearls. A chair can be sat on, but also stepped on, pushed to a place and stepped on, and crawled under, so that it is like a house, etc. All of this would, of course, contribute to a child's frustration tolerance or Ego-strength, as we may also call it. The likelihood that he could do something that may bring him closer to the satisfaction of a desire deprived for a given length of time is greater than it was before. He is not so much at the mercy of an imposed condition of deprivation as he used to be.

The Oedipal Phase

THE FOURTH, FIFTH AND SIXTH YEARS OF LIFE

WHEN it dawns on the child for the first time that mother is a woman and father a man, and he himself a boy or she herself a girl, that he or she is like one of the parents and not like the other, the "Oedipal period" has begun. We have been speaking of the infant and child as of "him". This was a convenience of speech. It meant "her" as well. Up to the third year of life the course of development is not too different for the boy and for the girl. They may already have referred to themselves as boys or girls correctly. In all likelihood they have. They may use the right pronouns when talking of themselves and they have generally begun to distinguish boys from girls even when seeing them for the first time. Yet they do not know what "really and irrevocably" makes a boy and what a girl and why they themselves are one rather than the other. As far as they are concerned, sex could still change, even repeatedly and at will.

What does make a boy or a girl? If this is not a facetious question, it is a very complicated one to answer. The combination of an X- and Y- chromosome in one case and of two X-chromosomes in the other, would be an aspect. Sub-cortical mechanisms that determine hormone production, would be another. That is, neurological and hormonal differences would supposedly make for the differences in sex or at least for some of them. But what are the neurological differences? There are more apparent criteria such as the so-called primary and secondary sex-characteristics. The sex-organs are different from earliest life on, and additional differences come with an individual's development. The girl's physique stays somewhat softer, her skin smoother, i.e. closer to hairless, her breasts develop and menstruation begins to inconvenience the growing woman periodically to various degrees. In mating the woman gets the baby, while the man "makes her one". Her incapacities increase as pregnancy proceeds and persists at least for a while thereafter. Of course, she is incapacitated only in some respects. In others she can do what no man will ever be able to do: she can bear a child and feed it "with her own body".

There are still other differences. Women wear skirts and show their legs, while men do not, at least nowadays. Women stay home, while men go out for work. In some parts of the world, however, men stay home or spend their time in pubs, while women go out to work, if necessary even with a child on their back, and do housework after they have come home. And in other parts of the world both men and women go out for work, but the man does the housework too and takes care of the children as soon as he gets home, while the wife tells him from the sofa or over the telephone how to do it. These are the exceptions, though. Where they become the rule, things may not be going so well. To continue, women are soft-spoken and kind, while men are harsher and aggressive. Women can tolerate pain, while men can inflict it. Women wait, while men keep them waiting (and can hardly wait themselves), not necessarily as far as dates and little favors, but usually as far as final commitments and marriage, are concerned. Women have taste, while men have strength and technical know-how. Women are artistic, while men are scientific.

So what makes a boy and what a girl? All these differences? Yes and many more. The examples could easily be multiplied and pursued further. But is that what makes a boy or girl, a man or woman, in the eyes of the growing child? Well, the four-year old would hardly consider the combination of chromosomes in the germ-cells or hormonal regulations as distinctive determinants. And he might consider others, but find sooner or later that they do not stand up. He may discover that mothers wear pants too, and fathers put on some kind of a dress on occasions. He means their robes. And sometimes mothers go out to work, say for a church organisation or to do the weekend's shopping, while fathers stay home. And what is soft-spoken or able to tolerate pain? What pain, how much, when? And if he does get the impression that mother is nicer than father, there are times, inevitably, when it looks the other way. Yet if one way makes the woman and the other makes the man, are they changing their sexes then?

There is only one criterion that would at once be plausible and, in the long run, stand up: the "anatomical sex-difference" or the primary sex-characteristics. That is probably why they have been called primary. The child is in a position somewhat comparable to a biologist who discovers an unknown species of ratlike animals on an uninhabited island. If he would want to make sure which one is the male and which the female and he could not wait for copulations—which may be seasonal—or for the birth of a litter by one of the two, what would he do? I think, he would inspect their sex-organs. He may venture guesses at their identities from other *data*. One animal may appear more aggressive and the other lazier or more timid. Or one may sniff at the other more often than vice versa. But obviously he would not know for sure. There is also a vast difference between this biologist and the child. The biologist knows all about sexes and their differences, whether it concerns men or mammals, birds, reptiles, insects, fish or even plants. He can make his test of a new species against an immense background of tested *data*. The child, on the other hand, knows very little yet and he draws primarily on his experiences with men, which means his family. There may be dogs around and dogs run about "naked". Their primary sex-characteristics are on display. Yet he has hardly noticed them so far and if he has, it means nothing yet for his parents, his siblings or himself.

Would not the secondary sex-characteristics come to his notice and be of help? After all, mother's breasts are on a kind of display. They are covered, but not hidden. And father has none. Furthermore he shaves, whereas she does not. She has no beard. And father speaks with a deeper voice than mother. Yes, but then the child looks at his little sister, or she looks at her little brother and none of these hold true. Yet she is a girl and a girl turns woman, and he is a boy and will be a man. So why can't he, the boy, become a woman in later life and she a man? If it is already fixed, what is it that has been fixed?

No, the only thing that can explain to the four-year-old why one is a boy or a man and the other a girl or a woman is the anatomical sex-difference. It may be baffling and hard to believe at first, that one kind of person should have "something" and the other "nothing"—and these would be the four-year-old's ways of phrasing it—but there it is, and it would make sense. "There it is" may also take the form of "Where is it?" when the little boy sees a naked little girl, and "What is this?" or "What has he got there?" when the little girl sees a little boy. With brothers and sisters in the house, this is almost inevitable. Without them other children, say on the beach, may offer food for thought. If nothing of the kind is available, if the anatomical sex-difference is hidden from him or her, he will begin to search all by himself for better explanations than the ones available so far. He will ask questions about why he cannot marry mother or why he cannot marry father for that matter and why grandmother is out of the question too. "You can't marry my *mother*," father may have replied. "But *you* have married *my* mother," could have been the boy's spontaneous answer, although he will get the point soon. And where do children come from? And how do they come about? Why does mother have to go to the hospital? Why doesn't father go instead? If mother gets the babies, what's the use of father? And if it takes two to have a baby, why not mother and grandmother? . . . To name only a few of the many questions with which the boy as well as the girl pursue their research, often much to the embarrassment of the parents.

What about children who have not been exposed to the genitals of the other sex? My counter-question: What about "What about them?"? What do you have in mind? Well, may be the reply, does that mean that they cannot distinguish sexes? No, they can. But their methods of distinction are not foolproof. They do not know enough about it. It may well be that the parents wanted it that way. Perhaps they hid the "facts" on purpose. So what will become of them? Well, they will learn about the anatomical sex-difference from other children in the neighborhood or in school, and if they get it straight, some of their experiences during the Oedipal phase will begin to make better sense at last. In retrospect, that is, but it is not too late. Now he knows why mother looks the way she does, why his sister has to always sit down when she goes to the bathroom and why boys have flies in their trousers. And the girl knows at last what that bulge is that one can sometimes see on men, say, when they wear swimming trunks. There are many more things that follow, but let us not step ahead of ourselves.

If the discovery of the anatomical sex-difference really is such an integral part in the child's world of people, if the parents' and his own sex are such decisive aspects, why does it occur so late, say in the fourth year of life, and what safety devices have been installed by nature or God so that it cannot be missed?

The first question first: Why does it not come about sooner? In order to pay attention to another person's sex-organ, the child must have learned about his own sex-organ in the first place. And when does that happen? We have seen that the child's cathexis of himself spreads from the mouth to the hands and later to the trunk including its extremities (see also p. 119 ff). By the end of the third year he has learned to manipulate and stimulate his whole body, so to speak. And just that would be necessary before he could manipulate and stimu- late as specific and inconspicuous a part as his sex-organs. The mouth must have relegated most of its authority to the hands and the hands must have had some practice in exploring the body, before they can focus on a part of it, leave alone relegate some authority in turn to that part. Only then, however, only if the hands can manipulate and stimulate the sex-organs, will the latter assume full psychological existence.

The second question was: What safety devices have been installed so that the discovery of the anatomical sex-difference and its prerequisite, this step-into- existence, psychologically speaking, of one's own sex-organs, cannot be missed? Well, the sex-organs are sensitive to stimulation to such an extent that they will eventually outdo all other stimulations. Besides they are the instruments of urination and the latter requires some genital stimulation, however small, some five or six times a day. Of course, the area of genital manipulation and stimula- tion has already been infiltrated heavily by counter-cathexis. All urination, washing or wiping of the genitals that so far came by the grace of the parents, usually stopped no sooner than they started. Apparently they wanted him to get no more than a minimum of stimulation. So how can the child attempt more without threatening to inflict punishment on himself (see also pp. 122 f, 85 f)? This is why the child usually does not plunge headlong into masturbation in spite of the discovery of his genitals and why most parents do not even have to prohibit it explicitly. They have, so to speak, prohibited it all along by refraining from stimulating their child genitally beyond the necessary minimum. That minimum, however, is inescapable.

All right, one might say, the child inevitably discovers his own sex-organs. They are located so that their discovery does not come too soon, but also so that they cannot be missed. Yet why would the child turn to somebody else? Why would he be interested in the sex-organs of other people? He does not really have to turn to somebody else. He has been turned to somebody other than himself before he knew it. From birth on he depended on mother even for the most primitive kinds of satisfactions (see p. 82 f). All genital satisfaction came from her too. So when he is capable also of doing it himself, why should he turn away from her? Why should he not try to get her to continue to help him with it, say, along with urination or otherwise, especially if she thinks that he needs it no longer. Nobody would give up anything enjoyable, any satisfaction at all, if he can help it (see p. 49f). As a matter of fact, if he has become able to handle and stimulate his own sex-organs, why should he not try to explore mother too for interesting parts and appendices? And how could he be content with the mere sight of such parts? Everything sufficiently new will have to be inspected by hand as well, and if it does not make sense, even the mouth may have to be consulted. No, if he knows of his own sex-organs, which means that he knows how to handle and stimulate them, he would try to get to know hers too. Horrible as this spectacle sounds, it would be the most natural course of events. If mother were a thorough moron, she might actually give in to her child's pursuits. Once the child has learned how to stimulate her genitally, he would gradually want both, stimulate and be stimulated genitally. And the safest way of achieving both would be to stimulate her genitally with his own genitals. At this point, the physical incompatibility would put an end to this savage pageant. Normally, however, counter-cathexes should prevent it all along.

This course of events, if unchecked by counter-cathexis, was summarised by S. Freud as the little boy wanting to sleep with his mother (Freud, 1905, 1916–17, 1924, 1933). While we are at it, we may ask as well, what the little girl does in that respect. Well, she does the same, or rather would do the same, if she could. She would also tend to turn to mother with desires to be genitally stimulated by her, but also to explore her and maybe achieve some kind of mutual genital stimulation. But what kind? The physical incompatibility is even greater, but counter-cathexes prevent such a course anyway. Wherever they are insufficient, mother will urgently see to it that they are strengthened. She will leave no doubt as to what her desires are. She wants to have a "good girl" as much as she wants a "good boy".

This is not the whole story. The discovery of one's sex-organs leads to an interest in other people's sex-organs. This precipitates the discovery of the anatomical sex-differences as well as of the sexes of mother, father, and oneself. And this discovery makes one thing clear: There are two of one kind and one of the other. There is a disequilibrium in the family, to say the least. The boy who pursues mother with his budding genital interests will come to think that father does likewise. What else can it be, if his parents put him to bed and stay up or even go out together; or if they share the bed with each other, while he is put up in his own little room; or if they lie with each other in thin pyjamas, as he can convince himself when, on Sunday mornings, they permit him to squeeze in between them for a little while. But if father wants the same as he does from mother, who will get it? In fact, "how dare he cross my ways?" the little boy may think. "I will dispose of him quickly and for good. But how? And what will he do to me ? Dispose of *me* quickly and for good, before I have a chance ? How dare I cross *his* ways ?"

How could the boy dispose of his father or his father of him quickly and for good ? If he wants genital stimulation from mother and father does not want him to have it, he could deprive him of it in some way, and the surest way of doing that would be to deprive him of his genitals. Father could also kill him, but that would not really be necessary. Of course, he, the boy, could try to do the same thing to father, but how would he do it ? Father is so big and strong. And if he is not mistaken, if what he caught a glimpse of is true, father's genitals are big too. Could he really deprive him of them ? Wouldn't he have to kill him first ? And if he tried either, but failed, would father not retaliate doubly. He better not go too far with mother. Otherwise father may "castrate" him, as Freud summarised it (Freud, 1905, 1916–17, 1924, 1933). As a matter of fact, father may do so even if he only caught him, the boy, playing with his own genitals.

The girl makes similar discoveries, not only of her sex-organ and of what boys have—they have more and they can do more with it: they can even urinate while standing up and aim—but also that mother is like her—a big disappointment; the most important object in the world is lacking something—and that there is only one man in the house, father. If one wants to have what a man has got, one will have to *have a man*. So who will get him, father, that is ?

Yet the girl is in a somewhat different position. The discovery of the existence of two sexes is linked to the discovery of what she is missing. While the boy may fear for what makes him a "man", at least if he does not behave, the girl has nothing to lose. She has lost it already. She was born a girl and mother bore her. So if anybody's, it is mother's fault. She is lacking the same thing. Secondly, father becomes important in a new sense. In fact, if she herself is to be a woman, father is all-important. And he has an advantage over mother. He tends to be a little nondescript. Mother has satisfied all desires so far, but never done very much in terms of genital stimulation. Here she stuck to the minimum necessary for elimination and cleanliness (see p. 168). Hence genital stimulation as well as mother's role in it have begun to be counter-cathected even before the girl— or the boy for that matter—was able to try it her- (or him-) self. The girl, how-ever, can turn to father now, who is some sort of a "late-comer" in the child's world. Her genital interests in father would tend to be slightly less "incestuous", if we may say so, than would be the boy's in his mother. Both, girl and boy, would come to look at the same-sex parent as their rivals for the favors of the opposite-sex parent, but the girl would be jealous of mother (i.e. desiring to be rid of her) only as far as she is a woman. She would usually continue to desire mother, and consume her for, her nurturant and power-aspects. And if mother succeeded in depriving her of father (say by hiding him in the attic or putting him up in another house), she would still have a lot of a parent left in mother. The boy, on the other hand, would be jealous of father as far as he is a man, but father is not very much more to him anyway. There are considerably fewer pre-genital aspects that could reconcile the boy to father's existence than to mother's. If father succeeded in depriving him of mother, he, the boy, would have too little of a parent left in father, or so it must seem to him.

All this would lead us to expect that the boy's genital interest in mother falls victim to more radical counter-cathexis or repression than does the girl's interest in father. This is enhanced by the fact that the girl has "less of a sex-organ" to begin with, as she tends to view her predicament, and does less with it than the boy. Her initiative in matters of genital stimulation and manipulation will be more subdued. She will tend to be less offensive even without the parents' implicit or explicit restrictions. Therefore the boy should come out of the Oedipal period with less of an attachment to mother as a woman (while mother as a "nurse" or a "power" may be unaffected) than the girl would have formed to father as a man, and latency period seems generally to show that.

Even after the boy has learned how to neither interfere with his father nor offend his mother by too manifest pursuits of his genital interests, he will still be curious about what it is that they do together. What do they exclude him from? What are their secrets? No, what is *the* secret of theirs? Sunday morning he is permitted to check up on them and their double bed—why is it a double bed?—but what about the other mornings? What about the nights, even Sunday nights? Sometimes one can hear them talk or laugh right across the hall and sometimes, if one sneaks up to their door, one can hear something very strange. Are they fighting? Why these giggles? And these . . . these gasps? But even if he is not quite as successful as a detective, he will wonder why they can undress before each other, but refuse to do so in his presence. And if they undress before each other, what do they see? And if they see something, what do they do with it?

There are still other things that might be on his mind, especially when he has been provided with a little brother or sister. Where did they come from? Where in general do children come from? And why do they come? After all, who needs them? But then what about himself? Where did he come from? Where was he before he was born? Is not a birthday, the day on which one was born, a gay reminder of something very mysterious? How was one born? Who did it? Mother? How? You were inside of mother? Is that so? But if you were inside of mother, where were you inside? Up here (he means mother's breasts)? And how did you get out? Can she spit a baby? Or does it come from the navel? Or from the behind? Where does it get out? And how does it get in to begin with? Why doesn't mother have a baby now? Why doesn't father for that matter? If she is the only one who can have a baby, what's the good of father? Why did she not have a baby before she met father? That would have been a smooth way of getting rid of him! Father is necessary? But how?

Well, gradually the boy learns why father is necessary for mother to have a baby and what they might be doing together in order to get one. A fuller knowledge often does not come until latency period which has sometimes been misconstrued to imply that there would no longer be any genital interests. No, latency period is the time in which "*incestuous*" genital interests, those involving parents and siblings, have generally been counter-cathected or repressed. But non-incestuous pursuits may well have substituted for them. Anyway, a fuller knowledge of the "primal scene" (Freud, 1905, 1916–17, 1924, 1933), the most secret and elementary interaction among the two most important people in the child's life, the interaction with the most miraculous consequences, well, a fuller knowledge may come later. It may, in retrospect, give final touches to experiences that hinted at it, but were not permitted to be pursued. Yet a tentative knowledge, however erratic and inadequate, is usually formed right on the spot. Even with parents who discourage such ideas bluntly, say, by telling him not to ask so many questions, or that he will find out about these things when he grows up, the child is bound to think up something. Siblings or friends may help him with precious whispers. "Father and mother kiss each other. Then they have a baby." And he has seen them kiss each other in different ways than they kiss him. Mother may get a baby in the hospital or from the doctor. But what about father? "Father pays the check." "Doesn't the stork bring some babies?" "Child stuff. Do you remember our cat? She had her kittens in the belly. Do you know how she got them? She went out at nights." "She went to the doctor?" "Don't be silly." "How did she get them?" "From a cat. From a he-cat. Didn't you know that?" Or babies may have something to do with the bathroom. The parents have a separate one, you know. Or with mother's little cabinet. She has all kinds of things there. She keeps it locked, etc.

The girl does something similar. She also pursues the matter of what parents do with each other and it comes as a pleasant surprise to her that girls can have babies while boys cannot. That is more than catching up on their advantage. "All right", they might think, "you have something that I do not have. But I *shall* have something much better, that you can never, never have." It comes as another surprise and disappointment to find that even then boys or men are indispensable. And if she learns in what ways they are indispensable, she may feel like little Ann of Concord, Mass., when she learned about it. She was a little older, though, about seven, when she stormed into the living-room one day proclaiming with tears of solemn anger: "Mother, I am *not* going to let a man stick a penis into me."

On the other hand, of course, she may already have accepted the fact that she cannot be a boy, but have one; that she cannot quite do what he can, say run as fast, climb as high, jump as wide, shoot as accurate or even urinate as well as he does, but that she might be able to make him do all these things for her. In fact—and here we are going off on a tangent again—she might even find it quite enjoyable to see him do all these things including urination. She might develop thoughts not only of seeing the organ do this magnificent job, but also of touching it, perhaps holding it for him and see whether she can do the same things he can do with it. Maybe they could urinate together, both at the same time, or even "together" in a deeper sense. Maybe they could exchange urine. Is that possible? Could they, of all things, touch genital by genital?

At this point the little girl might find it no longer so horrible that a man would "stick his penis into her". And if that is part of having a baby, so be it. In fact, she would want a baby very much under just these circumstances, would want it with, say, Jimmy from across the street. Or in more acceptable terms: She would want to marry Jimmy and have lots of children with him. All of these articulations might well be possible only in latency period or later, but in principle the problems originate now, i.e. in the Oedipal phase.

There is still another angle that the girl will tend to pick up at this time. She learns that the boy has something, whereas she has nothing, and that she will have something much better some day, which the boy cannot possibly get: babies. But that is a long way off. It will be years of school and other troubles before she reaches that stage. She must have something to show right here and now. Does she? Well, a person lacking something, say an ear, a nose, a leg, an arm, hair, a tooth, is *ugly*, isn't he? A person lacking what makes a boy would be ugly too. Wouldn't she? As a matter of fact, all girls would be ugly in that respect. But that is not so! It's the boys that are ugly! They are ugly for the very thing that makes them boys? *Girls are beautiful!* This is what *they* have got even now: their beauty. This is what they must cherish and cultivate, what they must be admired for. This is what they should guard. Girls *have to be* beautiful. It's a must. Why? Because they are not beautiful to begin with? Anyway, they have to wear ribbons and pearls, rings, pigtails and other fancy hairstyles, beautiful dresses and shoes, hats and the like. And they must not under any circumstances whatsoever lose anything at all of themselves, i.e. of their bodies or apparel. If they did, it would be absolutely shameful. Whereas a boy may be a hero, more admirable than he ever was, if he lost a tooth in a fight, a hand in combat or the like except for one thing: his sex-organ. In that case, he would really and truly be a cripple.

The girl's emphasis on beauty may be viewed as a reaction-formation to her "original ugliness" (Freud, 1933, esp. ch. 5). Quite in line with the characteristics of reaction-formation (see p. 46 f) the girl would tend to overdo the beauty and, in later life, give her husband perhaps many a headache over her beauty-purchases. In contrast to guilt which is a state of active expectation of, or a desire for, punishment (see p. 86 f), *shame* is the feeling of being ugly, i.e. of having been punished already in a way everybody can see or even feel. One could also say: shame is the desire to hide something of oneself or, under the worst of circumstances, oneself as a whole: a desire to sink into the ground; a desire to hide that one has been punished, and in what ways. Hence the girl would basically tend to be more bashful, and the boy more boastful. The greatest injury to her pride would be exposure of her predicament, whereas the little boy would do just that, expose himself, with the greatest pride.

In the course of the long and complex processes of derivation-formation, however, the girl tends to become the exhibitionist, poses in every kind of dress and undress, poses even naked for an artist, although this brinkmanship never goes as far as to expose her vagina. By the same token the boy renounces increasingly as he grows up to exhibit his physique or any part thereof, hides himself in standard suits and tends to show rather what he has got in a figurative sense, i.e. what he can *do*, how good he is at something, how strong he is and the like. (Of course, the most indispensable of all his strengths and accomplishments would lastly be his genital prowess.) And since he has literally got something that the girl has not got, he might start giving her things that she does not have. He might offer her presents. As a matter of fact, this is a rather regular course of events. The little boy learns how to make presents to his mother, how to be nice to her, help her in the house wherever "a man's hand" is needed or bring flowers so that she or her room would be even more beautiful. Later on it will be a necklace, a mink stole, a diamond ring or even a sports car for her private use, a house in a place where she had always wanted one or a trip around the world. He produces specifically what she, usually a girl other than mother, may desire. In a more sublime form it is giving the lady of one's heart all the comfort and protection possible both physical and psychological. It is being a king and yet her noble servant, a king who has only one superior to himself and the kingdom: *his queen.*

It starts out, though, with the boy's conscious recognition of his own strength in comparison to a girl's. While formerly he had to fight for his power position regardless of the sex of his challenger, it may now be sufficient to establish his maleness, provided he is dealing with a woman. Just show her what you are or what you have got and she will be quiet, crumble or even fall for you. Such attempts become manifest in almost every family that has a boy. Soon, of course, he catches on to the woman's or mother's sensitivity in that matter, and if he does not, father will help him to it. Finally he will refrain from using the last and winning trumps in his struggles with mother or any woman. She should not be defeated. She should be aroused by the way he plays his cards or knows how to defeat other *men.* She should fall in love with him of her own accord, the madder, the better. And she would probably tend to submit to it, if she sees that he, in turn, is madly in love with her, that she could do with him as she pleases, that he would rather tear up his trump card than abuse it against her. Because then she can even let him use it. He will learn how to establish his power over other men in forms already used before, but now the struggle will be over women. That's what it comes down to. Once the other men are out of his way, though, once he is with the woman, he will happily renounce plain or shrewd power and rape. He will want to be tender, gentle, kind, admitting to his dependence on her for the satisfaction of his desires, i.e. for his love, and thereby likely to win something much more precious than a defeated and humiliated woman. And she will learn how to submit to the wishes of this kind of a suitor.

We have overstepped the boundaries of the chapter. These trends will be truly articulate only after puberty has begun, but their precursors are already well on their way and can be recognised empirically without much trouble, provided one cares to look. These trends are claimed to be universal. If they derive from psychoanalytic theory which, after all, is a general theory of human motivation and its development, they should indeed be universal. Otherwise the theory would not be a general one. But they can be called universal also in the sense that there is no culture in the world where there would not be fathers and mothers and boys and girls, where boys would not be appraised somewhat higher than girls, where girls would not, in general, tend to prefer gentle lovers to brutes and tyrants, courtship and presents to having to court or make presents themselves. Where dowries are customary, the girls would still prefer to be desired for their own sakes. And where so-called matriarchates prevail, girls are not necessarily better off than elsewhere. It is mostly mothers to whom extraordinary privileges are extended, and this is done because of their children, particularly their sons. As a matter of fact, it is the children, especially the sons, who extend them, and in that respect all societies are somewhat matriarchal. Once she has become a mother, a girl is even willing to make presents herself, to give them rather than to take them. But she also is no longer in such dire need of something that she is missing. She has got her children. And whom does she give to? Her children? And what? Beauty tokens? Not for a long time, if at all. No, she gives them food. She mothers them. She makes them *her* children for good.

Do I mean to say that women are inferior to men and can only become their equals if they have children? No, I am not saying anything about what they *are*. I am only speaking about what they *look like* to themselves and to men. Psychologically, these are facts too, of course, and very powerful ones. But are you not biased then by these psychological facts and denying women their rights and appreciation? Well, if I may make an observation, I think that there is nothing more beautiful in this whole world than a beautiful woman. As far as I am concerned they deserve the utmost of appreciation, if they can wait for it or incur it passively, i.e. by what they are rather than by what they do. And they deserve all the rights that men have. Although perhaps no more. Even a beautiful woman cannot very well have her cake and eat it too. Except, maybe, when she is very, very beautiful.

Back to the Oedipal period proper. When do children grow out of it? Well, they will be out and in their latency period, when they have come to terms with their parents, when they know what they can get from, and do to, them and what not. They have solved their Oedipal problems, if they have reconciled themselves to the fact that they have to share the opposite-sex parent with the same-sex parent (they can neither have him exclusively for themselves, nor do they have to give him up altogether); that the parents are more powerful than they are themselves (but neither do they abuse their powers nor are they, the children, without any powers of their own); and that the parents are about as interested in each other as they are in them, i.e. their children (they are neither exclusively absorbed in each other nor in their children). Children have come to terms with such problems, when they have begun to see them through the eyes of their parents, i.e. when they have adopted the desires that their parents have for them, when the little boy has identified in as many ways as possible with his father and the little girl with her mother, when they have come to desire things and satisfy desires in ways of which the parents approve.

What is it that the child has learned that way from the parents ? Well, do not wet the bed, for one thing. Get up quietly, wash, brush your teeth, both without splashing or spilling water. Only in the bathtub may one do a bit of the latter, and only at the beach is there real freedom. Get dressed by yourself. Sit and eat properly at breakfast. Say "please" and "thank you", if you want something. Listen to requests by the parents. Keep quiet until they have finished what they wanted to say, i.e. do not break into their sermons or conversations. Let father go to work without fuss. Help mother with the dishes. Find your toys yourself. Do not make too much noise while playing. If something goes wrong, fix it yourself. Do not scream for mother. Do not tease mother just because father is gone. She may get angry, stay it all day and even mention it to father in the evening. Quit playing, go to the bathroom and put on a coat, when mother wants to take you along on a shopping trip. Behave in the store, in the car and with other people encountered on the trip. Don't fuss over lunch. Take your nap gracefully (provided you are still supposed to), even if you don't feel like it. If they let you skip it, be particularly good. Otherwise they may insist that you take one. Be good to another child that comes later in the afternoon. Let him use your toys. Play with the other child. Take turns where necessary. And do not scream or bang things. Greet father when he comes home. Let him rest, watch television or read the newspaper. Pester him only if he lets you lightly. If he says No, quit asking. Get ready for and behave properly at dinner. Take your bath, brush your teeth and go to the bathroom before going to bed. And from bed call on a parent once, maybe twice, but no more, or they will get angry.

And what has he learned to do in areas where the parents would not be quite so particular ? Say in playing with toys ? Well, he can use an erector-set by the end of his fifth year and can build something that moves, say a simple car or crane, in his sixth year. He constructs towers, castles or walls from blocks, draws or paints not only single objects, but even little scenes, say a house and a tree. He is observant of details, would tend to make eyes, nose, mouth, ears and hair on a face, arms and legs on a trunk, give them even shoes and fingers and buttons to the trunk (they represent the jacket), and if he has not been sufficiently discouraged, he may even add some sex-characteristics, e.g. breasts or a penis. He can handle simple tools such as a hammer, pliers, a screwdriver or scissors rather adequately, although some parents may not want him to do so. He could get hurt. He can engage himself in make-believe or identification games that imitate rather articulately the people and situations involved. Dolls are being dressed and undressed, put to bed, fed, wheeled, and two girls may get together, each with her doll carriage, rock it and play "mothers talk". Boys may set up battle fields with plastic soldiers, Indians, guns, trucks and the like, and they too would tend to be able to play together. As a matter of fact, the six-year-old cannot only tolerate but even utilise the company of contemporaries to the benefit of all involved. They will make and accept each others' suggestions, join on little construction projects and simple games and, perhaps all of their own, relieve their parents for an hour and more from their never-ending presence. That is they, the parents, can possibly have a peaceful game or chat of their own.

The five-year-old may, of course, be in nursery school and during his sixth year of life the child may have to attend kindergarten. These institutional regulations would not have emerged, if the child were not ready for the company of other children and the temporary exposure to substitute parents, mostly substitute mothers. But if we go by institutional regulations we might also say that the two-year-old is ready temporarily to be separated from his parents, leave home and somehow get along with other children just because there are some nursery schools that take them that early. Yet that is too early, indeed. Even the fourth year, the time when many American mothers nowadays part from their youngsters for the mornings, may be too early. The child should have achieved some solutions of his Oedipal pre-occupations and problems before he leaves home and mother for as much as three hours in a row, and he is unlikely to have come very far by the time he is four. But is that not saving him Oedipal pre-occupations and problems? No, the Oedipal period cannot be circumvented. The only path that leads to further development goes right through it. Just as there is no way of learning how to swim except in water.

The other-directedness of Americans diagnosed by Riesman (1950) may have one of its roots here. Children are expected to learn from the company of contemporaries at a time when they have learned too little yet from their parents. They have little to offer to each other and can hardly benefit at first from the parent-substitute in school diluted to serve some twelve children of about the same age. They learn to expect little from their companions except being together no matter for what and how boringly, and will become increasingly intolerant of being alone. Parents, on the other hand, will be likely to hand out their children as easily as they do, if they think they have little to offer themselves, and that may already be the outgrowth of a similar treatment administered to them.

We have spoken about the little boy and the little girl as if they were single children. Most children, however, have brothers and sisters, and that alone would complicate matters considerably. But then even parents differ. Some children have a strong father and a weak mother, others the reverse. Some have a very warm, sympathetic father and a cold, indifferent, eager-beaver of a mother, others a father who works so much that he is practically absent, while mother has to play both father and mother. Sometimes a parent is missing altogether and sometimes replacement of a parent occurs through remarriage after a death or divorce. What is more: all parents have been children themselves, with parents and siblings of their own, and the constellations of siblings may be considerably different not only for different parents, but even for a given pair of parents. Father may be the oldest of three children, two boys and a girl, while mother may be the younger of two girls. Which, by the way, may be no bad match as far as unconscious pre-formations go. Anyway, all this would complicate the Oedipal situation greatly. Freud has been accused of having given too little consideration to cultural differences. He was supposedly not prepared to deal with communities where, say, a godfather usually takes father's place, where children are thrown into a pool and may hardly get to know their natural parents or where the mothers have all the say and the fathers none. But I dare claim that there are no institutionalised family constellations anywhere in the world that would not have formal, though accidental, duplicates in our society or even in our city, and Freud and his disciples have become aware of many of them, although I grant, not always with the necessary didactic emphasis.

Let me outline a few of the complications of the Oedipal situation. Suppose a boy has a younger sister. What would that change? Well, it would give the family another girl. While father has mother, the boy may figure, he himself has his sister. Also if father caters to his sister, mother would cater to him or, if you like, he, the boy, could cater to mother. Furthermore his identification with father will not only apply to his mother—finding father so successful with mother that she has even become his wife, he will tend to adopt his ways of satisfying desires in order to improve his own chances with mother—but also to his sister. He will learn how to be like a husband to his mother and like a little father to his sister.

Or suppose a boy has an *older* sister. Well, the balance of sexes would be the same. The difference would be, however, that the girl would tend to adopt mother's attitude toward her little brother rather than would brother adopt father's attitude toward his sister. As a matter of fact, the older brother of a younger sister can "rightly" expect her to be submissive to him, to be obedient, to look up to him as the important one. After all, he has been in this world all along, while she has come only recently. She is dispensable. Why? Because she had been dispensed with until recently. She did not exist before she was born. Therefore her non-existence is possible, to say the least. Whereas the younger sister has had an older brother as long as she lived. He is an inevitable part of the world. The older sister of a younger brother will tend to use the same arguments. This little fellow is not really necessary. And he is so little. How can anybody dare to consider him more important than she is? Yet they seem to do so, and that brings the older sister of a younger brother into *her* conflicts. She will be reluctant to submit to a boy, will belittle boys' general advantages and perhaps become slightly belligerent with men when growing up. She may find herself able to relate satisfactorily only to "younger brothers". On the other hand, she may have motherly qualities that many men may like. Still, of the two constellations, older brother of a younger sister and older sister of a younger brother, the first is likely, other things being equal, to cause less trouble for both involved during childhood as well as in later life.

Or suppose a boy has a younger brother. This would intensify rather than mitigate the Oedipal conflicts as does the balance of sexes. After all, there are three men and one woman, which is more than the disequilibrium of the simple Oedipus situation. Three "men" are vying for the woman's favors and if one of them does not beat the other two once and for all, two of them, possibly with mother's support, may gang up on the third one, so to speak and forge him into a kind of girl. Which one will be the victim depends on the circumstances. The older brother will unconsciously look to his parents for clues. If father has mother, he may have found, then he himself could have brother as a sort of a little wife. However, if mother has his little brother, then father may want to have him, the older one, to himself. And for a while mother was indeed absorbed with the little one at the expense of father and himself. So he may have to be a bit of a girl for father, say, by helping with the beds or with breakfast, entertaining him before dinner, perhaps temporarily sharing the bedroom with him, while mother is obviously permitting her little one to be a real boy. Being a woman, how else could she possibly relate to the boy. So which way will the older brother turn?

Well, it depends on how much of a "man" he has already been permitted to be. If he has become four or five years old before the younger brother arrives, he may be more insistent on making the younger one the girl, especially since, in his phantasy, he might even have had a hand in the creation of the child. Father and mother had another baby, they say, but who knows for sure? After all, he himself was around too. It might have been he who did that which gave mother a baby. But he had better keep this a secret or they will shut him up. In fact, he may not even have to change his brother's sex too urgently, particularly if their age difference is still greater. Brother remains the baby toward whom he can behave simply like a parent, preferably father. If, however, he is only two years old when his brother arrives, things may turn the other way. His own sex is not established yet and as he approaches the Oedipal period it does become increasingly obvious that mother sides with his brother. He still requires more attention and consideration from her than he himself does. So his hope is father, and if they are to get along well with each other, it would have to be like a male and female, like father and mother. But then he cannot reasonably assume that he could change father into a mother. No, he himself would have to try to replace mother for his father.

Apart from the age difference of the two brothers, the parents themselves would also determine the course of development. If mother should be the oldest of her own siblings (say, with a girl coming after her, and then two boys) and a domineering woman, and father (himself the youngest of three children and the only boy) a somewhat submissive man, and if mother believes in the superiority of women—which is not unlikely with her family constellation—if, therefore, she would tend to prefer girls for children and she failed for the second time to get one, she may be angry about it and continue to wish for one. Of her two boys, however, the older one would be more likely than his brother to sense that wish of hers and try to satisfy it. He may try to be a girl for mother and a mother-girl for the little boy, say, by learning how to feed or change him, how to rock him to sleep or play with him. This may be reinforced by the submissive trends of father with whom he would tend to identify and by his little brother's probable failures when trying to be a man with mother. And the little one would try indeed. He might even attribute his failures to the existence of his brother and father, therefore combat them and continue stubbornly to try his luck with mother. If father should be a very tyrannical and dictatorial person, while mother has submitted to him so completely, that she does not have a will of her own any longer, so their friends say, then the boy's lot may be different. Such a father may want his boys to be both real men and yet submissive to him like mother. Again we would expect the older brother to be more sensitive to father's wishes and submit to him while, and even by, playing a man, whereas the younger one may challenge him more naively and therefore be forced to submit, forced to become more of a girl than his older brother.

What should not be overlooked, though, is a younger brother's potential advantage of having at least two identification-objects of his own sex: his father and his brother. He would not only try to be like father, but also like brother, even with respect to the latter's behavior toward his parents. He can learn from his brother how to approach his parents. Yet he often refuses as well to learn from him. Also these pressures toward sex-transformation should not be understood as inevitable or absolutely overpowering. Both boys would normally stay boys in a majority of aspects. In fact, they may be predisposed for more friendly and relaxed relationships with men than they might ever have with women or even, later on, with their own wives. They are sometimes the ones who would not give up their men's bars or poker clubs for anything in the world, but perhaps be willing to lend their wives to a friend for the mere asking. The wife, of course, might not like the idea at all. Or they may become "real" men, esteem women higher than their fellow-men, but be peculiarly awkward in approaching them. As if there were hidden in every woman a lioness, or as if she were the sweetest little thing on earth but had a lion waiting for her right around the corner.

Or suppose a girl has a younger sister. This would also intensify the Oedipal conflicts beyond those of its standard form. Three girls would be vying for the favors of the only man in the family, and if one of the three does not beat the other two into giving up, two of them may, perhaps with father's support, press the third one into becoming a boy, at least in some respects. The age difference between the two girls would again be one of the determinants of their choice of a victim. The greater it is, the more will the older have been established in her role as a female—if you like, even as an only child—but the more aware will she also be of the parents' wishes, once the second child is around and has turned out to be a girl. The greater the age difference, the more manifest and conscious will be the older sister's conflict between her desires of being a woman for father— especially since mother has been so absorbed with the baby at first, while she had father more to herself, and since it is not entirely inconceivable that she had something to do with the birth of the baby after all, since it is, perhaps, her baby with father to begin with—and her desire to please father, the parents, or the entire family by trying to become a boy, say, an expert on the tricycle and bicycle, in running, swimming, piano playing, in school or in father's shop. But then she may also be more successful in "passing that buck" to her sister. She may be the one to turn boy. The smaller the age difference between the two girls, the less of a female has the older one become yet and the easier may it be for her to renounce or not even develop at least some aspects of her sex in favor of what the parents seem to desire.

As pointed out before, these are not the only determinants. The parents themselves, by virtue of certain character traits which, in turn, may be partly determined by their own family constellations, would be another. The degree to which they should wish to transform the sex of one of the girls is also set by those traits. Another determinant would be hereditary differences, whether they concern their talents or their appearances. The really pretty or cute one will more likely be permitted to remain the girl. Just as, with two boys, the physically stronger and/or more intelligent brother would tend to stay the boy. Finally, even circumstances outside the family such as a neighborhood with more boys or more girls, or the sex-distribution among the children's cousins may determine the assignment or assumption of a second, secondary, sex role. Another consideration that should not be neglected is the relationship of the older to the younger sibling regardless of sex. The older one of two will, on the whole, tend to be the better and more cautious planner, the person who does know what he wants, the leader of others, the person who can form his own circle of friends, while the younger one will generally be the more erratic one, in his plans as well as in his social contacts, the person who likes to express himself without much care of the specific opportunities to do so. Yet he will also be more conspicuously competitive than an older one. This would hold especially for siblings of the same sex. The younger of two brothers or of two sisters would tend to be in a slight disadvantage over the older one as far as his social life, his career and overall success is concerned.

This may be different, though, where a whole culture appears to have protested against just that, where self-expression, individual freedom no matter for what, competition and denial of authority have become very high values. In such a culture, younger brothers and sisters might well stand better chances than older brothers and sisters or those who, by some calling, assume such positions. In any growing social system, of course, there are more later-born than first-born for the simple reason that it could not be growing unless a good portion of families have more than two children. It may be a matter of plain majority pressure that makes trouble for the first-born, the oldest, the unique ones. They are unique: a first-born's siblings are all his juniors, no matter to how many others they may be seniors, and by how much. They are more alike each other in that respect than they are to him. The only one who is unique among his siblings in a similar way would be the youngest. He is everybody's junior. Yet he can be dethroned any time by the arrival of another baby. Anyway, majority pressure may be against the first-borns and in favor of the rest. Whether that is good or bad for a social system is another question and remains to be seen. If we wait to see it, we should not forget, however, to consider the pressures exerted nowadays by all siblings against the authority of fathers and by mothers to step more and more into their husbands' shoes, to depose them if possible. These pressures accompany, perhaps even precede, the former.

This has carried us to the next-higher floor of complications. A third sibling may mean an aggravation of the Oedipus situation, if he is a boy coming after two boys, or after a girl and a younger boy, an alleviation if he comes after a boy and a younger girl or after two girls, although having two female masters among his siblings may not be too good for his prospects of becoming a man of his own. A fourth, fifth, etc. sibling would all add to the complications, although we might say that their arrivals become increasingly easy to handle for those already arrived, the greater their number, and the closer they bring the distribution of sexes to an even balance. A boy coming after three boys and three girls will do less to them than a boy coming after one boy and one girl. A boy coming after three boys will be less useful to them than a girl, although at first they may look a little more disturbed over a girl than they would have over a boy. They could have got too used to being a family of boys only.

The parents' own family constellations permit all kinds of combinations that would create different psychological milieus for their children. If father is the older brother of a sister and mother the younger sister of a brother, their relationship will tend to be different from one where father has a younger brother instead, or father is the younger one himself. The same will hold when mother has an older or younger sister, or a younger brother, instead. But father and/or mother may also be singletons, or one of any number of children (n) with any number of different sex-distributions among them (to be precise: with 2^{n-1}). At any rate, all types of matches that are theoretically possible will tend to have differential effects on their children and their Oedipal conflicts.

If that is so, however, the same would also hold for the parents themselves. The types of matches that *their* parents have formed must have had an effect on them. That is to say that even grandparents may, by their character (which is, among other things, a function of *their* sibling positions), influence the Oedipal conflicts of given children. But let us postpone the details. They will be taken up in the chapter on Marriage and Parenthood (see p. 236 ff).

One very crucial and radical characteristic of a parent may be his absence for good. The child may lose a parent before or at birth or any time during his infancy or childhood and will, accordingly, be affected differently by it. Losing father before birth is as much as never having had a father, but that would usually also be the case if he lost him during his first year of life. All provided that no substitute comes after. In his second year of life father has become more of an entity and his loss could already be directly experienced, not only via mother. She may, of course, convey to her child even a prenatal bereavement of her husband or lover. The child could be exposed to the consequences of a loss— one of which may be that his mother is a "forsaken woman"—but an experience of what it was that has been lost would be contingent upon concrete and sufficiently frequent exposures to father himself. In the child's third year of life a loss of father will already be a rather pronounced experience. He will recognise that he has lost the person that comes right after mother in importance, although it may still escape him that this person is male. During the Oedipal period, even the sex would be registered with the loss, and if the child is a boy, say the only child, this would leave him with mother. But would that really be a loss? Is that not precisely what the boy has wanted? Has he not tried to get rid of father and have mother for himself? Here he has got it.

No, this is not at all to be expected. The standard Oedipus situation, father, mother and child, is still the easier to handle for the child. If father has disappeared and the boy has ever wished for him to disappear, a desire that has begun to be counter-cathected almost as soon as it could first be distinguished has suddenly been satisfied. Hence the boy should feel quite anxious (see also p. 29f) and guilty (see also p. 86 f). He would be expecting punishment or even father in person to catch up with him any moment. No reference to the child's complete innocence, no matter how explicit, would be able to appease him very much at this age.

But is that true? Cannot children take a loss of a parent relatively easily? They often do not even understand what death is, if it should have been the cause for father's departure. Well, that would be precisely why a boy has every reason to fear his dead father. He is gone. The boy wished for his exit. Father must have sensed it. He may have complied, but only with a grudge, no, with the utmost of anger. He will inevitably get back at him. Sometimes adults get plagued by similar guilt feelings over deaths of close relatives, especially of those about whom they felt more than one way. The dead may haunt them even in their dreams.

What we can observe, however, with a boy of four or five who has lost his father is a period of gloom, sadness and mourning, during which he works unconsciously on the establishment of counter-cathexis, during which he strives to learn how to learn no more about father (see p. 37). And whatever impression the loss fails to make on him he can acquire from his mother. She will normally be the big mourner and this can hardly escape the boy's notice. She is sad, does not want to eat or drink much, is not attentive when playing with him, forgets things and never laughs. Even if he tries very badly to cheer her up, she hardly moves her mouth. If she does, she means otherwise. It's with tears in her eyes. There may be attempts on the part of the boy to deny either side of the loss, his own share and what he sees of mother. On the playground he may be gayer than ever, so gay, in fact, that he might not want to go home or inside. Why not? Because home is the place without father, the place where he and his mother would miss him the most. Things have changed a lot, whereas on the playground they have not quite so much.

But the real trouble begins when the work of mourning is already diminishing. Then he comes to realise that he has been left with mother. "Now I have her to myself," he may think, or: "Now I'll have to take care of her like father. Now I am to carry the trash cans to the street, chop wood for the fireplace, fix a broken window or an electric plug, etc. And if she takes a bath, I should be allowed to go in, see her, maybe help her wash her back. I should even move in with her at night. Father's half of the bed is vacant." Such thoughts would run through his mind and as he tries to implement them, he will find that mother does not adequately respond. She does not want him in her bedroom for one thing. Is that not strange? He had thought that *father* made it impossible for her and him, the boy, to get together, and this made good sense at the time. Apparently that was not so. It was *mother* who did not want him to begin with. But how can that be? Is he so unimpressive, so worthless? And if he cannot make an impression on mother, how can he hope to make one on another woman, now or any time thereafter? In other words, while all reluctance on mother's part to comply with his desires could have been father's doing before, it can no longer. Mother has primarily been his "love-object", the parent with whom he could hope to satisfy pregenital and especially early genital desires. Father was primarily the "identification-object", the obstacle to his desires for mother, but also the person from whom one could learn how to deal with mother, what desires to try to satisfy, and in what ways. Now the only person left for identification may be mother. He would tend to make her both, his love-object and his identification-object, but to the extent he succeeds they will be difficult to keep apart. While he could formerly try to have mother and be like father, he would now end up trying to have and be like mother. But how can this be done or ever disentangled?

A girl losing her mother would have a similar trouble. Her loss, however, would be more severe. Mother is the primal love-object, the nurse, the manipulator and protector, and the woman, while father is certainly not the nurse, at least in most cases. The girl would find that father is not more responsive and available now than he had been while mother was around. Now she could have her father, but he does not want her. How can she ever hope to make an impression on other men?

This is exactly what the loss of the same-sex parent during the Oedipal period tends to effect. The victim is discouraged in all heterosexual endeavors. Even much later he or she will stick more stubbornly to the same sex for friends. Furthermore, unable to get from mother what he has wanted as a child, the boy may also be unable to separate from her even as a grown-up. He can neither have her nor let her go. Which, by the way, would be a very common characteristic of a "neurotic" relationship. And the girl who has lost her mother may be unable in a similar way to get away from father and be pretty unhappy with him just the same. Both children had lost *and* been tempted too much.

Curiously enough, the same would hold for a loss of the opposite-sex parent. A boy who has lost his mother would tend to make father his love-object in addition to his identification-object and preserve his ties with him way into adulthood. Friends of the same sex would also be preferred to those of the other sex. After all, his first relationship with a woman led to a total loss, and what else could come of such a relationship now? Similarly, the girl who has lost her father would tend to make mother her love-object in addition to her identification-object, remain very closely attached to her and relate better to girls than to boys. She would also tend to expect unconsciously that, if she got involved with a boy, she may lose him, through death or otherwise.

There is a difference, though. The boy has lost his primal love-object, mother, whom he enjoyed for all her pregenital aspects before she became a woman for him and disappeared. He loses more of an object, but there is also more to latch new objects on to. It may well be that in his mind death or lasting absence, is linked to mother as a woman, while her other aspects remained relatively unimpaired, especially since father could, in principle, replace her on those. Therefore a girl who is motherly and strong (nurturant and powerful-protective) may well make a hit with such a boy, and given enough time and caution, her feminine (or her female genital) aspects may become acceptable to him too. The girl, on the other hand, has lost her secondary love-object which became important only later in life. She loses less of an object and, therefore, has less to latch new objects of the kind on to. Men matter mainly for the masculine (or male genital) aspects, and those are linked with death or loss. Therefore she will be more reluctant than might be a boy who has lost his mother to accept a heterosexual relationship. Or she may, in a reaction-formation to her reluctance, throw herself at man after man with little lasting luck. The effect will be the same. She will tend essentially to remain without a man.

There would also be some difference between the loss of the same-sex parent and that of the opposite-sex parent. The surviving son and mother or daughter and father are "heterosexual" couples to begin with, and a "non-incestuous heterosexual" object-choice will decrease the balance of sexes in the family. It will throw the burden of jealousy on the parent, and the parent's reaction to the loss, the original or the impending, is an important determinant under any circumstances. Mother suddenly has another woman to compete with, and father another man. Mother may end up without a man herself and father without a woman. On the other hand, a son who has lost his mother and survived with his father, or a daughter who has lost her father and survived with her mother, will find their balance of sexes improving with the entry of a non-incestuous heterosexual love-object. "At last there is a woman," may be the widow-father's comment and the widow-mother may say: "At last there is a man." There could be some rivalry as well. Father and son may both "want" the girl, and mother and daughter the boy. But they would not be so threatened in their own status. Father may think: "Of course, he must want her. She is a girl." And mother might think: "Of course, she must want him. He is a man." Whereas in the other case mother might say to herself: "What does he need her for. Am I not enough ?" And father: "What does she need him for. Doesn't she have me ?" All provided that the surviving parent has not remarried and thereby furnished a substitute parent for the child. Whereby the kind of substitute picked may be an additional complication of the child's Oedipal problems, although an easier one to handle psychologically than no substitution.

The loss of a parent at a pre-oedipal stage of development would aggravate the matter although the conscious experience of the loss may be considerably less pronounced. The extreme would be the absence of a parent from birth on (see also p. 28ff). If no substitute is furnished, if the child has never been exposed to that parent, there will be no conscious experience of loss. At the same time he would have the greatest difficulty in ever believing that such a parent-figure and a relationship with it is possible. If father was the person lost that early and the child, say a boy, never gets exposed to an uncle or friend of mother's, he will tend to behave as if there were no men, at least no steady ones, no men *for him*, in this world. Whatever men he would get in contact with he may perceive as some sort of mothers, and if they are not as indulgent, kind, forgiving and submissive as his mother has been, he will be inclined to attack them or run away and know in either case that men are not to be trusted or relied on. In other words, the effective loss will be the greater, other things being equal, and substitution more difficult, the less conscious the loss has been. The substitute object would be a *new* object. Cathexis would start from scratch, so to speak, while in the other case cathexis would merely be resumed after counter-cathexes due to the loss have been lifted.

All children who have lost a parent would tend to develop fears in correspondence to those desires that could have had something to do with his disappearance. On the late oral level the child may think that a parent—in this case mother; father would not be much of anything yet in his mind—has disappeared because he ate him, or rather her, up. In the second and third year of life he is more likely to think that he has manipulated the missing parent to pieces, disemboweled him, perhaps just severely mutilated him, whereupon he or she ran away, although even more primitive phantasies are not excluded, and in the Oedipal period he might think of all the other possibilities plus the mildest: father has run away because he, the boy, "castrated" him. Or mother has run away because she, the girl, took father away from her. Loss of the opposite-sex parent, on the other hand, would have to be accomplished in the child's imagination by more or less pregenital desires.

The fears of the child associated with any of these losses will correspond to the desires. The lost father may come back and "castrate" him, to say the least. And the lost mother may come back and take father away from her. The lost parent may come back and mutilate the child severely, kill him, smash him, cut him up or, the most primitive of all, devour him. Only the child who has lost a parent, especially mother, during his early oral period or never had one might have no such specific fear. His fear would rather be that of total disintegration (see also pp. 16 ff, 104).

Frequently the loss of a parent is made up for by a substitute parent. Father may remarry, mother may do likewise or keep a friend, uncles and aunts, grandfathers and grandmothers, etc. may come to a partial rescue, sometimes the surviving or the dead parent's mother or mother-in-law may take over with a vengeance. All of this would make for additional complications of the Oedipal situation, although not necessarily aggravate the conflicts. If the child has both his parents, but they have very little time and hand him or her over to nurses and governesses, those will become the mothers, and if there are turnovers among them, the child's impression will be that mothers are always being exchanged. They are not reliable. As for father, the child might recruit a male teacher or a sufficiently masculine female teacher, a grocer or even the janitor of the house they live in. Perhaps the child can get some stability there, although it is likely to be only second-rate. The child may be unduly vulnerable to their accidental losses, incurred, say, by the parents' move to another part of the country. He may cry for months after the lost person, and that would make sense only if a more severe loss had preceded it already. The second-rate relationship has become so important because a primal one has failed before. If a child has to be put up with foster parents, say, because he was an abandoned child to begin with, or if he changes his foster parents several times or if he grows up in an orphan's home altogether, where there is a constant turnover of personnel, things will be even more complicated and particularly difficult and sad. Such a child will grow up to believe that there are no mothers or rather that mother is something constantly changing. Mother is not giving the prerequisite of all satisfactions whatsoever, her steady presence. So how can one trust the food, the candies, the bed, the games, that one after the other hurries to provide? And fathers? What are those? The child may never in his life form any kind of relationship to senior males and soon find himself in trouble, either by turning criminal or prostitute, depending mainly on the child's own sex. They would be living and acting as if there were no fathers, as if there were neither authority and law nor paternal warmth and admiration. With foster parents changing, things may not be much better. Whatever increase of stability they represent, their exchange will be that more painful. The child of the orphan's home will be more or less immune and dazed, while the other may be acutely sensitive at least to the first and second such exchange. Thereafter he will also develop his callosities.

Not that foster parents are bad. If they stick it out with the child and adopt it within its first three months of life to begin with or within the first half-year, at the latest, they may sometimes be as good as the best natural parents. These children are the ones who, when finding out, say, during late latency period or perhaps after puberty, that they have been adopted, can take the shock in their stride. As a matter of fact, it may not be much of a shock at all. Only those children for whom good foster-parents came too late in their lives or have not been too good (e.g. unhappy with each other, or too old, too unresponsive or accusing each other for having no children of their own, or sometimes playing them, the foster-children, against their own children, and vice versa), only those children will not get over the shock of having been adopted. "That explains", they may figure, "why they did not like me or why I could never quite warm up to them; why I never had complete confidence. Now I know why they put me up in camp for the summer and went to Mexico themselves, why they forced this terrible piano teacher on me or why they bought me a bicycle only when it was too late."

All these complications are part of the theory of the "Oedipus complex". Everybody has one, but its forms may be very different with different individuals. Only the most basic aspects are alike with all men and women, but those are alike indeed. Investigation of a child's or adult's Oedipal phase, whether by psycho-analysis, a cross-examination or a short questionnaire, is indispensable, if we want to say something relevant about the person. Claiming of a person that he wants to kill his father and marry his mother or that she wants to get rid of her mother and have intimate relations with her father, is saying very little about the individual in question. Every boy or girl, man or woman, respectively, would have some such desires, unless these people have not even developed to the Oedipal stage. No, a person requires more consideration as an individual even if we wield a theory as our primary tool. Neither psychoanalytic theory nor any part thereof is that kind of a Procrustes bed. It helps us bring some order into an infinite variety of *data*, as a matter of fact, a fairly good one, but it cannot reasonably chop down all those that will not jump to comply.

Let us summarise briefly the Oedipal stage in its most basic and primitive characteristics. The *primal desires*, in addition to those formed during previous stages of development, are those of manipulation and stimulation of one's sex-organs, whether it is administered by or achieved with a parent, preferably the opposite-sex parent, or by oneself.

Object-formation has proceeded to the point where the parents' sexes as well as the child's own can be distinguished. The opposite-sex parent usually becomes the love-object and the same-sex parent the identification-object, but there are some aspects of a love-object also in the same-sex parent and some aspects of an identification-object in the parent of the opposite sex. As a matter of fact, the Oedipal period begins with both parents being either. Mother is male and fe-male ("phallic mother"), and so may be father, although as the second-most important object he would matter somewhat less. His potential "bi-sexuality" would be less persistent in the child's mind than mother's. But eventually, mother becomes predominantly a woman, father a man, and the child himself the third wheel on the cart. They, the parents, i.e. man and woman, do certain things together from which they want to exclude their child ("primal scene"). It may be more than a coincidence that, at the onset of the struggles involved, the child also learns how to use correctly pronouns such as I, you, he and she, mine, his, hers, etc. Beside the parents, relatives, uncles, aunts, grandparents, cousins, friends and other people and creatures of God will tend to be sex-typed in addition to other cathexes that have occurred and are still occurring.

Counter-cathexes center around the genital aspects of oneself and the parents, especially the opposite-sex parent, and around some aspects of their relationship to each other. The child learns how to forego genital self-stimulation, genital advances towards the parents, especially the opposite-sex parent and his ardent curiosity about what the parents do when they are alone together. His identifications have become sex-specific. To the extent that these counter-cathexes are established, the child has overcome his Oedipal problems and entered latency period.

The *primal fears* are those of being deprived of one's sex-organ. The boy fears that he might be "castrated", the girl (who "has been castrated already") that she might lose her man (and thereby his sex-organ) or that her man might lose his sex-organ. It should be understood that these fears are milder than all primal fears of previous stages of development, although when fully evoked they may be pretty tough by themselves. Yet the worst that can happen is that one turns sexless, so to speak, i.e. sex-unspecific, as one was not too long ago. But one would continue to live and would do so undebilitated except for genital endeavors.

Frustration tolerance has increased further. By the end of the Oedipal period the child can be alone for two hours or more even under unfamiliar circumstances. Of course, he can also keep himself busy in a larger than ever number of ways. He can draw more elaborately, build or sculpture more complexly, use tools more articulately. Objects in general have become richer and more diversified. His environment and time is more structured. He knows better where he is when he is with his aunt or, say, in kindergarten. He can spend three hours in a row there and know approximately, how long that is. For one thing, he can count up to five in his fifth year and expands his number concept to ten, eleven, twelve and even higher in his sixth year. So he can count the different things they do in kindergarten, perhaps even the dots on the clock that the clock-hand has passed, and thereby keep some track of time. He can get along fairly well with other children and play with them easily and constructively as long as an adult keeps an eye on them, at least from the distance. Even "why"-questions, one after the other, are a way of keeping himself entertained, and he also does not mind if they are put to him. He might occasionally evade them, say by "Why do you want to know?" or by playing silly, but generally he will have some fairly realistic theories already of rain, snow, the sun, food, the seasons, the stars, day and night, rivers, cars and other things that he might be asked about. Rain comes from the clouds. It turns into snow when it gets cold. The sun gives light and keeps us warm. Food grows on farms and we put it in the refrigerator. The seasons come about, because sometimes the sun is hotter and sometimes cooler. The stars are like the sun or the moon, but very far away; day and night are when the sun is on or off the sky; rivers come from the mountains and from the rain; cars have a motor that makes them run; etc. The child may have more phantastic or animistic theories on rarer events, say hail or a blizzard, a recording machine, a short circuit, lightning, a magnet and the like. But they would think about those things as well. In other words, they do not run out of subjects so easily any more. They can fill times of separation from parents or homes, siblings, pets or their own toys, with more different things and there is more to converse about, play-act or do, with other children or a teacher. He can stay away from home a whole day, if necessary, and, with proper preparation, even for a few days in a row. He will not like it and prefer the second-most familiar environment, say an aunt's or next-door neighbor's house, to a stranger one, but he might even be able to do that without suffering psychological damage. A prerequisite is that he has already come to terms with his parents on most of his Oedipal problems. As for tolerance of hunger and deprivation of sleep: the six-year old can forego a meal to the point of missing one, and he will tend to stay awake for an average of some twelve hours in a row, that is omit his afternoon nap regularly and stay up some seventeen or eighteen hours in a row on special occasions.

Latency Period

FROM SIX TO TWELVE YEARS

THE CHILD has entered latency period when his Oedipal problems are more or less settled, when the sexes of his parents and himself have been established in his mind and all the consequences tested and registered appropriately. The child has come to terms with his parents. He has learned what can be expected from the opposite-sex parent and what not, and how much identification with the same-sex parent is called for in order to offend neither. He is ready to go out to school and other places, ready to learn about new parent-figures—the teachers, the principal, a cub-scout leader, the gym- and music-teacher, policemen, doctors, nurses, new uncles and aunts or friends of the parents, etc.—as well as new sibling-figures such as his class-mates, the children from the neighborhood, the scouts, the children from Sunday school, etc. In fact, to the extent that he is able to do so he has outgrown the Oedipal phase.

Next to home, school is the most regularly and extensively recurring, hence influential situation, and it is almost as inescapable. Schools may be changed, but the new school is usually pretty much like the previous one. School is an extended home situation with a sibling-configuration that no family could possibly provide: some twenty or thirty children of one's own age. And one teacher has to be shared with all of these "siblings". In school the child becomes one of many like him, one of many equals, while at home he may still continue to be the only one or the second-oldest of three children, the only boy, youngest child or whatever he was born to be. What is more: teachers may change. As a matter of fact, they do change in most parts of this country. The child gets a new mother-supplement every year and if he is lucky, he may even get a man for the last one or two years of grade school. This is different from most European grade schools where there are more male teachers to begin with and where the teacher is trained to accompany his class throughout grade school. That means even less escape than there is in this country. Here the second-grade teacher takes over a group that has already begun to establish itself to some degree. She knows less about the children at first than they know about each other. This becomes more pronounced in the higher grades and tends to diminish her position of authority more insistently. She cannot get quite as much of a hold on the children as she could have in an earlier or in the first

191

grade or as the first-grade teacher actually got (although without "follow-up"). If she does not even know yet that Jack is the fool of the class and Milly the clown, and that Fred, Tom, and Sissy only pretend to quarrel—they are really good friends—how can she know much of anything else? This may be what the children figure and this, too, might contribute to the other-directedness which Riesman spoke of and to the American suspicion of and antagonism to authority mentioned (see pp. 177 f, 181f). With each move to a new grade the teacher tends to become less of an authority. Yet with American mobility, with moves carrying families sometimes from coast to coast, it may be a practical thing to learn that authorities are indeed evadable, easily capable of replacement and duplication and do not amount to much anyway. One might just as well get used to it early.

Children with lop-sided sex-distributions learn still another thing in school: how to have about as many brothers as sisters or, at least, how to have many more siblings of the sex that is scarce in their own families than they have at home. All provided, of course, that they are in a coeducational school. But coeducation, for whatever it is worth, has become pretty much the rule in the United States.

Is there any question about its worth? Let us see. Representing non-incestuous objects for each other, boys and girls at school may well try to pursue their genital interests that, with incestuous objects, have become counter-cathected. What makes a boy, what a girl, what can a boy and a girl do and what might they do together, would tend to remain active issues. However, they are not permitted to pursue these interests very far, at least not manifestly and under most circumstances. They cannot be boys and girls for each other in certain respects, as a matter of fact, not in the most primitive and vital of all respects. Since they are nevertheless exposed to each other constantly, they are likely to use very special measures of counter-cathexis. They are likely to play down the sex-difference, to minimise it unconsciously where it would matter and to tolerate it mainly where it does not. The girls will try to be like boys rather than girls and deny that there is anything a boy has or can do, which the girl would not have or could not do as well and better (see "Annie, get your gun"). Wherever they are not quite as successful competing, say in fixing gadgets, climbing trees, lifting heavy things or studying physics, they will tend to *have* boys rather than *be* them, and have the most successful ones first. They will want them, however, for boyish reasons and as long as they keep quiet about being boys. They will vie for the token values of boys rather than the boys themselves. The assets represented by a boy will be added to their own assets, so to speak. They will not like the boys for what they, the boys, could do for them, but rather for what they, the girls, could do *with* them. They will tend to be competitive in both ways, against boys and by means of them.

Boys, on the other hand, will tend to comply with this game. Not because their girl-classmates would necessarily make such a devastating impression on them. Rather because of the female teachers. In many grade-schools the only male figure available may be the principal who, however, is too remote to be of much direct effect on the children. Besides he often would not become a principal unless he could get along well with women teachers and, maybe, the parents' association to begin with, and this latter organisation is strongly infiltrated by women too. What is more, teachers and mothers alike may have been exposed to coeducation themselves and so may have the principal. He may well have learned already how to get along with them on their terms—after all, they are the overwhelming majority—and console himself with the fact that their terms are adopted male terms, anyway. Well, the boys will mainly be exposed to female teachers and these are likely to make an impression on them even if they change every year. Whatever (little) authority there is in school is being exercised or implemented mostly by females. The boys have not much choice but to identify with their female "masters". If they, the boys, do not become females, psychologically speaking, they will at least tend to adopt enough of what females think and desire in order not to offend them. It is in this sense that they comply with the girls' games. Some of them may even overdo it altogether. They may wish to become the girls' little boys, incapable of anything that girls cannot do, incapable even of some of those things which girls can do, and expect girls to nurse them through life. They may take to overeating and perhaps become the passive, chubby little boy who is growing more common in this country, who would like to be on television when he grows up or simply to win a whole lot of money somehow, say by making a quick phone-call to the television station and say "Roosevelt" in reply to the question: "What President of the United States has been re-elected three times?" A million dollars would not be too much for such an achievement.

Never should the boy of coeducation let the girl know that he is better off than she is, that he has got something that she has not got, that she is less complete without him than he is without her or simply that he is a man. And the little girl, in turn, will not resign herself to becoming a beautiful woman one day who, if she can wait it out, will have as much of men as she desires. No, she will have to be beautiful right now, she will have to manipulate her beauty, to use make-up (which, by the way, rarely fakes any longer what a few more fortunate individuals may naturally possess; it fakes what nobody can possibly have; it is conspicuously manufactured) and hairdo, to dress for "sex-appeal" even at the age of seven, and to be dying to hear not so much that she is beautiful—that is what every girl in the world would like to hear—but that she is the most beautiful in class, or the second-most beautiful in school outstripped only by Lilly who is two years older (a condition that will improve with the mere elapse of time; if only it would elapse faster!) or that she has the most beautiful hair, the prettiest nose or the most sparkling eyes, etc. And later on, after puberty has begun, the weights of their growing breasts and of their legs will be thrown around with even more fervor and clamor. The boy has long learned how to hide his sex-specific possession. He must not even hint at it. But the girl will take to exhibiting hers most freely. In fact, no means of augmenting the exhibition is too menial or obvious to use. Even measurements are important. And since society, mind you, rather than nature or God, and men rather than people in general, and everybody else rather than she herself behave as if men were indispensable, the hunt for the man with the greatest number of visible token values begins. They go from shoulder-width, muscle-size, etc., over suits or cars to social and financial position. This hunt will be followed up shortly by another and not too happy one: to be the first among the mothers of the neighborhood or among all girl-friends; to have the largest number of children and give up the least, if anything, of one's careers. She wants to become the most spectacular woman who can do anything in the world and extract the rest from her toiling husband. But she cannot do the very thing that makes for a happy marriage: wait for and submit to her husband's—or lover's, for that matter—desires until and when they come. And often she cannot reach satisfaction no matter how hard she tries. Not infrequently this is the miserable end of a long story.

I may have painted the picture blacker than it is, but that could still be better than painting it too white or not at all. The paradox about this country's women is that they are probably the most emancipated of the world and yet, on the whole, unhappier than all the rest over being what they are. And just that is to be expected.

Since I have claimed that coeducation may have something to do with this, do I advocate its discontinuation? No, not really. Separate education had its own shortcomings. But there was one advantage: by not being exposed to each other as overbearingly and persistently as boys and girls are in coeducational schools, they may have had a better chance to develop their own identities, especially if the boys had male teachers and the girls females. By implication they learned all along that there was a difference, indeed, between boys and girls. Why else would they be separated from each other in ever so many ways, see each other more or less from the distance, if at all, and do, study and talk, different things? And while they grew up in this kind of seclusion, they would learn from their teachers what to think of the other sex.

But what would they learn? Couldn't the teachers have warped minds of their own concerning the other sex? Why else would they have become teachers? Well, even an unmarried female who "could not do any better" but become a teacher would know much more about the other sex than the grade-school child. Most spinsters were pretty at one time of their lives, no matter for how short, were exposed to males, their courtship and some kind of propositions, and they must have gone through some experiences with them, no matter how slight and secret. They may have counter-cathected those experiences heavily since then, may make a big show of their antagonism to heterosexual relationships, but even then they will not only pretend, but tacitly reveal that they know more about them than any of their entrusted little girls. If relationships to men are that dangerous, if one can come out burnt and supposedly cured from them for good, well, even then the teacher would be conveying something worthwhile to know, something that can indeed happen to everyone of the little ones when they grow up. What is more important, if the teacher came out burnt and cured for good, she must have got herself into such a danger to begin with, and if that was so, there must have been a magnificent temptation, something wonderful and great that made her seek out that danger. Even a very defensive teacher could not help but convey some of this as well. In coeducation, however, such a teacher would probably be ridiculed. "What does she know? We have our boys right here in class, but she? What has she got? She does not even have a boy?" could well be the paraphrases of what the girls might think of such a teacher.

Things would be better and easier for the teacher and her girls alike, I mean the non-coeducational again, if she were married. But then she is likely either to quit teaching soon and have children of her own or to have returned to teaching after she had brought up her own children. In that case, however, she would probably be close to fifty years of age or older and perhaps toiling with the inner hardships of menopause. And if she were married, but could not have children, she would have another share of psychological trouble. She would bear a grudge against someone. No, the ideal teacher for girls was, and probably still is, the young woman who will get married before long, who might even be engaged already, but content and happy to work toward a home of their own or to wait until her fiancé is ready to support a family. If there were not such a nervous haste to get married and produce ambitious quantities of offspring—perhaps in order to populate more densely this still relatively empty continent—and if schools had not become such a waste of time, so that, e.g. they could turn out a well-trained grade-school teacher at the age of eighteen or nineteen—as most European countries are able to do—girls may well be available for six full years (please, do not leave in the middle of a school-year!) and still only twenty-five when they begin to make their own children. Such a girl would be ideal because she would, by being in a waiting state herself, make it seem sensible to the girls to wait for the time when they will be ready and to listen with joyful expectations for clues from herabout "love".

The same would hold for the male teachers of boys. They usually could and still can be married without having to quit teaching (although their salaries do not permit them too much of a family of their own). They too will tend to convey better what they think and feel about women and marriage than the boys of grade school could possibly convey to each other. We might go as far as to say that the very advantage of separate schools for boys and girls with teachers of their own sex, if at all possible would be that the child can learn about the more complex and intricate aspects of heterosexual relationships of genital love from an authority. It matters little that most of this learning is by implication.

All learning is to some extent, and the most relevant aspects of the world come to us almost exclusively that way. Let us remember that a child is not expected to develop his own alphabet or number system, nor to pick it up from other children. It would probably take them many many years to work out by themselves something only moderately useful, while even the most simple-minded teacher could convey the basic ideas involved within a few days or weeks. How much more true must this be of something as complex and intricate as a heterosexual love relationship. The very disadvantage of coeducational schools is that boys and girls are so close to each other that they find hardly time to look to the teacher for clues. They will try manifestly what they are not prepared for at all except in very primitive ways. They will date and dance, hold hands, play kissing games and neck long before they know what it means "to be in love", to be aroused from head to toe by the mere existence of a beloved or however we paraphrase the "real thing". They nibble long before they are hungry. Consequently their heterosexual relationships may tend to stay shallow and infantile way into adulthood. There may be little depth, little endurance and very little strength in a good proportion of present-day love relationships. They would tend to be flat, often made up by disjointed urges, pettings, mutual masturbations, the motions of orgasm or anxious failures to reach them and, if at all, summed up with the belligerent question: "Do you feel better now?" As if the whole thing was no more than some sort of relief or a medical prescription!

Even so I am not advocating to stop coeducation. I don't think the tides can be turned backward. Besides, boys and girls are not reacting all the way as outlined. In fact, boys of coeducational schools, especially of the better ones, have often as little use for girls during latency period as those of separate schools of fifty years past. And girls, with all their close exposure to boys, seem often to be able to let the boys work out their problems themselves. They do wait it out after all. They would prefer to be in on their games, but if boys won't have them, they can form their own circles of sorts, dream up their own stories and jokes and talk about boys from a distance. Furthermore every child has formed his basic notions about the other sex at home. School will only continue in a broader field, what the home has already established. If coeducation does not always work out, it may well be that what really failed was the home. If father is under the spell of mother and mother a dissatisfied woman who tries to make up for it by playing the man, the boss, the sergeant, the judge or what have you, they may be doing more harm to their children than school can possibly do, at least to a child who comes from a happy home. The same may be true for parents who believe that spouses can be switched on short notice and regardless of the children accumulated in the meantime, although a clean break may occasionally be better for the children than the preservation of a dragging marriage; or for parents who believe that children have to come in as rapid a sequence as at all possible, perhaps in order to "get it over with once and for all", or that girls are worthless, that boys are the only creatures that count and that they should not make a secret about these "basic facts of life". There are many other ways in which parents can do harm to their children merely by what they think, believe and desire, but let us stop here. We have sidetracked far enough.

In school children learn how to get along with their fellowmen, with new parent-figures as well as with "brothers" and "sisters", and it is here, in school, where the home is put to its most taxing and penetrating test. Only a relatively good home stands up. A poor home, psycholgically speaking, often means trouble in school. And all trouble a child gets into at school tends to have originated at home. In school the child learns how to be practical as well as moral about the pursuits of his desires outside of home. He learns how to satisfy them in such a way that they do not seriously conflict with the desires of others and nevertheless achieve the utmost for himself and how to apply all desires introjected from the parents and supplemented by those of the teachers in such a way that he cannot only avoid guilt and actual punishment, but preserve all the satisfactions he has been accustomed to consume and even earn new ones (see pp. 86 ff, also 90). He will desire to please not only his parents, but also his teachers, his principal, the coach, the team, the school, certain classmates (the "leaders"), in a way even the parents of his classmates whom they carry within them in school, and do so not only in reality, but also with respect to their introjections (see p. 86f). He will be steered in his actions progressively by what they might think of them or him, if they knew, rather than by what they actually thought in the past. He will become more and more active and successful in anticipating the reactions to what he does of the people who matter to him. He will find out more and more about their inner consistencies. As a matter of fact, all these later introjections have been grafted on those of his parents, and under favorable circumstances they will not only have taken, but continue to grow as one intimately coherent community. The parents, comparatively unconditional supporters of the child's interests, will be the trunk, if I may be poetic for a moment, the parent-supplements of latency period with their much more conditional support (they care about the child only along with many other children and only during certain parts of the day or of the week; at other times they are not even available) will be the major branches, and the twigs will represent all further, more passing and distant, objects of identification who might sometimes not even give a damn about the identifier. Yet they as a whole will be the ones who carry the leaves and communicate with the air and the sun. They will be the more conscious mediators of all intercourse between the world and a person's conscience.

It should not suprise us that a preliminary moral maturity is usually reached by the end of latency period. If there is objective consistency, i.e. if the home situation and the school situation as well as the objects chosen for identification have been stable and consistent, morality must become more or less objective too. The laws by which all desires abide which identification objects have for him become more transparent and can eventually be formulated. Therefore the eleven- or twelve-year-old cannot only name those things which are very bad—

to kill or injure somebody, to steal, to damage the property of others, to be in-chaste; but also to insult the parents, betray someone or tell lies about him, perhaps also to act against the will of God—but give some explanation as well. He might say: "One must not kill (or injure) somebody, because it would hurt him." "One must not steal, because it belongs to the other person." And if he is intelligent, he may continue: "He (the other person) will leave my things alone too. But if I take his, he will take mine." "One must be chaste or one would feel ashamed," etc. To the extent that these laws can be formulated, they may be-come rational. Their possible purposes are foreseeable. Practically all of them make life more productive and convenient, at least in organised and well-functioning social systems, we might add.

But this is only the broad and general background of what goes on in school or by the help of it. The explicit reason for sending children to school is to teach them something, subjects, say the three R's, or art, history, geography, biology, physics or what have you. Well, what else is there? Or why are these subjects taught to begin with? Why not skin diving, the Chinese script, the art of hard selling or radio engineering? These questions may sound absurd, but perhaps there is some use in asking them. Not only because anything that has been taken for granted too long might turn stale, but also because we can put the concepts of control of desires, derivative-formation, cathexis, and object-formation expounded at some length in the first part of this book (see p. 6 ff) to another and, what may be more, fairly neutral and unoffensive use.

Why are the three R's the three R's? Why are they so important to just about any child on this globe? Well, reading and writing are extremely powerful ex-tensions or derivatives of hearing and speaking. While reading

MAMA TOOK THE BABY
or
BUGS BUNNY ATE THE GIANT'S CARROTS,

the child learns about an event, but neither from direct sight nor touch nor by hearing about it from another person. No, the child learns about it from a piece of paper. Somebody told the paper and the paper tells it to him. Provided, of course, that he can read. And if he wants to say something to somebody who is not here or if he wants to tell a story for keeps, so that even he himself can listen to it again, he must be able to write.

These desires for extended communications with other people, extended in space and time, so that people at other spaces and/or at other times can receive them, must have spurred the invention of alphabets wherever they occurred historically, and they can also spur the first-grader's attempts to acquire his alphabet. As a matter of fact, the teacher who simply tries to pound it into the children's heads regardless of contexts will probably be less successful than the teacher who can make them aware of their desires to say something to people who are not present or to hear from them. She could suggest to them to write a message to their mothers which their mothers could read later on or suggest to their mothers that they should give them little messages to bring to school that could be read in class. Or they could learn how to hide messages from all people except the person they are meant for. All it takes is to fold the paper up, address and seal it, and give, pass or slip it to the person selected, say, to the teacher or another child. And one can also receive such secret messages.

But these desires would not be enough in themselves. Writing is also a kind of drawing, and reading a special way of looking at drawings or designs. And drawing has grown out of manipulation proper, of doing things by hand, no matter how primitive, and looking at drawings or designs is a derivative of looking no matter at what, as long as it amounts to visual stimulation. The child of beginning latency period has been drawing people, houses, cars, various animals, trees, etc. all along and he is pretty convinced by now that these drawings are not the objects themselves. They merely represent them. What convinced him ? Well, he might have shown what he put on paper to someone else, and that person had trouble recognising it. As a matter of fact, sometimes he himself might not recognise his own drawings of a year ago. Nowadays he would draw things differently or another person could show him what would make them look more like the objects he had in mind. Anyway, representing things on paper is a fairly established desire already. So why not represent or draw a ladder as it looks from the side with three lines, a rake with four, a flag with three again, a chair with only two, a moon with a single line, although a round one, or the ears of a mouse with four. And why not call the ladder A, the rake E, the flag F, the chair L, the moon O and the mouse-ears M ? And why not say "flame" to F L A M E or "Mom" to M O M ? Of course, in English the spelling method does not work too well. Writing and pronunciation are not in as close a relationship as they are, say, in German, Italian or Russian. In order to be able to read English, the child must give up this intimate relationship to the letter sooner or perhaps not even form it at all. Letters do *not* represent things. They are signs, period (or signs of sounds, to be precise) and even as such they depend on their contexts. Reading becomes guessing. There is less or only a very complicated logic in it. But then it should not be surprising that more English-speaking people than, say, Germans seem to be poor spellers and a few more fail ever to get to like reading or writing except in cartoon captions or perhaps on toilet walls.

Well, writing is not only an instrument. It is also a desire itself, at least under certain conditions and, under all circumstances, at a certain stage of development (see also p. 77 f). It derives from more primitive and less instrumental desires of manipulation and it will continue to develop further derivatives such as writing in capital letters, in small letters, in cursive script or even in a code, with red or blue ink, on black, green, or white paper, fast or slowly, in books, on sand, like some other person, etc. Still other derivatives would be to write beautifully and earn praise thereby, to write for an exhibition, for other people,

O

to show others how to write, to play secretary, to write a beautiful text, a letter, a poem, to write to different children in class, to children in other cities or even in other countries, to children of the opposite sex, to write in another language, etc. The good teacher will not only try to play into those desires of her children to which writing would be instrumental, but also latch on to those desires already formed in the children of which writing is or might be a derivative and to permit and even encourage further derivative formation or cathexis as soon as the elements of writing have been mastered. The good teacher would probably not do so because of psychoanalytic theory, but rather because of common sense. Which may show what I have tried to demonstrate all along: that psychoanalytic theory is indeed compatible with common sense. Why not stick with common sense, then? Because a theory is more articulate. It spells out what common sense may already be exercising and this may help with all those problems that are too intricate to be handled by common sense alone.

Reading will form similar derivatives once its most basic aspects have been mastered. The child can read books, funnies or even newspapers, can read about dogs, hunting, witches and ogres, about Hansel and Gretel or the story of the ugly duckling, about other countries, other planets, other solar systems, other forms of life, say, those of ants or bees, lions, zebras, whales, polar bears, trees, moss, wheat, etc. as well as about the old issue that has concerned him ever since he turned four (or rather entered his fourth year of life): What do men and women do with each other. Now, of course, this primal topic has assumed hundreds of different versions such as how Cinderalla lost a shoe and got her prince, how Tom Sawyer fares with his girl-friend, how a little girl liberates her seven brothers who have been turned into ravens, or how a prince brings sleeping beauty out of her sleeping spell. Adventure stories often have a love story as an aside, if they are not love stories in the first place. And the most moving and fascinating of all stories are about the vicissitudes of two people's love for each other and their final happy end or tragedy.

In other words, reading opens practically all doors of the world. Coming to think of it, we know about many aspects of the world as a whole only through books and magazines. Movies, television and radio are strong competitors to books, but they cannot really match them as far as intellectual storability and handiness are concerned. And writing gives potential access to all those parts of the world that are not here and now, and these parts are the overwhelming majority.

What about arithmetic? At five the child could handle the concepts of one, two, three, four and five, as serial indicators and as quantities. But counting or adding petered out right here. In his sixth year his command has usually jumped up to ten, eleven, twelve and perhaps a few more, and in his seventh year he is able to learn how to perform simple additions and subtractions as well as how to "construct" numbers by the arabic or digital code. In his eighth and ninth year he also learns about multiplication, then about division and at eleven or twelve he is able to perform all basic operations with just about any kind of natural numbers, no matter how complicated they may be.

But what desires does the exercise of arithmetic fulfill ? Well, it has grown out from simple manipulations of physical objects, from collecting them or taking some away, sharing them with another person, even with more than one, having everybody chip in his share, etc. Blocks, marbles, cherries, peanuts and the like, are the most handy objects for these kinds of manipulations. Arithmetic is a more indirect way of doing precisely the same. It is a manipulation of things that have at least one aspect in common (say, being marbles). Others may be ignored (their sizes or colors). And while the child manipulates things and counts the outcomes—which is a kind of manipulation itself—cathexis of the most frequently recurring relationships will build up an addition- and multiplication-table in his mind, so that eventually, he knows by heart how much $7 + 6$, $19 - 8$, 4×3, or one third of 18 is. At this point it might matter no longer what things are being manipulated. Only their numbers matter.

The better the teacher, the more inventive and sensitive will he be in "latching on" to desires already formed what he is supposed to convey. He would start with the most familiar countable things, and those are not even marbles and blocks, but, say, the children's ears and eyes, noses, arms, legs, fingers and toes, perhaps even teeth. Strangely enough, or actually plausibly enough, the two number systems that are in widest use in modern societies, the decadic and the dual, follow the trend of man's extremities, especially of the hands and fingers, to come in twos and tens. Then they could count and compare the number of people that constitute each child's family, the number of boys, girls and children they have in class, the number of classrooms in school, etc. and divide, sub-tract, add and multiply them. Then the teacher would try blocks, little sticks or pennies, then coins of other denominations, and exercise transformations of "amounts of money". Still later he may try to count "uncountable" things such as quanties of clay or fluids. How ? By counting, e.g., the number of weights that will balance it on a scale.

Once the elements of arithmetic have been mastered, opportunity for further derivative formation would have to be provided or sought. Otherwise it would soon get boring and require counter-cathexis (see p. 103f). Allowance money, scores at sports and in school, car miles, populations of cities and states, crops in agriculture, costs and other aspects of construction work, industrial production or labor forces, simple things again such as the prices of food, candies, bicycles, books, badges, etc. and their changes over time would be some of the available areas. Others may have to do with simple and later on also with more complicated aspects of geometry, say with painting walls (in units of square feet) or computing distances, surfaces or volumes, of landmarks, pieces or layers of land, and the air-content of a house or abstract geometrical bodies, respectively. And those with special talents are likely to go into algebra, analytical geometry, calculus, and even more complicated and abstract fields of mathematics.

In the course of this a person may have learned that a number, say 2, means actually $\frac{2}{1}$ (natural numbers can be expressed like rational numbers, that is as fractions). But any number can also be expressed as the power of another number, or as itself raised to the power of 1. Hence 2 could be written as $(\frac{2}{1})^1$. However, to be consistent with the suggested way of writing natural numbers we should write it $(\frac{2}{1})^{\frac{1}{1}}$. (This would, in principle, include irrational numbers.) Yet all this sophistication is not nearly sufficient even for simple mathematics. To be prepared for eventualities, it is necessary to assume that each natural, rational or irrational number contains within itself an imaginary number. This number is one of the other types multiplied by the square root of -1 which is equal to i. Hence 2 means actually:

$$2 = [(\tfrac{2}{1})^{\frac{1}{1}} + 0 \cdot i]^{\frac{1}{1}} \tag{9}$$

Even formula (9) is not the end of sophistication, but it will be for us. What should be demonstrated is how, through the continuous process of cathexis, a more and more complex and comprehensively adequate object, in this case a number concept, forms.

Let me briefly indicate how these notions apply to the other fields mentioned. Education for art, say painting or sculpturing, starts long before school. Scratching the sand with one's fingers or making cakes of it is already the beginning, and an even more primitive predecessor might be the holding or squeezing of food or one's own arms as it occurs during the first year of life. By the time he goes to school, he has already practised all kinds of paintings and sculpturings. He has colored printed drawings or his own with crayons, paint or strawberry preserves and by means of brushes, his own hands or his fingers. He has made balls, sausages, a meat loaf, perhaps even a little man, a dog or a house, out of plasticine, bread, wire, chocolate or even chewing gum. He has torn or cut paper, folded it, wrapped things in it. He has picked flowers and arranged them into a bunch or picked a ready-made bunch out of twenty others. He has dressed himself, one day this way and another day in another, and he may already have paid attention to some aspects of what he wore. He may have had the choice of the color of his room, of a toy car, a blanket, etc. Many or all of such things can be taken for granted with a first- or second-grader and would have to be picked up by a good teacher. And as for the introduction of new opportunities so that further derivatives can form (without which the whole thing would soon be boring and require counter-cathexis) or so that a better control over the art in question can be achieved, we would expect highly varied topics, realistic and abstract ones, also given or self-chosen topics, those to be handled on small scales, say in the sketch-booklet, and those on big scales, say on posters or as classroom decorations; also usage of different media (canvas, paper, wall, linoleum, wood, even birthday cakes) and instruments (brush, chisel, pencil, squeezers, ink or even acids); furthermore discussion and experimentation on dresses, cars, furniture, flowers, etc.; also very simple exercises such as artistically optimal placements of simple figures, squares, triangles, pentagons, in others that are larger, matches of two or three hues and shades of color, scattering of ten dots on a blank table, etc.; finally, of course, studies of historic and contemporary pieces of art, of adult and children's art, of the arts of other countries, etc. With the latter, possibilities are practically unlimited.

History also begins in earliest childhood. If the three-year-old can tell us that "Bobby fell off the chair" or that "Mother, Father and Bobby were at the ocean during the summer", he is a little historian already. He is stating and storing the past. Gradually, however, he will be able to learn about events that he has not witnessed, e.g. a few things that mother did when she was small or what house grandfather lived in and where he travelled, what country grandmother came from and, last but not least, how he, the child, came about himself. He will also pick for keeps some events concerning the neighborhood he lives in, the town, or his own country. He will learn when Massachusetts was founded and by what kinds of people, and a visit to Plymouth rock will provide him with further *data* to hold on to. He will learn about the pasts of other children, animals, trees, cars and boats, but also of the clouds, the skies and the stars. The teacher will have to pursue these cathexes which the children are likely to have formed and consolidate their knowledge in those areas first, that are most immediately relevant and evident to them, later on in others also, even in those that are very remote in space and time, such as Greece or China of the Shang dynasty. He will even have to acquaint them gradually with the search for and handling of historical sources. After all, history is not only what somebody tells you, but also what you find out for yourself. And here too he can latch on to experiences which the children have made by themselves, like sniffing around in a parent's notebook, browsing through the photo-album or exploring the attic for discarded things of the past.

The same would hold for geography or biology. The teacher would assume that the foundations of a child's geographical knowledge have been laid in earliest childhood, when he learned about the geography of his crib, then of his house and garden, then of the immediate vicinity, a few bits about the town or the countryside and some hearsay stories about other countries, distant mountains and foreign shores. And when he explored his first flowers or the big tree in the garden, tore out the grass, petted a dog or a cat, watched the birds and squirrels, etc., he had already become a little biologist in the making. The teacher would tend to resume any such threads, would have the children draw maps of their rooms, houses or of the classroom, locate their seats or change places on the map, then present them with maps of the immediate vicinity and have them take walks on those as well as in the territory itself. Finally map-reading of unknown and vaster lands such as the whole United States will be exercised. Questions like: "Which city is higher above sea level, Memphis or New Orleans?" "Why is Florida warmer than Maine?" "Why is the Salt Lake salty and Lake Michigan not?" "Why has

New York become such a big city ?" may be useful parts of these exercises. And for biology the teacher may bring in model animals, some live plants and pictures of others, he may have the children draw them, let them keep fish and a few greeneries themselves in the classroom and visit the Zoo or the museum with them. Later on they would also be encouraged to disect flowers and use microscopes. And finally they may study as much as the floras of their summer resorts and report about them in class next fall.

This may all sound rather trivial, especially since it does not mean that what the geographer does is nothing but infantile explorations of his mother and the immediate environment and that what the mathematician does is no more than manipulating physical objects or even excrements and that the painter's or sculpturer's preoccupation is plain and simple smearing. In each case the second derives from the first, but the long and complicated process of derivative-formation is precisely by what they are different. No, let me spell out, in analogy to some rules concerning the substitution of desires discussed before (see p. 28 f, also p. 30f), the rules that would apply to derivative-formation and implement them in some quite specific task of teaching. New desires can form more readily and easily (a) the closer they are to already existent desires, (b) the closer the latter would be to primal desires of the *continua* in question, (c) the larger the number of existent desires to which the new desire is close and (d) the smaller the number of different *substitution continua*, other things being equal, on which these desires are assembled. As for (d) we should specify, though, that desires tend to be more complex, the larger the number of *substitution continua* in which they participate and the larger the number of ways or combinations in which they do so. It is precisely these more complex desires that matter in education. Then, however, it is particularly imperative for the teacher to involve all *substitution continua* in question. Otherwise the prognosis for the desire to form is not so good.

Let us try to utilise these rules for a specific task, say, teaching the concept of gravity. We would expect that the teacher who observes these rules would probably do a better job than one who does not. What desires and experiences of satisfaction can he presuppose in the ten-year-old that may be pertinent ?

Well, a poor teacher might go about it somewhat like this: "Have you seen an apple fall from a tree ? You must have. Anyway, this is what got Newton started on the problem of gravity. He figured that the apple falls because of the gravitational pull exerted by the earth. He even assumed that the apple also pulls the earth, but due to its infinitely smaller mass its effect is totally negligible. Now, what holds for a falling apple holds for all falling objects, whether they are dropped or thrown into the air . . ." Obviously he is entering the topic like a blind elephant.

A good teacher, on the other hand, would start with an exploration of where and how gravity can be observed or even felt after assuring himself that the children have some idea of what the word refers to. Comments like "Gravity makes things fall" or "Gravity makes things heavy" may already be sufficient indicators and, at the same time, open up two important avenues that must be walked if an adequate and mature concept of gravity is to form. "What things have you observed falling?" may be a starter, and the answers may comprise: leaves or apples, rain, snow, things dropped from a window, and a smart child may summarise: "Everything that comes loose." Right, but maybe you can think of things that you observe every day. After all, apples and leaves fall only in the fall, it does not rain or snow every day, and you don't drop things too often from a window, I imagine. Or you better not. People may not like it. But what is there right around you and with you that drops, if it comes loose?"

Answers may be: A pen or a penny that you drop. A bicycle may fall. A dish may fall and break. Water, if you turn on the faucet. "Very good," the teacher might answer, "but think also of yourself. What is falling right on or with you?" The answers: Skirts. The tie. If you spit something out. If one goes to the bathroom. If you put something in your pocket, it falls to the bottom of the pocket. Hair falls, if it has grown long enough. If one jumps down from a wall. If you jump down the stairs.

"That's right," the teacher may say, "but perhaps you do not even have to jump down. What about walking down a flight of stairs? Don't you let yourself fall from stair to stair? Jimmy, come out and step down from the platform so that everybody can see it." And he may remind them of some of their numerous experiences with the fact that it is harder to go upstairs than downstairs. He may also ask a child to raise his arms sideways and hold them that way as long as possible or he may ask all the children to do so. And as they drop them one by one, he may wonder, for didactic reasons, why they did it. Anyway, the force they would be struggling against is gravity too. Then he might have them stand on one foot, keep their balance while walking along a ridge or a bar, if there is one, wonder why, in staggering or being tackled, hardly anybody ever falls to stand on his head and ask them why a child of one falls constantly or prefers perhaps to crawl altogether. He may also remind them of bicycle riding as a more recent experience of attempts to counteract gravity and stay erect.

After that or along with it the teacher may go into the problem of weights. If a stone we drop falls to the ground because of gravity, the force that pulls it, where is that force after the stone has reached the ground? If one does not go down the stairs, but just stand on the floor, where is gravity then? Or if one jumps in the air or throws a stone? Or think of a balloon, of an airplane, of a man swimming or floating in the water. How come they don't fall or sink? And he might take up weight changes that one can feel, such as when riding on a roller-coaster or carrousel, rocking on a swing, making sharp turns in a car or being under any other condition where centrifugal forces, buoyancy or a momentary thrust counteract gravity.

He may eventually resort to letting them make their own experimental experiences with falls and weights, have heavy and light things fall, have them fall through the air or through water, experience the impact by hand, then by some kind of scale, measure weights of different substances, compute their specific weights, observe and measure buoyancy in water, have them find out or formulate the principle (of Archimedes), play around with pendulums, their weights and lengths, with peg tops and their speeds, talk a little about the planetary system of our sun and finally expose them to or help them formulate some simple equations concerning, say, l, the length of a fall over a stretch of time ($l = \{g/2\}t^2$, where t would be the time of the fall and g the uniform force of gravity), the force with which it hits the ground ($f = mv^2/2$, whereby m would be the mass of the body in question and v its velocity at the moment of impact, and v, in turn, could be viewed as the first derivative of l or $dl/dt = l' = gt$), while w, the weight of an object, could be described as $w = mg$ or, if the object has been lifted by l, but is in a static state: $w = mgl$. In fact, some such equations are indispensable for an understanding of gravity adequate to handle any pertinent technical or scientific problems. Not everybody may form as articulate a concept of gravity as that, but everybody forms some concept. On the other hand we may say that the most proximal and intimate experiences of gravity are the most indispensable ones even for those with whom the concept does reach the articulation that affords mathematical formulation. It would be a serious mistake of educators, however, to think that children need not work for this greater articulation, that the most intimate, proximal and hence primitive, experiences are sufficient or even values in themselves. We shall see later on that some such mistake may also be prevailing to an extent in the field of psychotherapy (see p. 322f), although conditions there are different from ordinary teaching situations in a number of respects.

In what ways would the "good" teacher, in our sketch of what he might be doing, have obeyed the rules set up about derivative-formation (see p. 204)? Well, concerning rules (a) and (c) he has tried to link his discourse on to more different experiences that every child is likely to have had than the "poor" teacher did. Experiences, however, involve always satisfactions of desires (dropping and throwing things, jumping, moving on stairs, riding on roller-coasters and carrousels, swinging, making turns by car, etc., but even walking erect or getting up from crawling as well as after a fall), no matter how irrelevant *per se*, how purely instrumental, they may have become (such as staying erect, walking on level ground or on stairs, jumping with every step while running in a hurry, putting things where they do have support, etc.; see also p. 77f). These experiences include, of course, all those experimental ones that they are led to collect under the teacher's guidance. All these experiences also involve cathexis of conditions under which they have occurred, i.e. under which the desires concerned can be satisfied (see also p. 9 f). In such terms concept formation would be cathexis of the most indispensable and crucial aspects of all those conditions.

The "poor" teacher's lesson was sketched as much shorter. He might very well spend as much time as the other on gravity, but he would remain a poor teacher, if his strategy did not change. He may fill the time with anecdotes about Newton and other physicists, may prefer to read to the children some elegant formulations of what philosophers and novelists thought about gravity and perhaps tie it up even with religion or God, the ultimate mover of things, who also "makes" gravity. None of which would be too relevant to gravity as a physical concept or anything concrete that could be done with it.

As for rule (b) the good teacher has brought the children closer to primal desires than the poor teacher by taking up such simple and early learned things as walking, manipulating oneself and some primitive objects with or against gravity, experiencing sensations of gravity passively as infants and small children would have while being lifted and carried during their infancy, etc. The poor teacher, on the other hand, did little of this. Seeing an apple fall is his only paradigm, and this is a much more indirect experience of gravity than falling oneself, dropping an apple, throwing it, etc.

As for (d) we could argue that gravity in all its implications and ramifications is a complex concept and, therefore, likely to involve many different *substitution continua* in many different ways. If it is to form adequately, all *substitution continua* that might possibly be relevant should be tapped on by the teacher. Our "good" teacher has utilised various types of manual manipulation, kinesthetic stimulations and those of touch, vision and, perhaps, hearing (of the bangs with which objects end their falls). He referred even to something that the mouth can do, and he could well have expanded to the mouth's own gravity sensations such as when it holds a fluid, moves a bite from one side to the other or tries to get something off a tooth that is sticking to it, say a malt caramel. But, of course, the children in his class have long outgrown the stage in which the mouth is the major source of experience and activity. It still does the eating and speaking, but otherwise the hands and the rest of the body have become the chief executors, supervised predominantly by sight and hearing. The "poor" teacher, on the other hand, has utilised very little. "Have you seen an apple fall from a tree?" comprises about all of his sensuous referents concerning gravity.

To come back for a moment to our original questions (see p. 198), we would have little difficulty now with their answers. Radio-engineering, hard salesmanship, the Chinese script or skin diving are not commonly taught in grade school, because they fail on accounts (a), (b) and (c). They are neither very close to already existent desires, not even to a small number of them, nor to primal desires of the *continua* concerned (see p. 204f). And what other subjects are there than those mentioned (see p. 198)? Well, many others, but most of them can easily be traced back to those discussed. Typewriting or handling a printing machine comes from writing (and tapping, if you like), the use of computers or the exercise of higher mathematics from elementary arithmetic. Commercial art or great art derives from art practised in school, ultimately from primitive manipulations in general (although guided perhaps by its esthetic effects even in their earliest stages). Mythology or paleontology branches off from history or biology, respectively, geology from geography, microbiology or botany from biology, astronomy or nuclear physics from physics, biophysics from physics and biology, chemistry from physics or perhaps vice versa, although the handling of matter would probably precede manipulations of its composition. Yet the very first experiences of matter, say those of food, have been sort of chemical already.

I believe we need not continue this. The point is that the pursuit of any special field of knowledge can be viewed as a derivative of a broader and more general field and that these broad and general fields could be traced back to identifiable experiences and activities even of the earliest stages of development. Not that this would tell us very much, if anything, *per se* about the fields, areas or disciplines in question. Implicitly, this is all taken for granted. Also that fields of knowledge are inseparable from methods and experiences in those fields. Yet, in our terms, knowledge is the result of the never ending processes of cathexis and the methods and experiences refer, in principle, to desires, their derivatives, and their innumerable relationships of instrumentality. In matters of didactics, but even in those of clinical psychology and psychotherapy, this may be good to remember articulately.

I might have sounded as if there were nothing but home and school for the child of latency period. This is not so. The child is also on playgrounds, in the street, on bicycle tours, swimming, camping, hiking, in boys' or girls' clubs, or even in gangs. Yet psychologically speaking all this will be under the auspices of home and school, even if no direct supervision is maintained. After all, he goes home after every such excursion, continues to draw the most elementary satisfactions such as meals, warmth (even in the most physical sense), light, sleep, etc. from his home and his parents, and returns to school almost every morning. Where any of these extra-parental and extra-scholastic milieus get out of hand, the parents or the schools are, in all likelihood, the failing parties. The same might also hold true if the child does not develop or seek such milieus of his own at all, if he clings exclusively to home and school. In that case his home has probably planted doubts about the friendliness and stability of the world into his earliest years of life and, due to this, school cannot be a very safe place either. Thereafter, however, things can only be worse.

Summarising latency period, we might say that it is characterised by *further derivative-formation* of desires. Aside from all kinds of refinement of eating leading to distinctions of many kinds of food, candies and ice-creams, oral stimulation and manipulation branches out into still more articulate speech that is no longer only spoken but also read. Manual stimulation and manipulation develops into writing, more articulate drawing and painting than before, and many little mechanical skills such as using hammers, levers, glue, scissors and the like, but also numbers, more complex properties of physical objects such as weight, volume or surfaces, and causal relationships above those that are immediately apparent. Manipulation and stimulation of the entire body spreads out into all kinds of games and sports, fights and competitions, and makes for increasing familiarity with what oneself is capable of doing, and what the others are. Only genital stimulation and manipulation does not generally develop much beyond what it was at the end of the Oedipal period, although non-incestuous objects are available and make it more inviting than does the family at home. With respect to the family genital desires have become *latent*.

As for *object-formations* people are foremost as ever. In addition to one's parents and siblings new parent- and sibling-figures are learned about or cathected for secondary aspects of their sexes as well as for their powers and nurturance properties. But there are also considerable extensions of the child's spaces and times. He gets to know more and more about his vicinity, his town and his country and he gains some historical perspectives, some first ideas about the position of the present within the known past, and he can handle the times of the week or of the day with increasing accuracy. He learns better and better, how to live by the clock.

Counter-cathexes are mainly continuations of all predominant counter-cathexes established in earlier periods of development. There is no primal *substitution continuum* on which there would not have been some "drop-outs" of desires, some losses and subsequent counter-cathexes. Hence there are no losses now, that would not have predecessors in kind, or "guides" (see also pp. 30, 45). The same holds for *fears*. There are no primal fears except those already mentioned. Anything feared has been patterned already by the more primitive fears of earlier stages of development. All types of fears may be expressed manifestly, but they would generally be mild and temporary, playful rather than serious. Not even the loss of a parent would throw a child too much off balance now except when previous stages have not been passed through too successfully to begin with. Not that there would not be considerable grief and mourning. But we have already discussed that, developmentally the severity of conscious experiences of given types of losses are in an inverse relationship to the effective severity of the loss (see p. 155f).

Frustration tolerance has come close to that of the adult by the end of latency period. The child has learned how to *work* which, although always gratifying in itself to some extent, would also preclude or postpone temporarily the satisfactions of other desires. He can keep at a task up to several hours in a row, but he is also much more aware of the contexts of the tasks as well as of the time periods concerned. As a matter of fact, he may be able to work hard in order to gain some of the rewards only weeks or months later (say in the form of a good grade report, or a bicycle promised for the summer). Due to his improved time concept, temporal distances are structured and more manageable in his mind. The future can be foreseen and future events anticipated with considerable ease. Separation from his parents can eventually be tolerated for months at a time. Meals can be foregone for a day, if necessary, and he will tend to stay awake for an average of fourteen to fifteen hours and a maximum of thirty hours in a row, if required. That is, he will forego a night's sleep.

Puberty and Adolescence

STARTING from about twelve years of age subcortical and hormonal changes are making themselves known that affect the entire personality. The rate of body growth changes. Boys and girls alike shoot up and become the relatively tall and thin youngsters we all know. Secondary sex characteristics begin to develop. Boys grow the first fluffs of a beard. Their voices break. An awkward man's voice mingles more and more frequently with the child's. And they develop pubic hair and hair in their arm-pits. The girls do likewise except for the voice and the beard, and their breasts start growing. More important even are the changes in primary sex-characteristics. The genitals of both sexes develop too and as a consequence the boys become capable of ejaculation and the girls begin to menstruate. This makes them men and women, so to speak, and if they were living in primitive social systems, they may soon be permitted or encouraged to go ahead on these assumptions. In all more highly organised societies, however, inhibitions and restrictions of all kinds prevent such a course of events for plausible reasons. Here it takes much more to get into the positions of marrying and raising families, and offspring, the most vital generator and glue of families, is imminent wherever youngsters start consuming heterosexual relationships with each other. They have to find a place to live, the young man also a job or position that will pay him enough to keep it up and feed the family, and they have to be able to adjust to economic fluctuations which are inevitable, no matter how complex and articulate a social system grows to be.

But these external inhibitions and restrictions reinforce only what counter-cathexes, formed during the Oedipal phase and earlier periods, have already accomplished. All more primitive and destructive desires of oral, bodily and genital manipulation and stimulation have been repressed and could be aroused and satisfied only under various degrees of anxiety. This holds even for very simple social systems. It has been pointed out before (see p. 45, also pp. 123, 174f) that there is no culture where the parents and the circumstances of life would not impose some very definite counter-cathexes on each of the three primal drive systems. What complicates matters now, however, are the physical changes that accompany puberty. Not that there have not been physical changes all along. But now they are more drastic and rapid. They are hard to overlook, and they concern aspects of oneself that have been "forgotten". All throughout latency period boys and girls have been what they are for each other mainly for

210

secondary reasons. The primary sex-characteristics have largely fallen into oblivion, at least practically speaking, but they are the ones that obtrude now. They too change physically at a more rapid pace than ever and the capacity for orgasm increases considerably. Genital manipulation and stimulation would lead to a kind of climax before puberty, provided it had been engaged in to that extent, if at all. This climax, however, has usually been less intense and succinct than it can be now.

In other words, the body of the youth and especially the sex-organs command his attention. While the extreme sensitivity to stimulation of the sex-organs had been discovered during the Oedipal phase and counter-cathected in most of its aspects ever since, the impact of these changes is such that some of these counter-cathexes are "overrun" and others at least shaken (see Freud, Anna, 1936). That means that the person in question will experience unusually strong temptations for genital stimulations. Desires that had become non-existent for practical purposes, that had dropped out from their respective *substitution continua* or drive systems, either because of the impossibility to satisfy them or because of the punishment that had been pitted against them, come to life again to various degrees and attempts will increase to satisfy them after all.

Which are these desires? Well, the most basic and yet heavily forbidden would be the desire to engage in mutual genital manipulation and stimulation with the dearest and most intimately familiar person there is: mother; and in the case of a girl, to do so with the second-dearest person and the dearest of all men: father; to engage with the opposite-sex parent in what he has been suspected, and partly forgotten, to do with the same-sex parent; to have mother to oneself, now that one has become a man; and to have father to oneself, even to have a child with him, now that one has become a woman.

These desires, however, have been so heavily counter-cathected by the end of the Oedipal phase and throughout latency period that they are unlikely to appear that way. Or rather they do appear that way, but the parents are omitted. Objectless longings for a person like the opposite-sex parent are usually all the youth does experience and he or she makes the first, largely imaginary, attempts at filling these empty spaces. They try out in their phantasies how teachers, older friends, heroes and heroines of literature, of the movies, the stage, the newspaper or even of comic strips, would fit and feel. How one would meet them, what they would say, how one would respond, what one would insist on, where one would go for an evening, etc. Then how one would touch or be touched by such a person, whether and how one would kiss and be kissed, and what one would permit them or be permitted to do. Not infrequently in these earliest times of adulthood such phantasies are entertained even with persons of the same sex. And eventually contemporaries of the opposite sex will be chosen for such tests and games of imagination, and reality will come to implement them to increasing degrees as time goes by. It has been pointed out, as a matter of fact (see p. 192ff), that coeducational schools, and they are the majority, afford ample opportunity for that even before the onset of puberty. Yet strangely enough, or rather as is to be expected on theoretical grounds, these objects are not so eligible at all for the time being. Imaginary objects are dangerous in the sense that they appear more malleable to one's desires than do the objects of reality. They can come close to the very forbidden ones before the "dreamer" knows it. But they are also harmless in the sense that they are imaginary. They are more likely to do just what one wants them to do. They can be stopped and expelled whenever the desires grow too threatening. And whatever penalties they might inflict will crumble before the fact that all or most of the engagement was not real. This should not mean that there are clear-cut borders between the two lands, imagination and reality. The latter is inextricably infiltrated with the former, and the former is composed of elements of the latter. Even the most real and promising partner of the other sex is "filled" with a person's imaginations about him or her which are only gradually and sometimes reluctantly corrected in favor of realities as the contact develops. And all of a person's imaginations about such a partner draw heavily on previous and even ancient experiences with people of that kind, especially the incestuous ones.

In the course of this genital self-stimulation is pretty much the rule among boys and, to a lesser extent, among girls. Phantasies about heterosexual genital experiences accompany them and tend to be varied in a number of ways by the "tester". They are practically never purely genital. Desires for inspection of the object, by sight and manual, oral and/or bodily touch, but also for more indirect experiences such as different situational settings and all kinds of conversation might provide them, are pursued and satisfied in these imaginary plays. The objects themselves tend to be exchanged repeatedly, but nobody will get hurt from it and the dreamer himself will have to feel sorry for little, if anything.

Even so, however, fears and guilt accompany such practices. Counter-cathexes have been lifted and others shaken, but some remain intact even with the most uncontrolled and unrestricted individuals. The latter are the ones that may actively defy them. They may use reaction-formations against their fears and guilts, as if to prove to themselves or someone that, no matter how crazy and badly they behave, nothing is going to happen to them. Yet what they are trying to invoke unconsciously is precisely punishment for all they do and did, and usually they also get it (see Aichhorn, 1936; also Redl, Bettelheim, 1951). If nobody catches them, they do not rest until they slip somewhere and get their "arrests and trials" or, in the case of as harmless an offence as masturbation, until father or mother, a sibling or a highly esteemed friend finds out about it and puts them to shame, despises them, withdraws their affection and the like. If he is more reasonable about it and does not desire quite so badly to be caught, he may still fear to get sick from masturbation, to contract a venereal disease, to become forgetful, unable to work well, or lose his mind. He may expect that fate or God will catch up with him one day. And if he is still more reasonable, he may have no such fears, but feel badly about it anyway, feel unworthy in general for a while, undeserving of nice and pleasant things to come. He may even impose his own punishments, say deny himself food or candies for a day and longer, donate part of his allowance for a humanitarian purpose, take to hard and strenuous physical exercise, pray all evening, do some extra studying, promise not to look at girls for a week or merely never—or almost never, at least not for a long time—to commit the original offense again.

All of these fears could be called derivatives of castration fears or worse. It has been pointed out before (see p. 189) that the fear of castration is the mildest of all primal fears, since it affects only the sex of a person, not necessarily his powers in general nor his capacities to eat and speak nor his very life and subsistence. To be put to shame, despised, deprived of affection, to turn sick or crazy, etc., are all handicaps linked by the pubescent himself to genital self-stimulation, even if there is no rational evidence that they are connected. And all of these imagined or actual consequences would still be easier to bear than the real thing: injury or loss of the sex-organs themselves. If that happened, one would really and irrevocably be put to shame, despised, and deprived of affection. One would be sick, and one would indeed go crazy. What is that after all, a growing man without what, most unmistakably, makes him one? Only severe mutilations of one's physique or powers, only fatal accidents, being murdered, smashed, completely destroyed, and the like, would be worse.

All of this holds for the girl as well. It has been said before, however, that she is less prone to engage in masturbation during the Oedipal phase—there is "less" to do it with—and that throughout latency she remains more attached to her father than the boy does to mother as a woman (see p. 170ff). She stays somewhat more under his spell as a man. He is not as much out of the question as a heterosexual love-object as is mother for the boy. In puberty this means that her longings will not be quite as objectless, her search not quite as hopeless from the beginning and her need to support her imaginary tests and plays with physical shortcuts smaller.

What contributes heavily to this is the event of menstruation, which has its traumatic aspects no matter how carefully the parents, preferably mother, have prepared her for it. During the Oedipal period the girl had to discover that she lacks what a boy has got. Now she finds that whatever she does have for a sex-organ is even more deficient (Deutsch, Helene, 1944). It bleeds and soils one periodically and makes for other kinds of discomforts. The consolation that now she can and one day will have babies must look small at first. And if she was "originally ugly" (see p. 173), hence very concerned about her beauty, she is even uglier with this new predicament, and beauty will matter even more. Nature helps her, of course, and this help could not come at a better time. She does indeed become increasingly beautiful, a woman, but very, very young, a girl who may well find herself harvesting glances, whispers, compliments, whistles, dates, etc., from all kinds of men and even women. And if dresses, hairdo's, make-ups, the skin, the figure, legs, teeth, eyes and the like mattered before, they have now become many times as important and rewarding to attend to.

Gradually boy and girl alike begin to turn to more feasible and available objects around them: to friends, neighbors, class-mates, members of youth or church groups, of theater-, debating-, music-, ski-, sailing-clubs, etc. Toward the end of latency period they may have become fairly aggressive with each other. It looks as if they had a vague premonition of what they will soon mean for each other, as if they would sense already the first loosenings of their counter-cathexes of the other sex. That makes them anxious, and if they live it out, they would tend to behave angrily and destructively (see also p. 57ff). They may keep seeking each other out in order to insult and attack each other physically. At the same time they may be quite unhappy over knowing no better forms of satisfying their budding interests. At the onset of puberty, when more and more counter-cathexes are overrun or shaken, they may become so afraid of their awakened desires as well as of what they themselves might do in order to either implement them or prevent their satisfaction, that they sometimes decide to avoid each other altogether. But gradually the boy and the girl overcome this turmoil and learn how to find and settle temporarily for what is right around them. They will join with each other in activities at school, sports, dances, performances of various sorts (music, plays, debating contests), and they will begin to experience the more intimate aspects of the other sex on parties and party games, dates, dances of a special sort, movie theaters, car rides, walks, etc. The more articulate their personalities and the more articulate, disciplined and well-educated their parents, other things being equal, the longer will it take them to engage in direct heterosexual genital experiences. Even coeducation in school will not make too much difference in that respect. Inarticulate youths, however, especially when they come from parents who lead primitive, disinhibited, hence also quarrelsome and violent lives, youths without much intelligence, talent or the training necessary to develop either, are likely to come into heterosexual contacts, engage in genital intercourse and even become parents of children, much sooner than the others. If they should found a family rather than deposit their offspring in an orphan's home or put it up for adoption, they are not very likely to develop into mature and responsible parents. Hence their children are in for a similar fate soon after they, in turn, have reached the age.

The youths of puberty, boys and girls alike, do not only try to find a love-object. They are just as much in need of identification-objects, and the types they choose, the degrees to which they practise identification, and the concern with which they exchange them, will reflect again how articulate and well-educated they are and how well-equipped they have been by the parents that they happen to have. Imaginary identification-objects may be taken from history, politics or the armed forces, from literature, the stage, the movie- or entertainment industry, athletics, football, tennis, the fashion industry, etc. The means of identification are quite diversified too. They range from the adoption of mannerisms of speech and gesture, of dressing, handwriting, verbal expression, songs and trivial sentimentalities, all the way up to attempts at grasping the identification-object's outlook on life or the world, their moral principles, their strengths shown in defeat and depression, etc. And since all identification-objects have some kind of relationship to persons of the other sex—even no relationship at all, i.e. perfect rejection, is a relationship—they will inevitably introject those aspects of their heroes and heroines as well. They will learn from them what to think and how to act toward the other sex, what significance to attribute to it and what sacrifices to take upon oneself in order to get what one wants. We should not underestimate to what extent adolescents have picked up ways of approaching the other sex, of being seductive or seducing, of harmless or more conniving trickery, of embracing, kissing or handling more intimate situations, of dealing with tragedy, unfaithfulness, financial plights, extravagancy, triangle situations, disappointments, etc., we should not underestimate to what extent they have picked up all of this from sources other than themselves and their own direct experiences. On the other hand, we should not underestimate either to what extent these indirect experiences, these curiosities about and observations of the doings of others are determined by what a person has experienced himself and most directly in earlier life, especially in his immediate family. He will select only those identification-objects and only those of their aspects and doings that appeal to him on the basis of all previous cathexes and counter-cathexes (see also p. 30). His earliest identifications determine the realms and ranges within which he will choose objects for later and current identifications and the areas of the world with respect to which his identifications will help him along.

With all this the youth may still be under the subjective impression of breaking away from his parents and his whole family, from their business, their interests, modes and thoughts, and his, or her, parents may feel likewise. They may think they are losing their child because his pursuits are so different at times, so contrary to what they had had in mind for him or her. Yet the more contrary they are, the greater the likelihood that they are reaction-formations to pursuits and desires that seem too much alike those of the parents. And the more mature, responsible and happy with each other and the world the parents have been all along, the greater the chance that these reaction-formations are temporary. Once an English statesman claimed that a person who has not been a rebel or a radical in his adolescence, may not be much of a person at all. But the same would hold, he continued, of a person who remains such a rebel and radical way into, and perhaps throughout, adulthood. No. Mature, responsible and happy parents have already exerted all the influences that their child may need. No reinforcements are called for in puberty unless their sons or daughters ask for it. The best way of keeping up their parental control is to forego it explicitly. They should remember that the pubescent is indeed breaking away from his parents, although not in those areas where he shows it the most. He, or she, must find a love-object outside the family or at least get ready to search for one. If,

P

in the course of this, he rebels against his primal love-object and/or his primal identification-object on issues of schooling, music, politics, sports, vacations (that is, where and how to spend them), dances, dates, television programs, etc., these rebellions may well be the disguises and unconscious pretenses of more basic conflicts. As a matter of fact, these substitute issues may be kept alive because they contribute little to the original one. And they may well subside one day without any special and overt solutions.

Even so parents will have to stand ready to help, support, guide and advise whenever called upon, and these calls are sometimes quite devious and hidden. They will have to sense and listen more carefully and do less about it, or at least make less of a show of it, than ever. Even now they remain the most important people in their children's lives and they cannot possibly exercise their active interest in them too long, although so-called progressive education of all degrees has tried for a few decades now to do away with this. The longer a person has parents and the longer they care to be available and effective, the longer will a person grow up, and the more will he grow up to.

In the chapter on quantitative aspects we have raised the question whether libido, the energy that feeds into all of motivation and all of cathexis, does not increase in puberty (see p. 98f). If it did, our assumption about an intra-individually steady supply of libido, i.e. the simplest of all possible assumptions about motivation and cathexis as a whole, would be invalid. Is not the influx of genital interests, supposedly due to subcortical and hormonal changes, indicative of such an increase of libido?

Not necessarily. The assumption of an increase would be justified, if the genital interests would increase at the expense of no others. This, however, does not seem to be the case. Otherwise puberty would not be the kind of trouble that it is for the parents, school or the pubescent himself. And there is trouble. He becomes less interested, less willing to devote time to family matters, visits of relatives and the parents' friends, to father's business, his political tirades or matters of the church. His achievements in school tend to deteriorate. Subjects that require abstraction and concentration are affected the most at first. What's the use of physics or mathematics? What do I need to know Spanish for? What's the use of learning about the vegetation of the Southern Andes? Or about genes? Where are they? What have they got to do with what a person feels? That is the most important thing. Love, attraction, disappointment, mental pain and suffering, the mystic aspects of religion, the vastness of the universe or of the ocean, morality, repentance, asceticism, honor, bravery, sacrifice for a dear friend, defending him by every means against attack, dying in his stead, if that should be called for, or at least risking one's life, these are the things that count. And where these more spiritual aspects of the world are not so prominent, emphasis is on physical aspects, on sports, athletics, developing one's muscles, getting a tan, swimming long distances or swimming very, very fast, boxing, wrestling, etc. Team sports are not the favorites at first, although they had already been a little while ago, and sports that require very special skills and talents, say ski-ing, tennis, sailing are not either. The youngster is still too unfamiliar with his rapidly changing body, too clumsy and awkward to get anywhere in those areas.

Similar things hold for girls, although neither the athletic nor the "spiritual" aspects of the world are too important with them. It has already been said that they remain more closely attached to incestuous objects, that they are not so much in a vacuum and find ways more rapidly and quickly to contact, or at least accept the possibilities of contact of, the other sex.

Is that the point: the pubescent loses his interest in certain areas of life and the world in favor of his genital interests and their derivatives? Yes, but that is not the whole story. The genital interests are not the only ones that are increased. Interests in athletics, especially those branches that require brute strength and only primitive skills, could be called an increased interest in bodily manipulation and stimulation. Even the increased interests in feelings and all issues that evoke them strongly has a connotation of bodily stimulation. The youth is interested in all sensuous aspects whatsoever. He has become more sensitive to them. Hence he may be trying to heighten them. But there are even increased oral interests. The youth can eat excessive amounts, or "nibble" endlessly instead, i.e. all day long. He can also eat the same things day after day, as long as they are his favorite few, steak, mashed potatoes, bananas and gallons of ice-cream. All of which suggests not so much a shift of interests as a regression.

It has been indicated before (p. 103 f) that the psychological development of man can be characterised as a ceaseless travel to ever new lands of experience and endeavor. A person will find himself looking for new aspects of all those situations of gratification that have gone stale, that have recurred in uniform fashion and have been learned about or cathected close to exhaustion (see p. 103f). He will tend to like some degree of newness in whatever situation he finds himself in. This implies, on the other hand, that a situation may also become *too new*, i.e. new in too many different aspects at once. A new aspect in general is an aspect that has not yet been cathected, and that, in turn, means that it has not been experienced as a condition of satisfaction of desires. If too many aspects of a situation are new, that situation must appear too depriving, too difficult to find satisfactions in or too dangerous (see also p. 18 ff). Hence anxiety will prevail and mount. Anxiety, however, is a state of temporary regression (see p. 57 ff, p. 29 ff).

Well, the physical changes that are occurring now, in puberty, are that new, if by virtue merely of their faster pace. Therefore the pubescent must be somewhat in a state of regression on all basic drive systems, but especially on the *continuum* genital manipulation and stimulation. He will function more primitively and aggressively, the basic *substitution continua* will appear "accelerated", so that satisfactions have to occur more frequently, more thoroughly or both (see pp. 26, 27). And all that may well *look* to an observer like an increase of energy, i.e. of libido.

If children of nursery school age are already expected to learn from each other rather than from adults, even though there is less to learn from (see p. 177 f), and if the (adult) teachers in grade school have furnished little continuity and not too much authority (changing every year, joining as outsiders the group that has moved to a new grade; see p. 191 f), this should also be reflected in puberty. Boys and girls alike should have become more reluctant than those of all previous generations to look for, leave alone accept, the adults' desires for them. They would not want to understand what the adult, the teacher, the parent, the youth leader, etc., has in mind for them. All they want for the adult is to understand and accept what *they*, the growing adolescents, have in mind. And since parents and teachers alike are somewhat recalcitrant to such demands, they, parents and teachers, are discarded, and so are the youth leaders, unless they begin to sing or conduct the adolescents' own songs, such as, say, Elvis Presley or Dick Clark are doing, respectively. All that matters in life is to be an adolescent and have fun. What fun ? Well, the fun that other adolescents are having.

This should not be misconstrued to mean that the adolescents of other times have had no such ideas. Only neither parents nor teachers nor society as a whole would let them have their fun to the extents that they get it now. They would insist on their own ideas too, would let them "loose" only on occasions, such as when they have accomplished throughout the year what their elders wanted them to, and thereby actually do them a considerable favor. Part of the adolescent excesses of today, sometimes bordering on the criminal—such as physical or sexual attack of defenseless victims, pilfering, destruction of property, but even robbery and manslaughter—could well be interpreted as attempts on their part to extract discipline after all from the world. They are begging to be caught and penalised, to be forced into reason. Only if they fail to achieve that over a series of such attempts will they become as callous as some authorities in charge claim they were to begin with. No, they have not had parents who cared enough to have strong and definite desires for their youngsters. From early youth on they had reason to perceive their parents' *laissez-faire* as indifference, and perhaps they were right, although some parents have also been frightened into ridiculous degrees of tolerance by various pressure groups such as the neighborhood, the public, mass media and popularised "scientific" literature.

These trends are also obvious with their relationships to the other sex. Counter-cathexis will be effective under all circumstances. Even if we wanted to we could not raise a youngster without his forming counter-cathexes at least of some aspects of heterosexual contacts. In other words, there will be inhibitions even with the most disinhibited of them. But they may not be enough to prevent short circuits. I have pointed out before (see p. 192 ff, esp. p. 193 f) that heterosexual relationships could easily stay shallow and infantile way into adulthood as a result of too early and too intimate exposure to the other sex. If we can trust the adolescent's own songs—which are actually manufactured mostly by fairly sophisticated ex-adolescents who do not want to be "ex"; and who could blame them after the kind of adolescence they have, or might have, had, and after their scanty preparation for the dour years thereafter; manufactured pretty much with the primary intention to create smash-hits and cash the money—anyway, if we can trust the adolescent's own songs, then he wants to be with his baby forever—believe it or not—and she wants to be his baby forever. Also he wants to be her baby. He is as much in need of her as a newborn is of mother's milk and her hugs. And she wants to baby him like a baby. So we have: he a baby, she herself a baby, everyone a baby, but only "you and I the real, real babies".

That does not mean that they are not able to consume a heterosexual relationship. On the contrary. They want just that, and a little more: they want the world to pay for their living while they are being babies for each other, or not even pay. The world should just give them everything they want. Who needs money? And if there is as absurd a thing as a third baby growing in the belly of his real, real baby because of what he, the he-baby, did to her . . . "Well, parents, you have just become grandparents. Let us hand you a little newborn. Take care of it, will you? because we, its parents, are too busy making love to each other. And if not to each other, then at least to another baby, another he-baby, another she-baby, and if this damn thing grows again in her belly . . . Well, parents, or landlord, or mayor, have a baby! If you don't want it, we put it on your doorsteps at night. You know, we are too young to be parents. We wait until the babies come grown up. Then we'll keep them so that they can take care of us."

Finally these trends are also manifest in the kind of preparation for life that the school provides. Increasingly unable for various reasons to convey to the youngsters what they, in the name of society, want them to be and to do, the educators find themselves more and more at the mercy of their students. They, the educators, are requested to provide a kind of a University at which the thirteen-year-old can already feel like a grown-up. He can choose something like his own curriculum. He moves freely from lecture hall to lecture hall as they do in a real University. He has academic freedom to work or not to work and he can drop courses if doing no work for them turns out to be increasingly boring and not even the tacit permission to hold hands in class with his (or her) baby-darling is making a difference. The whole thing is the teacher's fault anyway. Why does he not make it a little more interesting, with cartoons, films, outings or dances, yes, rock-and-rolls around the clock, as a real, real pastime between making love? Why does he not give us *some* fun. His performance is worth a walk-out. Perhaps he should be given the works.

Well, the youngsters are getting everything but a University. In fact, they are not even getting what used to be a high-school. They often graduate with no skills, leave alone excellencies, whatsoever, with no conceptual knowledge to speak of, although they do so with cap and gown and receive a diploma. What is worse:

they don't know it! They don't know how very little they have learned, and how could they know?

None of this is the adolescent's fault. Adolescents of all times have wished for such an easy life in school and such wonderful comfort in matters of love and romance. Only they never got it. Or rather they had to go a long way for it. They had to earn it, and as they did, they also discovered that they were better prepared to take care of their own affairs. In fact, all they had been made to do, or much of it, was only for their own good. Sometimes they might even take to blaming the parents for not putting enough pressure on them. If they had, they would be in a still better position, they might have argued.

So what is it that has changed since those lucky times, when the adolescents were kept from their other sex and put to study and work instead? One of the things may be the adult's notions about adolescence. What holds for the baby who cannot do anything at first without his mother wanting him to do so (see p. 82 ff), is still valid to an extent for the adolescent. He would not have become what he is if we, the adults, had not wanted him to be that way. And why would we want it? Well, one reason may be that we just do not care to have more demanding desires for him. It is too much trouble. Let him grow up as he pleases. Or let the school do the work. After all, what are we paying taxes for?

Another reason that may, in addition, be used as an excuse for the first one, is: Why should they, the adolescents, not have what we never had? Why should they not enjoy their youth while they are young and satisfy all those desires that we were not permitted to satisfy, that were bluntly or tacitly, but unambiguously, forbidden. Oh, what have our parents done to us? They really and truly should not have insisted on anything. Does not age come soon enough? No, we do not want to be like our parents. Look what has become of them: old-agers. Why should we not, through our children, hang on to youth and its delights? In other words, we tend to believe that our parents have not only failed to be strict with us on certain issues, but have also been far too strict with us on all others, have forced us to do what we did not want, or even had little talent for, just because it fitted the ideas of some up-in-the-clouds scholars about general education. Why did they not let us ride as we pleased? Those with real talents would have discovered and cultivated them anyway.

Still another reason may be that we have less than ever to offer even if we wanted to. Through technological and sociological progress our lives have been greatly facilitated and compartmentalised. The institutions of industry, commerce and sale, have taken many a burden from our shoulders and reduced us to push-button men. We set the dial of the stove for temperature and time according to the prescription on the ready-made food package, say chicken pie, and get a ring or hiss when it is ready to be taken out and served. We are feeling a little chilly. So we turn the thermostat a few degrees higher and within minutes our oil-furnace makes us the temperature we want. And if there is something to talk about between Mr. Holiday in Canada and ourselves, we do not have to take a nerve-wrecking trip through deserts and mountains, but we pick up the telephone. We might even be able to dial him directly, etc. There may be important decisions to be made at times, yet all a child can see of it is that we use the telephone, and that he can do too. Just as he can set the thermostat, or even cook. If something goes wrong in our complicated households, we call the man who is needed, and he fixes it. We might not even see him while he does so. Well, that too can be done by a child.

There is little to learn from us for a child. But even as a boy grows up and gets a better idea of what we might be doing professionally, he will find that we have little to contribute to his understanding of the sciences, the arts, history, economics or even of the motors of our cars, a radio set, or a simple ballpoint pen. We might be authorities in politics, but just on the local level, he will claim. No, we are just physicians, managers, teachers, engineers, salesmen or whatever the profession, and beyond that we know how to wash dishes and watch television. That's about all.

The same would hold for girls who usually know by the age of twelve how mother runs the house (if she does) and to what welfare- and church-club meetings she has disappeared at given times. But that is about all one might learn from her. Often she has little to say about the more general and personal issues of life, very little about love, and nothing at all about a really great love. She has never had one herself, it seems. The only thing she really has is a man for good. Somewhere and somehow she must have grabbed that one. So she, the adolescent girl, better get one too. Get someone who will make her life worthwhile like mother's; who will do everything she wants him to do and provide all the money; and who cannot leave her unless he pays a fat alimony.

Needless to say that the adolescent boy, in his turn, will find it a small attraction to become like his father in matters of girls. If mother is like what they will grow up to, he better get himself a real baby of a girl who will take a long, long time to grow up. If he finds one, he may perhaps get a chance to be a real baby too at times, and as this continues, she will possibly begin to baby him, period, like a real . . . like a real mother would. Coming to think of it, he might never truly have had one.

Modern man may have been on the road of declining authority for decades, and he may well have overstepped an optimal compromise. Maybe it all started when he himself began to discard his own parents, either by leaving them for a new continent or by choosing his professions "arbitrarily" rather than simply taking after his parents. Probably the road will make a turn before long, if not for inner reasons, then because of political, economic, and other threats. In our social system institutionalisation has so far kept abreast with the decline of parental authority and the concomitant evaporation of general competencies on the part of their children. The institutions created are making up for what we seem to be losing otherwise. They are our crutches, so to speak. Yet a wind of warfare, of economic crisis and the like, could easily blow them away, unless we learn soon again how to hold on to them, to handle, repair, and even create them. May I be forgiven for such preachings and prophecies. Or rather they should be viewed as theoretical exercises. They have no final value in themselves.

Summarising puberty and adolescence, we might say that with the development of the drive system "genital stimulation and manipulation" the adolescent has at last embarked on all avenues of life. Both the pursuits of the Oedipal period, which remained mostly "incestuous", and the pursuits of latency period which were more "pregenital" again, more oriented toward the (more or less refined) power aspects of people, the rest of the animate world, and the inanimate as well, both pursuits are now maintained at once. The world has become peopled with males and females for good, and with some of them contacts seem indeed possible—even if only in the more distant future—that have been thought impossible ever since the acute conflicts of the Oedipal period had subsided. But males and females also have powers, those of plain and even irresistible attraction and those of rivalrous intrigue, brute or subtle strengths, capacities to win physically, materially, or in matters of people, sympathy, one's profession, etc.

As for counter-cathexes the situation is similar to that of latency period (see p. 209). The same holds for primal fears, although those centering around genital mutilation or incapacity are more pronounced again than they were before. The boy might find himself worrying whether he is really a man, and the girl whether she is sufficiently beautiful to attract and retain a man.

Finally frustration tolerance is potentially close to the level of the adult, although there may be still a lot of turbulence in the beginning. At times the adolescent appears already quite capable of withstanding long periods of deprivation. He can work toward graduating from high school, study a foreign language for years, plan on a trip to Alaska, stand heat and cold, i.e. the deprivation of the desire to be in comfortable temperatures, forego meals for two days and miss sleep not only for one, but even two nights in a row, if challenged to prove his manhood. Yet at other times he will also be quite restless and impatient, not only with the long school year, but with a single day or an hour of school, will not wish to hear a word of this wretched foreign language that he is supposed to pick up, be unable to make any plans, loaf in the sun for day after day, eat voraciously, sleep endlessly, and go right back to any of these feats after the shortest interruption. Not that the adult (or he himself at a later stage) could not outdo him(self) even here. But the adult is usually spending his energies on more worthwhile enterprises. He is not exploring and consuming his capacities with such primitive fervor and vehemence as the adolescent is. Of course, he also is no longer such a greenhorn at it. To the adolescent these capacities are new, have to be tried out in the most immediate and intimate ways, and, in that respect, are just as worthwhile for the time being. Everybody has to go through it in order to become capable of enterprises valuable also by the standards of society.

Choice of Professions

WHETHER a person likes to or not, he will have to fit into some useful place within the social system of which he happens to be a member. The vast majority of people do, indeed, find such a place. To an extent that holds even for the most incurable playboy as well as for the notorious criminal. If extravagant spending and consuming is the chief task of the first one, he will either have to check somehow on the people who keep him provided with spending money or take a look at his finances himself. That is, he will have to do *some* work. Moreover his investments must be aggregated in enterprises that are useful in some ways to the social system in question. Otherwise they would not last. And he, the playboy, would have to care *that* much about his future in order to last himself.

The criminal, on the other hand, is not altogether useless either. He tends to abide at least by some of the laws and manners of his society. He dresses. He usually pays for food, rent, transportation fares and the like. His conduct in the street or in the presence of most people may be unobjectionable. In order to prepare for a crime, he too has to put in work of some sort, and he cannot yet hit the man over the head from whom he gets his gun, some information about the bank or his welding gadgets to begin with. Often this is not even the only kind of work he does and the only kind of consideration he demonstrates. And if he has committed a new offense, been caught—which he does relatively often— and put to jail, he has found his useful place for the time being. Regretfully, to be sure. He would have it differently, if he had a choice. As a matter of fact, society would merely have to give him what he asks for and he might never have turned criminal at all. So he claims. But of course he wants more than what his parents and/or his society have bestowed or are willing to bestow on him. What is worse: he literally tries to get it, and fast as well as by force.

But most people find places in society where what they get and what they contribute in return is of fairer and more apparent proportions. Better even, most people do find places where they can do what they are best able to and what, as a consequence, they would tend to like best. And what is it that they may like best? Not just because of the money and prestige and not because of high-flung dreams that they might possibly realise in the distant future, if they kept at it and had some luck; but rather because of the intrinsic and direct gratifications that their profession or job gives them in their daily routines.

223

If we resort in our considerations to the primal *substitution continua* or drive systems on which all of man's desires are assembled (see p. 116 ff), we may not get very far unless we allow for most complex interactions among them. Only then will we be able to account for the great variety of professions by means of which people can satisfy their desires in ways useful to their social systems. Yet if we use only sociological or even technological characteristics, if we try to see how certain professions fit as institutions into the system as a whole or how the bureaus of labor might subdivide their lot, we could well be omitting psychological aspects of great importance. Let us, therefore, approach the problem of choice of professions from both angles at once and not even attempt a comprehensive picture. A method of looking, a viewpoint, an approach to the problem rather than a system or a solution, will have to suffice.

Take farming, the profession from which all others originated historically. To this day it might be the healthiest, most diversified and down-to-earth profession, literally and psychologically speaking. It satisfies broadly all primal *substitution continua* or drive systems, i.e. not only oral manipulation and stimulation, especially bodily manipulation or manipulation proper, and in a sense even genital manipulation and stimulation (see p. 124 f), but also most of the subsystems of which the drive systems are composed.

The animals and the fields have to be "fed", those by self-grown and other fodder and these by fertilisers, compost, etc. There is watching and waiting as livestock as well as crops are growing, and hoping for good weather. There is manipulation of simple substances such as earth, milk and butter, straw, thrashed wheat, flour, meat, fodder, etc., but also of more complex gadgets and tools such as the plough and the tractor to pull it, electric churners, thrashing machines and the like. There is manipulation on a more abstract and comprehensive level. The crops have to be diversified, have to be sown and attended to at different times of the year. The fields themselves are "rotated". Fodder production, other crop, meat-yield and market conditions have to be brought into proper balances and steadily watched out for. Depreciation, taxes, credits and loans, all have to be kept track of as well as envisaged for the future. Almost every day there is enough to do on every level of work. Even his children can participate, if they want to. There is sufficient sensuous contact with the products, the livestock, the crop and the machines, and plenty of variety of such contacts. There is even guided procreation, such as among the cattle, or free animal love prevailing among other livestock, although most recently—perhaps as a reaction against much freer loves among the people, if a little joke is in order—such love life has gone out of vogue. Artificial insemination is the last cry.

Furthermore, although produced for and brought to markets, the products do not evaporate, so to speak. The farmer does not only see where they go, grain, eggs, meat, wool, offspring, etc., at least to an extent, but he himself retains the fields, the orchards, the cows, the chicken, the machinery, that produce them. He can always replace what he gives away. In fact, that is the very idea. Besides he himself is a consumer of almost every kind of his own products. He may eat his own bacon at breakfast, but even the onions, the salad, the apple-cider, also the wood for his barn or the bricks of his fireplace, may be his own makings. What is more: he himself can produce almost everything that man cannot do without. He is more autonomous than any other profession. Hence economic crises or wars, though unpleasant for him too, will nevertheless leave him less affected than, say, the people in the cities, in big industrial centers or in very special professions.

The farmer has ample opportunity to form very elementary and well-founded relations to the objects of his work which, to an extent, are always his own products. After all, he himself is the breeder, the planter and cultivator, the carpenter, the mechanic, the electrician, etc. Everything on his farm can become dear to him. Dear in different ways, to be sure, depending on how subservient to his desires and purposes, and to how many of them, they happen to be. Little is left out and if it is, disposal is usually possible, drastic and neat. Cows that give no milk go to the slaughterhouse before others. Chickens that do not grow fast will be discontinued. No more breeding of those. Fields with low yields will be turned into meadows. Sick trees will be felled, vermins, rats and fungi exterminated, surplus cat litters drowned, etc., and all tools, machines, storing spaces and stables survive by the same tokens.

His life is embedded in a large variety of tasks with much overlap of time schedules that require something like orderly routines. Otherwise animals and crops may suffer or perish. Even more important: he has generally begun to feel his way into them from childhood on. As he grew up, he came to know and to hold on to more and more threads of the entire network. As far back as he can remember, living beings more dependent than himself have already needed his care. Maybe it was a puppy at first, then a little lamb, a calf, a few chickens, a wild duck with a broken wing, then all the young animals on the farm and finally the whole livestock. He may also have taken care of a few vegetables in the vegetable garden before trying his luck with greater lots and the chief crops themselves. And while riding on the tractor, regardless where, was already fun enough in the beginning, it gradually dawns on him what kinds of other and more specific things the vehicle is good for.

All of this would tend to be true of the farmer's own children. They have an inestimable advantage over the children of all those fathers who go away for work and whose work offers very little that would be immediately evident and plausible. The profession of a top executive was characterised by his little daughter as: "Daddy answers the telephone." The owner of a canning factory was claimed by his son to collect old tin cans and refill them with jelly and meat. And a congressman-father was supposedly doing "nothing at all'. The farmer's children see their father work on a lot of things that make sense. They can even do several themselves after a while, although not yet as well as father can. What is more, they learn implicitly that all these skills and techniques have room in one single person. Yet most other professions are characterised by fragmentation of some kind, and not only the children, but even their fathers themselves will often find it hard to make out what another person in the same field and even in the same branch office or plant is doing. For amelioration they tend to cling to teamwork, at least they do so in the higher echelons, and at times they appear quite desperate about it. Unfortunately this does not always do the trick, especially in fields where complex conceptual structures have emerged as indispensable tools of discourse, such as in the sciences, higher economics, finance or jurisprudence. The "great men", those who overlook the entire field, have become exceedingly rare these days.

Well, in farming they are still more or less the rule. If father could not see or do it, nobody would do it for him. By all evidence father is the man who knows it all. He *is* the great man. It matters little that there are millions of his kind. He was the only one at first, i.e. when the child was small, hence the most important one of all, and he really is an authority. He can do everything.

All of this holds for mother and the girls too. As a matter of fact, father and mother as well as boys and girls tend to cooperate and supplement each other in much broader and more sensible ways than they do in city homes or those of "professional" families. They step in for each other wherever help is needed, and not just by signing a check. The girls may not mind doing "a man's job" for a change and vice versa. Only when there is another baby in the house will mother or one of her daughters be excused from such extra duties and permitted to stick with her feminine tasks, or rather with the most feminine ones of them all: caring for a child. During such times the men might work even harder on other things. This has been so for thousands of years. Babies and their livelihoods have been the most discriminating of all issues between men and women. Not that men or boys would not occasionally have been enlisted for those purposes too. But probably at no times have babies been handed over so often, so easily, and with such a vengeance as they tend to be by twentieth century's emancipated women of modern societies and the cities.

The farmer's family does have another great advantage, though, that would help. Their children will be needed. In fact, before long they can be put to very good use. They may be a chore at first, no matter how lovely in kind, but they will soon pay part of their way, slowly take over, and develop into people to whom one can safely leave the estate. They will take good care of it. Why? Because they have done so already and they have come to love it through the years. This, however, is seldom the case with a city family. Here children almost never pay their way. They are growing up and trained in school for very little that would be of immediate use to the parents. On the contrary, the chore takes on momentum as they grow up, especially when anything like a higher education is aspired to. If father should have his own independent little business, his son's or daughter's cooperation is just about out of the question. And should he hope that one of them would take it over one day, he will get no more than a laugh.

"That crummy litttle store ?" they will be inclined to ask with amazement. They are heading for something much bigger and better. They could use the money after selling it out, to be sure. As a matter of fact, that is precisely what they plan to do as soon as the "old man" retires. But while he is in business, he may as well help them set up their own family, pay for their own new and huge house and chip in on a sparkling new office, an Austin or Cadillac or a trip to Europe.

This is not saying that we should all return to farming although, incidentally, some people do so in a sense. Presidents of big corporations, e.g., or even presidents of a whole nation. They do so as a pastime, or for retirement. Nor is it impossible outside of farming to develop a broad and well-rounded outlook on, and mastery of, life and one's environment. Millers, butchers, carpenters blacksmiths, and a few other trades may have afforded similar advantages, at least as long as they were all assembled in villages and small towns, and physical, economic or social, mobility were negligible. Even the teacher, the physician, and the minister, though more specialised already, could still participate in all of life, one might say.

Division of labor and compartmentalisation is not as far gone everywhere as it is in highly industrial countries and in the big cities. But even something like the steel-, textile- or food-industry offer plenty of diversification for those who seek them. Steel goes into almost everything, houseware, construction, tools, motors, ships, roads, even agriculture. The industry itself offers jobs in mining, at the furnaces, in workshops, at the conveyer belt, in selling, sales promotion, advertising, etc. The same holds for textiles, if for no other reason than that the industry must take care of all possible kinds of people and situations, work, school, entertainment, sports, armed forces and what not. And the food-industry is no different either. Knowing any such industry well would imply universality of sorts. How many people do, though ? Top executive positions might permit such an all around interest and knowledge, but this gets inevitably diluted to the extent that the executive really fills his post. He will sooner or later find himself reduced to bird's eye views dashing to the ground only at trouble spots or for jewels. And academics might have the breadth as well as the intimate contacts, but not with the primary data and facts. They usually draw on secondary and tertiary sources. If somebody is really good in his branch of the national economy, he will soon be labeled a wizard or, again, a great man. Only here they do not come by the million as in farming.

Well, if modern social systems offer little more than small compartments of their general productivity to most persons, which ones will suit them best ?

There are those people whose interests appear more passive and verbal, who like to appeal to *other people* for favors rather than work for those favors directly and with their own hands or brains. Not that they might not exert themselves in their own ways. They can wreck their minds too, but their chief concerns are to extract laughs, to be liked by men and women alike, to have everybody in a good mood or to stay in such a mood themselves. They want to win audiences, to be their pampered darling, to be able to wish for anything at all and get it. They are not jealous of others who win them too, or only when they find out that others can hold on to them better than they do. Secretly they tend to believe that the world owes them a living. Not so much for what they do, for what they contribute, but for what they are, even for the mere fact that they are at all, i.e. for the pleasure of their existence. In short, their *oral drive system* would tend to be the predominant one (see also pp. 124 ff, 126 f). They would not want to work so much as they would want to entertain, be entertained and win great fortunes.

Yet depending on their sub-talents they may take to all sorts of things. If they have always liked eating a lot, they may become owners of restaurants who feed and entertain people and see to it that the cook, the manipulator of, and worker on, food is good and does a fine job. They will taste whether his products can really be offered for sale. If they have always been great lookers and watchers, they may take to art. Not that they would produce it themselves. They would gauge it, be delighted or appalled, and buy, sell, or mediate the exchange of art. They love turn-over better than possession. As a profession they may take to becoming art dealers, managers of exhibitions, possibly editors of illustrated magazines or theater critics with special attention given to stage design. If they have always loved to listen, they may become music lovers and music critics, sometimes even conductors, although that might well call for more concentration and persistence of effort than they would be inclined to like. If they have come to love their own voices, they may become singers and even opera stars, provided they have enough of these ingredients, and a few more. They might even become composers, but remain smaller in stature than the really great ones of their time. In order to match them they would have to have stronger flares for hard work. They might also peddle in perfumes, soaps, and cosmetics or they might establish themselves in resorts as experts on leisure and amusement. They might be professional gamblers, owners of hotels or amusement centers, of beach facilities, or steam baths. They know so well what people frequenting resorts, convalescents, vacationers, loafers, and the like, want, because they want it themselves pretty badly. Only they could not get it and make a living at the same time. But one day they might be able to, and then they will even own the necessary facilities themselves. In fact, they may be working their pants off day after day in order to get there.

Talking is already a more active sub-talent than the others. It requires conceptual and motivational organisation of the world around, especially if it is not merely word streams or purely expressive gibberish. Such an organisation, however, is the outgrowth of some kind of work or its equivalents. A person cannot handle the world by speech unless he has had at least some contact also with the world as a complex system of things and people. All of a language's metaphors are borrowed actions of greater or lesser, but always of some, specificity. Only those talking very big in the most inconsequential fashions might never have had any such contact to speak of.

A talking-talent of this kind may become an announcer or a literal entertainer, a court-jester perhaps, or a poet. If his talents are small, he might also end up as a salesman, selling either just about anything, as long as he can make money with it or, on the other extreme, selling products that he has created himself, at least in part. In other words, he would also have a fairly strong streak of physical manipulation, and he could, of course, tell better stories about his products than the first one. If his talents are great, if in addition he has learned how to handle sounds, inanimate matter, concepts, ideas and feelings, as instruments for other purposes, and if those purposes are the loves and hatreds of people for their own kind, passion, tragedy, great deeds and crimes, death and the like, he may become a playwright or novelist, perhaps a politician.

Another way in which a person strong in the oral drive system might find lasting satisfaction is dancing. That too would be a considerably more active endeavor by itself than most of the others mentioned. The dancer does a lot of scurrying around, to put it mildly. But it is for no "material" purpose. It is expressive or illustrative. It creates illusions rather than realities, like all entertaining, even though consumers might be benefiting in reality, just as they would do from recreations of most kinds. Other trades not too remote from dancing would be interior decoration, fashion design or even painting. However, a stronger interest in manipulation proper or work is a co-requirement. Otherwise they might not amount to much.

All these avenues of professional satisfactions are open for women too, although often with modifications. The oral drive system tends, on the average, to play a slightly greater part with them anyway than it does with men. One of their most important desires is to be beautiful and attractive to men. They are the ones who do the waiting, whereas men have to come and get them. They, women, are the ones who can be what they are. Men must work and achieve in order to be somebody (see also pp. 170 f, 173 f). This condition requires from women that they try to stay beautiful, that they look after themselves with sophistication, lotions, baths, massages and plenty of rest. In fact, they should not work at all, if they can help it. Work emaciates the body, makes it too muscular, wiry, ungraceful. Dish-washing ruins the hands. To mention just a few of the reasons they might give. But besides all of this women simply tend to be more intuitive, more oriented toward people than toward things, more reactive than constructive, more imaginative and romantic than realistic, closer to art than to science and systematic labor, at least as long as they can have their own ways. If they are not, men often like to think of them as unfeminine, even when they are the ones themselves who heap the chores on them. Generally women are a little more willing to take on what another person wants them to, but somewhat less alert in scenting what the subject-matter may require all by itself. Men, on the other hand, tend to dislike being told what to do, but might not mind nor even particularly notice that they are putting in overtime. They can get carried away by their tasks, while it is chiefly people, that is males, who can do that to women.

There is another kind of persons. They appear less verbal, more active in specific pursuits and much less reliant on favors from other people. They would rather do it themselves than ask for them to begin with. They work hard, not in order to ultimately be done with hard work for good. No, they are inclined to keep it up beyond all necessities. They like to make plans way ahead of the present, work toward them in carefully regulated instalments or, sometimes, in big bursts of activity, be forever ahead of assignments and deadlines or very unhappy if for some reason they cannot, and to do their jobs well. Very well even, if at all possible. They love, and believe in, good work, and they love people who can put it in. They like no sales talks. Let the product, the piece of work, art or thinking, speak for itself. Public relations are for the kiddies and sissies.

These people are creators, collectors, investors, conquerors, explorers and the like. While others may be hazy and romantic about individual rights and properties, they have clear-cut and well-defined notions about these issues. While others tend to lose sight, sometimes almost on purpose, of their dealings with others, they tend to give and take by explicit rules. Their payments and receipts are usually in balance, their purchases and sales sober calculations. Where they exploit others, they do so shrewdly, but by some kind of justice or, at least, legality. Where they do get carried away by imagination, they usually end up in their aspired lands after all. The least that can often be said in their favor is that they truly had a point. In other words, their drive-system of *manipulation proper* would tend to be the predominant one (see also pp. 124 ff, 126 f).

But again, depending on their sub-talents, they may take up all kinds of very different things for a living. If gross physical strength is their asset and chief source of fun, they may become laborers of various sorts, steel workers, longshoremen, storehouse workers, masons, road builders, farmhands and even farmers. If their strength lies in the delicacy with which their hands can perform, they may become watchmakers and jewellers, producers of precision instruments, radio mechanics or workers in almost any field of electronics. If they prefer, or do not mind, to produce, create, or manipulate more indirectly, if they have abstractive capacities, if they can envisage broader contexts, those with manual talents may become engineers, industrial designers, architects, even city planners, whereas those of lesser manual skill, but greater physical force, or rather of stronger desires to exercise such force, may veer toward positions of executives in industry, heads of special task forces or perhaps toward military careers. If their abstractive capacities are very pronounced, if they love best of all to manipulate entirely by "imaginary hands", so to speak, if they prefer to operate in limbo—although they themselves will argue that they are moving in a much more meaningful physical reality than that of everyday life; and in a way they are right—they may become physicists, physical chemists, astronomers or mathematicians.

The material with which they do most of their work would play a part too. Land, wood, stone, steel, water, inanimate matter, food or living beings would all have different attractions for people with different talents and different predominances in their fields of experience. With land their chief object of manipulation they may become farmers, landscapers, dealers in real estate or land speculators. Wood calls for woodcutters, carvers, carpenters, perhaps paper manufacturers and the like. Stone might turn them into quarriers, sculptors, bricklayers, roadworkers, but also into miners or geologists. With steel and metals in general they may become junk collectors, autoworkers, bridge- or ship-builders, black- and silversmiths, coin-collectors, "gold-collectors" or rather collectors of gold and derived purchasing media, i.e. bankers, etc. Water may concern them as oceans to be crossed, in waterworks, electric power dams, canalisation systems, snow in ski resorts or as meteorology. Matter or substances are being handled or transformed by druggists, chemists, miners again, perhaps applied or astronomical physicists; foods by cooks, millers, bakers, foodpackers, storekeepers, liquor-distillers, etc. Living beings are the concerns of planters and gardeners, hunters, butchers, but also of all kinds of animal-breeders—although there may be some question as to whether they properly belong here—of veterinarians, even surgeons, especially the really fanatic ones.

Relations to people, to those who figure in the task systems of society, may be another important aspect. The choice of a profession might be less determined by drive systems or the materials of manipulation than by a person's own and earlier relations to other people and the chances prevailing in a profession of repeating them. What holds for long-range relationships formed in later life, such as marriages and lasting friendships (see pp. 241 ff, 258 f), holds in part for all formal, technical or so-called incidental relationships formed at work and in business. A younger sibling will probably be more at ease with authority figures than an older one, at least in effect, especially if the authority has been an older sibling himself. Yet the older sibling may identify with, and understand, the authority figure better than the younger one. A person who has grown up in an all-male environment at home may have difficulties with female employees. He might perhaps not treat them at all like women or he might, on the other hand, think that, literally, he has to seduce them all. Sometimes he will even try to do both things at the same time. Anyway, he may find himself better off in an all-male environment, say in oil-exploration or as a sailor on freighters. Some people have learned early in life to be quite tolerant of their peers, bosses, and inferiors, whereas others are always on edges with some or all of them. Hence the latter would do better choosing a profession where interaction with other people is negligible, where they can work pretty much by themselves and at their own pace, where they need not re-enter "public life" again unless when they have something to show and where shows may take no longer than the indispensable minimum. The former, however, would do better in professions that afford them ample contact with people. They would not be tolerant of and at ease with all kinds of them, if they had not been with people a lot to begin with, and it would amount to considerable deprivation if they could not continue to do so.

But even economic conditions prevailing in certain professions may well determine a person's predilection as strongly at times as special talents would. If somebody wants to enter the food industry, but finds that half of its entire work force is unemployed, he may think it over twice before deciding. And if there is a big boom in certain professions, if everybody is buying houses these days, or crazy about "psychology", this may constitute strong incentives for people to go into the construction—or real estate—business on one hand or into psychiatry on the other. As a matter of fact, economic conditions of such kinds will always have some influence. The more uniform a population's education and talents, and the more comfortable living conditions are in general, the stronger will be that influence, relatively speaking. This will at least hold true for people whose talents are average or, at any rate, not too pronounced. That, however, tends to be the majority in almost any population on earth. The great talents, those that find their fields even blindfoldedly and against any kind of adversity, are always rare.

There is still another dimension: the degree of *overall* talent or intelligence required by a profession, and the length of time it takes to learn it. There are jobs which anybody who has hands and feet at all can fill, and others such as neurology, investment, mathematics, international relations, history, etc., that one will almost never finish learning about. In between those there are professions requiring something like any old high school education or a good one, a special school, training camps, college, a graduate school or long periods of further training, internships, and practice, far beyond the awards of graduate degrees. Somewhere, though, there tends to be an end to all learning, and ultimately a decline (see also p. 114 f). Financial compensation is usually somewhat in accordance with the amount of training required, at least under comparable circumstances, in just about any social system. The higher developed the system, the closer will be this correspondence. Hence both desires, those to earn as much money as a profession promises to pay and to engage in those activities that one likes best of all, are likely to play a role.

The professional distinctions made in this context have, of necessity, been quite crude. For one thing, the level of overall talent or intelligence required, or the amount of training necessary to engage in a profession, have not been considered explicitly. Diversification can be shown to repeat itself on different levels of professional complexity. Medicine, e.g. offers opportunities for almost any special talent and interest. A person devoted to the miracles of all those many processes, reactive and regulative, that govern the work of the body may become a physiologist, while as an anatomist he would be more concerned with the architecture of the body. He may even specialise in sculpturing the anatomical models so useful in teaching. If the micro-architecture of the body is closest to his heart, he may go into histology. If his interests concern the genesis of this architecture or the ontogenesis of life in general, he may find himself accommodated best in embryology and obstetrics. If he wants to see how illness, this omnipresent enemy of man, can devastate in many different ways whatever part of the body is most concerned, he may end up in pathological anatomy. If diagnosis and therapy of illness is his favorite, he may specialise in internal medicine, and if he wants to pursue his favorites on a lesser level, if a sprained ankle, a blister or a simple cold, is not too small an issue, if it is people above all that matter, if he wants to help them in great numbers, he may become a general practitioner, and perhaps a pediatrician, if he prefers the little ones. If people's minds, their feelings and motives, even their deep innermost secrets and strangest aberrations, attract his chief attention, he may be in for psychiatry. But even the basic modes of stimulation (see also pp. 125, 121, 78) are all represented in the field of medicine. Sight concerns the ophthalmologist, sound the otologist, "sound production" the laryngologist, taste and smell the rhinologist, touch the dermatologist and general kinesthesis, among other things, the neurologist, in a sense perhaps also the orthopedist. And as for basic *substitution continua* or drive-systems (see p. 116 ff, esp. p. 124 f) we might say that the dental surgeon is concerned with the mouth, the internist again with the trunk and the specialist of gynecology as well as the dermatologist specialised in venereal diseases with the sex-organs. This may be stretching the point, though.

Those active in the field of medicine can also choose to be teachers, if they like the contact with students and have a flare for presenting their skill and knowledge so that others can learn and understand. Or they can go into research, if they strive for greater measures of truth than most others. Or become administrators, if they want to head hospitals, their services, their research, and their staffs. Or medical consultants to very special people, problems, or institutions. If they want to go to foreign lands, travel on boats, go on expeditions, there is always a need for physicians. And if they do not want to go through the long medical training, or if they are not able to, they can still become nurses, attendants, laboratory workers, dieticians, clerks, etc.

But medicine is not the only field of endeavor where this holds true. Any science tends to need people on all levels: very high calibre professors who are so good that they do not even have to teach (that is, they rather teach other teachers at their own convenience, maybe merely by writing a book); others who are good run-of-the-mill teachers, the "average college stuff"; others who by their scientific competency are "only" good enough for highschool and less; and still others who like just to potter around in their evenings. Or take literature. There is room for the comparative historian, the expert on a particular epoch or person, the college professor, the high school teacher, the literary columnist or critic, the librarian, the simple reader, but also for the person who contributes directly to the field: the writer. A foreign language may entice one to be a top linguist, another to be a literature expert, a third one an interpreter, and still another one a language teacher in an evening school. An emigrant of that country may find that he has something to offer in the country of his present residence even though he has learned very little else. He can teach his native tongue. Or take a news-paper. It assembles politicians, local, national and international, economists, art critics, amateur artists, sports enthusiasts and even good and intelligent house-wives and mothers who can write about dishes and family chores. The news-reporter who dares warfares, iron curtains, riots, wild animals, waterfalls and what not, is another pertinent figure. But then there are printers, engineers, typists, interpreters, stenographers, clerks, truck drivers, and deliverers. There is the chief editor, the financier, the director of advertising, etc. And all of them fulfill essential functions.

We have discussed some of the very general determinants of choices of profes-sion. However, the most immediate environment—especially its ol lest, stead-fastest and mightiest components: the parents and other family members—will ordinarily be exerting the greatest influences. Not only by what they themselves desire of the person in question—and if they claim they have no such desires, there may well be one that they do not want to recognise: the desire not to have to bother—but also by what they are themselves. Their own professions, or at least certain important aspects of them, will inevitably bear on a person's own choice of profession. After all, this is what *they* have chosen. Otherwise they would not be in it. Hence it will not help the parents very much to wish for their children that they become something they have not been themselves. A child cannot very well learn how to play the piano, if neither parent has the slightest idea about that or any other musical instrument and cannot possible appreciate his efforts. Of course, there may also be no talent to speak of in the family. And if they want him to become a lawyer, what good does that do when they themselves have been ex-peddlers and grocers? If they tell him that he, the son, must go to law-school or his life will be no better than theirs, how can he dare to be better than they are? And if he does, what else should he do but fail? If, on the other hand, he has no such pangs of conscience, the parents themselves may come to hate his success. He could fail to heap all those gifts of gratitude upon them that they may have been secretly wishing for all along. He may not even visit them any longer. In fact, he may pretend not to see or know them when they run into him by accident. As for a daughter, how can she marry a good and decent fellow, a person who is intelligent, honest and can make a fine living, if mother married this no-good bum of a father? Or how can she learn a trade herself, if mother, rather than doing likewise, got married in a hurry?

There are thousands of professions. There is one for every person alive and of only moderately good health. Even more than one. And yet some people end up with no profession at all. Their deficiency is not only that of many people living in any of to-day's highly structured social systems: over-specialisation. They do not even have a decent piece of work to offer. Not that they might not be able and willing to fill a number of jobs; but those would be of the kind that takes ten minutes or less to learn to perfection. And overnight, due to a tiny shake-up in the system's economic structure or its foreign affairs, there may be no such jobs available at all. Yet if they had acquired greater and broader competencies, things could look quite different.

This is where institutional help, not in the form of emergency relief, but as adequate preparation for a fair gamut of living conditions could really make a difference. Parents may fail. It will take long before the rate of such incidents of parental failures can be lowered noticeably. Some of the people to be trained and educated may be weak in their psychological set-up, hence tending toward mental disorder and ultimate hospitalisation, at least under stress, and prevention has not reached babyhood yet. But education as an institution could nevertheless insist that its subjects learn something well, and that they learn enough of their field of work so that no changes of the tides can throw them altogether off balance. If, rather than learning that life is fun, they would learn that there is no fun without work and that work can be fun too after a while, they will find themselves better masters of all of life, including their love-life. Contrary to wide-spread beliefs that love and work are mutually exclusive it should be emphasised more skillfully that these two partners are indispensable for each other. Where they appear singly, the people in question are in a state of escape, and they cannot do both, stay in that state very long and be happy. Really happy, that is.

People who are better prepared for all vicissitudes of work will sooner or later affect their working conditions in turn. They will no longer be content with jobs that all too often even a moron could fill. Nor will they like jobs where they can do little more than daydream of all those things that they would do if only they did not have to work at all. They will begin to do something about it, not just whine for undefined changes, and this will probably be to no disadvantage of their employers and the social system as a whole. In fact, this has been, and still is, the motor of a good share of all innovations, or of "creativity at work", if you like.

Marriage and Parenthood

THE most crucial and far-reaching of all decisions that people can ordinarily make is the choice of a partner for life, especially since the kind of union they enter is highly conducive to reproduction. Sooner or later children will be born to them. The possibility of contraception makes no principal difference. A mature and unconflicted relationship between man and woman will tend to arouse or rather liberate the desire for children of their own in both of them. After all, bearing a child is the way in which a woman's "intrinsic deficiency", if we might say so, can be undone (see p. 173, also p. 213f). Unconsciously this is more than her own beauty. She is really coming to par with her man as, in early life, she had hoped in vain she could do with father. But this is also the surest way of holding on to the possession of a man. Even if he should leave her, she will retain his child. But he probably will not leave her. She did not just bear a child. She bore it *for him*. He, on the other hand, will not only wish to fulfill her desire for a child. He would desire to get one himself. He cannot bear a child, but he can make her one. He can make her respond in the most emphatic of all ways: with buds of a new life. If he is really in love with her, they will find each other in harmony on this very issue: the most primitive, intimate and complete experience of another person, as a heterosexual genital union tends to afford, should be even more complete. It should bear fruit, lasting living testimony to their moments of greatest happiness.

Partners in love or marriage do not always reach that state of abandon for each other. To the extent they do not they may fall short of the realisation of such desires. Counter-cathexes of all sorts, fear of the other sex that may sometimes even be manifest in an excessive or extravagant consumption of the other sex, fear of the future, of failing to make a living or of losing a professional position, fear of heterosexual or any genital experiences, but also vain goals such as becoming the most admired woman in town or in the country or the woman who makes the most princely of all eligible men, or becoming the top man in one's field, the strongest, the roughest, the most powerful of all, may well prevent cathexes of a person of the other sex to the points where sincere desires for children would be (re)activated too. Some wives also think that they must have more children than their friends or they would be very jealous, and some husbands are convinced that a man has to have children in order to be a man himself, especially since all it takes is just to inseminate the wife. Everything beyond that is her obligation. Even such wives and such husbands have not really and truly formed desires for children of their own. They are being egged on by artefacts and unfortunately it is the children who will get the brunt of this predicament. Sometimes, however, children may innocently teach them lessons, through their infantile charm, the "primitivity" or naivité of their concerns, their utter dependence on their parents or whatever it is.

Once there are children that have truly been desired or to which the parents have "caught on" some time after they were born, it becomes increasingly difficult for parents to give them up or separate. Difficult on two grounds. They ought not forsake their family. Their consciences tell them so. They would feel very, very bad, if they did. And if the desires of other people, of the community or of the whole social system of which they are a part, have not really become theirs, these other people, etc., will see to it that they *do* feel bad. Secondly they have begun to cathect their children vehemently even before they were born. Going-to-be mothers can feel them growing within their bellies: a very unusual, hence frightening, yet, before long, familiar experience and finally quite delightful. Fathers, in turn, can see their wives get "out of shape" or perhaps one should say: get into shape for the final fulfillment of their and their wives' most intimate desires for each other. But the real feat begins after the child has been born. There it is, at last, a tiny little person, in fact not really a person at all, a tadpole, with a body all wrinkled, and the whole thing screaming with its little and yet so penetrating voice, wriggling helplessly along with it and stopping only from mere exhaustion by falling asleep. Again this experience should be frighteningly new, at least with the first child. But once the mother had held that tiny thing, felt its touch, its tender skin, its thin limbs and fingers and the only part of it that is really active: the mouth; felt it preferably on her own breasts which, lo and behold, *do* give milk; once the mother has begun to experience her baby with all sense modalities or in all areas of stimulation and manipulation, cathexis will accumulate rapidly, facilitate increasingly all further cathexes (see p. 102ff), and as a result the mother will learn how to love it more and more dearly. The father whose contacts ordinarily tend to be somewhat less immediate and direct, will at least learn how to love the two of them, his wife with her baby, but in the past decades the husband has been getting more directly involved too. He has begun to help feed, change and entertain the baby, or at least to assist his wife, say by warming the bottles, flushing the diapers, getting up at nights or even by taking over some of the chores of running a household.

At any rate both parents' cathexes of their child will accumulate in increasing quantities and sooner or later the possibilities of further cathexes might be exhausted (see p. 103), if . . . well, if the child would not grow himself. As the child's own cathexes of the world, which includes himself, progress, there is also more and more for the parents to learn about or cathect. Changes are slow at first, but gradually they take on apparent speeds the parents would never have thought possible at first, such as when, after only one kind of food (mother's milk) and only one condition of feeding (say, being held warm and tight, one side first, then the other), the infant of one year of age distinguishes a number of foods already, deals with them in a number of different ways (by hand, spoon or mouth, munching, biting, re-inspecting, etc.) and loves all kinds of feeding situations (in bed, in the baby chair, on mother's lap, in the car, etc.); or such as when, after acquisition of a few words in the second year of life, the child's language unfolds to a state of near perfection in the third (see also p. 148ff, esp. p. 159). However, as the child becomes more of an object in their minds, which implies an increasingly integral part of their relationship to each other, the parents will be less inclined to part with it or any aspect of their family situation.

And if they stick it out, *more children* are due before long. Their arrivals and early growths will be easier to handle than before, but at the same time there will also be more to watch, experience and learn about. The newcomers are not just other children repeating what their older siblings did to their parents. Inevitably they affect the other children too. There will be rivalries, jealousies, conflicts over power, affection and even sex-roles. The parents will have to cope with all these problems and that may again be quite strenuous and difficult at first, gradually easier, and finally quite blissful. Now cathexes will accumulate in large quantities, but they will not ordinarily reach states of exhaustion. On the contrary, possibilities for further cathexis are increasing. Why? Because all children as well as the networks of relationships that they entertain with each other and with the parents will grow increasingly complex themselves. One child, e.g., will go to school, the other to kindergarten and the third one will stay home. The home situation is relieved, but school and kindergarten create problems of their own. Friends will be made and not only visited in their houses. They will pay visits in return. The little one will not want to stay home alone with his mother although the others may have envied him for precisely that privilege. The teachers will want the parents to take an interest in school. The three R's are to be acquired. The little one, however, may not let the oldest do his homework. He may want to play with his siblings instead, while the middle one insists on learning the R's prematurely. In defense one may hit the other and the third one might go tattling.

Well, all parents will know what kinds of endless fusses I mean. Yet the children too learn about their conditions of home life and its extensions on the playground, in school, in little clubs and the like, and they also learn what it is that their parents want them to do. Gradually the fusses become fun and everybody in the family may be having a good time. This is, at least, what it looks like in retrospect and what becomes painfully apparent whenever losses have struck. Life with one's children gets more and more complicated as the parents learn how to handle them better and better, and it never gets boring, at least in the majority of all cases. Their children are growing up all between and around them.

Prospects may well be different with a childless couple. Although man is the most complex object in the world, the one offering satisfactions to the largest number and variety of desires, and although it may take years for a happily married couple to exhaust each other, to reach the point where nothing new is happening to them any longer, boredom will eventually loom. This is particularly likely with people of neither outstanding talents nor outstanding obligations, especially when they are rich. Yet even the most gifted persons, those interested in or committed to great and fascinating tasks, may well get tired of their spouses one day. A younger woman may catch such a husband's attention. She may not be up to him or his wife in all kinds of aspects, but she is beautiful, childish, extravagant or even admitting what she wants from him: an easy life or even just his money! And the wife may fall for a younger man, for his enthusiasm, fervor, abandon, devotion or whatever she calls it. It does not matter that he is entirely without means and spending every penny that he finds jingling in his pocket. Small wonder that he is always in need of funds. He shall have them, even if she has to sell her jewels. Because one day the two of them will elope together, that's what he promised, and in a distant town they may settle down for good. She does not know yet that he will not even show up at the station of departure.

There are brakes, however, working for both types of couples, those with children and those without them. They derive from the process of aging, not so much in the physical sense as in the sense outlined in a previous chapter (see p. 114f). Its most general characteristic is something like the eventual decline of the overall rate of cathexis by which a given individual operates. As he grows older, a person's zest for new aspects of the world, people and himself, to learn about or cathect diminishes. He gets "tired". His "energy" is beginning to give out. He becomes increasingly fond of routines, of the accustomed, and reluctant of adventures, even mild ones. At this stage parents are *no longer* so reluctant to let their children go off by themselves, become independent, set up their own homes and professions, even take over the business, an estate, a firm, etc., from them. And childless couples may find themselves content with what they have after all. It begins to look too cumbersome to start all over with a new person. Too much has been going on between the two of them and, what is more, things are running smoothly and comfortably. If there have to be digressions, why not satisfy them in non-committal ways, with a passing flirt, a hotel-room affair, a semi-business relation or the like.

Is all this not saying that people and their affairs tend to be just right as they are? And is that not trivial? Well, it was probably just as trivial to claim that man must eat, eliminate and propagate in order to be a potential subject of our study, let alone survive. And yet we have seen, I hope, that a fairly elaborate and powerful theoretical system can be derived from these, and a few more, principal assumptions (see p. 116 ff, also p. 6 ff). Everybody knows, of course, that marriage and parenthood is something tremendously important. But not everybody will feel quite so sure about the *details* of this "fact" on the basis of common sense alone. As a matter of fact, even the playwrights and novelists of all times and cultures, although greatly preoccupied with the vicissitudes of courtship and love and thereby underlining implicitly the importance and irrevocability of the decision to marry, have usually tended to stop right there. They might show how their heroes came to be what they are. They might show from what family backgrounds they have sprung and developed, although sometimes they are made orphans and foundlings for the sake of simplicity. And sometimes the heroes die, but more often they "marry". Next they "live happily ever after".

There are very many ways of "living happily ever after". In fact, we ourselves are already the products of what this meant for our parents. If I have really dwelled on the trivial in this chapter, perhaps we could, on the basis of our theory, try to make up for it and embark on some further elaborations of the fact that marriage is a very important and consequential event indeed (see also Toman 1959a, b, c).

There are many ways in which a person can be characterised. We could describe his looks, his apparel, his ethnic background, etc., but also his actions and thoughts in all kinds of contexts, say jobs, acquaintances, hobbies, diaries, philosophies or entertainments. We could write as much as a book about him or try to pinpoint him in a few poetic sentences. If however, we want to characterise a person relevantly, succinctly and with a minimum of effort, we should attempt to do so in terms of the most comprehensive and powerful of his determinants. Furthermore, if people are the most complex and, at the same time, the most indispensable of all objects, as has been suggested before (see p. 12f), and if a person is likely to be influenced the most, among all objects that might have effects on him, by other persons, people may well be these strongest and most comprehensive determinants.

Which people ? Those, of course, who have lived with a person the longest, most intimately, and most regularly. This includes those who have stopped doing so for good from some point on in a person's life. In other words, a person can be characterised relevantly, succinctly and with a minimum of effort by the people who have been living with him the longest, most intimately and most regularly, and by all incidental losses of such people. This will above all concern the parents and siblings. The people who have lived with him, in turn, can be characterised relevantly, succinctly and with a minimum of effort by the people who have been living with *them* the longest, most intimately and most regularly, and by the losses of such people. This will primarily concern the parents, although the people who have lived with them as indicated (their siblings and their parents) are usually no longer around. A person's siblings need no further attentions. They are part of a person's given family constellation.

And by what comprehensive, powerful, unambiguous and easy-to-obtain criteria can we say something relevant about any one of the people that constitute a person's family constellation ? Well, to make the game simple, let us distinguish only whether such a person is male or female, a characteristic the significance of which can hardly be overestimated, and whether he is the first-, second-, third-born, etc. of altogether one, two, three, etc. children.

That is to say that in order to characterise a person relevantly, succinctly and with a minimum of effort, we should know the skeleton of his family constellation, the order and the sexes of his siblings, something about the characters of their parents and all incidental losses that the person in question has suffered. And in order to characterise the parents, one should know the order and sexes of *their* siblings and at least whether their parents existed or not, psychologically speaking; furthermore all incidental losses that have been suffered.

These *data* will also permit an estimate of the kind of marriage that a person's parents have had, and this too is a basic and powerful characteristic. As a matter of fact, it may be the most powerful of all, since it provides the general psychological milieu, the matrix in which he grows up. But these *data* will also determine a person's own choice of a partner for life and the kind of success he can make of it or the degree of happiness he will achieve. And this, in turn, will determine the milieu or matrix in which his and her children shall grow up, but ultimately even the children's own choices of a partner for life and their own chances of happiness and success in marriage. The final criterion for a happy and successful marriage is the happiness and success of the marriage that its children will eventually be able to enter and maintain. Which should not mean that there are no signs long before that. We can often make predictions of the happiness and success of a marriage even before it is concluded, provided that no unusual circumstances prevail among all those *data* that we ignore at the time.

In order to do that, let us spell out an assumption that follows from another one made earlier (see p. 30). That assumption was that all pertinent cathexes and counter-cathexes formed so far determine how given situations will be perceived, i.e. cathected and counter-cathected. The new assumption is this: *An extra-familial (non-incestuous) heterosexual relationship will tend to have better chances of happiness and success, other things being equal, the closer it duplicates for both partners the earliest intra-familial (incestuous) patterns set for heterosexual relationships.* The same would, *mutatis mutandis*, hold for relationships among persons of the *same sex* or, generally speaking, for *any* kind of *interpersonal relationship*.

A person can be the first, second, third, etc., child of altogether one, two, three, etc., children and sexes may be distributed in many different ways. Varying only position and sex will allow for four different sibling configurations with only two children (male–male, male–female, female–male, female–female), for eight with three, sixteen with four, etc.

Expressed in more formal ways, the number of different configurations (c_n) of n children will be this (see formula 10):

$$c_n = 2^n \tag{10}$$

The same holds for each of a person's parents. Either may theoretically come from any one of 2^n sibling configurations. The number of different types of matches (m_n) that they can enter is expressed by formula (11), provided that both of them have had the same number of siblings.

$$m_{n,n} = (n\,2^{n-1})^2 \qquad (11)$$

If they do not, the formula would have to read like this (see formula 12):

$$m_{n_1,n_2} = n_1\,n_2\,2^{n_1+n_2-2} \qquad (12)$$

whereby n_1 would be the number of children in one parent's family, and n_2 in the other's.

The same relationships would prevail for any marriage that the person in question may enter with another person in question. Their match will be one of $n_a n_b 2^{n_a+n_b-2}$ types of possible matches and all of them would tend to be distinguishably different from each other. However, since the person in question may be the child of any one of $n_1 n_2 2^{n_1+n_2-2}$ types of matches, all of which would again be distinguishably different from each other and have differential effects on their children, we should actually say that a given couple's match is one of a much larger number of possible types. See formula (13) for the precise relationship:

$$m_{a,b} = (n_a n_b n_{1_a} n_{1_b} n_{2_a} n_{2_b})\,2^{n_a+n_b+n_{1_a}+n_{1_b}+n_{2_a}+n_{2_b}-6} \qquad (13)$$

Practically speaking, however, the parents' influences will tend to be diluted as long as a person has one or more siblings. Therefore formula (12) will usually be sufficient. Only with persons who have been single children, formula (13) will be imperative and, at the same time, not too difficult to manage, since both expressions, $n_a 2^{n_a-1}$ and $n_b 2^{n_b-1}$, are equal to 1.

It has been demonstrated that two children can come in four different configurations, three in eight, four in sixteen, etc., if no more than birth-order and sex are being considered. As for marriage matches it has been shown that there would be 16 different types, if both partners come from families of two children only, 144, if both partners come from families of three children, 1024, if they come from families of four children, etc. In other words, the number of different types of matches is the product of the number of sibling configurations that each partner may possibly have. In order to demonstrate the meaning of all this we shall pursue the 16 possible matches of marriage partners coming from families of two children each, and appraise their chances of happiness and success by the degree to which they duplicate already established intra-familial or incestuous interpersonal relationships. We shall assume that no unusual circumstances prevail.

If an older brother of a sister marries the younger sister of a brother, their chances of making a success of it would tend to be optimal. They are unlikely to get into conflicts over their seniority rights. He is used to a girl his junior and she to a boy her senior. And both of them are used to the other sex.

If an older brother of a sister chooses the older sister of a brother, things would not be quite so good. Both of them are used to the other sex, but each would try to be the older one for the spouse and to transform him or her into a younger sibling. There will be rivalries over their seniority rights, but once they have children, preferably of both sexes, they may henceforth be happy with each other. At last they have got their "younger siblings".

If an older brother of a sister marries the older sister of a sister, they would also tend to have conflicts over seniority rights. Both were "superior" to their siblings in childhood. But the wife would also have some difficulty accepting her man. After all, they had been three girls in her family (mother, sister and she herself), with only one male, father, to share. If they did not want to get into each other's hair, they had to learn how to like each other regardless of the man in the family. They had to become somewhat more "homosexual". Sometimes, of course, especially if they could not work out such a solution, the girl may be only too anxious to get a man of her own; which, by the way, is not the best condition for making such an important decision.

If an older brother of a sister marries the younger sister of a sister, they may have no problems over seniority. The wife would be used to having a sibling her senior and her husband to having one his junior. Yet she may not be too used to having a man.

Similar arguments could be raised for an older brother of a brother who marries the older sister of a brother or of a sister, or the younger sister of a brother or of a sister. Now, however, it is he who would tend to have trouble accepting the woman. The match with the least promise of success among these four would be the marriage of an older brother of a brother to an older sister of a sister. Both of them would have troubles accepting the other sex and in addition they would tend to be in conflicts over their seniority rights. As soon as they get children, however, they have their longed-for "juniors" and may be happier, although there will be a tendency for him to gang up with the boys against the girls and for her to do so with her daughters.

Similar conditions would also prevail for a younger brother of a sister who marries the younger sister of a brother or of a sister, or the older sister of a brother or of a sister. Among these there is one combination that would come close to an optimal one, namely the marriage between a younger brother of a sister and an older sister of a brother, although there will be a touch of a reverse authority relationship, i.e. of a dominant wife and a dependent husband.

Finally the younger brother of a brother may marry the older sister of a brother or of a sister, or the younger sister of a brother or of a sister. Other things being equal, the worst of these and, at the same time, the worst of all sixteen combinations would be the match between a younger brother of a brother and a younger sister of a sister. Both of them would have trouble accepting the other sex and they would be in conflict over their juniority rights. Both want older siblings. Therefore not even a child of their own would make a difference, as it does with an older brother of a brother who marries the older sister of a sister. In fact, they would not want one in the first place, and if they happen to get one, that may well be the end of it. Since they are so much in need of an older sibling, they will even tend to forge their child into such a role at the earliest possible time, and that means trouble.

Fortunately for life in general families do not only have two, but also three, four, five, etc. children and sometimes only one. In cases of $n > 2$ we can claim that these schematic relationships outlined above would tend to hold at least for the oldest and youngest siblings, while those in between would usually learn in their childhoods how to assume double and multiple roles. Consequently they should be somewhat better prepared for all eventualities of match-making than the oldest or youngest siblings are, although the latter may well be more exuberantly happy when they do make their optimal of all possible types of choices. Their happiness is somewhat more difficult to achieve, but it may be "deeper", if there is such a thing.

To pursue this a little further, let us introduce a simple system of designation. Let us call an older brother of a girl $b(g)$, the younger brother of a boy $(b)b$, the middle sister of an older brother and younger sister $(b)g(g)$. Let us symbolize a marriage (or any dual relationship for that matter) by a $/$.

> Example 1: $(g)b/(g)g(b)$, which means that the younger brother of a sister has married a middle sister of an older sister and a younger brother.
>
> Example 2: $b(g, g)/(g, g)g(g)$, which means that the older brother of two girls is married to the second-youngest of altogether four girls.
>
> Example 3: $(b, g)b(g)/(b)g(b, g)$, which means that the husband has had an older brother, an older sister and a younger sister, while the wife has had an older brother, a younger brother and a younger sister.

Let us see how we might inspect these matches for the degree of compatibility that they represent.

In example 1 the marriage duplicates completely for the husband what he had at home, whereas it does so only in part for the wife. She had two sibling relationships. She was an older sister to a brother, but also a younger sister to a sister. Therefore she should have a partial sex conflict. The two girls had to vie for their brother's affection. And she should have a partial rank conflict. She would also want to be the younger one to somebody older, which her husband is not apt to be.

In example 2 the husband has been used to girls. He had had two at his disposal, whereas his sisters are likely to have been rivals for his attention. The wife, on the other hand, would tend to have a full sex conflict. She is not used to male "peers" at all. And she would have a small rank conflict. Although she is used to somebody older (she has had two seniors), she would also want to some extent to be the older one herself.

In example 3 we find a more complex specimen of an optimal match again. The husband is in precisely the complementary position to his wife. A test of this could be made in the following fashion: reverse one of the spouses' rank order and convert all sexes in that spouse's sibling configuration including his or her own: $(b, g)b(g)/(b)g(b, g)$ will read like this after reversal of rank order: $(b, g)b(g)/(g, b)b(b)$, and like this after conversion of sexes: $(b, g)b(g)/(b, g)g(g)$. If the two expressions are identical, the match is optimal by the criteria under consideration. On analogous grounds a match such as $(g, g)b/g(b, b)$ would be optimal too.

At any rate, example 3 shows a husband who has been a junior to a brother and sister and a senior to a sister, whereas his wife has been a junior to a brother and a senior to a brother and a sister. She is somewhat more of a senior herself, we might say, and he somewhat more of a junior than the other. Since even sibling configurations like those of example 3 tend to split up into sub-configurations, into two couples each, we could also say that the husband is the older one of the younger couple and his wife the younger one of the older couple. There is a two-way complementarity of ranks which would tend as a result to yield no rank conflicts. A somewhat different match such as $b(g, b, g)/(b)g(b, g)$ would show more of a rank conflict. If it were not for the last two siblings of either spouse, their match would be perfect. With the younger siblings, however, the husband has been a senior to three others and the wife to two others. Hence both of them may also want to be seniors for each other to some extent, although the wife has learned to be junior to one. This couple, incidentally, would tend to be more anxious than the other to have children that could take the roles of their missing juniors.

If a match is only partially optimal, if other relationships than those duplicated in a marriage have existed in the spouses' sibling configurations, the degree of dilution can be expressed as a function of the number of relationships to siblings that each spouse brought into the marriage. This, in turn, can be determined conveniently by the number of "surplus figures" that remain after sex and rank of one spouse have been transformed and "subtracted" on both sides of the expression. Example 1, $(g)b/(g)g(b)$, transformed for rank: $(g)b/(b)g(g)$, transformed for sex: $(g)b/(g)b(b)$, leaves $b(b)$, or rather, "re-translated", $(g)g$, as remainder. If the husband had a younger sister in addition, and the wife an older brother, our two transformations, starting from $(g)b(g)/(b,g)g(b)$, would yield $(g)b(g)/(b)g(b, b)$ and finally $(g)b(g)/(g)b(b, g)$. This would also leave $b(b)$, or, re-translated, $(g)g$, as remainder, since $(g)b(g)$ is duplicated on the right. Compared to example 1, however, dilution should be smaller. Of three (in general: $n - 1$) sibling relationships that the wife has had, two are perfect matches for the sibling relationships of the partner, whereas only one of the two sibling relationships that the wife has had in example 1 is matched by her partner. Or of altogether five sibling relationships that the spouses brought into their marriage, only one found no duplicate, whereas in example 1 the same was true of altogether three such relationships.

What happens if a match is not even partially optimal, if the marriage relationship does not duplicate any of the spouses' sibling relationships? Well, example 2 would be one. Transforming sex and rank $b(g, g)/(g, g)g(g)$ will yield $b(g, g)/(g)g(g, g)$ and finally $b(g, g)$ $(b)b(b, b)$, and "subtraction" will not change a thing. In other words, the "remainder" will be $b(g, g)/(b)b(b, b)$ before re-translation. None of altogether five sibling relationships that the spouses brought into their marriage found a duplicate there. Yet with the same numbers of siblings things could even be worse. If example 2 would change to $b(b, b)/$ $g(g, g, g)$, two transformations will yield $b(b, b)/(b, b, b)b$ before re-translation, which symbolises a complete rank- and sex-conflict. If the example would change to $b(g, g)/$ $g(b, b, b)$, two transformations will yield $b(g, g)/(g, g, g)b$, which would indicate a rank conflict, but no sex conflict. And if it would change to $b(g, g)/(b, g)g(g)$, transformation to $b(g, g)/(b)b(b, g)$ indicates that we are dealing with a partially optimal match again, the remainder being $b(g)/(b)b(b)$, or rather $b(g)/(g)g(g)$ after re-translation.

In general we could say that a couple both partners of which have a rank- and a sex-conflict will be the worst off. If only one partner does not have a sex- or rank-conflict, things may already be a little better. He or she can help the other overcome difficulties in matters of rank or the other sex. This will be even more true if one partner has no conflict at all. If one partner has only a sex conflict and the other a rank conflict (which, incidentally, can only be a partial one, since a full rank conflict is mutual), they could help each other. And if only one partner has only one type of conflict and the other none, things are already pretty good.

This, however, may be worth still another more articulate formulation, especially since all sibling configurations with $n > 2$ may make for some dilution of the conflict involved. A person's sex conflicts will have to be multiplied by d_s, the coefficient of sex distribution, expressed by the number of same-sex siblings over the number of siblings (see formula 14):

$$d_s = \frac{n_s}{n - 1} \tag{14}$$

In formula (14) n_s would be the number of same-sex siblings of the person in question, and n the number of children that constitute his or her sibling configuration. Hence in a marriage of, say, $b(g, b)$ and $(b)g$, the husband would have half of a sex-conflict, whereas in $b(b, b)/(b)g$ his sex-conflict would be one, and in $b(g, g)/(b)g$ it would be zero. In $b(b, b, g)/$ $(b)g$ his sex-conflict would be two-thirds, and the same would be true of $b(g, b, b)/(b)g$, although proximity of the sister might well make some difference in practice. In $b(g, g, g, g)/$ $(b)g$ the husband's sex conflict would also be zero. But is that true? Must it not get increasingly difficult for him to get married, the larger the number of sisters for which he is the lone wolf? We shall see later (p. 246) how such dilution of an optimal match can be appraised. If the wife should have sex-conflicts too, it would add to the trouble already existent. We might say that the degree of overall sex-conflict that prevails in a marriage is perhaps well expressed by formula (15):

$$d_{s_m} = d_{s_h} + d_{s_w} \qquad (15)$$

whereby d_{s_h} is the husband's sex-distribution coefficient and d_{s_w} the wife's. The maximum value of d_{s_m} is 2.

Similar considerations would hold for rank conflicts. If there is one at all, it would have to be multiplied by d_r, the coefficient of rank-distribution, expressed by the difference between the number of junior and the number of senior siblings over the number of siblings of the person in question (see formula 16):

$$d_r = \frac{n_{jun} - n_{sen}}{n - 1} \qquad (16)$$

In formula (16) n_{jun} is the number of siblings that are juniors to the person in question, and n_{sen} the number of siblings that are senior. If d_r is positive, we are dealing with a person who is more of a senior him- or herself. If d_r is negative, he or she is more of a junior. The absolute value of d_r indicates how much. Thus $(b)b(g, b)$ would have a value of $d_r = 0.33$, and $(b, g)g$ a value of $d_r = -1$. The man would be somewhat of a senior, and the woman a complete junior. In analogy to formula (15) the overall rank-conflict that would prevail if those two, or any two for that matter, got married would be d_{r_m} (see formula 17):

$$d_{r_m} = d_{r_h} + d_{r_w} \qquad (17)$$

Therefore $(b)b(g, b)/(b, g)g$ would have an overall rank conflict of $d_{r_m} = -0.67$, i.e. a certain degree of juniority conflict. Similarly $b(g, b, g)/g(b, g)$ would have an overall rank conflict of $+2$ (which is the maximum of a seniority conflict), whereas, say, $(g)b/(b)g$ would have -2, the maximum of a juniority conflict; $b(g)/(b)g$ would be zero in rank conflict, and so would be, say, $(b, g)b(g)/(g)g(b, b)$.

Another kind of conflict will result from the fact that marriage, at least in most parts of the civilised world, is a relationship between no more than two people, whereas sibling configurations may, within reason, be composed of any number of persons (n). Hence marriage will, for many people, differ in number from the "peers" they had at home. The discrepancy coefficient (d_n) expresses the relationship (see formula 18):

$$d_n = \frac{n - 2}{n} \qquad (18)$$

In formula (18) the numerator should actually be $n - n_m$, whereby n_m would be the number of people that constitute a marriage. But as long as neither polygamy, polyandry, nor any combination of the two, are customary, formula (18) is sufficient. Single children will, of course, show negative values. They get literally more in marriage than they had at home. With spouses having one sibling only, d_n will be zero. The larger n, the closer will d_n approximate 1.

For a marriage as a whole overall discrepancy in number would be expressed by d_{n_m}, the discrepancy coefficient of husband and wife together (see formula 19):

$$d_{n_m} = |d_{n_h}| + |d_{n_w}| \qquad (19)$$

Thus with 2 being the asymptotic maximum of d_{n_m}, a match such as $b(b)/(g)g$ will represent a discrepancy of zero, $b(g, g, g, g)/(b)g$ one of 0.60, $b(g, g)/(b, b)g$ one of 0.67, and $b(g, g, g, g)/(b, b, g)g$ one of 1.10, whereas $b/(b, b)g$ would be equal to 1.33.

Coefficients d_r and d_n might, as a reasonable alternative, be computed from the same-sex siblings only, rather than from all siblings, particulary when d_s is being considered anyway.

A compound estimate of rank-and-sex conflict prevailing in a particular match is expressed by formula (20):

$$d_{s_m, r_m} = \frac{d_{s_m} + |d_{r_m}|}{2} \qquad (20)$$

If discrepancy in number (d_n) is to be included too, the estimate of all conflict (d_t) existent in a given marriage is expressed by formula (21):

$$d_t = d_{s_m, r_m, n_m} = \frac{d_{s_m} + |d_{r_m}| + d_{n_m}}{3} \tag{21}$$

The maximum values of both d_{s_m, r_m} and d_t are equal to 2, although d_t will approach it only asymptotically. The minimum values are zero.

We shall see later on how losses of siblings and parents, for that matter, can be treated, either in their own rights or as aggravators of already existent conflicts. Yet how can formulas (14) to (21) be applied when, say, a sibling has been lost at a certain time of a person's life? Including it would ignore the loss. Excluding it would ignore the sibling while he was existent. Well, interpolation would obviously be a solution. Interpolated values of d_s, d_r, d_n, etc. could be computed as the means of d_s, d_r, d_n, etc. before the loss and thereafter. These values could even be weighted in proportion to the time lived with a sibling as against the time lived without him. But the simple mean and sometimes even one of the alternatives, may often be sufficient.

Children are more the parents' product, psychologically speaking, than anybody else's. Parents will tend to affect them basically in ways deriving from what kinds of people they are. Their sibling configurations will, in turn, be very important determinants. For all these reasons it may often be found desirable to include the parents explicitly in our computations. "Algebraically" this could be done, say, by writing the husband's parents' sibling configuration on one side and that of the wife's parents' on the other side of the "equation" that represents the couple in question.

Hence $b(g)/g(b)//b(g)/(b)g//b(g)/(g)g$ would mean that the husband's father was the older brother of a sister and had been married to the older sister of a brother, whereas the wife's parents had been the older brother of a sister and the younger sister of a sister. Subtracting identical relationships on identical sides of each expression for two adjacent matches at a time will yield $O/g(b)//O/(b)g$ and $O/(b)g//O/(g)g$ as remainders. The relative number of zeros will indicate the degree to which the match of the couple in question duplicates their parents' matches and the remainders the types of conflicts that prevail. Another example, $b(g)/(b)g(g)//b(b)/g(b,g)//(g)b/g(b)$, will yield $b(g)/(b)g$, $O//b(b)/g(b),O$, and $b(b)/O, g(g)//(g)b/O$.

Another important aspect will be the conflicts that have existed among the parents themselves. They can be appraised by transforming sexes and ranks on the same side of each match and subtracting identical relationships within each match. Thus the first example will yield $b(g)/(g)b//b(g)/b(g)//b(g)/b(b)$ and, after subtraction, $b(g)/(g)b//O/O//b(g)/b(b)$ before re-translation, indicating that the couple in question was optimally matched, but that they have inherited conflicts from their parents. The second example would yield $b(g)/(b)b(g)//b(b)/(b, g)b//(g)b/(g)b$ and $O/(b)b,O//b(b)/(b,g)b//O/O$, which shows something of an opposite: the parents have been well matched, whereas the couple in question is in for sex- and rank-conflicts.

The same would hold for all formulas with which the degree of rank-, sex-, and number-conflicts can be appraised. The parents may be included. In fact, they ought to be. The coefficients d_{s_m, r_m} (formula 20) or d_t (formula 21) should be computed for both sets of parents and a quarter of their sum-total added to the value computed for the couple in question.

The single child has only his parents to draw on, so to speak. This does not mean that children from other sibling constellations do *not* draw on their parents. On the contrary, parents are the most important people in any child's life. Psychologically speaking they sometimes manage to change their children's seniority-juniority relationships and even their sexes. As a matter of fact, circumstances other than the parents such as looks, talents, handicaps, etc., may also interfere, but we have ruled them out for the time being and expect them to cancel each

R

other with larger groups of cases. What happens in families with two, three, four, etc. children, however, is that they tend to turn to each other for what they cannot get from their parents. If the parents are happy with each other, they are prone, psychologically, to move into their children's backgrounds. It is easy to come to terms with such parents. Hence the siblings will become relatively stronger determinants. Only parents who are unhappy with each other may keep their children anxiously focused on them, i.e. unable to find even fair satisfactions with each other.

Well, normally the single child is in that position even with happy parents. We might say that such a family is already a mildly deficient one. The child has only his parents to turn to. He does not learn what children of larger families can learn from their parents: how to treat children. He or she is the only one around who is being treated as a child. Therefore singletons may rather look for a father or mother in a potential spouse than for a sibling and more often than others be content without children of their own. They want to remain the children themselves. Under certain conditions, however, such as when he, the only child, marries the younger of two sisters, they may break out of it and have children of their own, even ambitious numbers of them. Younger siblings of same-sex seniors tend to be diffusely, hence restlessly, competitive. The diffusion derives from the fact that they do not quite seem to know what they want. Why don't they, incidentally? Or another question first: What *might* they want? Well, to outdo their older siblings, preferably once and for all. And the safest way of achieving that would be to have them disappear, to drive them into non-existence. And why don't they know that this may be what they want? Because they have never had a time when their older siblings actually were non-existent, whereas their older siblings have certainly seen such times. Therefore they would tend to be much surer of what they want and also much more specific about repressing their desire for abolition of the second-born. Therefore the older sibling will be inclined to have just as many children as he, or she, and the spouse desire and feel they can care for, whereas the younger one may well find no end to his attempts of outdoing the senior sibling.

It has been indicated already that consideration of the parents' sibling configurations is imperative with the only child (see above). There is nothing else to go by in terms of our skeleton criteria. If the parents are optimally matched, the child will tend to learn through identification to assume the sibling role of the same-sex parent. That is to say that an only child, a girl, may grow up to behave somewhat like the younger sister of a brother, if that is what mother had been in her childhood and since. If parents have entered their marriage with sex- and rank-conflicts, or both, their only child is likely to get the brunt of it. Two, three, and more children would also tend to be affected and less able to consume each other, so to speak, but then the mere existence of their siblings might appreciably mitigate the situation. In the worst of all cases, entailing conflicts over sex and rank in both parents, with both of them having been juniors to older siblings, the parents would be inclined to confuse their child as to his sex-role, hence to make him basically afraid of marriage and to transform him into an older sibling. This he cannot possibly be at first, but he will try to catch on to it at the earliest possible moment. He will pretend to be much more mature than he is or can be. But underneath he will perhaps be as much of a younger sibling as both of his parents have been and still are. The same would hold for a girl.

The reader may note that a single child could be represented symbolically by the "equation" of his parents which, however, should be put in special parentheses. A single child's marriage may be represented, e.g., by $[b(g)/(b)g]/(b)g$, which, incidentally, would be an optimal match. The only child's parents have been perfectly fitted for each other. Therefore he will learn from his father how to be like an older brother of a sister, and he is married to the younger sister of a brother. Among the worst possible matches would be the following: $[(b)b/(g)g]/(g)g$, or even $[(b)b/(g)g]/[(b)b/(g)g]$; in words: the match between an only child of a younger brother of a brother married to the younger sister of a sister, and the younger sister of a sister; or the same only child married to another only child with precisely the same predicament. In the latter, and a few other, cases it may be convenient to indicate explicitly the sexes of the person in question. This could be done like this: $[(b)b/b/(g)g]/[(b)b/g/(g)g]$ (see also p. 256 ff).
A single child could also be appraised by the kinds and amounts of conflict (over sex, rank, and number) that prevailed among his parents. Formulas (15, 17, 19, 20, 21) could all be used to do so. In cases of optimal matches among the parents the same-sex parent's sibling configuration may substitute for the single child's missing one. We can assume that he or she, will tend to grow more after his father or after her mother, respectively, than anyone else.

It may be important to consider the age spans between siblings in addition to their mere ranks. This could be symbolized by indices such as $(b_9, g_2)g(b_6, g_8)$, whereby the numbers refer to the age differences in years from the age of the person in question, or a semi-colon could serve to signify all differences of more than five years: $(b; g)g(; b, g)$. Any interval of, say, six years or more will be a sufficiently severe incision to separate the siblings involved, e.g. to make something like single children of two siblings, or two pairs of altogether four, perhaps even if the first pair may be two boys and the second two girls. As a matter of fact, other things such as looks, talents, handicaps, etc. (as mentioned p. 247), but also the social strata to which the parents belong, their ethnic backgrounds, their race, etc., let alone all specific events and individual experiences, would certainly matter. Ranks and sexes of siblings, however, as well as the sibling configurations of the parents and their bearings on marriage would tend, in general and as a whole, to be incomparably more decisive and powerful characteristics than those, at least with groups of cases where particular circumstances would either be uniform or make up for each other.

There is one more characteristic, however, that must be included by all means: losses. Any person who is a constituent of a given family constellation may one day drop out for good. Death or its equivalents such as divorce, chronic mental illness or simple desertion, might ask their toll. Not that temporary losses, i.e. absences for months or years at a time, would not matter too. But they will tend to be milder. The victim can ultimately "latch on" to where he left off, although

people who have suffered final losses usually do not go entirely without substitutes either. Yet the others get their original objects back.

There are other traumatic conditions such as accidents, surgical operations,
seductions, physical attacks, etc. They may not even appear as losses on first
glance, although they always are, no matter how negligible. An accident or
surgery may leave a scar or nothing where formerly there was something, say
the tonsils. Both may involve separations from home, i.e. hospitalisation, and
being handicapped physically or even orally for some time after. Both may imply
pain, thus depriving temporarily the desire to be painfree from the incessant
satisfaction that usually characterises it (see also p. 21). And both will teach the
victim that such things are possible. They have occurred and they may occur
again. Hence a tendency will result to avoid situations that could conceivably
lead to such things again, and that is loss. As a mattter of fact, all counter-
cathexis that has become necessary involves learning how to learn no more (see
p. 23f). It establishes that there has been a loss, indeed, whether this is objectively
true or not. Psychologically it is true by definition.

As for seductions and physical attacks the same reasoning would hold. If an
uncle, a neighbor, a neighbor's child, can make one do things that must not be
done, that person will have to be avoided, even though it had been terribly
thrilling, wicked and so on. If there is no guilt, of course, seductions may lead to
further seductions and active seducing in turn. Then, however, there would be
no loss, technically speaking. And if one discovers that a dear person is capable of
great anger and violence, the victim will learn how to avoid, or how not to
provoke, such situations. That too is equivalent to establishing a loss of certain
aspects of a person or of a person as a whole, especially if it has not been such a
dear (i.e. familiar and close) person to begin with.

Yet all these traumata are usually small compared to final losses. It is still
better to have a father who sometimes is drunk, violent or very, very impatient,
than to have no father at all. I remember a case conference dealing with a young
woman complaining about frigidity who, when about five years old, had been
thrown out of the window by her father because the house was on fire. This had
been interpreted by her (young) psychotherapist as an act of violence that the
little girl must have construed to contain a sexual, or more specifically a genital,
meaning besides. This was what father could do to her or what she, in her unconscious desires for him, may have wished him to do. There was even an intimation that the girl may have wished for fire to be around the house, "the fire of
passion perhaps", the psychotherapist ventured to surmise. Since it all ended
in violence and (minor) burns, she must have concluded that this is what sex is
about. Hence her frigidity. In the course of treatment it turned out, though, that
father had seen to it that the mild damage which the fire had done to the house
was repaired, but that he had left a few months later for another woman considerably younger than the girl's mother and that this development of things must
have been heavily in the making by the time of the fire. His departure had been

impending and he left for good. Mother became a forsaken woman, and she herself, her child, could only learn from her how to be a woman. A forsaken woman, that is, a woman without a man (see also p. 183ff). These facts were obviously more powerful than the incident of violence. This incident could have been interpreted by the patient as a perfectly reasonable thing, as a sign of father's love for her, if only he had loved her. But instead he left.

Death or its equivalents are the most powerful losses a person can suffer. So powerful are they, that even losses that only a person's parents suffered and that did not affect him directly, such as those of his parents' parents or their siblings, may still bear on him. An important aspect of what he experiences and thinks of such a loss will always be how the parents and even his own siblings take it. As for general rules we can say that losses will be severer in their effects—although not necessarily in their conscious experiences—and more conducive to subsequent psychopathology, the closer they cut into a person's immediate family, the earlier they do so, the smaller the family in which they do so, the greater the number of losses that have occurred before, the more they have moved the balance of sexes in the family toward disequilibrium, and the longer the responsible survivors took to secure a full-fledged substitute.

Let us try to capture some of these rules in a more articulate expression (see formulas 22, 23, 24).

$$l = \sum_{i=1}^{n_i} l_i \tag{22}$$

$$l_i = \frac{1}{-\log(k)} \tag{23}$$

$$k = \frac{a_l\, t}{a_o\, a\sqrt{a(\bar{n} - 1)}} \tag{24}$$

In these formulas (22, 23, 24) l stands for the overall cumulative loss a person has suffered; l_i stands for any one of n_l individual losses that a person has suffered; k is the measure of each individual loss. As for the determinants of k, a_l is the age of the person lost, a_o the age of the oldest person in the immediate family. The ratio a_l/a_o could be called the age coefficient. The length of time that the lost person has lived with the person in question is represented by t; a is the person's own age. All of the determinants of k can be measured in years for the time at which the loss occurred. The number of persons that constitute the family (parents plus siblings plus the person in question) is represented by n.

In order to take into account what a given loss has done to the balance of sexes in the family, l_i should be multiplied by the reciprocal of c, whereby c is the change-of-sex-balance coefficient (see formulas 25 and 26).

$$c = 1 - (s_b - s_a) \tag{25}$$

$$s = \frac{n_{s_l}}{\bar{n}} \tag{26}$$

In formula (25) s_a stands for s after occurrence of the loss and s_b for s before the loss. In formula (26) s is the sex-balance coefficient, n_s is the number of persons in the family (including parents, siblings, and the person in question) that are of the lost person's sex, and $\bar{n}$ the number of persons that constitute the family. Perfect balance will yield an $s = 0.5$. The closer c approximates l, the smaller the effect of the loss in question. Hence formula (22) should actually read like this (see formula 27):

$$l = \sum_{i=1}^{n_l} \frac{l_i}{c_i} \qquad (27)$$

A brief example will illustrate this. Suppose the older sister of a sister has lost her mother at the age of 4 years. Mother has been 30, father 33, her sister 2 years old at that time. Hence $k = \dfrac{(30)4}{(33)4\sqrt{4(3)}} = 0.15$. Therefore $-\log(k) = 0.82$, and $l_i = 1.22$. The change-of-sex-balance coefficient would be $c = 1 - (\frac{3}{4} - \frac{2}{3}) = \frac{11}{12}$. Hence l_i as computed by formula (27) would be $l_i = 1.33$. Had father been lost instead, c would have been equal to $c = 1 - (\frac{1}{4} - \frac{0}{3}) = \frac{3}{4}$, and l_i accordingly larger ($l_i = 1.64$, if we ignore the changes that this situation would also create in k).

If that girl would also lose her sister, say, five years later and after her father had remarried a woman his junior and turned 38 himself, her sister 7, she herself 9 and another child, a boy, had been born to them three years ago, the following values would result: $k = \dfrac{(7)7}{(38)9\sqrt{9(4)}} = \frac{1}{82}$. Therefore $-\log(k) = 1.91$, and $l_i = 0.52$. Now c would be equal to $c = 1 - (\frac{3}{5} - \frac{2}{4}) = \frac{19}{20}$. Hence l_i would be 0.58 according to formula (27). And the overall loss l that this girl has suffered would be $l = 1.33 + 0.52 = 1.85$.

One might argue that in these formulas substitution of another person for the lost one has not been accounted for. This is not quite true, though. If no new person is recruited to take the lost person's place, the remaining ones will, of necessity, substitute for that person. Only if a family should consist of no more than two persons, mother and child, would the loss of mother leave nobody to substitute for her. In that case, however, the child would have small chances of survival. In terr s of our formulas a four-year-old's predicament of this kind would yield $k = 0.5$, $-\log(k) = 0.30$, and $l_i = 3.33$; c would be $c = 1 - (\frac{2}{2} - \frac{1}{1}) = 1$. Hence l_i would remain the same. This is plausible in the sense that the loss of mother will not change anything in the balance of sexes. There was no male to begin with and there is none now. If that child were only one year old, the following values would result: $k = 1$, $-\log(k) = 0$, and $l_i = \infty$.

If a new person takes the lost person's place for good, any subsequent loss will reflect this fact as it did in our example. If new persons substitute only temporarily, such as in the case of hired personnel, nurses, maids, tutors, and the like, each change will, in a sense, be an additional, though small, loss and appear as such in our computations. It may be desirable, however, to include the present age of the person in question. After all, the effectiveness of losses does seem to fade as time goes by. Hence formula (27) should perhaps be re-written to read like formula (28):

$$l = \frac{1}{\log(a_p)} \sum_{i=1}^{n_l} \frac{l_i}{c_i} \qquad (28)$$

In formula (28) a_p would be the present age (in years) of the person in question.

The amount of loss prevailing in a marriage (or, *mutatis mutandis*, in any interpersonal relationship) would be equal to the sum of losses suffered by its partners (see formula 29):

$$l_m = l_h + l_w \qquad (29)$$

In formula (29) l_h is the loss suffered by the husband, and l_w the loss suffered by the wife.

At this point an overall formulation shall be ventured in which the conflicts over rank, sex and number of siblings, as well as the losses suffered are included (see formula 30):

$$P_m = (d_t)^{1+l_m} = \left(\frac{d_{s_m} + |d_{r_m}| + d_{n_m}}{3}\right)^{1+l_m} \tag{30}$$

In formula (30) P_m expresses the overall prognosis for a match. All other symbols have already been explained (see formula 21 etc.). P_m will vary between zero and infinity, but the vast majority of cases will be between values of $0\cdot1$ and 100, and a large bulk of them between $0\cdot5$ and 20. The smaller P_m, the better will the prognosis tend to be.

Losses that a person's parents have suffered could, of course, be included too. In fact, the same would hold for all conflicts that they may have had over rank, sex, number of siblings and configurations of children. Hence rather than compute the parents' influence in each of the component measures of P_m, the values of P_m could be computed for the parents, the grandparents, the great-grandparents, etc. and added to P_m of a given couple. Formula (31) describes the relationship:

$$P_{m_t} = P_m + \frac{\Sigma P_{m_1}}{4} + \frac{\Sigma P_{m_2}}{16} + \frac{\Sigma P_{m_3}}{256} + \text{etc.} \tag{31}$$

In formula (31) P_{m_t} would express the overall prognosis of a match when the matches of ancestors are considered too. P_{m_1} would be the sum of values of P_m computed for the husband's and the wife's parents, P_{m_2} the sum of values of P_m computed for all four grandparental marriages, P_{m_3} the sum of values of P_m computed for all eight great-grandparental marriages, etc. In practice it will be found, though, that the third summand is usually quite small and the fourth one already negligible. As a matter of fact, it may suffice to use formula (30) after all, at least as long as l_{m_t} is substituted for l_m, and l_{m_t} computed in analogy to P_{m_t}.

As for losses affecting relationships between persons of the same sex, formulas (22–31) would be applicable as well, although l_i in formulas (27 and 28) would have to be multiplied by c rather than by the reciprocal of c. On the other hand, formula (22) may be considered sufficient by itself.

We have investigated how a person's own and his parents' sibling configurations as well as all incidental losses of people that have been suffered might determine that person's character and, ultimately, even the kinds of matches that he is likely to enter in marriage, and the kinds of successes that he will be able to make of them. There is one more aspect remaining to be studied in these matters: the children that they are going to have.

Both happy and unhappy couples will attempt to have children. The happy ones because children will crown their relationship, so to speak. Husband and wife are likely to have strong and direct desires for them. Both long for completion of their marriage through children. The unhappy couples, however, will often also attempt to have children, if for no better reason than that they, their children, might help them to get a little happier with each other. Probably they won't. On the contrary, such parents may, without meaning to, try their best to make the children unhappy too.

And both, happy and unhappy couples alike, have no direct control over the arrival times or the sexes of their children. They can only *try* to have children, and although many couples in all more articulate and highly organised societies succeed in having them pretty much at the times they had in mind, the sexes of their children, but also the number of children they can or will ultimately have and a few other accidentals, are not at their discretion. Hence there are all kinds of possibilities of conflict between what they want and what they happen to get. And on the basis of everything that has been said so far in this chapter, we should not be surprised to find that those parents who carry conflicts among themselves are also the ones who will tend to get in conflict with what they have for children. But even the happy ones may well find it hard to accept at times that they should have, say, five girls in a row and still no boy or vice versa, or that they should be able to have no more than one or two children, if any, perhaps due to some injury, anomaly or particular economic circumstances. This, however, will not be the rule. Only extreme circumstances can put them at a loss, and even then they will learn how to be gracious about their lot. It is the unhappy parents who really make trouble for their children.

The children's fortunes could be rated in analogy to what has been suggested for a person in general. The parents' conflicts will come upon them, and their own sibling configurations as well as all incidental losses will do the rest. It has been demonstrated how these conflicts could be estimated clinically or even computed by the "algebra" proposed (see p. 244ff) or by a few formulas (14–31; see p. 245ff). But we could also appraise clinically or more formally, to what extent given configurations of children would tend to contribute to the troubles the parents had already been having.

In order to do that we must adapt our general rule about interpersonal relationships and their chances of happiness and success (see p. 241). We can say that a configuration of children within a family will be conducive to a happy and successful family life to the extent, other things being equal, that it duplicates for both parents the sibling configurations that they have come from themselves.

This is assumed to hold true for two reasons. First the children will be less conflicted about their own position if they can learn straight from their parents how to be what they are themselves by fate, namely boys or girls, but also juniors, seniors or a combination of both, and how to behave toward the other sex and other ranks.

Secondly, the parents themselves will be less conflicted about their children, if they can recognise in them their own sexes and ranks and/or those of their own siblings. Other features would matter too, of course, but they would tend to be less pervasive and general. Therefore they can be ignored in this context.

Let us remember here (see p. 82ff) that the child cannot satisfy any of his desires without the parents' very explicit and active cooperation. The infants desires and the parents' desires for him are one at first. As a matter of fact, the parents will often know better than the infant what it is that he wants. To the extent, however, that the child's desires develop and form, the parents will find themselves adopting those in turn. They will introject or identify with whatever they can make out in their infant. This means, as has been indicated before (see pp. 83, 87), that they will actually introject their own versions of his desires, but they have not outgrown their most primitive and delightful forms of satisfaction to the extent that they would be unable to match their infant's. Simple drinking, cooing, wriggling and—worst of all—elimination, become an unproportional source of enchantment, as friends of new parents may sometimes witness with estrangement. In short, the parents identify with their infant's desires, and they continue to do so throughout life. Transitorily they turn into their own children again and again in ever so many ways, entertaining their children's desires themselves or, at least, supporting them emphatically. And with particular specimens of their children, preferably of the same sex and similar rank, they will tend to do so more readily than with others.

Suppose the husband is the older brother of a sister and the wife the younger sister of a brother, which would be an optimal match by the criteria of rank and sex alone. If they have a boy and a girl themselves, the situation would be ideal. Both children can learn from their parents how to be what they are as well as how to treat each other and the other sex.

If they have a girl first, and then a boy, there will already be conflicts. The girl will have to learn from father how to be a senior, and from mother how to be a woman and vice versa for the boy. So she might either become a somewhat too masculine senior or a feminine junior with a grudge against boys and their imagined superiority. And the boy could either become a somewhat feminine junior or a masculine, but belligerent and inconsistent "master of females". Still another solution may be that they, brother and sister, will refuse to have very much to do with each other. Both parents, on the other hand, will tend to confirm these trends in their children. They will recognise their sex in one and their rank in the other of their children, hence get confused in their identifications with as well as in their desires toward them, be inconsistent and even inefficient in their thinkings for and about them and generate for their children the troubles mentioned.

If these parents have two boys instead, they, the boys, will of course develop conflicts on their own grounds. They may find their sibling configuration a good preparation for friendships with other boys, preferably those with complementary positions of their own, but a poorer one for marriage. Yet the parents too will have their troubles. Mother will search in vain for the girl that will grow up to be like her or even better and luckier than she has been, and father will find no girl for whom he can be a great, big, wonderful daddy. Therefore both of them may attempt to transform psychologically the sex of one of their children, but they will thereby not only go unsatisfied; they will even make life somewhat difficult for the victim.

Similar conditions would prevail, *mutatis mutandis*, if the parents had two girls instead. With three children in all their problems would be more complicated. One would tend to be the spare one, the child with whom neither parent identifies too strongly and whom neither understands too well. However, if the parents let them, the children themselves may compensate for it. Those two who can easily identify with their parents and whom the latter, in turn, identify with, may take the third one as their own play-child. Four children might already split up into two couples by themselves and that could well make it easier for the parents again to be the objects of identification and of (heterosexual) love for them and to identify with, and "love" them, in return, etc.

If the parents themselves had come from families of three children, they may be happy with two children whether those happen to duplicate the sibling relationship that they themselves have already repeated in their marriage or the one which they did not, provided, of course, that fate cooperates with their unconscious desires. With three children things would tend to be even better. There is a possibility that their children supply at least one of them precisely with what they had at home and what they could not get from the spouse as long as two people only, rather than three or more, constitute the family at the start.

If parents have made a poor match with each other, say, because father was the older brother of a brother and mother the older sister of a sister, even an optimal configuration among their children, say, two in all, a boy followed by a girl, will not be sufficient to prevent conflicts over rank and sex. The boy will learn from father how to be a senior, and since he is one himself, this would be fine except that mother wants to be one too. Being a senior will come to mean fighting over one's seniority rights with a woman. His sister, on the other hand, who would not put up a fight of her own accord, will learn from mother how to be a senior even though she herself is not. She will put up a fight for something that does not even make sense. And both of them, boy and girl alike, will not learn too much from their parents about how to treat the other sex. The parents themselves do not know it too well. The parents, in turn, will recognise themselves in their children, but both would tend to "gang up" with their same-sex child against the two other members of the family and prevent him (or her) from availing himself (or herself) of the sibling. The mother, however, might find her daughter particularly inept, disappointing, even unfaithful, all because she is indeed a junior.

If we want to use our "algebra" again, we might designate $b(g)/b, g/(b)g$ to be the marriage between an older brother of a sister and the younger sister of a brother who have two children, a boy and a (younger) girl. "Subtracting" the children's configuration will leave $O/b, g/O$, which means that the children create no conflicts for their parents. With $b(g)/b, g/g(b)$ subtraction will yield $O/b, g/g(b)$ which means that the mother will have a rank conflict with her children. Family $(g)b/b, g/g(b)$ will permit no subtraction, even though the parents would be optimally matched for each other. Both of them would have rank conflicts with their children. Family $b(b)/g, b/g(g)$ will also permit no subtraction, but the parents are having rank- and sex-conflicts with each other in addition. Family $b(g, b, b)/ g, b, b/(b)g(b)$, after subtraction, would be $b(g, b)/g, b, b/(b)g$, meaning that both father and mother find one of their sibling relationships duplicated with their children. In another sense father gets precisely what he had at home, provided he imagines himself in the position of the oldest sibling. This could perhaps be expressed like this: $b(O)/g, b, b/(b)g$, but it may be too confusing to do so. Obviously, the number of sibling relationships that parents find duplicated with their children, expressed in proportion to the number of sibling relationships that they brought into their marriage, will be a measure of the amount of conflict which the configuration of their children will create for them; in addition, of course, to those conflicts already prevailing among themselves or handed down to them from their own parents.

This could also be expressed by means of formula (32):

$$d_{ch} = 1 - \frac{n_d}{(n-1)} \tag{32}$$

In formula (32) d_{ch} is the coefficient of conflict between a person's sibling configuration and the configuration of his children; n_d would be the number of (dual) sibling relationships of a parent that has found (one or more) duplicates in his children, and n would be the number of children that constitute the parent's own sibling configuration. With $b(g, b, b)/g, b, b/(b)g(b)$ the husband would have two relationships, both $b(b)$, repeated with his children. Hence $d_{ch_h} = 0.33$. The wife would find only one relationship repeated, namely $g(b)$. Therefore $d_{ch_w} = 0.50$.

Formula (33) might be used as an alternative to formula (32):

$$d_{ch} = 1 - \frac{2n_{d'}}{n(n-1)} \tag{33}$$

whereby $\frac{n(n-1)}{2}$ would be the number of all dual relationships that prevail among n children constituting a parent's sibling configuration (including those of which the parent is not an immediate partner); $n_{d'}$ would be the number of all those of their relationships that find duplication in any of the relationships prevailing among their children With formula (33) the above example would yield $d_{ch_h} = 0.17$ and $d_{ch_w} = 0.33$. Yet formula (32) is not only simpler, but probably just as meaningful.

Note, incidentally, that the number of children that the parents have is not reflected directly in either formula. If parents $b(g)$ and $(b)g$ should have five children, say, b, g, b, b, g, their d_{ch} values would be the same as if they had just two children, say, b, g. If their children are to be included in number, formula (32) would have to be re-written to read like formula (34):

$$d_{ch} = 1 - \sqrt{\frac{n_d}{n-1}} \sqrt{\frac{2n_d'}{n'(n'-1)}} \tag{34}$$

whereby n' would be the number of children that the parents have, and n_d' the number of all dual relationships prevailing among their children for which the given parent has (one or more) duplicates in his or her own sibling configuration. Hence example $b(g, b, b)/$ $g, b, b/(b)g(b)$ would yield $d_{ch_h} = 0.18$, and $d_{ch_w} = 0.29$. Example $b(g)/b, g, b, b, g/(b)g$, however, would yield values of 0.37 for both parents, whereas with $b(g)/b, g/(b)g$ d_{ch} would be zero for both of them.

In most cases, especially where the number of siblings that constitute each parent's sibling configuration and the number of children they have themselves are not too grossly different, formula (32) may be sufficient. After all, the chances of duplication of the parents' own sibling relationships will tend to be greater, the larger the number of their own children. Hence the latter is at least indirectly taken into account anyway. And parents may continue having children regardless of whether they have already got the constellations of children they wanted and are trying again—in that case because all went so well—or whether they have not yet got what they wanted, but keep trying.

For a marriage as a whole the degree to which the configuration of children duplicates their parents' sibling configurations is expressed by formula (35):

$$d_{ch_m} = d_{ch_h} + d_{ch_w} \tag{35}$$

Thus d_{ch_m} of $b(g, b, b)/g, b, b/(b)g(b)$ is 0.47, of $b(g)/b, g, b, b, g/(b)g$ 0.74, and of $b(g)/b, g/(b)g$ zero.

If conflicts with the configuration of the couple's children are to be included in d_t or P_m (formulas 21 and 30), the estimate of all conflict (d_t) would be expressed by formula (36):

$$d_t = d_{s_m, r_m, n_m, ch_m} = \frac{d_{s_m} + |d_{r_m}| + d_{n_m} + d_{ch_m}}{4} \tag{36}$$

The maximum value of d_t would still be equal to 2, although it will approach it only asymptotically. The minimum values are zero. An example of $d_t = 0$ would be $b(g)/b, g/(b)g$.

A few words should also be said about relationships between people of the same sex, or friendships. Not that there might not be heterosexual friendships too. But homosexual friendships are different in one basic aspect: they can never lead to "anything", i.e. to a heterosexual genital relationship and children, whereas most of all heterosexual friendships, no matter how platonic they may look, are not altogether bare of such possibilities and intimations.

In treating friendships between people of the same sex, the formulas concerning ranks (16, 17) and discrepancy of number (18, 19) can remain unchanged, except that they might, as an alternative, be computed from the same-sex siblings only, rather than from all siblings. In the formulas concerning sex, however (14, 15), n_s will obviously have to mean the number of siblings of the opposite sex rather than of the same sex. Formulas (32, 33, 34) do not apply at all, although one's children might matter somewhat with friendships among parents of different families. The treatment of losses (formulas 22–31) would essentially remain unchanged, but there is some reason to assume that in formulas (27) and (28) l_i would have to be multiplied by c rather than by the reciprocal of c. On the other hand, formula (22) may be considered altogether sufficient.

In terms of our "algebra" a test for fit of a "homosexual" relationship can be made by transforming only ranks (see also p. 244 f) and "subtracting" identical sibling-relationships. Thus $b(b, b)/(b, b)b$ would yield $b(b, b)/b(b, b)$ or O/O after rank transformation, which could be an optimal match. Identical positions such as $b(b, b)/b(b, b)$ or $(g)g/(g)g$ should make for strong conflicts of rank, represented by transformation to $b(b, b)/(b, b)b$ or $(g)g/g(g)$, respectively. Heterosexual sibling relationships, on the other hand, should create conflicts over the (same) sex of the friend regardless of rank complementarity. Thus $b(g)/(g)b$, although yielding $b(g)/b(g)$ after rank transformation, cannot be an optimal fit because of their sisters. Each friend would tend to transform the other into a girl, or rather not to become friends at all. As a matter of fact, they would be better suited for each other's sisters. Friendship $b(b, g)/(b, g)b$, however, transformed to $b(b, g)/b(g, b)$, would indicate a partly optimal fit, and so would $b(b, g)/(g, b)b$. The latter would even be better.

Hence we might say that optimal "homosexual" friendships will lie somewhere between identical and fully complementary sibling relationships of the partners involved. Identical sibling relationships would leave the friend "cold". The two can identify with each other, but they cannot live together, so to speak. Fully complementary relationships, on the other hand, are impossible by definition. The partners of a homosexual relationship cannot be man and wife for each other, although they might sometimes try very hard.

We have demonstrated more formally how the configuration of children that the parents happen to get would affect their relationship to them and to each other. We have also indicated how all our propositions would hold, *mutatis mutandis*, for friendships between people of the same sex. Yet none of this should mean at all that family constellations are the only determinants that matter, nor that they are completely inescapable. An older brother of a sister may marry the older sister of a brother, which would make for a rank conflict. But she is ten years his junior. She is a younger one at least by chronological age. He would probably tend to assume the role of a father for her to a greater than usual extent.

A supposedly reverse authority relationship as represented by the younger brother of a sister who has married the older sister of a brother may not show at all, say, because she has taken over the household affairs and finances, whereas he has been permitted to be a star in political showmanship. Even severe conflicts over both, sex and rank, may sometimes be mitigated by relationships established with in-laws and friends. A marriage is not *a priori* exclusive of all kinds of friendships that may continue and/or be formed anew. The partners may build an "extended family" around them with their friends and thereby get to an extent at least what they miss with each other, including the big clan that they might have had at home. A sibling configuration of three boys only, supposedly conducive to psychological sex-transformation of at least one child, may be a very happy one for all involved, because the first one wants to be a scientist, like his father, the second an artist like his mother—and he happens to have considerable talent—and the third the strong man, the football player. Or they may have three girl cousins of an appropriate age and a fair amount of contact with them, so that they do learn how to deal with girls at least to an extent. At times losses up to a certain severity may also appear as sources of strength. Not that any loss can ever be completely made up for. But losses are, or at least will be, a part of any person's life, if only he lives long enough himself, and when they occur, that person may be stronger in taking them. Yet of two people the one who has suffered the heavier loss under otherwise comparable circumstances, will still tend to be affected to a greater degree by a new one. If a person's parents and/or siblings have had very severe conflicts, he might well try to "run away from them as far as possible" in his own choice of a partner, and he may sometimes be lucky to succeed. But more often than not he will manage to set himself up for the same kinds of trouble that his parents and/or siblings had with each other. Whatever he had at home tends to be stronger than anything he can think up "by himself".

At the same time we should be prepared to discover the effects of family constellations even where we would not think of looking for them at first and to find them very persistent, even stubborn, sometimes quite mischievous agents in the bustling city of life. They are, perhaps, the most crystallised and clever of the unconscious gyroscopes built into our motivation.

A System of Psychopathology

ONE of the most ambitious "tests" of psychoanalytic theory has been the system of psychopathology that Freud, Abraham (1924), Fenichel (1945) and others have tried to derive from it. Historically the opposite may be almost as true. The many different forms of psychopathology called for more order than had been accomplished, say, by the turn of the century, and psychoanalytic theory emerged in these attempts. Not as a system of psychopathology at first. Rather as an elementary theory of motivation, normal and pathological alike, or shall we say: as a theory of the pathological, primitive, unconscious, in all motivation. But as time and clinical work proceeded, psychological symptoms and syndromes began to show common trends and finally to fall into place. As they did they sometimes challenged the theory, but the latter would respond by further articulation.

We have seen that man's desires develop around three *substitution continua* or drive systems. These are oral, bodily and genital, manipulation and stimulation (see p. 116ff). Furthermore, that the processes of cathexis and counter-cathexis determine a person's particular course of development (see pp. 6ff, 23ff, 30), that people are the most important single items in a person's psychological environment (see p. 13) and their losses, other things being equal, the severest of all traumatic events (see pp. 28ff, 182ff, 249ff). And finally, that early influences exerted over given periods of time are stronger than influences exerted over the same lengths of time in later life. Hence the severest forms of psychopathology should stem from losses suffered in the earliest stages of development, and the mildest from losses suffered relatively late. As a matter of fact, from a certain time of development on, losses should no longer have pathogenic effects at all, provided they are the first losses the person has experienced. That does not mean that there will be no suffering and mourning. There is no loss whatsoever without them. Where there has been no suffering and mourning, there was, in all likelihood, no loss to begin with. Nor does it mean that losses of a given objective severity will have identical effects on different people. The basic rates of cathexis by which a person operates are given with birth and may vary greatly (see p. 126ff). Frustration tolerance shows considerable individual differences from earliest life on. What may amount to non-existence of a parent in one case, can well be a non-traumatic series of temporary absences with another. Physical punishment may be a token of love in one person's mind, and the utmost of humiliation and defeat in another's. Or weaning may never really have been accepted by one child, while another may almost have weaned himself.

The key concept in this system of psychopathology is regression (see also p. 48ff). It should be noted, though, that this is a very broad term. It means return to earlier levels of motivational development. However, a person may be involved to very different degrees. The loss that precipitates regression—and every loss does—may have affected a *sub-continuum* of a drive system, a considerable portion of a drive system or even more than one drive system. The object lost— and it will always be an object that is being lost; i.e. more than one drive system will almost inevitably be affected—may have been known moderately well for only the last small portion of a person's life. It may be a more crucial figure, say an intimate friend, a cousin or a sibling. And it may be the only object yet formed in a person's mind, say mother during the later part of the first year of life.

Hence only losses of a certain severity and pervasiveness will really have pathogenic effects. Others will be overcome quickly and without much difficulty unless they happen to be reminiscent of earlier and more severe losses. That, however, is precisely the pathogenic effect of a more severe loss: it predisposes a person to interpret even harmless losses and minor adversities which other people might take in their stride as duplicates of the original. A boy who has lost his mother through divorce may run away from a date where the girl kept him waiting for a few minutes and not approach a girl again for months. Or a little girl who has often been brutally beaten by her—as it happens: hard-drinking— parents may go into a fit of rage or perhaps of deep gloom and brooding when hit by a pingpong ball during a game.

The earlier and more severe loss has caused regression at the time it occurred. The person has since grown out of it, but if no loss can ever be entirely made up for—and it cannot—there must be a lag in the accumulation of cathexis. A *substitution continuum* or a particular area of the world has been infiltrated by counter-cathexis. This regression of the past *is* fixation (see p. 48). Hence we may also say that, under the impact of a new trauma, a person will regress to earlier fixations, but this is only another way of saying the same thing: that earlier re- gressions, like all counter-cathexes in general, "attract" later ones (see pp. 30, 31, 38). Situations become traumatic and precipitate regression because they are being interpreted in terms of all pertinent cathexes and counter-cathexes, and regression was among the latter. As a matter of fact, it was the last resort after other devices had failed. Hence it will appear to be the only thing that could conceivably help at present.

If a person without any hereditary deficiency, psychologically speaking, has reached latency period un-traumatised, nothing much can happen to him any longer. He is past all danger spots, past all rapids that might damage or possibly overthrow his boat. He has reached calm waters. Only very unusual forces of the order of torrential rains, typhoons or earth-quakes, could still do him harm. Not that puberty would be an easy water to cross. But its troubles are mostly in the open, visible from great distances, so to speak, and generally quite manageable. Only where there have been lesions before may the present turmoils be seriously aggravated and quite hard to handle.

If a person has been *traumatised during the Oedipal period*, specific psycho-pathology may result. The trauma could be the loss of a parent or of both, or merely an impending loss. A parent may always be on the verge of leaving, whether for a trip, for the hospital or for anywhere, though for good. But even poor, quarrelsome and destructive or merely cool relationships prevailing among the parents can be pathogenic. They may become obvious only now, when the child discovers that the parents could also behave toward each other as man and woman, and they don't. Until then, however, he might have thought that every-things was fine. They were at least correct and polite to each other. Or there may have been violence between the parents and it may have spilled over on the child. There may be specific seductions, such as by parents who are too liberal in exposing themselves and their most intimate affairs to the child, or parents suffering from perversions, perhaps from some mental illness that became crudely apparent at that time, or from pathological jealousy. Even the mere arrival of a sibling may be pathogenic under certain conditions, such as when it is of the sex or general character that one or both parents desired very badly, whereas the child in question was not, or vice versa. The same would, of course, hold for the loss of a sibling.

The most general effect would be that the victim, the child, would have to resort to regression repeatedly and, if at all outgrowing the Oedipal stage, he may be heavily fixated. He has not succeeded in finding out what he can get or hope for from his parents and what not. He has not really come to terms with them. Hence confusion will prevail also with his non-incestuous or extra-familial relationships. He will not know what he can reasonably hope for and what not, and as a consequence seek for, suspect, and at the same time defend against, the worst: heterosexual genital relationships. Every contact with a person of the other sex and sometimes even of the same sex will be misconstrued to have genital connotations. And since the ordinary use of counter-cathexes will prove insufficient to handle such pervasive a predicament, special devices will be resorted to. These are phobias and conversions (see also p. 52ff). And the overall syndrome within which they occur, is *hysteria*.

A person, say a girl in her late twenties, an only child, unmarried, may have been struck by a strange attack of anxiety one day and this may have been repeated several times. It came out from nowhere, she claimed. Upon closer inspection by a neutral outsider—in this case a psychotherapist, but sometimes a teacher or a friend might also be helpful—it turned out that the preferred days were Fridays and Saturdays. Secondly, that it was on those weekends when her parents expected visitors. Because of her anxiety states, however, the parents started either to call their invitations off, or their daughter was given permission to withdraw to her room. Thirdly, it looked likely that it was the guests themselves who had something to do with her attacks, especially one bachelor friend of her father.

Her anxiety was *"free-floating"* at first, but gradually it developed into a fear or *phobia* of people visiting the house or of being visited by them. Then the people of the office where she worked as a typist and secretary were drawn into this. She could tolerate the office, but became afraid of all outside contacts with her colleagues, just as she could tolerate complete strangers in places like movie theaters, libraries, the subway, etc., but got very anxious if she was with friends. Ultimately her phobia got aggravated to the point where she would not wish to mingle with people at all, neither at her office nor at any public place. She quit working and stayed home most of the day. She would go for walks only at nights, just to catch some fresh air, as she said, and in order to avoid people—now she did not even want to see or be seen by them—the loneliest streets and darkest lanes were just good enough.

Well, this is how phobias develop. Quite often they have to expand in order to keep anxiety from mounting. The afflicted may end up utterly incapacitated. Somewhere along the line however, they usually do seek help, either of their own accord or upon advice or even pressure by the family. With the girl described above an assault by a man during one of her nightly walks brought her into therapy. She escaped. As a matter of fact, it was not too much of an assault, but it made it consciously obvious to her what it was that she had set herself up for. All her avoidances had brought her closer to the only way in which she could ultimately, though unconsciously, conceive of the possibility of contacts with men: rape. Why rape? So that she would not be responsible. Under all other conditions punishment must follow. The original traumatic condition, or worse, will be re-instated. In fact, the very purpose of the phobia is to prevent just that.

Phobias may take on various forms. The afflicted may fear open places or closed rooms. He or she may be afraid of great heights, of elevators, trains or airplanes, of blushing, but also of dogs, mice, dirt, germs, certain kinds of dishes or food, etc. Yet in all of them the person's unconscious preoccupation would be somewhat the same. He may fear open places because of the many people crowding them who, he or she fears, will inevitably get out of control. They will seduce the female phobic. Or they will tempt the male into approaching them. Yet he may also fear open places because of the scarcity of people, because he really wishes for their company, even for more: for "illicit" contact with the opposite sex, particularly with one very special (mostly parent-like) person. The same would hold for claustrophobia, the fear of closed rooms. Somebody may come and seduce the afflicted, or nobody may come; but this is even worse. Then he or she may get desperate for people, forget him- or herself, perhaps masturbate with phantasies too terrible to be even named, and finally everybody or at least somebody, will know, laugh, reproach, punish, even . . . oh, again this is too terrible to be named (even mutilate genitally; put the stamp of his evil right on

S

his body so that everyone could see; or, in case of a female, expose her pitiful genital predicament; either one might put an end to all of these crazy hazy desires).

If it is not one thing, it is the other. But isn't there something wrong with a theory in which two different things can be equally true? Is it not too unspecific, hence not really subject to empirical test? Well, the alternatives mentioned are not all that is theoretically possible. The afflicted does not think, e.g., that somebody may come without "illicit" intentions or that nobody may come and the afflicted's intentions may remain secret. Nor does the afflicted seem to get in reality what he wants, and that is precisely why he has to keep maneuvering around it so much. Any person could, under certain circumstances, be seduced by, or tempted to seduce, another person. The phobic, however, believes that this could happen to him at almost all times. Or take a symptom such as extreme untidiness which, incidentally, is usually *not* hysteric. It may be motivated by a desire to smear, to wallow in dirt, or by a reaction-formation to the desire to be tidy, neat and orderly. Inversely a person who has been deprived or traumatised in his desires to use his body and especially his hands may either turn to very primitive or to overly controlled manipulation. In other words, the theory cannot be wrong, a critic might say. He overlooks, however, that according to the theory both extremes may be equally remote from a realistic variety of compromises. Normally a person would be somewhere in between tidy and messy and appropriately lean more toward the one or the other at given times and under given circumstances, say in his business or on a camping vacation, respectively. The disturbed person tends much more strongly to be only one or the other regardless of circumstances or to switch overnight and for no good (external or objective) reason from one extreme to the other, or to practice both extremes at the same time. As a matter of fact, all neurotic symptoms are always doing both: satisfying a primitive, aggressive, destructive, hence counter-cathected, desire, but also satisfying the defense or counter-cathexis established against it (i.e. the desire chosen to substitute for the original desire when its satisfaction became impossible; see also p. 53). What is more: all behaviour whatsoever, whether neurotic, psychotic, "normal", and even most specific and technical, is a compromise between more primitive desires and their (less primitive) controls (see also p. 62ff). What distinguishes the normal from the disturbed person is the kind of compromise he manages ordinarily to achieve. The more "reality" is taken into account and the more complex, organised and efficient that "reality", the smaller the likelihood of psychological disturbance. This is what psychanalytic theory would truly imply.

Back to phobias. The fear of blushing, too, is the fear of revealing to others and even to oneself one's "real" desires. In minor degrees this fear is not too uncommon and can easily be seen to concern other people, mainly of the opposite sex. Much to one's inconvenience one blushes at their sight, at the mention of their names, at the mere thought of an event where a more intimate contact was or might have been possible. In fact, secret lovers would tend to do and fear just that on occasions.

The fear of heights, like those of rooms and open places, focuses on spatial aspects of its "real" concerns. It should be mentioned, however, that these aspects may well be both pregenital and genital, in meaning. Experiences with space and gravity have been made from earliest life on and they will soon be experienced with delight, though passively at first. The infant gets used to being lifted, carried, turned or, in other words, to floating through the air without his own doing. In fact, he does so usually before and after every feeding. Hence experiences with space and gravity are a part of the earliest and most gratifying satisfactions he can yet consume: sucking, munching and swallowing. The same holds for the other primal *substitution continua* or drive systems which begin to form from birth on—but are more complicated, hence take their time—and with active manipulation being minimal at first. All bodily and genital stimulations that he does experience passively—and even those do not amount to much yet—are also linked with spatial and gravity experiences. In order to change his diapers, e.g., an infant must be taken out of his crib, handled, turned, etc. Hence spatial and gravity experiences may very well attach themselves also to genital stimulation and, later, to genital orgasm, quite apart from the possibility that all orgasms, oral (swallowing), eliminatory (sphincter-passage) and genital, do "create" physiological conditions all of their own accord that are, in turn, reminiscent of spatial and gravity sensations. At any rate, these experiences can assume representative functions. Therefore fears of heights may, on the one hand, indicate that counter-cathected desires of passive movement or of various sorts of bodily stimulations learned to have followed them, are being tempted; on the other hand, they may represent genital experiences and climaxes or rather desires for such experiences. Both kinds will, of course, have to be avoided in all disguises by the phobic.

Fears of elevators, trains or airplanes may not only involve other people, but also counter-cathected desires of bodily manipulation and control. The afflicted may wish to handle such powerful gadgets, but believe himself unable to or expect punishment to follow suit. Punishment for what? For his desire to wield undue power, but also, of course, for his desire to handle something more specifically forbidden or impossible, say sex-organs. Furthermore there may be an element of a desire for being the object of power, the passive recipient and "beneficiary", and the fright may stem from this one. "How can I possibly have such a wish?" may be his reaction.

In animal phobias dogs may be feared because they can chase you, bite, charge and even assault genitally. Children of both sexes may develop such fears, but among adults women are somewhat more prone than men. After all, do they not speak of *men* who behave like that as "wolves"? Mice, but also snakes, are feared (especially by girls and women) because they can sneak up, crawl over you and worse. You don't even notice them and suddenly they are on you. Oh, it is too awful even to think of what might happen (namely genital stimulation, even penetration). Needless to say that these afflictions may vary greatly in degree. Some queezy feeling at the actual sight of some such animals is fairly widespread among women, while incessant fears of mice or snakes that may come from anywhere, crawl up your chairs, try to come into bed with you, etc., would be rare and more seriously pathological. Fears of germs may be fears of dirt, hence pregenital in character, but also fears of the most vicious of all tiny animals: those that make children.

The other major hysteric device is *conversion*. The primitive and basically incestuous genital desires or defenses used against them are "transformed" into physical manifestations (see also p. 52 f). Any mode of stimulation and any drive system may be used to implement the unconscious purpose. A person may turn blind or at least be impaired in his vision (dimness or restriction of the visual field) in order not to see. See what? The primary but forbidden love-object or its equally forbidden substitute. Or that love-object's secondary or even primary sex characteristics. A change occurring with the love-object such as pregnancy, but also physical illness, a crippling injury or ageing. There is even biblical, mythological and proverbial, reference to the fact that one can turn blind upon looking at the wrong thing.

The same would hold for hearing. Rather than listening to wicked rumors, say about one's parents, about beloved but unreachable substitutes or about how children come about, the person "renounces" hearing altogether or in part. He might, e.g., develop a peculiar difficulty for understanding speech, but remain intact as to hearing sounds and noises.

But then, rather than not seeing or hearing, a person may also see and hear things that are not there. He might be the victim of hysteric hallucinations that produce for him, sometimes in little disguise, the very things he is concerned about: his love-objects, scenes that he might wish to happen, or words that he may want to have heard. So lively may they be that he can confuse them with actual events, at least in retrospect, and think that they have really happened. By similar tokens he may also blot out from his memory events that have occurred indeed. His capacity to use and influence wishfully his experiences and actions remains greater than it does normally (see also p. 53). He does not quite outgrow it as he emerges into adolescence and adulthood.

Other modes of stimulation, especially touch, including sensations of tempera-ture pressure and physical pain, are even more pliable. Hyper-, par- and anaes-thesias may serve to produce or deny sensations reminiscent of, or related to, incestuous heterosexual contacts or preliminaries to such contacts. Hands may be painfully sensitive to all touch or numb. They may even feel as though gloves had been pulled over them. Large parts of the body may be afflicted temporarily by red patches, even by mild eczema. There may be intestinal sensations, pain, even false pregnancies. The mouth may be afflicted by periodic or constant dryness, sensations of hairs or little crumbs, by "nervous" yawning or burping, even by a loss of the "voice" in speech or sometimes of speech itself, etc. There may be a lump in the throat, something like a frozen sensation of mild choking. However, these phenomena involve already kinesthesis and striate-muscular afflictions. There may be spasms or paralyses of arms, legs and fingers, of eye muscles (accommodation and convergence may not function properly) and occasionally even of sphincters, but also disturbances of the respiratory and circulatory system.

In contrast to psychosomatic disorders where the physical conditions are the "normal" outgrowth of abnormal or abnormally prolonged psychological conditions (see p. 282 f, also p. 53), specific unconscious desires and designs are not too difficult to recognise with the hysteric. The symptoms represent heterosexual or even homosexual genital desires, also attempts to prevent them or, most frequently, both. But a person's motor apparatus may also be involved more dramatically. His entire body might turn cataleptic or he may have a hystero-epileptic fit. The latter resembles a true epileptic attack, at least superficially, but its onset is almost always determined by the acute psychological situation. The hysteric usually throws his fit for an audience, so to speak, especially for those with whom he is unconsciously preoccupied. The fit is a piece of showman-ship and not infrequently the convulsions reveal specific conscious and uncon-scious intentions. While collapsing he may still avoid bumping his head against a chair or he may sink right into somebody else's arms. The convulsions often seem to bear out his (medically inadequate) ideas about convulsions. Sometimes they seem clearly to simulate genital intercourse. All of this, incidentally, holds for males and females alike, although females tend to be slightly more common as hysterics.

Sometimes a hysteric may neither suffer from any particular anxieties or phobias nor from any specific conversions. He might use both types of symptoms on occasion, but he can easily exchange them and often forego them altogether. Yet his entire character may be hysteric. Such people usually look extremely suggestible. They seem to lie incessantly. They may change their emotions and plans on a moment's notice, even on no notice at all. Being preoccupied with a relationship that they can never consume—because it is incestuous—they appear egotistical, insincere, unreliable and forgetful to the point of having fugues or even "two personalities" between which they may switch forth and back.

A person traumatised in the Oedipal stage may also have regressed to the earliest portion of that stage in which the parents were still perceived somewhat sex-unspecific and his own role had not been established either (see pp. 165, 188f). Both mother and father appeared to be both: love-objects and identification-objects. In case of regression to this part of the stage, however, one will not have to embark on these earliest "facts of life": that there are men and women, that oneself is either male or female, hence in a rivalry situation with the same-sex parent for the love and possession of the opposite-sex parent. "Maybe," a male may continue to believe as he did then, "one can love father and identify with mother", especially when mother has in reality been quite masculine and father quite feminine. The female, on the other hand, may love mother as a genital love-object and perhaps identify with father on similar grounds. Both regressors can thereby escape incestuous heterosexual genital desires, their derivatives and their commitments. Hence they may either develop hysteric symptoms against their homosexual genital desires or give in to them and satisfy them manifestly.

In other words, practised homosexuality, at least that of the active partner, stems from trauma and loss suffered in the Oedipal stage or from conditions such as, say, partially reversed sex-roles of the parents which become obvious to the person in question during that stage. Consequently, a male may look for another male to engage with in genital relations and the woman for another woman. He would try to be a mother for his male love-object, but a "male mother", of course. And she would usually try the same thing. She would try to be a male (or "phallic") mother for her female love-object. Remember that mother is the primary love-object for children of both sexes and father only the second-most important of all people, the most important merely of all males (see p. 188f).

There are other perversions, although ordinarily homosexuality would still tend to be the mildest. The preferred object of the pervert's genital desires may turn out to be a much older person of the opposite sex or of the same sex, or a much younger person, a little boy or a little girl, or even more eligible hetero-sexual objects, but very many in succession. Or the person must be dead before genital relationships can be consumed; or he or she must expose him- or herself laboriously or very specifically, i.e. genitally (in cases of males) or watch the afflicted's own exposures, or torture him or be tortured. Or the person must defecate in order for the pervert to reach his satisfaction. Sometimes the afflicted may also take to enacting the heterosexual love-object himself and become a transvestite or to concentrating his efforts on much remoter and, therefore, less anxiety-provoking representations of his heterosexual love-object such as shoes, ear-rings, pigtails, a piece of underwear and other fetishes.

In some of these cases Oedipal problems blend heavily with others. Sadistic, masochistic and coprophilic desires, e.g., have strong components of bodily manipulation. Primitive power relationships are involved too. The same holds for fetishistic desires, although here the afflicted may have been even more intimidated in his early life. He looks for genital satisfactions in a still more indirect way. To be sure, he is concerned with the love-object's body, but dares to approach and touch it only by mediators: the fetishes. These, incident-ally, tend to represent the male sex-organ which the male afflicted refuses to see as missing with the woman and the (rarer) female as being separable from the man as a whole. By focusing on the fetish he can continue to believe that the woman has got "it" after all. In milder and closer-to-normal cases he may be preoccupied with women's legs or breasts in a fetishistic manner. They may be more important to a person than the women themselves. The woman, on the other hand, by holding on to the fetish, by keeping it in lieu of an entire man, is thereby trying to convince herself that her own body is "lacking nothing". More often, however, she becomes a kleptomaniac instead (see p. 280f).

It should also be noted that mild perversions of all sorts are a normal part of ordinary love-play. As long as they remain the preliminaries of ultimate hetero-sexual genital satisfaction, they are a tribute to the love-object as a whole, we might say. Pregenital desires and their satisfactions would create a considerable deficit to a love-relationship if they were missing. Feeding, catering to, even dressing (and undressing), one another, loafing together, even sleeping side by side in the literal sense, but also wrestling for a change, playing, watching people, sceneries or each other, even cooperating in work of all sorts and in planning of the future etc., are all part of a mature heterosexual love-relationship. Homosexual or transvestite features are also more pervasive than one would naively assume. Some men like their women to look like boys, to have haircuts like them and to wear slacks, uniforms, etc. and women may wish their men to be a bit feminine somewhere, to wear silk robes at home, to let their hair grow longer or to take good cosmetic care of their hands. Different historic periods have emphasised sex specifications to very different degrees for all contemporaries. Fashions tend to change in accordance.

All these perversions have in common that genital orgasm is sought and usually reached and that the sex-distinction is clearly made regardless of the person's final preference. This distinguishes perversions from so-called impulse neuroses (see p. 280 f) where primitive pregenital desires are being satisfied without necessarily involving genital desires at all. The person might have them, to be sure, but they are secondary in importance and not linked to the pregenital desires in question.

If a person has been *traumatised* in ways similar to those already mentioned (p. 262) during the *late stage of bodily manipulation* (the late "anal-sadistic" stage, normally occupying about the third year of life), he might never fully enter the Oedipal phase. He may have to resort to regression repeatedly and remain fixated on the drive system "bodily manipulation and stimulation" and all those aspects of the world and people to which this system would be more immediately instrumental. Although he may grow to make sex-distinctions and sense remotely the pleasures and delights that people of the opposite sex such as father and mother, but also he himself and mother or, in the case of a girl, she and father, might find in each other, pre-sex-specific power aspects will dominate in his outlook on the world and people. Genital gratifications are conceivable, but would have to be bought or sold, extracted or given away like possessions or inanimate objects. Humans can be handled like things, is his contention, and this holds even in the most physical sense. They can be kicked around, beaten, mutilated, even killed, provided you are strong enough to get away with it. Women make no exception. They may be less actively engaged in it, but they would not wince when somebody, preferably a man who is obedient like a dog to any one of their desires, does all this bullying of others for them. Or the afflicted, the person traumatised in the late manipulatory stage, may prefer to wield more subtle powers such as money, industrial capacity, political influence, prestige and the like, and do so supposedly for subtler purposes. But just cross such a man and he will flare up to furies you would not have suspected. He may lose a foreign investment and be willing to wage war on account of that. Or he may have been let down by a friend and will be working for years to close in on him for the kill. Nothing less would do. In point of fact, he wants to shred him to pieces.

Well, if a person fights these cruel ambitions of his for power beyond reason and for power's sake, he may take to *compulsions* and *obsessions* in order to prevent the worst from happening in reality.

Take a young man, a college student, brother of a girl six years his junior, who has developed the compulsion to touch certain things. He cannot predict which, but once the idea has struck him, he must go through all possible and impossible detours in order to bring it about. Once, while still in high school, it was the button of a policeman, another time a letter opener on the desk of the person who interviewed him as a college candidate. At some later time it was a car that did not have the right of way, but made him stop. He had to follow that car until it was parked. Then he got out of his, walked by and knocked at it passingly. Gradually he also developed the habit of touching wood and ultimately carrying around a piece of wood or rather a little elephant carved of ebony. If he could not touch the thing or person whom he might otherwise have felt compelled to pursue until he had done it, he could now touch the elephant in his pocket a certain number of times—increasing numbers of time, to be sure— or touch something *like* the thing or person concerned with the elephant. Even touching himself with the elephant would sometimes do. In other words, with the small image of the animal in his pocket everything got under some kind of control and might have remained that way, but one day, due to very unlikely circumstances (which, nevertheless, he might have instigated himself), he lost the elephant. This was so upsetting that he sought psychotherapy.

Treatment revealed slowly what the reader may already have suspected: the afflicted had had to touch those whom he hated acutely. The policeman had yelled at him. The interviewer at the college had kept him waiting and appeared generally condescending, and the car that made him stop could have hit him. Like all neurotic symptoms, touching the offender accomplished two things. It gave him the contact with the object of his unduly destructive desires. He actually wanted to wrest the head from that policeman's body, stab the interviewer and smash the fellow-driver's car. Yet he consoled himself with a button. Tearing that one off would have been much less of an offense. Hence he could dare to touch it, whereas with the original and more primitive desire he might have preferred not to go near the policeman at all, both in order to save him and himself. Similar considerations would hold on the other two examples. To touch the dagger or the car is just enough doing and not-doing to be "satisfactory". But actually the satisfaction value is so small that he has to do more and more touching over smaller and smaller offenses. The wooden elephant, the image of a strong and powerful, though tameable, animal, is a compromise with practicality, but without it, anxiety is high.

What traumatised the person in the manipulatory state? One event that could be established in this case was the birth of his sister. But by that time he had already been at the end of the Oedipal phase. So why did he not become a hysteric rather than a compulsive neurotic, if psychopathology was inevitable to begin with? Well, the other trauma was a less conspicuous, but even more chronic, hence powerful, condition. His mother had been a belligerent female, sister of a younger girl and the daughter of a weak and partly paralysed father and a domineering mother. Father had been the oldest of two boys and two girls, but had lost his father in his late childhood. According to the patient the parents must have been in constant struggles with each other over their seniority rights, mother even over acceptance of the other sex. Two of her many derogatory remarks she had made to the patient were: "Men are ugly enough as they are" and: "Where would you be without us women!" Father, on the other hand, had found himself in an unusual position of seniority: at about ten years of age he had lost his father and had turned the oldest male in his entire family, guilty of desires to that effect that had come true (he had got rid of his father) and hence particularly touchy on the subject.

The patient had grown up with a fierce and awesome mother and a relatively quiet and reticent, though by no means uncertain, father. What is more and to be expected, he had been strongly intimidated by and identified with his powerful mother before he even entered the Oedipal stage, and remained so upon actual entry. Heterosexual relationships contained little beyond power aspects. This was the impression he must have got. There was nothing specifically female to look for in a woman. But this somewhat shaky and half-hearted position taken in the Oedipal stage was shaken altogether when his sister arrived and when it became obvious that she was something different. She was a *real* girl. She was liked and attended to by both parents merely for what she was. She did not have to enact a girl or rather some kind of a pre-genital creature, as he did.

Well, from there on he seemed to have focused on power, on authority derived from power only, on hating unconsciously all masculine females and finally anybody wielding power of any kind against him. Without knowing he was very very angry at his mother. He could have killed her for thwarting of her own accord and without any interference from father every effort whatsoever to approach or even see her as a woman. And yet, but also because of it, he could not let go of her at all.

Compulsions to wash, to check incessantly whether everything is locked or contained, to keep counting one's money, to insult at least one person at every meeting or gathering attended, to cheat everybody at least once, be it only by a penny and cost it many dollars even to get into the position to cheat, all work by the same devices. Here too desires and the defenses against them blend to form the neurotic symptom. The compulsive washer is defending against primitive desires of manipulation, such as soiling, crushing, killing, destroying, sometimes also against primitive genital desires, but he is also satisfying primitive desires, although to a very moderate degree only: he is wallowing in soap and water, squeezing his hands, the soap or the towel—should the reader know a compulsion-neurotic, please watch the vehemence with which he is usually practising his symptom—and killing the dirt, the germs, etc. Since such moderate and, in principle, legitimate gratifications can do little to quench his thirst for much greater violence, the symptom is recurring rapidly again and again (see also p. 27).

The compulsive locker as well as the counter of his money, other possessions or even anything, does not want to let go of what he has. Yet why should he be worried about it? Nobody is going to take it away from him. Such may his friends wonder. The trouble is, though, that he wants to possess so much and to hold on to it with such force that he must fear punishment all over. He is usually fearing the very same things that he would want to inflict upon others. Underneath he himself wants to rob them of everything they have and pile it up in his own treasury vaults. Why would he want so much? In order to be really and truly in power. The chief object of his unconscious fury and hatred, however, is a parent or both or some close psychological descendant. Originally *they* wanted to rob *him*. They would force him into all kinds of things including even his very own elimination. He would have to give whether he wanted to or not. Well, they were not too lucky on that count. And as if to prove this, compulsion neurotics are often constipated.

Obsessions refer to compulsive thoughts rather than actions. The afflicted may be unable to get rid of the idea that something terrible is going to happen to his parents, or strange words such as "You will sizzle in hell", "Spit on his grave" or "Kill him" pop up against the will of the person in question. But they are not his, he claims. They come from elsewhere. He would never do anything like that nor say it, nor even think of it. Again we would assume offhand that the obsessed must, among others, have desires aspiring precisely what these strange ideas imply. He cherishes the severest hatred for the person who should sizzle in hell. Only he could not possibly admit to it. Otherwise he would be the one to sizzle there. It is he himself who tries not to spit on that person's grave, but wishes him dead in the first place and spit on him in the second, and the lonely thought "Kill him"—he claims he has not the faintest idea of whom that refers to; he does not want to do even the slightest harm to anybody—is his own deliberation. All of these obsessions, however, occur in isolation, just as do compulsions. The afflicted is not aware of what he is doing or in what ways these ideas that haunt him so crazily could conceivably have meaning for him. Counter-cathexis of those desires that are being fought by the symptom is incomplete.

They are not abolished. They are more in the open than he or anyone in his position would like. Hence dissociation, i.e. isolation, of those desires or repression of their connection with oneself, is a prerequisite of a successful symptom. Without it nothing at all would be accomplished. With it, however, the magic is possible.

Other types of symptoms pertinent to this level of fixation run under *pregenital conversion neuroses*. They comprehend such phenomena as stuttering and tics which may be said to be even more isolated than obsession- or compulsion-symptoms. The stutterer gets mixed up in his verbal intentions because of some insufficiently counter-cathected primitive desires for power and destruction. He stutters when challenged by an authority, whether in reality or in his imagination. He stutters at the mere thought that somebody will test him. A question put to him by a casual passer-by, no more than "Where is Bucyrus Avenue ?" may come as enough of a surprise to incapacitate his speech for the time being. Each response on his part suffices, of course, to stigmatise him as a stutterer in the eyes of the other person and that is already part of the punishment he takes along with his symptom. His bad intentions are atoned for right as they come out. His fury at the authority figure in question, his wish to dispose of him most drastically, so that he will never forget, to say something very crude and violent to that passer-by—how dare he address him, the stutterer ?—are being penalised by the ridicule and pity that they earn him. But more atonement is often found necessary. The stutterer tends to go out of his way to please, to say much more than is requested of him, only in order to display his affliction in its full grandeur.

Needless to say that even a person without a pregenital conversion neurosis may stutter on occasion, such as when he wants to say too much at once, or something too complex and difficult, or when he is using a jargon or a language that he is not too familiar with. Sometimes even a hard-to-pronounce word will do. The conversion neurotic also wants to say "too much", but in a vastly more intensive way.

A person suffering from tics will respond similarly to specific situations. His twitch of the face, his shoulder shrug, his "bite" (an upward snap of the lower jaw), endless throat clearing or his neck wriggle, will occur or get aggravated when the desires against which they have been installed are acutely tempted. A sudden threat to his own power, reprimands, but also undue expectations, may trigger him off. Again the symptom represents both, desire and defense. The desire may be to stab the challenger or monitor, but his arm remains in place, even limp. Only his face simulates a grimace that would accompany his stab, if he really delivered it, and the shoulder shrug the blow that he meant to land. The "bite" or the throat-clearing could stand for an aggressive shout preceding a primitive attack, and the neck wriggle perhaps for an attempt to shake off his jacket and shirt in order to mete out his physical tortures without handicaps. Yet at the same time the tic is looked at as a physical disability. He, the afflicted, is a minor invalid. Hence how can he possibly do any harm or have any wicked intentions. As a matter of fact, his symptoms may even represent the physical punishment too that he wishes guiltily to receive for his designs. He would wince like that—i.e. twitch, shrug, "bite", cough or wriggle—under the slaps, blows, stabs or mutilations, even genital ones, that he himself deserves.

Here too the chief object of the afflicted's unconscious aggressions is a parent or some close psychological substitute as well as the unreasonable power that they exercised in his opinion. Even so his responses will be somewhat appropriate to specific situations. Appropriate in neurotic ways, to be sure, but things could be much worse. Where they are, where pregenital conversion symptoms are extremely massive and more immune to influences by the immediate situation, fixation is likely to have occurred on the early manipulatory or anal-sadistic stage.

If no specific symptoms are resorted to, a person may be more broadly, though less specifically, affected. He may develop a compulsive character. He will tend to be meticulous, excruciatingly thorough, monotonous and conscientious in his endeavors. Some will be engaged in unending debates with themselves as to whether they should do one thing or the other and mostly end up doing neither. They become compulsive deliberators and doubters. Others may be full of all kinds of superstitions and magic beliefs, often in religious disguises, or they attempt to gamble and bet with fate or God by means of peculiar and secret sacrifices, oracles, prayers or some kind of hypnosis. Others are sarcastic and weirdly witty, but incapable of relating to people in any other ways. A caustic politician, a skilful rabble-rouser, a gruesome cartoonist or a master spy, would be among the examples.

Perversions corresponding to this level of fixation are represented by the sadist of all colors, but also the masochist. Their distinction from sadism and masochism on the genital level would be the relative irrelevance of the opposite sex and genital relations. Not that such a pervert might not seek and have them. But they will be merely a sideline. He prefers orgies of power and violence and he can never get enough. The only stable relationship a sadist can build would be with a masochist, but even then he cannot really be happy. The most primitive and gratifying of all his desires would be to mutilate and perhaps even kill his love-object. Yet if he does, it will depreciate in value (the more there has been mutilated, the less remains) or be lost altogether. He will have to get another one and start all over. If he does not, however, he will always stop short of ultimate and final gratification, and this is not a very happy state either. The same would hold for the masochist who is, of course, the more likely one to die if a love-object must be killed. What these two often do in their union, whether it is homosexual or heterosexual and whether genital relationships do or do not play a part, is to torture and be tortured psychologically. This can be more devastating than physical torture, but also has a great advantage: recuperation is possible. On a primitive level nothing has really happened. The physical person remains intact.

The more pronounced masochist, the person who does not want to be punished so much as to be overwhelmed and even raped for the glory of it, preferably by a superior power, is fixated on the early manipulatory or anal-sadistic stage of motivational development. He is the truer masochist. He gets more immediate delight from being the victim of mutilation and destruction, unless he is putting up a fight against such desires to begin with. But even the sadist differs from the sadist of the earlier stage in that the former is overtly more concerned with a particular person and sometimes content to exercise his powers with him or her. The latter, however, wishes to wield much greater power, happens to be more diffuse in his intentions except that he himself is to be the very greatest of all and would not hesitate to dispose of hundreds or even millions of people like mud, should doing so enhance, defend or restore his own stature. The same would hold for the person defending by means of neuroses against sadisms of either kind. The obsessive or compulsive person's symptoms are unconsciously geared toward a parent or both, or parent figures of his early life, but they tend to be specific. They apply to present and partly real situations. The neurotic of the early manipulatory or anal-sadistic stage is less specific, wilder in his unconscious wishes and "crazier" in his defenses against them.

Other perversions, those with genital components, have already been mentioned (see p. 268 f). Coprophilia (love of feces smearing, also of the person who does it or provides the wastes) and necrophilia (love of dead bodies), but also fetishism, are concerned with desires pertaining to the drive system "bodily manipulation", with possessions of objects as well as with their exchanges, including the most primitive kinds of property: sex-organs, at least in symbolic representations, and excrements. But even manifest homosexuality among males with its frequent emphasis on anal-genital contacts belongs here too, whereby the active partner would represent fixations on the early part of the Oedipal and on the late manipulatory stage, whereas the passive partner is likely to have regressed, at least partly, to the early manipulatory and/or late oral stage of motivational development, if he is not merely the accidental victim of homosexual seduction and ready to step out of it at his first real chance. One might wonder, though, what traumatic condition made him amenable to such seductions in the first place. Female homosexuals, like all females, tend to be generally somewhat less active in the drive system "bodily manipulation". They remain slightly more oral than males, whether this is due to constitutional differences that come to bear in later childhood and adolescence or due to their disappointment during the Oedipal stage with genital manipulation and stimulation which, after all, would be the natural continuation and favorite of bodily manipulation and stimulation (see also p. 170 ff). Hence the active exercise of power for power's sake plays a smaller part with women in general, at least under ordinary circumstances, and they rank somewhat less frequently among obsessives and compulsives as well as among the perverts of that stage. This holds even for the more primitive early manipulatory stage of motivational development, although here female representation is a little more at par with the male.

It should also be mentioned that minor pregenital perversions such as nose picking, squeezing of blackheads, scraping the scalp, enjoying bowel movements, even their smells, and many others are widespread and seldom *per se* indicative of pathology. The same holds for kissing, say, odd body areas, for nailbiting, having one's back scratched, and other more oral and passive desires. As a matter of fact, there is no desire whatsoever whose satisfaction might not, in turn, look like a perversion, like something improper, rude, wicked and even utterly impossible, in certain contexts.

If a person has been *traumatised during the early stage of bodily manipulation* (the early "anal-sadistic" stage, normally occupying the second year of life), say through the loss of a parent, through extreme violence exercised by his parents or used to stop his own infantile assertions of power, or through great indifference on the part of a parent or both, he might never fully have moved on to the late manipulatory stage or to the Oedipal stage. Such a person will also be preoccupied with power and destruction, but in its very primitive varieties. A whole city or industry, an entire nation, all of mankind or the world at large want to be grabbed, shaken, forced into obedience or destroyed, and any attack whatsoever is good enough as long as it leads to results. The afflicted wants to wield powers far beyond the amount of work that he would be able to put in. Tremendous deals, revolutions, and *coups d'état* figure foremost in his imagination. He does not want to get something for something. No, he wants all and he is willing to invest all that he has. And he will show them all. Anybody who ever crossed him will pay, and lives are the least that some of them will have to give.

If that person does not find the world responsive, though, if what he desires with a remnant of reason cannot be had, he will raise his demands to the utterly impossible. And if the utterly impossible proves impossible indeed and all his pent-up wild and primitive fury goes unspent, that very same impossible may get him in return. Perhaps, he begins to wonder, there is a power greater than his own that has no other design but to thwart him, to do to him what he wanted to do to the world. As a matter of fact, the world can never be at his command because it is already at the command of that superior person. So great is his force that it can control him down to the silliest little chores of everyday life. A match does not strike. That's because of him. He planted such matches in his pocket. The milk is not cool enough. That's him again. A button came loose. His wife forgot to pick up their winter coats from the cleaner's. His child flunked a subject in school. His nephew broke a leg. Well, all that comes from the great "persecutor" and his agents. They have even fixed his toothbrush!

Why does the afflicted not give in to that superior power? Would it not be reasonable to quit fighting and ask that person what he wants him to do? Not really, because all this is merely that person's preparation for the big kill. If there were any use in trying to appease this persecutor, he, the victim would certainly try to. But he knows that this power is without mercy. How come he knows? From his own desired power (which, unfortunately, has been conquered by a parent's power quite early in his life). He would tolerate no mercy himself. After all, the persecutor *is* his own creation (built, however, from his own experiences with such a power in reality). How would he be killed? Oh, he would be attacked from the back. He is sure about that. He would be assaulted and slaughtered. His intestines would be ripped apart. He would be torn to pieces. In fact, among the mildest things that could happen to him would be a merely genital assault from the rear. Hence fears are sometimes focused on that aspect alone. After all, anal manipulation and stimulation was the most impressive and gratifying of all the things that the body was found able to do during that stage of motivational development (see p. 148 ff). The name of the affliction: *paranoia.*

As has been pointed out before (see p. 273), *pregenital conversion neuroses* indicate fixation on the early manipulatory stage, if they are very massive and highly independent of specific situations. The afflicted seems to be closer to an all-or-none struggle for power and survival than the person fixated on the late manipulatory stage. Besides his preoccupation with a parent-figure, usually the really cruel one of the two, is more pervasive. Their psychological descendants or substitutes matter much less. A chronic and irresistable tic recurring automatically or being omnipresent, or a very persistent stutter regardless of any particular contexts and the kinds of people addressed, is more likely to belong to the early manipulatory stage.

Perversions of the early manipulatory stage have already been mentioned (see p. 275). Profuse killers and reckless attackers, but also the more emphatic masochist are examples. The sadists may get themselves killed in the process, but they do not originally intend to. Nor does the masochist. He may have wishes to be killed, but he would not do it himself.

If the entire character is affected, a person may become hopelessly querulous and righteous, an inarticulate reformer, political, religious or social alike. Evangelists of active christianity, prophets of expropriation, but also fascists, terrorists and haters of all mankind would be among them (see also p. 285 f). The less they are checked by their own defenses, the more do they live for power and try to build it up to devastating proportions. The stronger the reign of defenses, the more paranoic will such persons tend to be.

If a person has *suffered traumata during the late oral stage* (i.e. the "oral-sadistic" stage, about the last two thirds of the first year of life), whether due to losses in reality or their equivalents or whether due to hereditary weaknesses that make even mild environmental difficulties intolerable, he will be prone for the severest disorder yet. It has been mentioned that the only object to speak of that exists in the infant's mind is mother. Anything drastically peculiar with her, such as extreme neglect of her child, a strong aversion to feeding, repeated longer absences or even her disappearance for good, will have most direct and immediate effects on her child. Father's absence, disappearance or other peculiarity would not go unnoticed, to be sure, but the child would hardly be the primary victim. Mother would suffer, though, and may well communicate to her child a measure of her grief, dread, worry or whatever it is.

At the late oral stage mother is the great mediator between the child and the world. One might even say that she *is* that world. All good things of life come from her. What is more, they come by her grace alone or all by themselves, but at any rate they require no work to speak of on his own part. Not that the child would not be active. Considering how little he has learned yet and how uncooperative a servant still is his own body, he is trying as hard as he will ever do (see also pp. 140, 145). But his efficiency is negligible. He controls only very few and the most immediate of the conditions of life. He can scream, but mother will have to come to his rescue. He can pull himself up to stand on his own, he can even get up again after he fell over, but beware of getting caught between the bars or in a blanket or of losing the pants. He can eat from a spoon all right, but the spoon as well as he himself must be held by mother, etc. In other words there are almost no good things in life that would not come from her and for free. The only effort required at times is anger. Getting angry, that is trying again more primitively and aggressively (see also p. 58), brings the desired in a jiffy. If it does not, a little tantrum surely will.

Remember that gentle sucking and violent biting, respectively, represent the most advanced and the most primitive of all desires yet formed (see p. 145); also that the most ferocious thing in his imagination that the child could conceivably do is eating up the object of his desires; finally that the worst thing that could happen to him in his imagination is being devoured and destroyed even in substance (see p. 146). Considering all this we have already the main ingredients that figure in *mania* and *depression*, the two outstanding disorders of this stage of motivational development.

Mania is a state of excessive, gaily aggressive excitement, of feeling great and wonderful, of being intoxicated with omnipotence. Thoughts fly so fast that there is no way of checking whether the track of pursuit is right. In fact, there is no one pursuit. A hundred tracks are being followed almost at once, so quick is their succession. It looks as if realistic considerations would not enter at all, partly because too many different aspects matter all at once. The afflicted promises to a nurse who smiled at him that she will meet the Shah of Iran to-morrow—he himself will throw the party for the Shah—and that he will give her a Cadillac for a present so that she can visit the Shah, but he is in isolation in a mental hospital and does not even have a dime to his avail, nor a telephone, nor a place to throw a party, etc. What color should the car be? Snow-white, replies the nurse. He could also get her a mountain of snow, if she preferred that, he might continue. That would be too cold, she says. But then he could ship Greenland ice to the hospital. Enough for all the cold drinks of the world. And so on.

It looks as if he believed that somebody endowed with absolute powers of every kind possible will take care of things or rather of all his things. That person will arrange for his phantasies to come true. No further effort will be necessary on his part to deserve such incredible services. His word is enough. He feels so fine that he thinks he must have accomplished great things. Small wonder then, that he is being swamped with all those favors and distinctions. Anything else would merely make no sense.

The world does not respond, though. It fails him even on the most irrelevant particles of his dreams. So maybe he is not in such a splendid state after all. Perhaps he has accomplished great things, but they were bad. Coming to think of it, they must have been very, very bad, in fact the worst of all possible things. If that invisible, but omnipotent gratifier of his gives out, he himself must have driven him away. But would the great sponsor let him? And if he really had, wouldn't he come back on the first occasion? No, he must have done something much more violent. He must have become that "god" or "goddess" himself. But how? He must have incorporated him. He devoured that god. He must have done so literally. That is perhaps why he had all this power. Or could he only swallow him, because he had it to begin with? Oh, these things are inextricably intertwined!

If he has really swallowed him, that god is gone, and without him he himself is nothing. Finding himself still alive and moving is an error. He should be dead. He should be disposed of for good, and his own god, whom he abused so very, very gravely, will dispose of him. He, the patient, will be devoured in return and the whole world is going to be devoured with him. Everything will disappear. This is in progress already. There is no hope (except that the god in him—the same one?—is getting the treatment too). This is how far his guilt will carry him. And the god with whom he is engaged in such gruesome deals is . . . his mother.

Depression is the name of this process, and while it lasts the patient is retarded in his overall behavior, although sometimes also diffusely agitated, at least for periods of time. He appears dejected and infinitely sad, cries easily and for a while is a serious suicide risk. The temptation is great to punish himself together with the love-object that he thinks he has incorporated. This, incidentally, is in contrast to the paranoic who might rather get himself killed in pursuit of his delusion than to lay hand upon himself, although the latter can happen too. Depression may follow mania, and often it does so in rather regular cycles. People who look fairly normal during their intermissions may get their raptures, mania, about every six months or every other year and they might either return directly to normal or slide into a depression and "atone" for their mania before doing so. The closer they are to normal in their "free intervals", the more likely is it that they get both mania and depression in succession. If they are normally somewhat on the sad side, they may only get a mania. They atone all the time, so to speak, but once in a while they have to break out of it. If they are normally

T

on the hypomanic side, they may only get a depression. Things can go well for a long time, is their philosophy, but not for good. One cannot keep away from gloom altogether.

These cycles are usually quite independent from the environment or, to be precise, from the present environment. They have been set up long ago, in early childhood, and then it may have been an environmental influence indeed that brought it all about: some severe trauma or loss, as indicated (p. 277f). The cycles set up will tend to grow in length with the afflicted's age (see also p. 97 f), but once adulthood has been reached they may remain fairly stable. They may also go unnoticed for a long time and come to the fore only when life gets serious or begins even to close in on a person a little. Sometimes, however, the attacks seem to be solitary, especially with depression. They may be precipitated by an acute loss, but mourning over it goes on and on. The bereaved cannot recover. Usually this indicates that an early, though perhaps overlooked, loss has been re-activated.

These psychoses, however, are not the only manifestations of fixation on the late oral stage of motivational development. Another important group are the so-called *impulse-neuroses*. They comprehend recurrent morbid desires, say, to wander off to other places on no notice at all, settle down in another city or town, get oneself moderately established, and suddenly drop everything and wander off again. It looks as if this town or city had not been the right place either; as if something were still missing. Impulse neuroses comprehend sudden and irresistible desires to set fires, to prostitute oneself profusely, to get drunk, to gamble, in a sense even to steal. In all of them it looks as if the afflicted resolved just then that he cannot stand it any longer. What? His plight. His boundless deprivation. Of what? Of an all-powerful god, or goddess rather, of an all-providing mother who would set the world straight for him and give kindly and indefinitely without asking for anything in return. They are all engaged in intensive searches for that paradisical semi-union with mother which was shaken too soon in their lives.

In the late oral stage mother appeared as an entity separate from oneself for the first time, and yet remained in such intimate harmony with oneself that it was still she more often than oneself who recognised one's desires and fulfilled them. But for the impulse-neurotics this goddess, good fairy or mother (sometimes also a very motherly father) should still be there. She should not exercise any power except unswervingly in their favor. There should be no struggle over and fight for the goods of the world. They should just come. Needless to say that this goddess would not be a genital love-object. For all of them sexes matter little. That holds even for the prostitute or the girl who becomes one in spells. She is not looking for a man at all. She is looking for a very kind and warm gentleman or rather for a gentle woman, a mother. But women don't care, she has come to believe, and men do only under certain conditions.

Pyromania and especially kleptomania may have genital connotations too.

The kleptomanic girl steals something that she has not got (see pp. 268f, 170ff). But if it had not been for mother, if she had not born her to be a wretched girl, she might have had from the beginning what she is looking for so desperately. Actually mother has let her down in many more respects, in fact in all those that would make one feel comfortable and secure in the world. Hence the stealing (often fairly indiscriminate, with subsequent discarding or disinterested storing of the stolen objects) is an attempt to extract anything from mother that supposedly she did not want to give, or to forge mother into a kind and generous goddess at last. That holds even more for (rarer) male kleptomaniacs. With pyromania the pre-genital aspects are even stronger. Fire devours its objects, houses, barns, perhaps even people. That takes care of the hatred with which the afflicted pursues mother who has not given him enough. At the same time fire furnishes a very elementary sensation that goes with mother too: warmth. The warmth she should have given him or continued to give him.

The dipsomaniac, drunkard or addict of any narcotic drug including even sleeping pills, is trying to reinstate his infantile happiness and bliss by artificial means which, incidentally, he would prefer to take orally, where possible. He is fabricating his own mania, so to speak, but it will inevitably be followed by depression: the hangover, guilt over the relapse, and still no motherly person around for keeps; although the drug-addicts often call their peddlers "mother". So he takes to the drug again, and due to chemical and neurophysiological factors greater dosages or shorter intervals become necessary all the time. All this may hold even for such perfectly acceptable "drugs" as coffee, tea, cigarettes or pervitin. To the extent that the person fails to get what he wants or, generally speaking, to extract the kindness from the world that he desires so badly, his addiction will mount. However, these drugs are so acceptable, among other things, because they do not only delude the consumer about his well-being. They really exhilarate him temporarily. They make him more alert and even more efficient so that his chance to wrest from the world what he longs for is at least not diminished.

One could call these addictions some sort of perversions of the late oral stage, but in regression to the earliest stages of motivational development neurotic and perverse solutions of the basic problems of life lie closer together. The psychotic, borderline case, or other psychological relative, is readier to think and do those primitive and impossible things than is the neurotic of the manipulatory or of the early genital stage. Inversely, the real perversions of that stage of fixation, thorough delinquency and all-round aimlessness, criminality of the most explosive, but hardly contemplated variety such as manslaughter of the person who dared to slight him, blowing up dams and railroads in order to get even with the grocer or a station-master, but also inciting others by sweeping demagoguery to do so, placing a bomb in an airplane in order to have mother, an aunt, etc. shredded to pieces and swallowed by the air or a mountain desert, but also impulsive suicide, are usually manifestations of a psychotic or borderline character. What is known as the "psychopathic personality" has also been fixated on that stage.

Still another type of disturbance are the so-called *organ-neuroses* or *psycho-somatic disorders*, to use a more recent term. The person with whom the afflicted is unconsciously preoccupied is also mother or whoever came closest to having filled her part for him (and ultimately let him down). This person or the world in general, is not giving freely enough, if at all, and he is either wildly furious about it or outraged with himself, i.e. dejected, guilt-ridden and begging for punishment. However, rather than admitting to one or the other, he does something that the child of the oral stage could normally accomplish too. He lets his body be affected. As a child he may have developed acute stomach burns and pains or colics, say, over a temporary replacement of mother or over a change of routine, but that would have been gone as soon as she returned or the old routine was resumed. As an adult he, the afflicted, can keep his gastro-intestinal tract in a state of constant expectation and develop ulcers, colitis and the like. Yet no food can quench his thirst. He yearns for something that he could not get in early life and that, as a consequence, he could not accept now even if it were served to him on a platter. With other cases it may be the heart that is affected. They may come down with pseudo-angina pectoris or they may develop essential hypertension. Both reflect the infantile and tantrumlike rage with which he would like unconsciously to respond to a balking world. The respiratory system may get the brunt. A person may get asthma bronchiale, which represents the eternal wail or scream with which he wishes unconsciously to accuse the world or mother in particular for letting him down. He may develop very ugly and/or itchy eczema, sometimes all over the body, with two chief unconscious meanings: mother left him or the world is not kind to him because . . . well, just look at him. Look how ugly he can get. That shows how ugly and bad he *is*. And that is why he has been left by mother and why the world is doing nothing for him. Secondly, he is giving himself the stimulation of the skin that goes with any kind of mothering and that, he feels, he had so little of. He has to provide it himself by this strange device (see also Alexander 1950, Deutsch, F., 1953).

A similar meaning can be attributed to hypochondria. The afflicted is so preoccupied with his own body and its most detailed welfare in order to substitute for what his mother failed to give him, in his opinion, but also in order to account for the reason mother left him: because he was so weak and sickly to begin with. Unconsciously he hopes even to be able to summon an unbelievably kind and ubiquitous mother by all his achings.

In short, the problem is more uniformly the same with all these disorders and their chief longings more primitive than with hysteric conversions, although even here different sufferers choose somewhat different angles and different organs to play on.

Still another disease that belongs here is *epilepsy*. In contrast to all other disorders it is identifiable by neurophysiological means, i.e. by the electroencephalogram. This does not mean, though, that other forms of psychopathology might not one day become identifiable by similar or other neurophysiological means, nor on the other hand that differential diagnosis and theory of psychopathology would have to wait until that day. It is not even hard to see why the more complex phenomena of psychopathology are quite unlikely ever to be fully amenable to neurophysiological treatment alone. Why? Because they are so very, very complex, and so little of what is easy to substantiate and handle psychologically shows at all on any set of oscillographs, no matter how intricately arranged. Whether and why a person loves another person, what he loves about him or her and what would follow from it for his behavior in a given situation, say an offer of a mission to a foreign country, is beyond all neurophysiological concoctions. Psychologically, however, a few more *data* permit already some fair predictions. If we know what kind of relationship prevailed among the person's parents and siblings, to what degree the love-object fits incestuous patterns, how much loss has infiltrated the person's as well as his love-object's past, for how long he has known and how much he has seen of her or him, how much separation, first from the beloved person, but secondly also from other customary aspects of life, the mission may involve and how big the premiums for such sacrifices, we might be able to tell what that person is going to do and how he will manage. Many more data may flow into our appraisal, as we investigate the matter, but those data mentioned lend themselves easily to the treatment of groups of cases, say soldiers going to overseas bases, but even missionaries or diplomats, and wherever we have groups, predictions can be tested with much greater convenience and scientific elegance than is possible with individual cases. I hope, though, that these comments are not misconstrued to be antagonistic to neurophysiology. Speaking personally for a moment, I have great respect for whatever little I know of it.

Well, full-fledged epilepsy as a psychosomatic disorder or organ-neurosis can be said to have affected the entire motor apparatus. It is a most violent fit of anger over extreme and most basic deprivations. The non-compliance of mother and, indirectly, of people and the world in general makes him mad, but he has learned to be calm and complacent about it. Outwardly, of course, but in a way also inwardly. He feels no anger. He relegates it to his motor apparatus, to his body, so to speak, for execution in isolation and unconsciousness. He resorts to this most primitive and destructive of all ways of doing something and obtaining satisfaction (see p. 57 f) at last: the fit of panic. As a matter of fact, if anxiety can be viewed as temporary regression, and temporary regression, in turn, as an attempt to satisfy the desires in question by more primitive means (see p. 58, also pp. 25f, 27f), utter panic would be the attempt to satisfy all basic desires at once on the most primitive level possible. Specific desires could no longer be maintained on such a level of regression, and all primal *substitution continua* or drive-systems should be involved with their most elementary specimens. Hence, in addition to the tremendous spasm of violence that constitutes the epileptic fit and would represent the drive-system bodily manipulation, there should also be oral manipulation, biting, and elimination, the most impressive of all things that the body can do (see also p. 124 ff). This, however, is precisely the case in a full-fledged epileptic attack. There is "biting", a powerful jerk of the jaw, not infrequently leading to injuries of the tongue, and there is urination and defecation. One might say that the epileptic fit is the attempt to reach ultimate satisfaction or orgasm by global bodily manipulation and stimulation. Yet this cannot be genital orgasm, the most gratifying, but also the relatively most difficult to achieve, of all (see p. 121 ff), no matter how hard may be the try. In that respect, if I may digress for a moment, he is in no better position than the rock-'n'-roll fanatics who sometimes work themselves into frenzies, or certain African tribes that are trying in their religious festivities to reach ecstasy by global and primitively rhythmical bodily manipulation. Both may end up on the ground, completely exhausted and delirious, but still not "really satisfied" unless ultimate cohabitation is part of the rite.

There are many sub-forms of the epileptic attack, such as psychomotor, autonomic, abdominal, even sensory seizures, *petit mal*, and other so-called epileptic equivalents. They represent only certain selected aspects of *grand mal*. Brain injuries may lead to epileptic attacks too. All of these syndromes and conditions are distinguishably different from each other and could be accounted for, in principle, by psychological means. Since these sub-forms are all occurring in isolation, just like *grand mal*, and are very difficult to reach psychologically, these accounts will not be attempted. Epilepsy is a domain of the neurologist. He can control it by a few pills of dilantin. Only its occurrence or non-occurrence at all must concern us psychologically, if for no other reasons than its hereditary vicinity to schizophrenia and other psychoses as well as the changes that the attacks—their frequency, severity, and even their quality—tend to undergo with the afflicted's motivational development.

If a person, fixated on the late oral stage, "chooses" none of the pathology discussed, his entire character may be infiltrated by the concerns and preoccupations of that stage. If he is not a passive clinger, whiner and drone altogether, he may become the person with ever new and more grandiose schemes of what could be done in order to transform a field of trade, a science, or even the world as a whole. His mission would be outlining the dimensions of the paradise to come, and it would be a vast one. The details? Who cares except for those millions of small fools who will execute his ideas, and even elaborate them for such a course in the first place. The credit goes all to him. Not in a possessive way. He would not want to wrangle over it. No, he simply takes it for granted, even if it concerns the remotest outgrowth of his ideas such as the sewer-system of a house in town which he thinks he has built, perhaps because he moved there, or because he invested some money.

If he fails throughout, if people do not take up his gorgeous inspirations and visions, he may become the prophet of gloom and doom, the great vilifier of his people, his colleagues, or the world, not seldom in the name of God who he still believes is steadfastly on his side. If people do not heed his terrible threats either, he may try to redeem them, possible by his own ultimate sacrifice: death. He may desire at last to be eaten by a whale, or to jump into a volcano and be consumed by its fire, or he may wish to be crucified, that is to die on display and be buried, but swallowed symbolically and ceremonially ever after. All in order to atone for the evil and bad wishes of mankind which, incidentally, may well be his own bad wishes for mankind that has failed him, or for God who could have helped him by the move of a finger. Why, of all things in the world, didn't he?

Revolutionaries always carry some such features in their characters, but they often also wield power more pertinently, even love the other sex, and tend to be men of great talents in the areas of their endeavors. Although all new houses become old after a while and may finally have to be torn down rather than patched up forever, the revolutionaries often under-estimate how much repair the house could still stand, and how much good it may still do its tenants. The Pharisees against whom Jesus Christ preached and even raged were not all that bad, and the revolution that he proclaimed—love even your enemy, do not strike back, not even in your phantasy, forgive him who robbed and killed you and your family, abandon all earthly possessions—has been waiting until this day to be truly implemented.

Similarly so-called capitalistic societies could not be, or in the long run remain, quite as bad as Marx and some of his spiritual sons have perceived them. It looks as if they had been loath to credit any ability whatsoever to individuals and groups in stronger positions, and as if they had thought it possible to reach such positions without being of any service at all to other people and the society as a whole. Similarly, of course, "capitalistic counter-revolutionaries" have often been loath to see any resemblance between state capitalistic societies that have emerged historically, and their own. Yet on closer inspection the structural and functional similarities have increasingly seemed to outweigh the differences by wide margins. Some of to-day's economic and sociological theories which Western democracies have produced are perhaps conceptually bolder and logically more penetrating than all the writings of Marx (who, incidentally, produced his own theories in a Western democracy too). Yet single pieces of his work such as the Communist Manifesto or as little as its concluding slogan ("Proletarians, you have nothing to lose but your chains!") have reached and moved more people directly within a few decades than to-day's economic and sociological theories may ever do. This does not say anything, though, about the number of people that may ultimately benefit from such theories.

Finally, to give one more example, even Freud, a key figure in this book, was not as new and revolutionary as he liked to see himself, and as followers might often have insisted with a vengeance. This concerns at least his basic concepts and notions. His early writings are full of substantial quotations, references, and credits to others (e.g. Freud, 1900), and in some of his late writings (e.g. Freud,

1912–13, 1920) his speculations, say, on the primeval family or on life and death are of no compelling theoretical import. In his thoughts about religion it may have escaped him that atheism and even sciences, especially in their early and anthropomorphic forms, can be religions too for all practical purposes. Of course, the large bulk of his writing is extremely significant both theoretically and practically, not by world-encompassing images and wisdoms, but by very specific and bold new assumptions, careful articulations and elaborations, and detailed implementation in practice. As a matter of fact, the lines of his writings are sometimes only the treasure boxes. The treasures themselves are between the lines, so to speak, and in the tradition of clinical and psychotherapeutic work that has originated from him (see preface). In that respect he has indeed created a new creed of sorts.

This should not mean that revolutionaries are wrong. Due to their strong desires for passivity and contemplation, which characterise them in all fields in one way or another (if by virtue of no other fact than that their only activity is talking about their grandiose ideas, whether through books or oral addresses), and due to their relative detachment, they are often very astute observers. Obviously they could not launch revolutions if they had no points to begin with. Usually they play on desires that everybody has. Not only in the sense that everybody has all of the primal desires and their most basic derivatives. This would be trivial. Rather in the sense that at certain historic times certain desires are being deprived more universally and pervasively than others, and if that has gone on too long, a little tap on some of the habitual constrictive forces may well make them crumble.

If a person has been *traumatised in the early oral stage*, his chances for a normal motivational development are small, particularly since it is hard to traumatise an infant during that stage without jeopardising at the same time even his very survival. During this stage mother can still be substituted for without too much of an experience of loss. She has not become an object to speak of yet, and other females stepping in may be able to duplicate her in every one of the few ways by which the infant would recognise her "blindly". However, if an infant is fed very irregularly or weaned very early and abruptly, sometimes permitted to cry until he falls asleep from exhaustion (in these early days of life believing even that perhaps his own tantrum was the feeding after all), and other times fed even before he wakes up by himself; if he is sometimes kept cold, other times too warm, or treated very roughly, as if he has earned a spanking and were actually getting it, if "mother" holds and carries him a lot one day, but does not take him out of his crib during another day, not even for the feedings, and does not change his diapers at all; if she decides to wean him overnight and goes back to nursing after a few days, only in order to try to wean him again, etc., a severe trauma in this earliest stage of development may be in the making.

What mother would do that, though? Perhaps a mother who does not want her child, or a mother who is a very disturbed person herself. Possibly a woman who is not even the child's mother, but the only one left to adopt him, or a number of employed persons, nurses, taking care of him in an orphan's home. If he stays there long enough to form an object relationship to speak of, he will cathect even this turnover of people, the fact that there is no *one* mother. We might say that traumatisation of children growing up in orphan's homes may become effective only in the late oral stage, but it should be noted that the object relationship he develops is "defective" from the start, and that the stages are not succinct. The groundwork for the ultimate formation of the object "mother" is still laid in the early oral stage, and toward the end of it his peculiar predicament has already begun to dawn on the orphan. Not that he knows any different; he has no way of comparing. But that is even worse, as far as the effects are concerned. A conscious loss, i.e. the loss of something or somebody whom one has come to know and love, is more painful, but after mourning is over, substitutes can be sought, possibly found and finally accepted. The person who has never had something or somebody, has no real idea of what to look for.

All of this holds for any of the conditions mentioned. It will begin to transpire on the infant what kind of a mother he has got by the time he can distinguish her from the rest of the world at all. His trouble starts already at the entrance to the late oral stage, which forces him of necessity to rely more heavily only on his "pre-object" relations of the world, whereas with the person, say, who finally develops mania or depression, the trouble starts in the midst of the late oral stage. During his development a child may not only regress *within* a given stage of development, if deprivation becomes overbearing and all other defenses are insufficient, but also, of course, to an earlier stage. As a matter of fact, all regression usually does both. Hence this is true also of all regression of the past, i.e. fixation.

The disorder representing fixation on, and acute regression to, the early oral stage of motivational development is *schizophrenia*, and its chief characteristic is the fragility of the afflicted's relations to any other person whatsoever. Once regression has really been achieved, there are no object-relations left. So it looks at least. The patient is extremely autistic, hallucinating, unresponsive to all stimulation, although not really insensitive, and totally reluctant to engage in any of the risks that even the most casual relationship to another person would entail. There are risks, to be sure. If a person has a luncheon appointment with the representative of a firm with which he may want to do business, there are a number of uncertainties such as: Will he like the man? Will the man like him and his product? Will the firm be a good choice for him? Will the financial aspects be satisfactory? Will he and his wife be able to buy a house now? But also others such as: Where in the hotel will they get a table? What will they eat? How will he start the conversation? Will he be able to be on time? And will the other person be? Or will he be late? How late? What if he does not show up at all?

How long will there be hope that he might still come? etc. The schizophrenic has withdrawn from all such enterprises. Even the risk of waiting a few minutes is too much for him to tolerate. He would rather not meet such a person at all. If he has regular appointments with a hospital staff member and that person is late once, this is just what he knew from the very beginning, and what he has been waiting for all along. That person too would not be reliable. It was foolish to hold out as much as a finger. So why not tilt the unwelcome visitor's cup of coffee with that same disappointed finger? Or why not pour the whole thing in his face? Why not attack him? In another case the visitor may be altogether innocent. He may just have had a haircut. Yet the clipping of anything, the lawn, a dress, finger nails, or wires in the hospital workshop, may have taken on the meaning of severance which the world keeps imposing on man. So the visitor has been severed from something too. As a result of this, he must be sick. As a matter of fact, he, the visitor, is really the sick one. He is covering up, but beware of him. They are all mad. The most vicious things are to be expected of them. So attack him! Or don't speak until Spring!

The schizophrenic does not rely on any person other than himself. He does not even rely on himself as a person, but rather as a kind of primitive man-world flux or a bundle of sensations. He is highly autistic and narcissistic. He has little, if any, interest in what is going on around him. Not even his closest relatives can make an impression, except for the piece of cake that they bring him regularly. He grabs that, to be sure, and devours it on the spot before he wastes another word. Politics, spots, the hospital, friends, doctors, nurses, fellow-patients, are all of no concern to him except where they touch him most immediately and directly. Politics and sports are simply something on television. If television can be turned on and off like light, that's why politics and sports have to do with electricity, also with him, and why he really does not care. Electricity has been irritating him all these years. Currents have been going through his body and influencing his own will. He would not be here, if it were not for those currents, except that sometimes they whisper to you, and they also try to hypnotise you. The hospital is not a hospital, it is the place where he lives. It may be a resort, Buckingham Palace, or a prison. In fact, it can be all these things within the course of a day, even within one single trend of thought or conversation. Friends, doctors, patients, they are all the same. They may be government officers, or messengers from hell, soldiers, Russians, they may even be snakes in human disguises. And the nurses? They are white little angels. But they can be scared. All it takes is to urinate against the wall when they come in, and off they go. But so what? And how long has he been here? Oh, two hundred years. Or maybe a day. Days, years, centuries, they are all the same.

Before a psychosis becomes manifest, a person may sometimes appear highly gifted and extremely sensitive to people, their intentions and feelings. So sensitive, indeed, that it might come as a small surprise to his friends that he slams at last his "inner door" to them. Their capacity to exhilarate and to disappoint him was just too much. He could tumble from extreme affection for a particular person to extreme hatred, and vice versa. He was so ambivalent toward them that he could ultimately save himself from his unbearable conflicts only by regressing to a *pre-ambivalent* stage where objects do not exist.

It has been pointed out before that, starting at the late oral stage, the infant begins to have a certain choice as to the intensity and destructiveness with which he can satisfy at least certain desires (see also p. 145). He can suck gently, and he can bite violently. As he develops further, intermediary degrees of destructiveness fill in, not only for the drive system or *substitution continuum* "oral manipulation and stimulation", but for its sub-systems as well as all other drive systems too. Besides, while at first everything comes from, and goes to, mother, other objects can at times take her place to increasing extents. Desires from a certain intensity or destructiveness up could be diverted to them. Both trends help to decrease the (potential) ambivalence which is maximal at its first appearance, an all-or-none affair, in spite of, or should we say because of, the relative inefficiency of the infant's general behavior (see also p. 64f). Gradually the infant learns how to try more violently for something withheld in proportion to the amount of deprivation, and the increasing number of people and circumstances that he has come to cathect or know opens more gates for detours and substitutes. This does not mean that a person can ever be completely unconflicted about his love-objects. But in adult lasting heterosexual relationships, in marriages of long standing, the traces of ambivalence may be nill for all practical purposes. With respect to primal gratifications, any enduring heterosexual love-relationship tends to be post-ambivalent. The conflicts and furies stemming from frustrations of the partners' desires to be caressed, comforted, and nurtured, but also of those involving power and control over the other, extracting favors and goods from him or her, etc., will tend to submerge in view of the fact that, as man and woman, they can be pure bliss for each other. They supplement each other. They need not fight over any aspects of their relationship once the most gratifying of all have been accepted.

On the other hand, it is not really true that the early oral stage is altogether pre-ambivalent. Conceptually it would not quite make sense. And indeed the infant can be observed after a few days of life to have and exercise a choice on such matters as what he will and what he will not eat, and when. At the regular feeding times very little in kind will pass, and almost everything else will be rejected, but he can make the distinction and either swallow or spit out. Swallowing is permitting stimulation to occur, and spitting out is destroying it. Hence the infant may very well be ambivalent to a particular offering that is similar to both "good" and "bad food", or ambivalent to any offering, if the "bad kind" has been furnished too often along with the good one, or if the "good kind" has been coming erratically. Any infant who does not seem to eat somewhat properly and reasonably and is keeping his parents confused may be having that problem, usually thanks to the parents' or mother's behavior.

"True" ambivalence, however, is distinguished from this in that the destructive desires affect an object rather than a barely cathected condition of satisfaction, and in that other types of satisfaction as well as desires other than the one concerned would suffer with the destruction of the object (see also p. 9 ff).

Symptoms like hallucinations, feelings of estrangement from the world and oneself, unresponsiveness, negativism or blind obedience, or the disorganisation of speech to the point of producing no more than stereotypes, neologisms, and "word salads", or merely grunts and noises at last, are all reminiscent of the early oral stage.

Every normal person is capable of experiencing some of the phenomena that constitute the psychotic's hallucinations. In the twilight before falling asleep, but also in states of extreme relaxation and rest, we may experience vivid images, so vivid in fact that they can be mistaken for real as long as the daze lasts. While lying in the grass we may hear all kinds of murmurs and rustles, chirps, twitters, and soft little scratches, that would ordinarily pass for plain silence, and if we approach sleep, our own thoughts may mingle with them as words, sentences, and even voices. We may wake up with a jerk because we heard somebody say something, but as we look around we find nothing. Off the Adriatic coast fishermen have been reported some fifteen centuries ago to have heard the loud announcement: "The great Pan is dead." They heard it at a time of the day when the great Pan together with his assistants, the satyrs and nymphs, was supposedly busy playing pranks on dazed men and women trying to rest through the hot afternoon.

If we would pay attention to sensations of touch that we experience and respond to mostly without being conscious of them, we would find ourselves swamped by little taps and tickles, itches, squeezes, etc. In sleep or in hypnagogic states these may well be interpreted hallucinatorily as leaves stroking against us, an out-of-place button, a tight belt, or a rope around the neck, as ants or mice nibbling on us, etc. The schizophrenic, however, having turned away from people and the world at large, focuses on these sensations as safer entertainments. This, as well as the degree to which his *rapport* with reality, his world of objects, has deteriorated or softened morbidly, distinguish him from a more or less normal person.

Feelings of estrangement remind us of the times when the infant did not know yet that, say, his own hands and feet were closer to him than the face of mother, the crib-bars, or the window (see p. 143 f). The schizophrenic may feel that some of his sensations do not belong to him, that his own movements, e.g. catatonic mannerisms, were not really intended by him. They come as if he were under a spell, perhaps under hypnosis, as if he himself had nothing to do with their activation. The world, the skies, the millions of blossoms that Spring scatters all over the countryside, the moon and its dead light, but also the one thousand withered leaves of which Mr. Fall is composed, what are they all? What do they mean? What are their consequences, except, maybe, that they are part of him, that he himself is the blossom and the withered leaves, that the moon is dead because *he* is dead, and light emanates from his own eyes. Yet if that is so, what does he himself need his toes for? He might as well cut them off, or his fingers, or his entire body, for that matter. Is not even his body far, far away? Farther than the stars? And if he smells a beautiful scent, what is that? What is the essence of scents or of smelling? How can they ever get through to him? But then, what is he himself? Perhaps no more and no less than a fleeting scent.

Unresponsiveness is the state in which the infant of the early oral stage finds himself with respect to almost all aspects of the world except for those instrumental to his most primal desires, particularly oral manipulation and stimulation. Blind obedience to orders, echolalia, echopraxia, (automatic repetition of words as well as gestures and actions, respectively), and flexibilitas cerea (waxy rigidity or catalepsy; the patient tends to remain in any position in which he is placed), reflect "emptily" a state of semi-unison with the environment and especially with mother that has long been lost (see also p. 82ff). The undertone or meaning of these symptoms is usually that of utmost indifference to everything around him.

Negativism, "paralalia", and mutism, are symptoms of a lesser indifference. The patient engages himself actively in something else or tenses up in his posture in order to resist whatever imposition somebody is making (negativism). Or he gives conspicuously contradictory and antagonistic replies ("paralalia"; not to be confused with paralalia as the result of certain cerebral injuries or tumors). Or he refuses to speak (mutism). All of which would be infantile, though later than oral, ways of interaction with other people and the environment. Mutism, to be sure, may also occur with a patient suffering from psychotic depression, but with him it looks as if he just cannot talk for the time being, even though he wishes to and might be relatively cooperative otherwise, say in the workshop. The schizophrenic does not wish to speak, or thinks it entirely unnecessary.

In his verbal behavior the schizophrenic may deteriorate to a highly unintelligible language of his own, full of neologisms, syllabic play, and verbigerations (morbid repetitions of meaningless words and phrases), all of which are reminiscent of the expressive "babbling" of the infant in the latter part of the first year of life, when he used to experiment with his ability to produce sounds, and when his sounds had still very little, if any, specific meaning (see p. 138).

Schizophrenics in their end-states may be literally reduced to the most primitive desires within all of their drive-systems. Monotonous grunts, tireless rocking, uninhibited elimination, smearing, eating of his own wastes in addition to a few edibles, and excessive genital self-stimulation, may be all he cares to do. Only sleep, the oldest of all of man's desires, the state from which waking life emerges in increasingly larger stretches in order to submerge at last where it came from, only sleep will interrupt his animal life for a while at a time.

Obviously regression to these earliest stages of motivational development is not an exact duplication of those stages as they appear in the normal course of development. Certain skills and a certain amount of knowledge acquired in later life remains preserved even in the most unfortunate cases, although temporarily the similarity may be striking. But even the end-states know fluctuations and small recoveries after which some communications with other people may again be possible. One might say that even the most acute and radical regression such as the one described is above the early oral stage by appearance, if for no other reason than that smearing and eating of excrements as well as genital self-stimulation are impossible during the early oral stage except fleetingly and by accident.

What causes fixation so that, at later times, regression may occur? The pertinent literature is full of contradictory claims. Too much deprivation of desires, too little deprivation, too much after too little, too little after too much, both too much and too little in alternation, have been mentioned (see, e.g. Fenichel, 1945, p. 65 f). If all were true one may wonder under what conditions fixation would *not* occur. In our context only one relationship makes sense: fixation is the result of *too much* deprivation. Losses of objects or modes of satisfaction will cause temporary regression, and fixation is regression of the past. This does not preclude that there may not be normal gratifications in other areas and with objects other than the lost one. It is questionable, however, whether the opposite, *too much gratification*, is even possible. Too much gratification is more than the individual would want himself, and how could he want more than he wants? It may well be that parents tempt their children unduly, say by being subservient to any little wish or mood the child might go through, or by running around naked and making love to each other in the child's presence without inhibitions. Yet as the child continues to take them up on these things and to want more, they will get scared one day—telling themselves: "What have we been doing?"—and change it all. This holds for all parents in principle, who do not end up by making adult love to their child, even if they are aware of no such fears. They have communicated their restrictions implicitly. That, however, is deprivation, and too much, to be sure, after what they had led their child to expect.

In other words, a person may well have uneven opportunities for different drive-systems, say plenty of comfort and fancy goods, and from early adolescence on even paid-for prostitutes, perhaps because he happens to be the crown-prince of a corrupted oriental court, and yet very little opportunity to find out what he can do by himself, what he can create or endure. An overprotective mother may pamper her child to become a chubby and helpless baby, but she would also be depriving him of other basic types of gratification such as activity, work, and achievement, on the one hand and "genital love", contact with the other sex apart from mother, search for an appropriate mate, and ultimate marriage, on the other. "Too much" gratification can only concern a part of a person's motivation, and it implies inevitably that in other parts there reigns deprivation and frustration.

Regression will generally tend to stop at that stage where the decisive trauma occurred, but under certain conditions regression may never proceed that far. A person might be floundering perversely in the early genital stage, although he has actually been fixated on issues of power, control, giving, and getting. Or another person, say a girl, may drag along as a hysteric, but her real trauma has possibly occurred during her late oral stage. If the life situation worsens considerably, the first case might indeed regress to where he "belongs", and in the second case the girl may even bypass the manipulatory stage and slide all the way down to a mania or depression. As a matter of fact, there is a certain slight preference among females to do that, although recently, with decreasing parental and educational emphasis on the virtues and delights of work and achievement, men may have joined this group in growing numbers.

All psychopathology based on fixation and regression is capable of recovery, at least in principle and to an extent. That does not mean that there is new hope for psychotic end-states. It does mean, though, that with appropriate and refined devices of prophylaxis something could be done in order to prevent at least the worst courses of mental illness. Besides every now and again a fairly chronic and far-gone case surprises us by considerable remissions and recovery, sometimes even to the point of inconspicuous normalcy and no relapse thereafter. This may be due to various forms of treatment such as insulin shocks, sleep therapy, and sedation of all kinds, or to some hard-to-account-for psychotherapeutic influences, and occasionally recovery may be "spontaneous", i.e. validly traceable to no specific agents at all. Which should not mean that there were no such agents.

Psychopathology resulting from identifiable organic disturbances such as arteriosclerosis, luetic or other infections, tumors, and chronic intoxications, have not been discussed in this context. They often show resemblences to psychogenic disorders and are psychologically plausible in many of their facets, but any psychological account alone, without resort to chemical, physiological, and neurological factors, would be inadequate.

Summarising, we might say that the psychoanalytic system of psychopathology distinguishes comprehensively all major forms of ("non-organic") psychopathology by a set of aspects the most important of which are: (a) the level of motivational functioning, (b) the predominant desires, (c) the principal fears, and (d) the character of the most elementary object-relationships.

The anxiety hysteric, *the conversion hysteric*, and the *genital pervert*, have been fixated on, and have regressed to, the early genital or Oedipal stage. The predominant desires are genital manipulation and stimulation (against which the neurotic fights, whereas the pervert satisfies them deviously). The major fears are those of being deprived of these satisfactions for good, through "castration", and hence changed in sex, or changed to sexlessness, and the primary struggle is with the afflicted's sex-specific parents and their (intolerable) attachment to each other as well as with all parent-substitutes.

The obsessive-compulsive neurotic, the pregenital conversion-neurotic and *the pregenital pervert* are fixated on the late manipulatory or late anal-sadistic stage. The primal desires are those for physical manipulation and control (over parents and their substitutes, one's own body, and things, i.e. products, including one's own and most primitive: wastes). Again the neurotic fights against them, and the pervert satisfies them. The leading fears are those of being manipulated, severely mutilated, hurt, tortured, even killed. The chief struggle is with sex-unspecific powerful parents and their substitutes.

The paranoic, the very severe pregenital conversion-neurotic, and *the radical pregenital pervert,* are fixated on the early manipulatory or early anal-sadistic stage. The predominant desires are those of physical manipulation to the point of destruction, the wild exercise of force (with parents and their substitutes, one's own body, elimination, and the world as a global whole). The primary fears are those of being crushed, smashed, ripped apart, killed in terrible ways, attacked from the rear. And the principal struggle is with sex-unspecific all-powerful parents and their substitutes.

The manic and *depressive psychotic, the impulse neurotic,* the *drug-addict, the "organ-neurotic"* or *psychosomatic patient* (including the *epileptic* and the *hypochondriac*) are fixated on the late oral or oral-sadistic stage. The primal desires are those for oral incorporation and general omnipotence, the major fears those of being incorporated, devoured, destroyed even in substance. The primary struggle is with and for the (sex-unspecific) all-giving mother and her substitutes.

The schizophrenic is fixated on, and regressed to, the early oral stage. His primary desires are those for oral (and other utterly primitive) stimulation, his ultimate fear something like that of disintegration of all stimulation, or of total panic. There is no object to speak of. In a sense the afflicted is beyond (below) all struggle and ambivalence.

All disorders are complex defensive maneuvers to avoid anxiety and final panic. Without regression to levels of previous fixation, deprivation involved in acute stress would be experienced as intolerable as it has been in the past, even if objectively it would not seem to be at present. The avoidance of anxiety and panic is the primary gain accomplished by the disorder. In contrast, secondary gains are all those resulting from being ill, such as special privileges, extra care, getting even with the spouse or a family member, etc.

One might raise various arguments against any system of psychopathology: The field is too large and complex. Even a given disorder by which a given individual is afflicted may look very different at different times. A person, no matter how sick, remains an individual in the first place and is unique also in the way in which he handles his sickness. Yet all of these arguments have not prevented various authors from trying to bring some order of their own into this large and complicated area. Most of them would even raise all these arguments themselves against their own systems. What can be mentioned in favor of the psychoanalytic system of psychopathology, however, is its greater scope, its more penetrating analysis and grasp and the magnitude of evidence collected in its favor (although no single piece of it would be conclusive by itself; yet this holds for all theoretical systems in any field of knowledge) and the techniques of clinical treatment from which the system emerged. The latter are distinguished, if by no other aspects, by their durations. The authors of no other system have dealt so thoroughly and expansively (as well as expensively, I am sorry to admit) with individual patients, their individual problems, and their uniqueness within, and in spite of, all general relationships and laws that were found. Perhaps more than any other one, the psychoanalytic system of psychopathology is just a guide-book, in spite of its volume.

Psychotherapy, General Considerations

IN ANY science or field of research, manipulation of the conditions in question and correct prediction of outcomes are still among the most persuasive arguments in favor of hypotheses and theorems concerned with these conditions and outcomes. The same holds for psychoanalytic theory as well as its system of psychopathology. As a matter of fact, if a theory is really articulate, a single experiment yielding results other than those predicted might require a revision of the theory. After all, what sort of theory would it be that predicts something that does not come true? All provided, of course, that there were no flaws in the experiments themselves.

Obviously psychoanalytic theory is not quite in that state of articulation, and although this book has been an attempt to ameliorate this condition to some extent, there is still a long way to go. It looks, though, as if at the present time there were no other theory in the field of human motivation, its development and pathology, that could match psychoanalytic theory for that matter. This includes the theories of the deviationists, Neo-Freudians and others, who usually pretend to have proof that a certain hypothesis or theorem in psychoanalytic theory is wrong. Yet the only thing that can often be said in their favor is that they had a point. The hypothesis or theorem they picked from psychoanalytic theory was at least poorly stated and perhaps misleading in its implications. Their own proofs, however, tend to be theoretically no more convincing than those for which they were meant to substitute, no matter how emotionally intriguing and even Messianic some of their arguments may be to some people. They are theoretically no more convincing, among other things, because these deviationists furnish less of a theory themselves. If they claim that man is basically good rather than bad and/or vice versa, that genital desires play no part in the development of the female psyche or that culture is more important than a person's parents and the experiences made with them in early life, and if these claims were true, they would still be saying little more, *mutatis mutandis*, than a physicist who avers that the sun stands higher in the sky during summers than during springs or winters (which is not correct for all geographical latitudes) or that the subject of physics is the physical world (which is understood anyway). Basic assumptions matter in any theory, especially where they are few and non-redundant. Yet its real test of distinction will always be the grammar developed to apply and elaborate these basic assumptions, the elegance and economy with which it can do so and the breadth of specific *data* which it organises or with respect to which it makes a difference to have the theory. On all those counts most deviationists seem to stumble and fail almost as soon as they take off by themselves.

Even so nomothetic investigations have not been the favorites of psychoanalytic theory either. My elaborations on quantitative aspects (see p. 92 ff) and on family constellations (see pp. 178 ff, 240 ff) would probably pass as fair examples of those not-too-numerous studies that are both nomothetic and general enough to have larger portions of the entire theory at stake. In the field of psychopathology proper the situation is considerably better. There is a vast, although predominantly clinical, idiographic, and sometimes clumsy literature, not only in the English language, but also in German, French and others. But the true testing grounds are still to be found with psychotherapy in progress, so to speak, with the practice of psychological and other forms of treatment, that goes on in semi-secrecy or privacy and, for the most part, neither has nor will be handed down to others except by oral and mostly implicit communications, if at all.

General nomothetic studies in the field of human motivation could well be experimental in the true sense of the word. Nomothetic studies in psychopathology could at least utilise the experiments which Nature or God have performed for us. The experiments may consist of appropriate selections among what is already there, say, children who grow up without fathers, because there is a war on and the fathers have been drafted or they have just left (see, e.g. Anna Freud and Dorothy Burlingham, 1943; Bowlby, 1951, 1953); or convicted adolescents who have suffered losses of a given or greater severity, say the break-up of their homes before they turned seven years old or the incidence of prostitution among their mothers; or first admissions to a mental hospital and their relation to types of marital matches prevailing among the parents, to losses suffered, to sibling positions, to income groups, ethnic backgrounds, etc. Anything beyond such selections among the given could amount to playing with human lives.

Psychotherapy cannot even do that. As an institution it is moving on a front of millions of little combats, with overall progress being noticeable only over decades. Yet all sorts of implicit experimenting, predicting, explaining and interpreting, goes on in each instance of psychotherapy, even in each one of its sessions or contacts. It looks as if an entire species, earthworms, were engaged in this and as a whole accomplishing more than the surface can ever show except by infinitesimal increases in something like the yields of the soil. Therefore let us try to pursue those, the changes in yields, or the overall trends which psychotherapeutic work seems to be following.

As for the treatment of psychoses, the conservation of the mentally ill until they die or until they have spontaneous remissions has given way to a much more active and imaginative concern with them. Hospitals, at least those with enough staff and endowments, provide them with an easy and comfortable life. With the help and advice of hospital staff members the patients can set their own pace of entertainment, social contact, work or other activities. Even short leaves from the hospital may be given. They serve the purpose of keeping the patients in touch with the environment from which they have come and which had been too much for them, too taxing to be withstood, leave alone handled. In addition to all this, insulin- and electro-shock, sedatives, hypnotics and stimulation conducive to sleep (slight rhythmic rocking, dim light, monotonous visual and acoustic surroundings, etc.) may be administered at the discretion of the psychiatrist in charge. If sleep is the most primitive of all satisfactions, so primitive indeed, that it can only be consumed without consciousness and requires no acute effort at all in order to be maintained, and if it is regenerative to all cathexes established during the day (see p. 106 f), it might well be a chief agent in the therapy of all who are seriously over-strained, too tired and exhausted or whatever one calls the mentally ill. In that respect, incidentally, psychoanalytic theory would help us arrive at a conclusion quite similar to those cherished by Russian psychiatry, supposedly on the basis of *their* learning theory: the theory of conditioned reflexes (see, e.g. Pavlov, 1927).

Certain stimulants have also been used with success. Yet they may not really be therapeutic, especially since they will often have to be taken indefinitely. Lobotomy, severance of certain nervous connections between the frontal lobe and other (deeper) parts of the brain have also been used, e.g. in cases of irrepressible agitation or pain. But that is not therapy either, even though the patient may be calmer and socially more tolerable. In fact it is an irreparable mutilation. Both kinds of treatment will not concern us further.

Insulin treatment, through mobilisation of glycogen and depletion of all glycogen reserves of the body, achieves a coma, i.e. an unusually deep sleep in which cortical regions active even in deepest sleep—so that they can, e.g., transform milder sleep disturbances into dreams—are rendered completely inactive. Electro-shock treatment does something similar. It induces an epileptic fit, we might say or, neurologically speaking, a very primitive pattern of neural activity: global synchrony or big bangs of neural firings, rather than the delicate crackling that characterises it during waking life. Appropriate sedatives calm down excitement and agitation, whether manic, depressive, paranoic or catatonic. They can even do something for stuporous states which are usually extremely active states in spite of their apparent inactivity (the patient fights with himself, or stalls such a fight with someone else). Sedatives bring the patients closer to sleep, so to speak, and often they do lie down and doze off. Hypnotica are even more radical.

Yet all these treatments do have their side effects. Insulin comas may recur spontaneously after the treatment series is over. Electro-shocks, when administered too generously, lead to memory disturbances and other indications of mental deterioration. After all, the shocks are something like a very violent shake of the clock that stopped running properly. Sometimes it removes a speck of dust or rust and other times it may loosen a wheel or break a few cogs. Sedatives and hypnotics may make addicts or produce prolonged sleeplessness. Natural sleep would, of course, be best, but that is often precisely what the patient cannot properly consume, and physical manipulation of the environment, no matter how well done, is usually insufficient to produce sleep by itself. But in combination with mild sedatives and gradual weaning from them as soon as the patient seems to catch on, it may well be the best compromise.

However, none of these treatments will ordinarily be effective by themselves. Some form of psychotherapy is almost indispensable. It should be noted, though, that with psychotics psychotherapy will not work in the same way as it does with milder disturbances. Conversation is not meaningless to them, but its motivational undercurrents are much more important than the spoken word itself or the rational content of the topic. It is often obvious that the patient does not care what they talk about as long as there is contact. Illumination of the conflicts that he could not solve in his life are less important at first than the simple physical presence of the therapist, his unswerving reliability, steadfastness and friendly acceptance regardless of the patient's moods and overt demeanor. Tokens like cigarettes or candies, certain phrases, rituals of starting each contact, etc., are often clung to with infantile fervor and should not be treated lightly by the therapist, especially when he is dealing with schizophrenics. They are too afraid of people anyway, so ambivalent indeed that they prefer a pre-people world, a life in which people do not exist or in which they appear only by signs and symbols, but remain in a distance themselves.

Under these circumstances it comes as a small surprise that the bulk of therapeutic work with psychotics, if attempted at all, is not accomplished altogether by those who see the patients just once or a few times a week for some psychological "chitchat". Attendants and nurses, occupational therapists, art therapists and teachers of trades, English, basket-ball or whatever it is, can claim a considerable share. Sometimes they do it all alone, while the young and fanciful trainee-psychotherapist is too theoretical or ambitious and impatient to be of much use. Yet he may be officially in charge of a ward or of a particular patient, and in hospitals with low endowments no others but trainees are often available. That does not mean that an experienced and competent psychiatrist cannot, and will not, convey his presence to staff and patients alike even while he is absent.

These problems are very different with persons who are less disturbed, need no hospitalisation and can even run their own affairs adequately. Their range may still be wide. One person, say a man in his thirties, is unmarried, quiet, withdrawn, with fits of locking himself up in his apartment, not wishing to see anyone at all for days and telling his office that he is sick. He is, to be sure, but not in the ordinary sense. Another person of the same age may be married and have two children with his wife, but suffer from anxieties and impotence after his second child, a boy, has arrived. Still another person, the wife of a wealthy and considerably older man, may suffer from spells of nausea, mild fugues, depression and frigidity. And a child, a person in the making, so to speak, may suffer from nightmares, bedwetting and supposedly vicious impulses to steal and even destroy things at home.

The first person is probably the most severely disturbed, perhaps a borderline case, i.e. one bordering on psychosis. Yet if he seeks psychotherapy himself, pays for it, works harder than before in order to be able to pay and shows gains, if of no more than a minor kind—say, having somewhat more courageous phantasies about girls and less destructive ones with respect to authority figures than he had in the beginning—his chances of improvement may be good. He will not become a dashing lover, to be sure, nor necessarily marry or even found a family. As for genital gratifications, masturbation, occasional contacts with a prostitute and frequent homosexual temptations and phantasies to which he does not give in, may be all he can ultimately permit himself to consume. Yet even that may be progress. He dares to realise now what he has been missing, although he prefers to forgo it to this day except in occasional small and non-committal doses. But that is more than nothing and more than being utterly defensive about the other sex.

The second case has a relatively mild problem. His first child was a girl. He had thus remained the only man in his family. With the arrival of a son, however, his psychological situation became somewhat reminiscent of his own home where he was the only child of a gentle, kind and subdued mother and an extremely demanding father. That man wanted no less than excellence, would easily turn abusive and not seldom include the patient's mother in his reproaches. She would usually end up crying quietly in her little sewing room or finally take to drinking. With the arrival of a son of his own, the patient felt tempted, at least in part, to assume his father's role. And what other role would be more available and familiar to him? He caught himself developing tremendous schemes for the education and final career of his son. He should end up as the president of a large concern, perhaps of the whole country. He would beat him to it if necessary, and he would beat his wife too, if she tried to spoil him. Yet on the other hand he did not want to be like his father at all. Besides he had married a strong person, the older sister of a sister and a brother, who would not let him abuse her even if he wanted to, say because she was spoiling his son or *their* son, to be objective. So how could he be like his father even if he wanted to? Still another aspect was more hidden—he was afraid of his son. He would grow up and one day reduce him, his father, to nothing, was one of the phantasies recurring in his dreams in various disguises. But how could he possibly have such a fear? How could he think that anybody would wish to do this to his father? Well, obviously because he himself had wished to dispose that way of his own father. It was not really obvious to him. As a matter of fact, it took some time before the patient could accept it in spite of the logic that would make it perfectly plausible to an interested outsider or to the therapist.

The troubled wife of the wealthy older husband may need no more than to get rid of her husband for good and inherit his estate, in order to be happy again. This is at least how common sense or folklore would have it. And if it were so, the problem would be a mild one indeed. She could get a divorce, relinquish part or all of his riches and marry the person she loves. Yet why did she not do that in the first place? This would be among the chief questions to be solved by her psychotherapy, provided she really wants to be helped. She may rather wish some entertainment or "permission" to go astray or perhaps just to heap another bill on her husband.

And the child who has nightmares, wets the bed and steals, may well be protesting against his divorced mother's new date. He does not like the man. Coming to think of it, he does not like any man but his real father. Why can't he stay with him, he wonders. Yet while father was still around he had sometimes wished he could get rid of him and have mother all to himself. He has got at last what he wanted. Has he? Not really. I have pointed out before (see p. 183) that in spite of all the rivalries existing between the child and his same-sex parent, the complete family, father, mother and child—preferably several children—is still the optimal psychological environment in which to grow up. His trouble is not that father left him and that his bad wishes had come true, but rather that his home situation had been a tense and fragile one as far back as he could sense such things at all. Father was often away. When he was home, there were always quarrels. Dinner took the shape of a frostly and often wordless event. So, if his home should break up, whom would he stay with? Whom should he side with now? Who will take him? But then, if one parent had left him, what reason is there not to expect the other one to do likewise? He may end up with no parent at all. Right now this new man whom mother is dating may want to take mother away too. He is going out with mother a lot, while he himself has to stay home with a baby sitter. And father too has another woman by now. So it comes as no great surprise that he is causing trouble. He thinks he *is* in trouble.

With such problems it is imperative for the psychotherapist to see one or both parents too, in addition to the child, or to have another psychotherapist, with whom he can have regular contacts, see the parents. Sometimes it suffices to see only the parents. If they can benefit they may, in turn, be able to help their child. Clarification of the problems that the child may possibly be having will be an important part of the parents' benefit and it is likely to be effective as long as some of the parents' own problems in the areas concerned are illuminated too, tactfully and wisely. Usually it does not take too much work before these connections can be established, and if parents are only moderately well matched for each other, not seriously regretting that they took each other for spouses, and of average or better intelligence, they will recognise these connections too before long.

But how can psychotherapy work at all? What are the aspects and devices that make it possible that one person helps another person solve his psychological problems? Well, in a sense by the same token by which one person can help another one at all in any way. In order to do so, he, the helper, must know what the person to be helped desires. A mother can help her child by recognising that he is hungry and feeding him or by helping him get back on his feet after he has fallen. The difference between this plight of a child or of an adult who, say, wishes to borrow and gets money in order to buy a house, and the plight of a person who needs psychotherapy lies in tne fact that the latter's present situation, as viewed by a neutral observer, is no plight at all. He, the "neurotic", does not seem to be deprived of any of the things which he claims he cannot have or does not even try to remember.

He cannot relate to girls, date them or enjoy more intimate relations with them. Yet there are plenty of girls around, he is a handsome young man, and some may even be very anxious to meet him and go off with him. Or he cannot defend himself against obvious injustices and even tortures administered by another person. Yet he is physically stronger than that person. He could beat him up or leave the place where this is happening. Or he cannot hold a job for long. Yet there seems to be nothing wrong with his job. There is not a single trouble that he can put his finger on. Or he cannot get up in the morning nor go to bed at night. Yet all he would have to do in order to get back in tune with his fellowmen is to go to bed earlier. And then he may have anxieties, phobias, peculiar physical sensations and other symptoms, compulsions, obsessions, tics, etc., all of which seem to come from nowhere, to have no realistic reason and to handicap him just the same in very absurd ways. All of these problems may, of course, also haunt girls.

Ordinary help won't do in these cases, because it is difficult to know what the person in question wants and desires. And he must want and desire something other than he gets. Otherwise he would not be unhappy, anxious or even in trouble. And he himself does not know what it is that he wants and desires, at least not offhand. Yet without realising it consciously, his actual behavior is precisely the compromise between his desires and fears attached to them that he feels he can handle best.

Then at a party, after a drink or two, the girl-phobic may find himself talking to a girl quite freely and animatedly after all, very much to his surprise, and this may either teach him that one does not have to be quite so afraid of girls or, on the other hand, that he must not drink at all, because look where that gets you: right in the crocodiles' pit. Another person, too afraid to assert himself even in the face of crude injustices, may find himself hollering at a bus driver who offended an old lady. Again this may either launch him on other attempts to defend himself and others against "assault" or it may worry him no end that he did let himself be lured into a counter-attack. It could also be an isolated gain. He may be able to deal with bus drivers from there on, but with no others.

It has been pointed out early in this book (see p. 30) that cathexis and counter-cathexis are processes going on as long as a person lives. They are building on all cathexes and counter-cathexes established already. As a matter of fact, situations cannot be perceived but in the light of all pertinent cathexes and counter-cathexes established so far. That does not mean that *revisions* within the system are impossible. On the contrary, they are *occurring all the time*. All new cathexes are cathexes of something new, something not yet learned about, even when the *data* or aspects concerned may have been present in many or all previous exposures. Sometimes, however, more far-reaching and dramatic revisions occur and if they are in the direction of lifting counter-cathexes and opening up more avenues of cathexis, rather than the opposite, they are usually therapeutic. It matters little that there often is no professional psychotherapist around. The overwhelming portion of all "psychotherapy" is going on in everyday life, in parental and school-education, in social relations, friendships, dates, competitions, work, but also through the theater and the movies, through literature, magazines, etc. Parents and teachers are in key positions, and if there should ever be an effective prevention of mental illness, it will have to be through them. Not just by recognising problems and referring them to psychiatrists for solution. No, by understanding better their children's and their own minds in their intricacies, and by steering clear from wars, intimidations, inconsistencies, indifferences or even fears of their own children.

Where the plights and deprivations imposed on a person by no apparent external circumstances are gross and pervasive, professional help will, of course, be more or less indispensable. Yet even then it sometimes happens, as has been indicated in the examples above, that help comes from elsewhere. A person may be talking lively to a girl even though he is supposedly afraid of girls or speaking up to a bus driver for the benefit of an old lady. A friend may bring it to his awareness or he himself may notice, either at once or in retrospect, although both, the friend and he alike, would have a certain unconscious interest in keeping things the way they are. He himself because otherwise he would get very anxious. His friend because perhaps he has chosen him for his fear of girls. Anyway, he *can* do it, talk to a girl, because he *has done* it. The girl may even have expressed a clear wish to see him again. He might have it in writing. With all this evidence it really cannot be true that girls do not want him. This may be his sudden revelation. And the old lady may have smiled very kindly at him and thanked him in a way a woman had never reacted to him before, he might feel. With these "desserts" added he might well venture to believe that there are opportunities after all and that one can possibly get what he had "resolved" to see or seek no longer. Of course, if the girl does not show up at the next date or if the old lady or perhaps other passengers should not have appreciated his intervention, or if his friend who originally helped him see his change of attitude takes a strong stand against it—fearing perhaps that he himself might lose his friend—our timid one may be where he was at the beginning or even a trifle worse. This is not infrequently the moment where he realises that he has some trouble that he cannot handle by himself, and tries to find some expert help.

The psychotherapist, whenever consulted by a person with "neurotic" problems, will try to help the patient find out what he wants and why he thinks he cannot get it. At the root of all neurotic problems are real problems of the past, losses of one kind or another that the person in question has suffered. It may have been a parent or merely some heretofore gratifying aspects of a parent, that got lost. The parents may have hated each other, and this is what they could not hide from him. A younger sibling who had come to dethrone him may have broken a leg or died, as he had wished for with one half of his heart. Mother may have liked him, the patient, very much at the expense of his sister, which—partly —he must have felt quite guilty for. The parents may have left him in a hospital for six weeks without visiting him except just to look through a window in his room. He had contracted scarlet fever, etc.

If that is the case, if there have been concrete and circumscript traumatic events, the chances for psychotherapy are usually good. If, however, the patient has something like a constitutional deficiency, a low overall frustration tolerance —i.e. a lower rate of cathexis which would make itself felt especially with all more complex objects to be cathected, above all people (see also pp. 96, 112 f, 126)—there need be no specific and "objective" traumatic events. His early life, however calm and uneventful on the surface, may still have been too much and too difficult for him. Since his hereditary constitution is likely to be unchanged (I would say: by definition), his chances of benefiting from ordinary psychotherapy are small. He might still have use for some kind of supportive psychotherapy, in which he would learn to appraise himself more realistically, to console himself to the fact that he will be unable to get some of the things that many others can have and, above all, to take it easier than others, if necessary by explicit permission or even order of his psychiatrist. He is in danger of regressing into psychosis without such guidance and care and in a way he may be considered to have been a borderline case all along.

The neurotic, however, has usually been exposed to concrete losses (including conflicts prevailing among his parents and losses that *they* may have suffered), and he has expanded his counter-cathexes whenever he found he was still being tempted, i.e. led to believe or hope that the lost could be had after all. Psychotherapeutic work with him will start with a general conversation about his own life. A detailed example will be given in the next chapter. Suffice it here to indicate the kind of course it takes.

Suppose he mentions briefly what his immediate troubles are. He has fits of restlessness and irritation. They are connected with nothing at all, he claims. He also feels depressed much of the time. He is not getting anywhere and yet he will soon be thirty years old. And he has lately been afraid of swimming. He does not venture into open waters any more. Something might happen. Somebody may drown, he may want to rescue him and get dragged down with him. But this too has connections with nothing.

The therapist could explore any of these symptoms further, but the patient has already indicated some reluctance to go into them: he claims that his troubles are related to nothing at all. This means that he prefers it to be connected to nothing at all or to *have* the symptoms rather than to explore their genesis, and why shouldn't he? He is a little freer with the swimming, although he might not be aware he is. He has possibly expressed already what or rather whom, he is fighting against: a man. The person who may drown and drag him down is a "he". This could be a linguistic accident, but it might also not. If fears derive from wishes—and we cannot really imagine anything happening to us that we have not imagined ourselves doing in some ways to somebody else (see also pp. 83, 87, 146)—and if, on the other hand, our patient might wish to rescue someone, he could well imagine that someone light and weak, a child, or perhaps a little dog is drowning. Then there would be no danger to him. However, the danger is probably an integral aspect of the whole thing. He may wish someone in particular, possibly someone big and powerful, to drown. Yet he cannot do this without wishing to inflict punishment upon himself as well. So he would go down with him.

If, however, the therapist were to pursue the issue as far as this, the patient may stubbornly renew his claim that even that particular fear comes from nowhere and has no connection. The therapist could argue that obviously he would have to be in the water in order to be in danger and even as little as that would be a connection. But he cannot make it hard on the patient so soon without losing him in all likelihood. The patient may decide: "This man's crazy", even suspect the therapist of wishing to drown his patients. He may express this in a passing remark to others or in a dream, but, at any rate, fail to come again.

No, the better course would probably be to ignore the symptoms altogether for the time being and ask him about his life, especially since he has indicated in his starter that he has not been getting something in almost thirty years of life. The patient tells, for instance, what he is doing right now for a living. He is working as a chemist in a big company, his special project is synthetic fibres and he is working under Keating. And if he stops here, waiting for further questions, and if the therapist's expectant look and nod does not prod him to go on, the therapist has a choice of (a) asking about how he got into this, what other jobs he has held before and how he started out; (b) asking about his particular tasks, perhaps with the hope of getting at some of the patient's relations to colleagues; (c) ask about Keating, apparently an authority or boss and about bosses he has had before. As a matter of fact, the patient has the same choice, should he just ramble on. Only he might not be able to avail himself of it with the same kind of psychological objectivity as the psychotherapist can. He may, for instance, go into the subject of synthetic fibres, into their industrial significance, into their chemical composition, etc. or he may dwell on the economical and financial position of his employer firm. All of which would be perfectly fine in ordinary conversation. But this is not what he has come here for.

If we assume that people figure eminently in all psychological problems, whether pathological or normal, and that among all people those who have lived with a person the longest, most intimately and regularly, that is members of the immediate family, will be the most important (see also p. 240 ff), avenue (c) may be more promising than the others. If the patient "rambles on" in that direction anyway, the therapist will, or course, let him. After all, the patient will have to learn from immediate experience, in addition to possibly being told sooner or later, that here, in the therapist's office, he can speak about everything in any way he wants, and that whatever he says will even be kept strictly confidential. In either case, whether the therapist has to emphasise (c) or the patient takes it up all by himself, the therapist will be interested in other bosses, even in "bosses" in school, in gradeschool, on the playground and finally at home.

In the course of this the patient may soon come to talk about high school and his interest in science. Again the therapist's assumption would be that people must have figured strongly in addition to talent in developing this interest and as he inquires, the patient may begin to speak about one particular teacher, Miss Hartwell, a young person who taught biology, and get somewhat enthusiastic about her. He says, among other things: "She was the best teacher in high school. She could make everybody in class work. Even the poorest students picked up in their marks." "What about you?" "Oh, I was an A student. I assisted her in preparing material for demonstation. I remember I once brought snowdrops for the entire class. We dissected them."

Here he stops, ignores the therapist's expectant look and again the therapist will have to decide which angle of this topic he should pursue further: (a) that she was such a wonderful teacher; (b) that he was a very good student, possibly her favorite; (c) that he did her favors which were apparently accepted; (d) that the particular favor he had in mind was handed to others and "went to pieces" or (e) that he stopped talking right here.

And again the purpose of any of these pursuits would be to trace the neighborhood and past of the desires or objects in question. As a matter of fact, among all other areas of life where motivation matters, it is here, in psychotherapy, that the concept of drive-derivatives and object-development is of utmost significance.

Some critics, incidentally, have protested against all derivation of a person's present from the past. The person is more than the product of his past, they claim. He is future-oriented. Well, psychoanalytic theory implies no different. But this has not prevented its authors and followers from trying to develop some kind of model of how the past might possibly bear on the present and future, with "elements" that carry their future-orientation in themselves: desires. That is precisely it, these same critics tend to say. There is no model that can account for the person as an individual. And again the authors and followers of psychoanalytic theory would agree in a sense. No model can explain the individual fully. If it were not so, psychotherapy might well be unnecessary. Conveying the basic structure of the model could possible do it all by itself. It is maintained, on the other hand, that there are no aspects and dimensions of both motivational development and concrete motivational behavior that would not be common to all individuals. A theoretical system in terms of which the individual can be understood and distinguished from others need not be a Procrustes bed. If it is well constructed, it is likely to do a better service to the individual than those "advocates of the individual" who say no more, in ever so many (often pompous and empty) words than that the individual is unique, that it should not really be studied and explained and that, above all, nobody should dare to study or explain them, the advocates. It may seem unfair to resort to psychological interpretation in a theoretical argument, but as long as I am not saying that there must be something in their past or something to their entire past, that they do not want to remember, things are not so bad. My point would be that those advocates are not interested in any theory of man at all, and unless these premises of theirs are brought to the fore, all discussion would be meaningless. Besides, who would want to study and explain them, unless they themselves wanted to be studied and explained in the first place, say, by presenting themselves to the public in any one of a number of ways (as actors, playwrights, commentators or even authors of psychology books). But let us get back to our case.

When taking up how wonderful Miss Hartwell, the young teacher, was (a), the patient is likely to get not only into the problem of teachers, but also of girls, both those older than he himself and those approximately his own age. Ultimately the conversation may or could be made to drift to his mother and sister. It turns out that he has one sibling, a sister five years his senior. When picking up his relationship to the teacher (b), they might again be dealing with his relationships to teachers and girls, but more specifically with his ways of ingratiating himself as well as doing good, fair or whatever kind of, work. Also his relationship to rivals, whether for the favor of an authority (more or less regardless of sex) or of an (attractive) person of the other sex, will inevitably be tapped on. Going further into the ways in which he won the teacher's favors and her possible acceptance of his efforts (c) will elaborate on (b). Can one win women's favors in general? Or is it a very uncertain affair? Can one do so through work? Or does one have to have power, money, physical strength, and make her very personal flattering presents? Or is it better to try to be a little boy, dependent, needy, desperate for love or what have you? All these questions are implicit in (c) and waiting to be clarified some time. If the fate of his snowdrops were taken up (d), it may become obvious that he was not only helping the teacher implement her plans for teaching, but possibly also giving her flowers which, however, she passed on to the others. Even more, she let them cut these flowers up. It could be that this is why he stopped talking for a while. Or it could be that this incident was reminiscent of an even more disappointing event. And in order to pursue that one further, aspect (e) could be explored. Why was it that he stopped? The therapist may ask this or also: what is he thinking about?

Which course does the therapist choose, if the patient is waiting, or which of these aspects would he come back to a little later, perhaps as soon as he has a chance, if the patient should wander on, say, to some more technical problem of biology?

Well, as has been indicated before: the ones leading most promisingly to the male and female friends of earlier periods of life and, finally, of his home, or to early forms of desires apparently underlying the events mentioned. And by this time almost all aspects, (a), (b), (c) and (d), would seem to get the patient "somewhere". However, there is another very important principle that must be observed by the therapist. He will forever be on the lookout for acute emotional involvement in the present situation, no matter how fleeting the signs. If the patient is getting a little more enthusiastic, as he speaks about his matters, or if he slows up and slides into mild melancholy or if he shows no mood at all where, by all sense and reason, he should have one, the therapist will latch on to it. He will take up the subject or that angle of it, to which the patient seemed to respond that way, and he may do so right then, though with caution, or later, say after the patient got himself worked up for a second time on a similar topic. If, in principle, feelings are always the feelings of desires (see p. 67 ff), emotional involvement means stronger desires or fear of desires, i.e. desires and fears aroused by stronger opportunities to satisfy them, if only in imagination. Stronger opportunities, however, have been furnished by the patient's conversation with the therapist. And if there is more to "feel" all of a sudden, there should also be chances of conscious awareness, of understanding and possibly handling the desires and fears in question a little better.

Well, in our case there is obviously some emotional involvement with (d). And as the therapist explores it further, it turns out, e.g., that Miss Hartwell got married during the patient's junior year and left at the end of that year. Even more, already before that she had been discouraging his fervent interest in helping her, in being called upon, even in getting more contact with her than school could afford. One day he stood in the door of her apartment with a request, supposedly concerning the biology class, that could easily have waited . . .

Enough to be sad or angry about, although surely not all there was to it. Older problems were linked to this incident and had been revived by it. One was his own sister, an attractive girl close to Miss Hartwell's age, with whom he felt he had never had much luck. He had been in love with her as far back as he could remember. He would talk to others about her in the most glowing terms. He would not leave the house for the playground before she had not come home from school. He needed to see her or he could not go out for the afternoon. At dinner he tried to engage her in conversations. At outings and beach trips he would try to cling to her. And she was friendly, but always brief and had never had much use for him.

Never? Really? the therapist would tend to ask himself. How then could he keep at it for so long? How could he be sure that what he was trying to get from her was not impossible to begin with? Or does it mean that he actually got it, although a long time ago, may be when he was one and two years old and his sister six and seven and when she was delighted to have a baby brother to play with. But it may be a long time before the therapist and patient could embark on recapturing that and what it might have been that led him to believe that this could come again or had continued all along.

Or was another problem of life, his mother, the really important one? Could it be that he insisted on pursuing his sister unsuccessfully because, at the bottom of his heart, it did not really matter; or perhaps it mattered only insofar as he could thereby indicate to his mother how much he was still willing to do for the person he loved and with how little in return he would already be content.

But then, how could mother be such an impervious woman? Maybe, someone forced her to? And who could that possibly have been? Father? And what about father? What did he do? At a later time it may turn out that he just did not have very much use for the boy. Father had grown up in his own family, consisting of father, mother, himself and three younger sisters, as if girls were forever available and as if there was no room for another boy. Except for father's father, of course. But that man had always been occupied and seldom home. Whenever he was, he spent all his time with his wife. He had had little patience with children.

Well, the patient's father behaved similarly toward him. For the patient's sister, however, he was a doting daddy. She could do anything at all to him. If she wanted him to, he would even stay home from work. But she was also ready in return to do just about anything for him. Once she presented him with a pipe just when he was getting ready to complain about the old one and he was delighted. *They* were in love with each other.

What is worse, father kept mother too. As a matter of fact, even mother was sometimes jealous of her daughter, but she was a reticent, slightly bitter and not very affectionate person anyway. She, incidentally, had been the only child of her father's first marriage. Her mother had left father and her for another man, when she was only three years old. There were two half-sisters from father's second marriage. All of this the patient may have heard about, but it can make little sense as long as he has not found out (but will in the course of his treatment, at least by implication), that his mother had once been a sad and motherless child, that she did not have much trust in herself, that she could not let herself fall in any great ways for either her husband, her son or any man for that matter. Why? Because in her own childhood, when she was "at last" alone with father, he got himself another woman and had two more girls. Consequently it was not even his father who prevented the patient from having mother more to himself. She did it herself.

All of this may be hidden in the patient's dealings with his young teacher, but it will have to be unburied slowly. Otherwise the patient may well find the procedure too painful—repressed desires being tapped on before he could tolerate even as much as their general and non-incestuous implications—and stop coming. But while they are still talking about the patient's shy endeavors, the therapist may venture to state the desires involved, i.e. to interpret: "It looks as if you had been quite fond of Miss Hartwell. Were you?"

The patient may admit to that and proceed to mention more about her including that she left that year. And again the therapist may comment after a pause of the patient: "This must have come as a big disappointment to you."

And after nodding, perhaps with a sad shrug and another pause, the patient may continue to speak about chemistry, the field to which his interests may have shifted after he had been fed up with biology. And the therapist may let him for a while.

By his comments or interpretations the therapist has done something that is of utmost importance for the patient's treatment. He has indicated to the patient that he, the therapist, understands his feelings about his unhappy friendship or "love affair". He has named it a little more poignantly than a person might do in everyday life. He has indicated furthermore that neither the fact of his love for the teacher nor its sad ending changes anything in their, the patient's and therapist's, relationship. Even more important, he has also conveyed to the patient that he, the patient, will not be pressured (unduly) into anything. He can get away, if he does not want to stay with a painful event too long.

All of this will contribute to building up what Freud discovered at the onset of his work and called *transference*. The patient will have to experience that revivals in phantasy of past traumata will not be quite as traumatic as he had automatically assumed and that the desires thwarted by the trauma in question and "forgotten", i.e. counter-cathected or repressed, are not so impossible after all. Every area of his life that has been covered up by repression will give him pain or anxiety as soon as reopened, but gradually lose its frightful aspects and make possible the uncovering of traumata in which still older desires had been deprived "forever". And since the therapist is an integral part of the situation in which such things occur, and inconspicuously guiding the whole process, he will of necessity be associated with the pain, fear and anger that is being revived and with the elation that may follow the discovery that nothing, or not too much at least, has really and "forever" been foreclosed by a particular trauma. Hence the patient will get afraid or angry with the entire situation including his therapist, if he discovers unexpectedly, or is being pushed too hard for, underlying desires and more primary and still frightening objects or aspects of objects than the ones that have so far been talked about. And to the extent that new opportunities seem to open up before his eyes, he will love the entire situation including the therapist. As a matter of fact, since the whole situation is kept externally uniform by intention and since the therapist is the only person around with whom the patient interacts in reality, the therapist is likely to be made the object of it all, of fears, hatreds and of all desires that are being released from repression. As therapy continues, he will come to love the therapist in all major respects of interaction: as an all-giving mother, as a power who can make demands and as a lover, although the therapist's actual sex will ultimately make a difference. Not that the therapist *is* all these things. But at different times the patient will make him into any of these things to various degrees.

The handling of transference is perhaps the most difficult part of psycho-therapy, if any parts can be isolated. The most important guiding principle is *not* to give in, i.e. *not* to satisfy the patient's fears and desires in reality. If the patient is afraid of what he might have done, still do or what might happen to him, the therapist is not, and if he dreads his father or his wife, the therapist does not. If he hates the therapist, the therapist does not hate him in return. And if he wants to see the therapist for a weekend, be praised by him or scolded, get favors, control him, win his approval for a contemplated prank or adventure, be friends with or, sex permitting, even marry, him (or her), the therapist does not comply. He will instead continue to focus on the desires and fears that may make the patient wish for such things just now, i.e. at this time of psychotherapy and while concerned with such and such a topic, say his mother, or appealing to males, proving himself a man, etc.

In order to be able to do that, the therapist should, of course, be "master in his own house". Otherwise he ought not even to start working in other people's "houses". How this condition can best be brought about is another story (see p. 313 ff), but generally he ought to have achieved in his real life what he could reasonable hope for. He should be happily married, have children, if at all possible, be financially comfortable and fond of his work. The same would, of course, hold for a woman, although she might get herself into realistic conflicts with motherhood, at least for a while. The therapist should also know his own history and life well enough in order not to run into any of the common everyday pitfalls, whether they come up in his real life, in the patient's life or in the therapeutic situation itself. Even then the therapist will always have to keep an eye on his counter-tranference, i.e. on fears, hatreds and desires aroused in him by the patient and/or the topics talked about. That does not mean that he is not supposed to like the patient. If he would not to a fair degree, at least as he comes to know the patient, he may not really be able to do very much for him. But he is not supposed to let his own feelings and wishes determine his dealings with the patient. Otherwise the patient may well be cheated of his ultimate—and paid for—benefits. That would hold even where the patient does not pay himself. Someone, parents, relatives, the city, an agency, the government or even the therapist himself are paying the bill one way or another.

"*Acting out*" has been Freud's term for the patient's attempts to try out barely released desires either in his daily life or in the therapeutic situation. The purpose is usually obvious to the therapist, but not to the patient. He knows he is doing something, but he does not really know what or, as we could also put it, why. If he did, if he *knew* it, he would not have to *do* it. He would not try to "re-test reality" prematurely, i.e. long before he has inspected most or all of the pertinent realities of his past. He may wish to marry a girl he has just met, chiefly because he dared to address, invite and date her at a time when, in therapy, his ineptness with girls had been the topic. He may wish to give up his job as an accountant and embark on the Bohemian life of a painter, even start painting, because that was the thing his parents had discouraged him from in effect, if not by intention. However, there are a few more things they discouraged him from, but he does not want to see those. He is too frightened.

Or he may get obstinate in the therapeutic situation, burn a hole in the carpet of the waiting room "by mistake", come late consistently, refuse to pay or quit the treatment altogether without notice. Yet he may, underneath, be trying madly to win the unconditional protective friendship of the therapist in reality. He may want to move in with him and could be hostile chiefly because he does not get what he wants. But even that is not the crux of the story. He is "really" afraid to admit to himself that he has always wanted to be taken care of without prerequisites, to be a careless, pampered, lazy little child. And if he were not so afraid he would gradually discover that this is because he had not been permitted to be one even at a most tender age. But how could he, then, form the desire at all? Because at a still more tender age he *had* been permitted to. Thereafter, however, maybe around the time when he turned three, things changed.

All of this must be considered by the psychotherapist. He must know how to scan the material the patient brings up for all its associative and derivative properties. He must observe the emotional behavior of the patient, the degrees to which the desires and fears involved are acutely aroused in the patient's mind. And he must keep an eye—and ear—on the patient's and his own interaction in reality, that is on the therapeutic situation itself. Every decision, whether to ask, what to ask first, whether to point out something, to summarise, to return to a former topic or to keep quiet, whether to interpret, whether to do so on the topical or on the transference level or both, or whether to discuss aspects of the agreements made at the beginning of treatment, every such decision requires considerations and weighings on all dimensions of the therapeutic situation. And hundreds of such decisions are being made within a *single hour*. Not consciously, of course. That is, the therapist, as he makes these decisions, does not enumerate explicitly in his mind nor weigh by some explicit measuring scale the determinants involved. He would get as stuck as the centipede when asked how he managed to walk with so many legs. Yet if inquiring retrospectively into any of his decisions, say, because he is puzzled by something or because he is still in training and has to report to his supervisor, he would be able to elaborate sensibly in ways I have tried to outline, and his elaborations should make sense. They should be consistent with most or all that is already known and understood by the therapist. The longer therapy has gone on, the more is there to remember and to consider, but the clearer will also have become the trends in the parent's motivation that are strongest and most repetitive.

Small wonder that a lot of experience and learning is necessary before the therapist is really competent to do his job. Small wonder also that the best way of learning it is still the apprenticeship with a psychotherapist who has already learned and has had all the experience. No book nor even any kind of presentation of how it is done, no matter how articulate, can accomplish competence, although both types of exposure may help. No, just as the going-to-be swimmer will finally need real water in order to learn, so the trainee-therapist has to come to grips with his subject-matter and medium directly. He will have to take on cases, preferably those over whom he has initial advantages. They could be children or at least younger than himself or less intelligent or hard stricken by fate or very poor or very severely disturbed and hospitalised or all of these. Even if he had no intentions of becoming a therapist, he would tend to have something to offer to them in any of these respects. He might have some difficulties with married people, if he has not been married himself, but on the other hand, if he is not seriously dating or engaged, he may be too far yet from a solution of this problem in his own life and hence possibly "disqualified" anyway, at least for a sizeable group of patients. He could see children, one might say, but in order to do so effectively, he or somebody would have to see the parents too and their marital conflicts may well be the children's chief trouble. He knows something about marriage himself, of course. His parents were married and if they had been reasonably happy with each other, he is likely to have learned a good deal from them. He may be able to handle his cases, but the neutral observer or supervisor of his work would wonder nevertheless why his parents' happiness has not encouraged him yet to try for marriage himself, seriously and full-heartedly. He may also be too young, no more, and that is a counter-indication all by itself to doing psychotherapy.

Even if he were seriously dating or engaged or even married, he may find himself uncomfortable with people coming from the "lower and lowest strata of life", with people who have seen drinking, brawls, violence and death, but also abuse, perversity, prostitution and rape, in their own homes, even participated in it actively or passively and finally embarked on similar lives of their own. Yet this need not be so. One of the most general assumptions in psychoanalytic theory concerns the universality of all basic psychological phenomena, no matter how varied the timing, the intensity, the composition or the degree of control achieved over them, may be. Potentially everybody is everything and there is no potentiality to speak of that would not be based on something actual, something that has really happened and been experienced. There is nothing on earth done by anybody at all for which a given person could not find a fair analogue in his own life and experience, if only he or she searched long enough.

This, incidentally, may perhaps be the most foolproof preparation for the practice of psychotherapy: to search that long or, in other words, to find all of one's own potentialities, whether buried or hidden or even in states of exercise. And the surest way of getting such a preparation would be to undergo psychotherapy oneself. This would also have the advantage of doing no wrong to others, as might be the case with psychotherapy practised on another person under the supervision of an expert. After all, the supervision applies only to the reports of psychotherapeutic sessions. The therapist cannot interrupt the therapy whenever he is in doubt, call on his supervisor for consultation and rush back properly enlightened. All throughout the session he is on his own. Yet if he is qualified to start learning psychotherapy and under the control of a competent teacher, the risks of harm done to the patients is minimal. In fact, they cannot even be averted by the trainee-therapist's own psychotherapy. Even then he is prone to err on occasions, not to see something, to get a bit anxious, to interpret too early, etc. No psychotherapy regardless of length and "depth" can solve any of his psychotherapeutic problems in advance; nor can it do so with any of his real life problems, for that matter. Both his own practice of psychotherapy as well as his own life will remain an unending challenge while they last.

The first few exchanges with the patient of our example have opened up all these complexities and we are not nearly at the end of them. What might be mentioned, though, in order not to leave the case altogether on loose ends is how the first hour might have continued (see p. 309). After returning to the problem of girls and conveying a little about his luck with them—lots of good luck, he claims for the time being, as if to dispel the failure and disappointment with his biology teacher—he resumes the topic of chemistry, which he chose in college possibly because of a "magnificent man" of a teacher, and about various factual and personal details of his career as a chemist. There is also some discussion of his living arrangements during all these times. He went to college in his home town and lived in his parents' home for three of the four years. He has been sharing small apartments with men about his own age ever since. His first room-mate had also been a chemistry student, the second a law student and the present one a writer and journalist. Under the latter's influence the patient had lately taken to writing himself and had even succeeded publishing a few popular articles on chemistry in the Sunday sections of a middle-sized daily. Upon questioning, it turned out that he had also been interested in law. He remembers several long discussions with his previous room-mate, especially on marriage and divorce laws. Further inquiry into this interest of his is shoved off by him as just one of those things. But at the end he remarks passingly that he will visit his sister this weekend. She is having a somewhat difficult time. One of her two boys had developed a squint in his right eye, supposedly stemming from measles he had had a year ago, and the other boy had just broken his arm falling down the stairs. Dave's (her husband's) business is not too good these days, but he is not the brightest guy anyway. He is a bully and a bit of a bore. Well, this may have something to do with the patient's interest in marriage and divorce. It may even have something to do with the symptom he mentioned at the start: his fear of drowning, possibly while trying to rescue someone. In fact, one more question may provisionally confirm this clue: "Where do they live?" "In Portland.

They have a house right by the beach." But it was already too late for it and besides there is really no hurry. Sooner or later everything of relevance will inevitably come up for discussion and work under the appropriate guidance of the therapist.

The therapist of some experience can often sense and outline a patient's major problems after a few contacts. Occasionally even one is enough. Without knowing some of the *data* developed as possibilities with our example, one can say already that one of the patient's chief concerns is his disappointment with women, especially with those in his own family, and among them mother is likely to have played an even greater part than his sister. Another concern is his own relation to men, characterised possibly by an unusual degree of submission and sub-ordination which, again, will ultimately have to do with his father. As a result of this he should be confused about his own psychological sex. He is not sure whether it pays to be a man and try his luck with women. But if one, henceforth, focuses on men, how does one do it? Will one have to be like a woman oneself? Submit to him, the wonderful and strong one, whoever it is? Perhaps even die? Be drowned by him, even after a fight, if there is no other way of reaching him?

More generally speaking, it may already be apparent to the therapist that the patient has problems on the Oedipal level of development. He may have been fixated on the early portion of it, where sex-differentiation and sex-identification has barely begun and is still quite unstable. But there is also a trend of trouble on the early manipulatory stage, indicated by unconscious desires of submitting passively to men or anybody powerful, for that matter. If that is so, however, there may also be someone in the family, a parent in all likelihood, who appeared un-duly passive compared to the other parent, and in this context this may have been mother. That person may have disappointed him even on the late oral level, say by offering too little nurturance and bodily comfort, at least from some time on. This has perhaps been indicated even by the symptoms mentioned at the outset (see p. 304): the depression, the infantile rage that could well be lingering be-hind the patient's fits of restlessness and irritation, and his fear of drowning, i.e. of being swallowed by by the water (which would be an oral fear; see p. 278f). His difficulty with leaving home even for college might also bear on this. On the whole, however, the patient's predicaments do not look too bad. He *is* dating, he *is* working in a highly articulate field: chemistry, he *is* away from home now and he *can* make a living. His prospects for psychotherapy are good.

Yet it is a very long way from this first diagnosis made by the therapist which could well be perfectly accurate, to the patient's own understanding of what it is that he wants, hates and fears. In between lies all the piecemeal work of pursuing desires and anxieties to earlier and earlier origins at a pace which the patient's defenses can take. Anything too fast will get the patient scared and force him to tense up again or to adopt methods of superficial compliance, of acting out in real life, in transference and both, or of quitting the whole thing. During the first twenty years of his therapeutic work, no lesser expert than Freud got himself into these troubles at times. Enthused by what he had diagnosed (more or less for the first time in history), he was often tempted to confront the patient squarely with his discoveries, leaving out all tests of how much the patient could possibly take. Yet without such tests, even the most appropriate interpretation can sometimes make no sense at all for the patient, and where it seems to, the patient may well be hypocritical and get something altogether different from psychotherapy than what his guide has in mind. Where the patient appeared to resist, Freud would accuse him or her precisely of that, of resisting. Later on, however, he understood more of the reason for this. He conceived of *resistance* as a more or less normal front set up against all attempts made by anybody to loosen or shake well-established counter-cathexes. The patient who does not show it, is likely simply to resist in other more deceitful ways. Gradually, however, as the patient experiences that the unconscious dreads and losses of his past are not quite as devastating as he has assumed, i.e. as he can perceive opportunities where, formerly, he would believe there were none and as he takes them up and succeeds in getting what he wants, no matter how moderately, his resistances would weaken. In fact, they would do so in proportion to the transference that is building up.

How does psychotherapy ever end ? Well, in the course of treatment the patient will find out what he really wants and why he thought he could not get it. Not just rationally, but in effect. Otherwise he has not really found out yet. This will be documented by increasing attempts to get in reality what he had so far been afraid of. Sometimes he may even discover that he has been getting it already, but that he could not see it as such. These attempts have been called *"reality testing"* by Freud and they must be distinguished from "acting out", although the difference is often hard to recognise without close inspection and careful appraisals. Misunderstandings in these aspects may sometimes prolong psychotherapy unnecessarily or even jeopardise whatever has been accomplished. To the extent, however, that the phenomena in question are evidences of reality testing, the patient himself will be able to judge it as such. He will no longer make a fool of himself in reality or public, as he is likely to do while "acting out".

Psychotherapy approaches the end, if the patient can perceive and understand his own behavior, past and present, imaginary and real, more or less objectively. Then he can see himself with the eyes of an outsider or even of the psychotherapist. Ultimately there is always some adopting of the psychotherapist's attitudes and viewpoints, but it is no blind adoption. Everything has been tested and compared to alternatives, particularly to those that the patient has lived by so far and not been too happy with, and the least absurd, the most sensible and promising, are the ones that survive. In a way one could say that the two, psychotherapist and patient, have come to understand—even identify with— each other on all major issues of life including also the more subtle facets of the patient's own, even though the psychotherapist has ordinarily revealed very little of himself. But the patient has finally learned how to sense what's coming next in the psychotherapy sessions. Slowly, bit by bit, he can anticipate the therapist's questions, comments, interpretations, even the modulations in his voice, and that means that he does not need the therapist so badly any longer, provided it is not a mock-imitation, i.e. a defensive maneuver, altogether. If it occurs in the beginning of treatment, it may well be.

But the identification with which the patient manages at last to part from the therapist, could itself be seen also as a defense. Against what? Against the desire to continue the relationship forever. As a matter of fact, it is. Yet by degree and complexity this is a very different process from the identifications of early life, some of which may well have contributed to the patient's original troubles. This identification should be slightly easier to accomplish, by the way, if the persons parting are of the same sex, than when of opposite sexes. In the latter case there sometimes remains an implausible remnant: why couldn't they, the patient and the therapist, get together, make love to each other and even marry? Yet due to the peculiar conditions of psychotherapy this would be among the unfairest things a psychotherapist could do to a patient. It has happened, to be sure, and then the patients often wanted that more badly than really to understand themselves and get well. But that is not a good excuse. Not even the implicit promise of the psychotherapist to remain his or her healer for the rest of their lives makes it any better. It would hardly work under any other premises, but on the other hand that is the last thing any patient would realistically come for: to make psychotherapy permanent. Incidentally, while termination of treatment is somewhat easier when the persons involved are of the same sex, its beginning would tend to be a trifle easier with many cases when they are of opposite sexes.

If it is true that successful psychotherapy ends with some kind of adoption of the psychotherapist's attitudes and viewpoints of life and the world, very much indeed will depend on the attitudes and viewpoints he holds. And if psychotherapy is really what it purports to be—a liberation of all of the patient's unnecessarily and fearfully fenced-in desires—these attitudes of the therapist should concern only the most obvious and undisputable aspects of life and the world. They should be self-evident. Assumptions like the following would probably pass as such: Man wants to live. While living, man prefers pleasure to fear and pain, satisfaction to deprivation and destruction, enjoyment of all aspects of life to that of only some and the co-existence with other human beings to their annihilation. Above all he wants to love a spouse lastingly and, if can be, have children.

Hence psychotherapy would have to accomplish no more than to enable the patient to loaf at his discretion, to work according to his capacities and to enjoy heterosexual relationships, preferably lasting ones, and even to desire children of his own, and likewise for women.

If any of the assumptions above were omitted, we would be at a real loss explaining how come we live at all. I have tried to show that psychoanalytic theory assumes no more, although its more essential component is its "grammar" which permits considerable, clear and fairly unambiguous elaborations. In fact, the "grammar" is the thing that makes it a theory, worthwhile and teachable to begin with. If it were not, I personally would rather spend my time with the Bible, other wise books and world literature, for they too contain a lot about man's motivations and troubles!

Anyway, psychoanalytic theory assumes no more than the evident. Other theories of bearing on psychotherapy do likewise, although by my experience their "grammar" may not be as good or a few less evident assumptions may have been added or both. Some such less evident assumptions would be the following: There is a God. There is no God. There is a thereafter. There is only matter. The President, the Pope, the party, the people's will, money, capital, social class, nationality, race or what have you, come first, etc.

Hence a therapist basing his position on such theories will objectively be weaker, at least explicitly. He might not be as free to take anyone who would really need his help. He would also have learned less well how to think most efficiently and usefully in matters of psychotherapy and his patients. And he would tend to be a poorer teacher of his trade.

This is not to say that they could not do psychotherapy, at least with certain groups of patients and up to a point. Under particular conditions that may be all that is needed. They would even tend to be better psychotherapists with a theory and general premises about man that they feel they need rather than with a better theory and a stricter set of premises that they have trouble accepting. Once in a while I have even found psychotherapists who, while claiming to adhere to another school of thought, were nevertheless operating as if they had adopted psychoanalytic theory. This is not too surprising. I have pointed out in the very beginning (see preface) that even psychoanalysts and psychoanalytically trained psychotherapists have had trouble to this day spelling out the theory by which they are working and communicating with each other. As a matter of fact, some so-called theoretical issues discussed by them have little to do with the theory they use. It should also be mentioned that occasionally psychotherapists are incompetent, untalented, psychologically disturbed or at least slow-witted. This holds for all schools of psychotherapy, although those schools with the most thorough and careful training should have the fewest of those.

Who becomes a psychotherapist anyway? What chief motives might bring him into this field of work? What desires can possibly be satisfied by his profession?

Well, there is the desire to help other people. However, this is what people in all branches of medicine, in science, in trades, in public service, etc., may also wish to do or at least claim to wish. Even so, helping by psychotherapy is obviously of a different kind than most of these others. In a way, it is like cheering someone up who is sad or scaring someone who is recklessly happy. It is like helping someone handle his affairs with another person or other people in general, like giving him or her advice on how to approach the others, how to write, what to think of such and such an incident, etc. It is like teaching a person, but also like controlling him, like having power over him, although in a quiet and secret sort of way. Yet it must be great powers, if their effects may be a happy or unhappy future life, success of personal relationships or failure, professional accomplishment or doom. Psychotherapy must impress the person who aspires it for a profession as a kind of help where you do almost nothing, you just meet and talk, and yet mountains may be moved; or as if the work put in and the effects achieved are way out of proportion in favor of the effects. In other words, there seems to be strong "oral component" (see also p. 227ff).

Can this be confirmed in other respects too? What does a psychotherapist do in his daily work? Well, not very much, it seems. He sits and listens. A joke has it that often he does not even listen! He does not have to go out for work. People come to see him. Even if he works in a hospital and makes his rounds, he either gives out instructions to the attendants and nurses who carry them out for him or he has the patients come to his office anyway for the "real thing"; or at least the out-patients do. His office is nice, comfortable and warm. It had better be. In his dealings with the patients he has them do most of the talking. They are the ones who struggle and fight with their problems. They bring in their lives and all their adventures, whereas the psychotherapist just looks on. He gets the fun without the risks. Whenever he does open his mouth, however, he can produce day and night, joy, fear and hatred, and he can potter in his patients' pasts, shove around their friends and relatives, praise or discredit them by implication, etc. But perhaps the best thing is that the patients pay him for all of this. No more than ten or twelve of them at a time will do. If he sees them a few times a week, he will be splendidly maintained.

There are other aspects, of course. There are chances of making patients over, to "work" in their minds, to exercise magic. There is the phenomenon of transference in which the patient may, so goes the rumor, be utterly at the mercy of the therapist, madly in love in cases of different sexes, sometimes even in those of the same sex, or lost in admiration. For the therapist-to-be this may even look like a way of shutting out all competitors of the patient's favors, but also of knowing the innermost and even humiliating secrets about particular people, about the social circles in which they live and move around, about the city or town, etc.

In reality, of course, things are usually not that simple and "wonderful" at all. For the most part psychotherapy is hard work, requiring an alert mind, considerable flexibility and, at the same time, discipline. That does not mean that it cannot be interesting, challenging and gratifying throughout, but certainly not in the sense of the naive expectations outlined above. There are also great variations among patients, and even the same patient is very different at different times. Some are delightfully intelligent and others are not, although a minimum of about average intelligence is very instrumental for the progress of treatment. Some are engaged in professions and dealing with people that would be fascinating all by themselves. Others are not. Some have had fates that arouse immediate sympathy and others have not. Some are quite attractive and others not at all. The trouble of some is that they *have* had and done "everything", they had to give up nothing, although, as the reader will remember (see p. 260ff, also p. 27f), there would be no trouble, if that person had not been missing something somewhere, maybe a kind mother or even one that was available at all. His or hers happened, say, to be a movie star. Some are pretty disturbed and others only mildly. Some can easily pay for treatment and others not so easily. As a matter of fact, the sickest of all are very frequently also the most likely to have no money whatsoever. A fair compromise between the patients' needs of treatment and their abilities to pay is sometimes difficult to accomplish, although some psychotherapists, especially in big cities, tend to impose no other limits upon themselves than what they can get away with. They may even feel proud about it. They claim to be realistic, but are they?

Many an ambitious aspirant for that profession has ultimately been bogged down by the realities of this profession. Some find that psychotherapy is not really for them only after they have passed their board examinations and become psychiatrists, although the cynics among them keep at it anyway and may settle right where the customers abound: in the big cities. They are the ones who often abuse their profession, meddle incompetently in people's lives, prolong actively the transference relationship way beyond termination, accuse the world of non-cooperation if their clients should fail in reality, advocate that everybody should go for psychological treatment, work as consultants for producers of psychiatry thrillers, etc. Other aspirants of psychotherapy quit sooner. And still others do not even go through the prerequisites of proper training in this field: medical school. Which is not to say that medical school prepares anyone for psychotherapy. Yet it is a more reliable and grinding test of the student's sincerity of interest than other avenues such as clinical psychology, social work, teaching, the ministry or merely having been around a lot in life. In all guidance centers, clinics and hospitals there are some excellent psychotherapists who have come through unconventional channels, and the profession as a sociological entity cannot really afford to lose them. But they are the exception rather than the rule. One indispensable qualification for psychotherapy is age. A person under thirty years of age cannot really hope to be able to cope with the kinds of problems that he is likely to encounter, at least with adults. If however, he is to turn thirty before he can be let loose, he might as well spend his time in an orderly and maximally useful fashion, i.e. in hospitals and with the sick of all kinds first, later with those of his contemplated profession.

Psychoanalysis is different from (psychoanalytically oriented) psychotherapy only by degree, although by degree on a number of dimensions (see also Alexander and French, 1946; Kubie, 1950; Glover, 1952; Menninger 1958). It lasts longer. The sessions are more frequent. The patient reclines on a couch, so that he cannot even see his therapist. And he "free-associates". With duration of treatment and frequency of sessions the difference by degree is obvious. With respect to physical position it is too, on closer inspection. Both, sitting and lying, are comfortable positions, more comfortable e.g. than standing, although lying is the more comfortable of the two or the more ancient position, as we might also say. A person was able to lie on his back from birth on, whereas it has taken him or her more than half a year to be able to sit at all and close to two years to sit down in a chair all by himself. Whether lying is also more comfortable before another person who sits and watches is another question. There are implications of passivity, inferiority and submission. Why doesn't the therapist lie on another couch or even on the same couch with me? the patient may well wonder. But even in ordinary psychotherapy there are such connotations. The person who is in trouble and comes for help at all is thereby submitting to another person, supposedly one who has greater powers than himself. Otherwise what would be the point of coming? Also the patient reveals everything about himself, whereas the therapist does nothing of that sort. Similar considerations hold for visual contacts. The patient cannot see the therapist while on the couch himself, but he sees him when entering and leaving, and in Europe they might even shake hands. While lying, he may also turn around, if he thinks he has to. The therapist may ask or explore, why he did it just then, but he, the patient, is not outright forbidden to do so. If he should be, he certainly continues to *hear* the therapist. Whatever the therapist's face might betray under different circumstances, his voice can now. The patient may even hear the rustle of his notebook or the scratching of his pen, the squeak of a shoe, the lighting of a cigarette, if the therapist smokes—which, actually, he should not during the session, if he can help it—the clearing of his throat, etc. Lacking visual cues, the others will tend to be heightened.

Finally, as for free association, there may be as much of it in psychotherapy as there is in psychoanalysis, at least for all practical and therapeutic purposes. The explicit instruction to say everything that comes to the patient's mind may or may not be given in both forms of treatment. In most cases it makes little difference. The patient is doing it anyway, and if he does not just now, if he seems to ward off some thoughts that have come to his mind, he has certainly free-associated before, e.g. in hours of reverie, even while working, driving or listening to music, although he usually does not keep much of a record nor does he even have or wish another person to be witness. Every conversation is free association to some degree. If it were not, if it consisted of nothing but logical derivation, it would probably be rather boring. Just imagine that, in reply to a friend's "Hallo", a person would say: "By my intuitive impression you look at my face. You may or may not know me. Your verbal expression is often used to address people one knows. Hence you *may* know me .... etc". And even that is no true logical derivation.

On the other hand, if the patient who comes for treatment could really say everything that comes to his mind, if he could think in every context of his life, whether in reality or in imaginary revival, of everything that is or has been pertinent, he would not have to come for treatment. In other words, by the time a person has really learned how to free-associate in his therapeutic sessions, he may well have been cured.

One could argue that in psychoanalysis he learns free association faster than in psychotherapy. The extent to which his controls and defenses are loosened is greater and he stays in this state of "induced regression" for longer periods of time.

True enough, but first this would only confirm the point I tried to make: that psychotherapy and psychoanalysis are different from each other by degree. They may appear different in quality, to be sure, but then there *are* differences in quality among any two patients undergoing the very same type of treatment.

Secondly it can be said that if a particular case of psychotherapy turns out a success, it must have involved all "induced regression" that had been necessary. For purposes of psychotherapy, psychoanalysis could not necessarily have done more for the patient, as some popular and even professional opinions might have it. There is no absolute value in "delving deeper and staying down longer" in a patient's past, except that it may be easier for the therapist. He can take his time, he sees fewer patients more often and he can possibly charge more. Even in psychotherapy all major fixations will, of course, have to be reinvestigated, but the farther they lie back and the more pervasive they have been, the smaller the chances anyway that the usual forms of psychotherapy or psychoanalysis can help (see also Freud, 1937).

I have stressed these aspects because the signs of some moderate sociological abuse have been multiplying. Maybe they have always been there, but checked by circumstances. They all point to a somewhat unrealistic overestimation of psychoanalysis, at least in the big cities of this country. As a *profession* it has come to appear much more distinguished than "plain psychiatry", as a form of treatment about the only thing that can save mankind, and as a philosophy of life, child rearing and education, the most modern and progressive thing there is. Yet the psychiatrist who does nothing but psychoanalyse (wealthy) patients in his elegant suite at an increasingly rapid rate (nowadays often only 45 minutes at a time, with no time in between) is a kind of an artefact, just as is his status of psychoanalyst, legally and in other respects, even though it may bring him considerable financial and even some social success. As a *form of treatment*, psychoanalysis is a neighbor of others such as psychotherapy, counselling, group-therapy, group discussions, clubs (including Alcoholics Anonymous), but even of social contacts of many kinds, of friendships, old and young, of contemplation of times gone by, whether alone, in company or over some wine, even of praying to God or of playing with children (if attended to, they are among the best "therapists" there are; if officially adopted they can even "give" their foster-parents children of their own; i.e. then, all of a sudden, the foster mother gets pregnant), but finally even of "distractions" like hiking, sports of all sorts, particularly those practised in the countryside, literature, art, music, raising of fruits, flowers, puppies, fish or what not, but even good old napping and sleeping.

And as a *philosophy of life*, child rearing and education, it has been misunderstood to no small degree. In some cases it furnishes no more than a vernacular for justifying why people do all those things that they should not, such as let off steam forever, live a life of impulses, attack freely all those in one's way, dispose of one's children in order to consume every square inch of available sensuous comforts, indulge children in every little whim of theirs and whine over the restrictive functions of social institutions. As if any institution could do otherwise, but also as if it had emerged for no purposes of gratification at all, only as a nuisance.

It is perhaps no mere coincidence that psychoanalysis has blossomed where psychopathology and especially psychoses, but also delinquency and crime have been on the increase too and that the growth of psychoanalysis as a profession, a form of treatment and a philosophy of life, has hardly slowed down the increase of the other. One might argue that it could not, because it is neither dealing with psychotics nor delinquents nor criminals, that the means of diagnosis have probably been refined (Of what, however? Of delinquency and criminality too?) and that it would, of course, blossom where there is more need. True as this may be, there is one additional sign of alarm: the increase of the average length of psychoanalytic treatment. Have patients become sicker? Can psychoanalysis treat sicker people than before? Or is pure psychoanalysis more and more climbing out on a limb? Perhaps getting there without moving?

I may be accused by some of my colleagues of making poor public relations when saying all of this, but in another country than the United States, or ten years ago, I would not have said it. At that time psychoanalysis could still use more support than it was able to get.

The psychoanalyst is a person who has undergone psychoanalysis himself and psychoanalysed a few patients under supervision of at least two experienced psychoanalysts. In that respect he has done more than the ordinary psychiatrist. One might say he has also read Freud and the most important of his disciples and he has learned the theory, but the reading can, of course, be done by any psychiatrist or any layman, for that matter, and the training in theory is usually not very theoretical anyway. It need not be, one might say, but why call it then a theoretical training and make a point of it? Every psychiatrist, on the other hand, has learned psychotherapy chiefly through the supervision of his work by more experienced psychiatrists, and if the supervision was any good the crucial personal problems of the trainee must have come up and been handled somehow. Explicit psychoanalytic treatment of the trainee's own problems—and he might not be in the field, if he had not got some—would probably achieve more, although not necessarily in proportion to the time spent by both supervisor and "candidate". Psychotherapy may be sufficient and, above all, relatively more instructive for the trainee's own practice.

The trainee-psychoanalysts usually undergo psychoanalysis with the intention of graduating to candidacy and ultimate membership of the "club", and this intention has always been a slight problem with psychoanalytic training institutes. If they do graduate, the trainees' own psychoanalyses have done something in reality for them that they should not. Hence, their transference relationships may never be totally resolved, although they may get into conflicts with the transferences of other graduates, and all that could be responsible for some of the peculiar social tensions that are often prevailing in such training centers. There is more irrationality seething under the surface than the naive observer would ever expect. After all, these people have supposedly solved their emotional problems. The training analysts have gone through their own "training analyses", the older ones among them usually in a less formal and extensive way, and consequently they sometimes have their own problems among themselves, particularly when the Almighty of that group, Big Father or Big Mother, has just resigned or passed away.

This flavor of irrationality has not always been conducive to the theoretical nor even to the practical and didactic growth that might have been possible. Occasionally there have been feuds over theoretical trifles and irrelevancies of practice or conduct. Among excellent efforts there have also been signs of some ostrich approaches to the problems of mental hygiene, education, preventive medicine and the like. To some psychoanalysts it looks as if all that would be needed to help the people is to have psychoanalysts in all leading positions of medicine, public health and perhaps even education, and as if world affairs would be fine if only all leaders, economic, political, scientific, etc., would be psychoanalysed. Why would it help? Because it has helped *them*, both directly and indirectly. A few interpretations passed out to the world as a whole, to a political party, an ambassador, a school system, a general hospital, would be all that is needed.

Fortunately the explicit advocates of such positions are not too many. As a matter of fact, other schools of psychotherapy and psychoanalysis (Jungians, Alderians, Neo-Freudians), though smaller in club membership, have them too, and some groups among the Neo-Freudians have almost only those. Mild delusions about one's own omnipotence as well as a stubborn blindness to some of the complexities of the world and the unending tasks it sets us seems to be among the hazards of the entire trade.

My recommendation for the training of psychotherapists would be this: Separate the psychological treatment of the trainees from their training. Let them go through their own psychotherapy and psychoanalysis to the extent they find it necessary, either before they even start their own work with patients or while they are already doing so. In the latter case, let the supervisors have a word on this too. Let them be supervised in their own therapeutic work, with a larger and more diversified group of patients than is customary, including children and parents, by at least two experienced psychotherapists who are, at the same time, good teachers. Let the supervisors be the professors of psychiatry at the medical schools. Make appointments of such professors on the basis of their scientific and medical accomplishments. Let them be good therapists by the judgements of *their* supervisors, superiors and colleagues as well as by more direct evidence of cases they have dealt with, rather than by their ability to handle their possible appointment "therapeutically". Not that the latter would not prove something about their qualifications too. Yet it should not be enough by itself. In other words, let the training and selection be *work-oriented* rather than *feeling-oriented*. Let the leading persons in the field be those who excel as general psychiatrists, as psychotherapists and as teachers, but also as hospital directors and real, not would-be, researchers. Let the leaders not be those who are essentially anonymous and can, partly because of it, hold the largest number of "club members" in unresolved transference, whether directly, through intermediary generations of "club members" or even through the influential outsiders whom they have treated; not those who are essentially interested in little but their own material and limp intellectual comfort; not those who want to make their trade ever more expensive, seclusive and impregnable, to the disadvantage of the public.

I dare make these recommendations not only because they would make sense, but also because things seem to be moving in that direction anyway. I would not be surprised to find a majority of psychoanalysts among those leaders. They have, on the average, gone through the most thorough of all formal trainings in the field. But I would also expect others to be among them, people who have come from Jung, Adler, or Sullivan or who may merely be very gifted, kind, wise, broadly experienced, intelligent, etc. men and women in the field.

And let us not forget about the curative forces that work outside of formal psychotherapy, that surround us everywhere in our daily lives and can often be realised by a minimum of comment, advice, interpretation or even manipulation. Let us not forget that by far the largest portion of work necessary to promote health, strength and well-being among all members of our social system is still, and will always be, resting with the parents and secondly with the schools. Anything that parents and teachers can learn in that respect, would be very welcome and helpful, but let us also remind ourselves of the fact that they know a great deal already, even about psychological conflicts and problems, that most of them have handled them reasonably adequately most of the time and that they do not deserve to be bombarded with semi-psychiatric trash by playwrights, actors, producers, entertainers and occasionally even psychiatrists, all perhaps of no other distinction than that they have supposedly been psychoanalysed. Perhaps they only think they have been. Otherwise they might recognise their talents and limitations for what they are and not be so anxious to sell psychiatry. Mind you, I am not against lectures, discussion groups, even so-called group therapy gatherings, but I would say that the very best people, the leaders in the field, rather than its enthusiastic toddlers should be engaged in this, and all their therapeutic skills should be mobilised in order to really reach the parents.

But still more important than this, at least in breadth of effects, would be adult education in general, particularly in the arts, in literature, in history and, if you like, in religion, even when conducted through mass media. We should not forget about the cultural riches that make up our heritage. Most of it is dealing in very direct, impressive, and yet sublime, ways with the eternal psychological problems of man, and these classic, and some contemporary, solutions have a lot to offer too. Even Freud has drawn some of his most ingenious theorems from them. They are often more appropriate, more passionate, more moral and altogether more elevating than what most people can provide by their own doings and from their own experiences alone, even if a psychiatrist is helping them. In some of these cases a good reading guide would be more timely and adequate than the custom-tailored treatment that they get, with little material to do the tailoring.

Again I would not want to be misunderstood. The literature of the whole world may mean nothing to the person who is acutely in grief, regression, or despair. A person's own experiences are still the most intimate of all to him. But even so they are infiltrated with his cultural heritage. He cannot accuse, swear, repent, appeal, try to seduce his beloved, etc., without using the language, the metaphors, the gestures or even the instruments (daggers, jewels, explosives, flowers, stationery, etc.) of his present and former times and without finding even more gratifying specimens of accusations, swears, repentances, seductions, etc., should he ever, or just a little later, wish to look for them. Furthermore, if he is in a really bad condition, neither psychoanalysis nor ordinary psychotherapy, but only a mental hospital may be of any immediate use to him.

At last we should even consider the psychotherapeutic and generally in-vigorating character of *work*—believe it or not—at least as long as it is even mildly meaningful. The alarming rate in the United States of mental illness as well as criminality in spite of all her psychiatry and psychoanalysis should give us something to think about, when we compare it, say, to the corresponding (official) rates in Russia, where people work longer and harder for much less immediate gratification and where psychoanalysis is non-existent. Again, this is not advocating that patients should be given the rough treatment and forced to work. By the time they have become patients, this would usually be too late. But while they were still children they might already have learned about the delights that are potentially inherent in work, especially for greater contexts, but also about those contained in any kind of accomplishment and excellence, from their parents and the communities in which they happened to grow up. The parents and communities would, of course, have to know enough about these delights and be willing to let their children participate. Too often, however, they leave their children to themselves for "free expression" (of very little to express) or to impatient, despised and underpaid teachers, or both. They are too concerned with their own comforts, even psychotherapies, and plots to wrest a still greater slice from the meats—or should we say puddings?—of happiness, than they are already getting.

Concluding, may I mention that all considerations concerning the sociological strategies of psychotherapy are irrelevant in any case where psychotherapy or psychoanalysis is really indicated and has begun.

A Case of Psychotherapy (A Brief Glance)

AFTER making an appointment by telephone and sounding very urgent, in came Elsa H., an attractive girl in her early twenties, smiling sweetly as she begged the therapist's (*Th*) pardon for being rather late, without further explanation. The patient (*Pt*) was well, though not elegantly, dressed, sat down, searched flightily for something in her purse, but gave it up and began:

Pt: Let me tell you how it all happened. We had been together all summer in K. (an inexpensive resort on a lake). We swam and hiked. Once we even rented a sailboat, but he did not like it too well. Perhaps the wind was too strong that day. I know nothing about it. He wanted me to stoop down under the sail so that he could make a turn, but I pretended I did not want to. So he got angry, and I complied. I always do, when he gets really angry. It was a very nice summer, but at the end we ran into this Susan at the dinner table and the two got into a conversation. On the weather, of all things. That is what you talk about, if you are bored or if you have fallen in love. Next came sailing. Obviously she knew something about it and she said something about the calm. She had had to wag the rudder in order to get back to the pier, she said. It served her right. But Bob tried to explain to her, why sailing would soon be better again. He moved up and down with his hands and spoke like a professor of meteorology, all this stuff about cold air, warm air, weather fronts, turbulence and all these clouds. I never could remember their names.

Well, the next thing I see is that they sail across the lake for a whole morning. That was a few days later. Five days, I believe. By that time I was already glad that we were leaving shortly. He had become cool and absent-minded with me. So much so that I wondered whether he had ever loved me. Then I usually get irritated and gloomy and he hates that. You know all about that.

Th: Do I?

Pt: He can't stand crying, but I think I even cried. Or maybe I didn't. And then, that evening, I danced with Arthur a lot and Bob sat there all alone. He would not dance at all, not even with me, when I asked him too. So that was that (*she looks for something in her purse again, but does not seem to find it*). . . . Well, and now, a month after we have been back, he wants to leave me. That is what got me so upset. That's why I called you. . . .

Th: How does he want to do that?

Pt: What do you mean?

Th: How will he leave you? Didn't you say he wanted to? Will he not see you again? Or what?

Pt: He will move out.

Th: You live with him?

Pt: Yes. . . . Yes, oh, didn't you know that?

Th (smiling): How can I? You did not tell me.

Pt: Of course (*she looks out of the window and strokes lightly over the back of her left hand*). . . .

Th: What is "of course"? That you did not tell me?

Pt: No, I mean I did not mention it . . . I should have. . . .

Th: You have. Haven't you? Just now?

Pt (after looking sideways at the floor for a little while): We have been living together since last spring. My father would not let me go. But I went anyway.

Th: Your father wanted to hold you back, but you would not let him?

Pt: That's right. . . .

Th: So he had to let you go? He had no choice?

Pt: That's right . . . I am curious where Bob will go. He can't live with her. That's for sure. She is quite religious. She was brought up in a convent.

Th: Who?

Pt: Susan. But I am not even sure he wants to. I don't think he really goes for her. He just wants to break off with me. That's all he wants.

Th: And you? What do you want?

Pt: I don't know. I don't care. . . . Maybe I do. I think this is foolish of him. Perhaps he is jealous of Arthur. Or maybe he is just upset.

Th: Would you want him to be?

Pt: At this point I am not sure what I want. . . .

Th: So you came here?

Pt: Sort of, yes.

Th: So that we can, perhaps, find out what it is that you want?

Pt: Maybe, yes. . . . No, I am not sure. I think I just came for some advice.

Th: Advice on what?

Pt: On what I should do.

Th: You mean, you want me to advise you on what you should do?

Pt: Yes.

Th: What would you want me to tell you?

Pt: Whatever you say. I don't know whether I will do it. But I want to know about it just the same. Maybe I'll do the opposite. . . .

Th (smiling): Now you have become a little angry with me. Haven't you?

Pt: Why should I? You have done nothing whatsoever that could make me angry.

Th: Maybe I did. Not that I meant to, but this is how it might have appeared to you.

Pt: I don't know what you are talking about.

Th: You said you wanted to get some advice on what you should do. Didn't you?

Pt: Yes.

Th: And then I asked you . . . What did I ask you? Do you remember?

Pt: No, I don't.

Th: Just a moment ago? No?

Pt: I don't remember.

Th: I said: "What would you want me to tell you?"

Pt: Oh yes.

Th: Now, if you ask me for advice, and I ask you back: "What do you want me to tell you?" you may well have inferred: He is not going to give me such advice. And then you may have become angry.

Pt: Well, maybe I did.

Th: If you did, how come I knew?

Pt: You saw my face. But I wasn't angry. Not really. I am sure.

Th: Remember, you said you would not necessarily follow my advice. You would just want to know. You may even do the opposite. . . . But I don't think this is what you have really come for. I think you do want to know what it is that you want yourself. What you want from Bob, for instance. What you want from Arthur, perhaps, or from other people. It could even be that you want these people to want something from you? To let you know what they really want. Bob, for example? Hmmmm?

Pt: I am not sure I care. Not really. . . . But I would like to know. Yes, I would like to know what he is up to.

Th: Now, is there someone else about whom you are curious in that respect?

Pt: Arthur? Or Bill R.? No, I haven't mentioned him.

Th: Somebody you have already mentioned?

Pt: I have mentioned Bob and Arthur.

Th: Somebody else?

Pt: Well, Susan, of course, but she is a girl.

Th: What do you mean?

Pt: You are talking about boys!

Th: Am I? I asked you for somebody whom you have already mentioned.

Pt: Bob, Arthur, Susan. That's all the people I mentioned.

Th: You mentioned someone else too.

Pt: Did I . . . I don't remember. . . . Whom *did* I mention? . . .

Th: Your father.

Pt: Oh?

Th: In what way did you mention him?

Pt (*pauses, then shakes her head in slight astonishment*): I mentioned him. But what did I say about him?

Th: Are you sure you don't remember?

Pt: Funny, I know I mentioned him, but I can't recall it.

Th: You said your father would not let you go to live with Bob.

Pt (*astonished*): Oh. . . . He told me not to go. . . . I did. . . . Yes, I did. . . .

Th: What? Mention father? Or go and live with Bob anyway?

Pt (*with a smile*): Both, I guess.

Th: You mean you did the opposite of what your father told you to do? Did you?

Pt: I guess, I did. But it was getting intolerable at home. My mother was always bickering. I should wear this, I should take a coat, I should do the dishes. I should learn how to cook. I should come straight home from school. As soon as I began to work with S. (a publishing firm), she wanted me to contribute to the household. And with her permission I could never bring anyone to the house.

Th: She said so?

Pt: No, but you could tell anyway. It was written on her face.

Th: But *without* her permission you could?

Pt (*after a surprised look*): As a matter of fact, I did. Bob came to the house when she was not home. . . . (*looks ahead pensively*). . . .

Th: Where was mother then?

Pt: Oh, she was working. She still is. Both my father and my mother work.

Th: So you brought Bob home while both your parents were out working?

Pt: Yes . . . (*she looks down at her hands and to the floor*). . . .

Th (*while nodding repeatedly*): And you did it, because you could not bring him home when they were there!

Pt (*with a faint smile*): Yes.

Th: You really had no choice, did you?

Pt: Well, I don't know. We could have gone for walks. We could have gone to a movie. . . .

Th: But? . . .

Pt: I don't know.

Th: You wanted to be by yourselves?

Pt: I guess so.

Th: If you were not permitted to bring anyone home, what about Bob? Could he take you to *his* home?

Pt: No.

Th: Why not?

Pt: His parents did not approve of me. That's why we moved to the apartment.

Th: So both of you left your parents at the same time in order to be together?

Pt: Yes. Bob even quit T. (a state engineering college) and took a job. Mine is not paying very much and you know how expensive apartments are. He got himself a pretty good job with P. (an electronics firm). But now he does not like it any more. I think he also wants to go back to *school*.

Th: In addition to what? What else does he want to do?

Pt: Besides leaving. Or what do you mean?

Th: He wants to leave you and he wants to go back to school. Something else that he wants to do?

Pt: Isn't that enough?

Th: Is it?

Pt: What more do you want?

Th: I don't want it. But you may have something else in mind that Bob wants to do besides leaving you and going back to school.

Pt: I have nothing else in mind.

Th: Well, if he leaves you and does go back to school, where will he live?

Pt: With his parents, I believe.

Th: T. has no dormitories, has it? So he will go back to his parents?

Pt: Once he said so. I don't really know.

Th: Would they . . . would they take him back?

Pt: Oh yes. They have been pleading with him to return ever since we took the apartment. He would not listen. He would even hang up the telephone on them. Once his sister came to talk to him. I left for a walk, but when I returned she was gone and he told me that he had thrown her out.

Th: Is that an older sister?

Pt: Yes, the only one he's got.

Th: Apparently they tried hard to get him back and you assume that they would still be anxious to have him?

Pt: I am sure.

Th: Now what about you?

Pt: What do you mean?

Th: What will you do, when Bob leaves you, probably for his parents, and goes back to school?

Pt: There is nothing much I can do.

Th: Does that mean that you will stay where you are?

Pt: I guess so.

Th: Even though the apartment is so expensive?

Pt (pensively): So it is, I guess . . . I don't know. . . .

Th: What are your possibilities?

Pt: Well, I could leave too. I could go elsewhere.

Th: Such as where?

Pt: Anywhere. There are cheaper places. I could take a small room. Or I could have a girl move in with me.

Th: Any other possibilities?

Pt: Is that a game? What's the point of all this?

Th: Well, didn't we agree that you might wish to find out what Bob wants to do—you have told me a little about that—but also what you yourself may want to do. So one thing we can do is inspect the possibilities. Would you agree?

Pt: Are there other things we can do?

Th: What do you mean?

Pt: I mean, can't we change the topic?

Th: Yes, we can, if you want to. . . . What would you suggest?

Pt: Oh . . . well. . . .

Th: . . . Why don't you tell me a little more about your parents?

Pt: Well, my mother is not my real mother. She is my stepmother. They got married when I was five years old, and when I was seven, my father adopted me and I moved to them. You see, I was an illegitimate child, but then I got my real father's name.

Th: You became his legitimate child?

Pt: Sort of. I had lived with my mother until I was four. Then my father's sister took me, but after a year I was put up with friends of father's who had a girl of my age. Her name was Joy, but she was no joy at all. She was selfish, boy! She would not let me touch a single toy. But she always asked me to play with her. She would show her dolls to me, how she fed them and undressed them and I had to watch. Just watch. Aunt Nellie would say (*imitating a sweetly timid voice*): "Don't you want to let Elsie play with you?" And Joy said "No" and that was the end of it. That girl could do anything, and it was fine with her parents. It was unbelievable. Once she threw a hammer at me, hit the toilet bowl instead and broke it. I had wanted to go to the bathroom and she had wanted to go first. So we ran, and I was first, but right after me came the hammer.

Th: She could really have hurt you!

Pt: I had tried to slam the door behind me. The hammer bounced off the door.

Th: And what happened then?

Pt: I don't remember. She may have cried. Aunt Nellie may have argued with her. I don't remember. Anyway, it was not my fault, although I remember hearing that girls do not run to the bathroom. . . .

Th (*after a pause*): Did something come to your mind?

Pt: Oh, I was just thinking of my mother and her nagging. . . .

Th: Which one?

Pt: Which nagging?

Th: And which mother? You have had a number of them, haven't you?

Pt: Yes, I had my real mother, then my stepmother. But Aunt Patricia and Aunt Nellie were also mothers in a way. I lived with them and that makes them mothers, I guess.

Th: But there was only one real mother?

Pt: Yes. . . . But I remember very little about the time I lived there. Later I kept visiting them, and when I did not come too often, it could be a real treat. Especially when the children were in school and Mr. D. at work. They have four children. Bob came after me, then Linda, Mary and Esther.

Th: One boy and three girls? With you it's even one boy and four girls?

Pt: Yes, but they are only my half-brothers and -sisters. My mother married when I was two years old. My brother had already been born, I understand, and then came the girls.

Th: So your half-brother had been an illegitimate child too?

Pt: Yes . . . that's right, but he bears his father's name, of course, and so do the girls. With them there was never any question.

Th: But with your brother and you there was?

Pt: Actually only with me. I did not get my stepfather's name when they married. I believe my real father had objected, but my stepfather did not want it anyway. One of the few things I remember about this time was that he said: "You go and stay with him!" I have forgotten why he said it, but I am sure he meant my father. He never liked me. Later I heard something about his refusing to marry mother before she hadn't got rid of me. He wanted no girls anyway. Maybe that's why I was put up with Aunt Patricia. . . .

Th: What else do you remember about that time when you were still living with your real mother?

Pt: Not much. Let me think. Once I remember I held on to a tub that was filled with water. I slipped, fell and the whole thing came over me. Once I fell into a dry sewage hole in the yard. That was awful. I believe Bob and I had played hide and seek, and when he could not find me, he played something else. So I stood at the bottom of the pit and looked up and waited for someone to pull me out. It must have taken ages. At last I even started to scream for help. Then I heard voices, I remember. Finally I heard the voice of my mother calling for me, and then the face of my stepfather appeared above me and he laughed and laughed, pointing at me and saying in between: "Look at that! Look at that!" Then they pulled me out. One man had to hold another one, while he reached into the pit, and up I went. My father sat right by and laughed even more, because I was all covered with mud. But then my mother told him to be quiet, took me to the bathroom and dipped me in, clothes and all. Actually, she was quite nice about it. . . .

Th: Did I get that correctly: you called for help only after quite a while?

Pt: Yes. At first I thought Bob would come and get me out. I mean he would tell mother or someone that I was down there. But he didn't come. So I thought I would wait and see.

Th: But that must have been pretty frightening.

Pt: Was it? . . . Maybe it was. But I don't remember being frightened.

Th: Not even when your stepfather's face appeared above you? Or were you glad?

Pt: I was more upset about his laughing. First I couldn't figure out what he was laughing about, except that it was about me. He made me feel very badly. Not only then, but even much later, when I came to visit. "You again," he would say. I usually left right after he came. Actually I left before he even got home, but sometimes we ran into each other. Once, when he was drunk, I believe, he said: "There is Elsie, look. There is Elsie! Isn't that a pretty dress? I have been treating you badly, Elsie. Come here, let us make up!" I sometimes can still hear his words and smell the beer he had drunk. I wanted to sneak past him quickly. That was in the hall. But he grabbed my hand like a bulldog and I froze completely. I thought he was going to hit me or kill me. But then I heard my mother's voice saying: "Is it you, Frank?" and that was like . . . like sunshine almost. He let go of me and I rushed out.

Th: What did he have in mind?

Pt: Oh, I don't know. . . . He is an ugly man, fat and pretty bald. Mother has also grown heavy, but she is all right. She cannot do much for me, but she will try whatever she can.

Th: Such as what?

Pt: Oh, when I was still in school, she would give me money. And there would always be cookies or candies. And I would tell her how school was and how I got along with my friends. I remember speaking to her about the first boy I had a crush on. She was wonderful about it. Only later when things got more serious she seemed to change her mind a little. She would switch to saying: "That is for you, Elsie, to decide." Or: "I can give you no advice, dear." And I wondered why she couldn't. Even with Bob she had really nothing to say. I told her what we had planned to do, and she crossed herself, but at the same time shrugged her shoulders and smiled, almost foolishly.

Th: You wanted her to tell you what you should do, but she wouldn't. Is that it?

Pt: Yes.

Th: What plan was it that you had told her about?

Pt: About the apartment.

Th: So she also knew about your problems with your stepmother? That she wanted no friends of yours in the house?

Pt: I told her, yes. That was when she said: "I can't give you no advice, dear." That's the way she would say it: "can't" and "no". She is not a very educated woman. That may have been one of their troubles, my father's and her's, I mean. My father graduated from business school. He is an accountant. And his father had been a district judge. But he is dead now.

Th: By their troubles you mean what?

Pt: That they never got married.

Th: Well, that alone would not necessarily be a trouble, would it?

Pt: What do you mean?

Th: Many people never get married to each other. They get married to others instead and some don't marry at all.

Pt: But that is different when they have had a child together.

Th: Such as you?

Pt: I haven't been thinking about me in particular.

Th: Not as a child, but perhaps in other ways?

Pt: I am talking generally about the problem.

Th: Yes, but if it is a general problem, it could also be your own problem. Could it?

Pt (*slightly impatiently*): If you imply that Bob and I might have a child, you are wrong. There would be no accidents. Believe me.

Th: I believe you, if you say so. But remember, you said your father's and mother's trouble was that they never got married, either after they had a child together or before they even planned to have one.

Pt: They never planned me.

Th: But they planned on a relationship with each other that could lead to a child. Would you think that they knew that?

Pt: That was in those days. I don't think that could ever happen to me.

Th: And from this you concluded that you would go and live with Bob? What happened to mother, could not happen to you? So there was no need to get married? . . . Or no wish to get married? . . . Or are you married?

Pt: No (*she casts her eyes down and strokes over the back of her left hand*). . . .

Th: And now he threatens to leave you?

Pt: He will (*she nods almost eagerly*). . . .

Th: You sound as if you are sure he will leave you, almost even as if this would be all right with you. Is it?

Pt: It is not all right with me.

Th: In some ways, of course. You don't want to lose him. But in other ways you perhaps feel it is?

Pt (*softly and slightly depressed*): Maybe it is. . . . Maybe I deserved it. I should have listened to my father. . . .

Th: Yet if you didn't, there must have been reasons. . . .

Pt (*looks curiously at the therapist*): Oh. . . .

Th: Maybe you didn't just want him to *tell* you. . . . Maybe he should have *held* you back? Literally, I mean (*makes a light gesture, as if holding someone by the arms*).

Pt (*swallowing possibly with tears in her eyes*): He would never do that. . . .

Th: . . . Hold you *back*? Or *hold* you?

Pt (*fingers in her purse, gets handkerchief and blows her nose*): Perhaps he *wanted* me to leave. What do *I* know about him? . . .

Th: That is what you may have thought: that he wanted you to leave. But of course you have also evidence that he wanted you to stay. Don't you think so?

Pt: What evidence?

Th: Well, he did tell you to stay when you contemplated leaving. But he also had you stay with him for how many years? . . .

Pt (*pouts and shrugs shoulders*).

Th: Since you were seven years old, you said?

Pt: He had waited long enough. And he had married this woman before he condescended to take me in.

Th: He should not have married? He should have stayed *single* and taken you into the house?

Pt: Well, that may have been difficult for him. I couldn't do much in the house when I got there. I was too small. But he could have married someone else, someone nicer. Someone who would stay home rather than work like a man.

Th: If it hadn't been for your stepmother, things would have been easier all these years?

Pt: That's right. They would be easier even now!

Th: Our time is up. Could you come again on . . . ?

Let me add a few comments about this interview. It was chosen for presentation in this book because the therapist was more active and probing than he would have been in other cases, except those seen mainly for purposes of quick diagnosis. A patient with a stronger and more conscious desire to get help could have been left more to himself and to the pace he finds comfortable. Hence the interview with Elsa shows more variety of content and cruder interactions with the therapist than other first sessions might. More activity and probing was necessary, on the other hand, because the patient appeared somewhat flighty and "delinquent" from the very beginning. It was necessary to prevent her from doing what she set out to do unconsciously: minimise and evade the issues she had come for; possibly flirt with the therapist; even try to move in with him fast. It was important to make her realise by experience that she had a problem, and that there might be some point in coming again. Apparently this was successful. As a matter of fact, the reader may have observed as much as a change in her, within one session, from a "silly" girl to a slightly more intelligent and realistic one.

As she speaks about her trouble, it becomes obvious to the therapist that this is not the real trouble at all. He would, of course, assume no different with any contemporary and acute problem that any patient reports. Not that it may not be a severe one in its own right. But even more severe ones of the patient's past have made the present one what it is. Elsa's acute problem is being left by Bob, her boy friend, with whom she has been living in an illicit relationship. So one question to be pursued would be: What are her previous experiences with being left? Another question: Why is the relationship an illicit one? Why is she not married or, if that cannot be, a little less ostentatious about her love relationship. And if both questions pertain to the same problem—as they seem to—we might ask: Why does she have to engage herself in an illicit relationship in order to end up forsaken?

In the pursuit of these questions, factual content and motivational reaction or immediate experience of the patient are equally important. As Elsa admits to living with Bob with some misgivings, another girl, another boy and her father come into the picture. Bob leaves for the girl and she is ready to run for the other boy. Has father also left for another woman, so that she had to look elsewhere in the first place? Has he not loved her enough to stop her from the adventure with Bob?

On the level of transference to the therapist she reveals that she wants the therapist to take over her life, to tell her what to do, and she gets angry and evasive when the therapist does not quite comply. In order to bring her back, the therapist takes up that little episode and promises implicitly that therapy may have something to offer after all. So assured, she has "forgotten" her father and his lack of concern for a moment, is made aware of this, not unpleasantly surprised and, when helped to recover it, more confident about her psychotherapy as well as the topic. She speaks freely about her home and father's "other woman", and the therapist, by implication, "permits" her to have (had) a boy of her own. Hence she can admit to his parents' dislike for her, especially since she has meant so much to Bob that he gave them up for her. But the triumph was short, probably by her own doing. She feels guilty, as she must have then, can recognise Bob's wish to return to the parents, but is resistant to admitting to a similar wish of her own. When pressed, she gets slightly angry and the therapist has to explain again. This time, however, it is not sufficient. She really wants to get away from this one, so much so that she cannot even think of another topic when encouraged to pick one. So the therapist suggests one, in a way the same he is after, but it appears like a different one to the patient. What a mean trick? Not really. This as well as everything else that the therapist tries to bring about is in the interest of the patient.

And now the patient tells her "secret" and her story which, among other things, helps to explain why she thought she could not return to her home and had run away in the first place. She has been, and still is, an illegitimate, i.e. an undesired, child. Her mother could not keep her because of the man she married, although she could keep her other children. Her real father did not want her either, although the person he disliked even more was her mother. He takes the patient at last, but how sure can she be, especially with this woman of his? What is worse, her real father had been no more than a rare uncle, if anything, in her early life. Mr. D. was her father, psychologically speaking, and he never hid his feelings before her or anybody. He wanted to get rid of her quickly and for good. His interest in her at a later time and while drunk could probably do little to correct that impression. When Elsa had fallen into the pit, she may have thought that this was it and gave in to her fate, at least for a while. Yet how can a child or anybody do that unless he or she had already accepted the fact of being utterly despicable, as later on she learned her mother might have been to her father. Toward the end of the session her wish to lose her dear ones (introjected from wishes of her early love-objects to get rid of her, but also from what happened to

her mother) comes ever so slightly to the fore, and now the therapist suggests
and even implements by gesture what she had wished her father to do. There she
is close to tears. She can admit to such a wish that was not fulfilled, because
her therapist—by as little as naming the wish—has implied and she has unconsciously registered that he, the therapist, will be somewhat different from
father. He will be a more interested and benign father.

In order to wind up the session and not let her leave too depressed, the therapist
reminds her also of some good things she knows about her father and that her
stepmother could be the real culprit. The patient feels comfortable enough to
agree heartily.

Well, we have already tapped some of the crucial problems that will have to be
dealt with in Elsa's psychotherapy. The work will be long, provided she does
not stop coming, but there is no room for further details. May I, however,
present a dream that she had about half a year later, after some noticeable
psychotherapeutic progress, after Bob had gone back to his parents and to school,
and after she herself had moved in with an older girl friend of hers and her
parents, paying punctually for her small room and breakfast. And may I illustrate
roughly what the dream might "mean" and how it would be handled. She
reported:

I dreamt that I was going down to a basement.
It was a strange spiral staircase.
It went around a greyish-white column on one side (left).
On the other side there was a wall following the staircase.
It was like a staircase in a church-tower.
I went down, but the staircase didn't seem to end.

Then I noticed that somebody was behind me.
So I stopped and looked, and there came this man.
He looked much like my father, except that he was dark-haired and lighter in
     complexion than he actually is.
Besides he wore a funny cloak or something.
He looked like a priest. Almost . . . almost like a woman.
He gloated over me from head to toe, then turned around and disappeared.

So I kept walking downstairs, but there was someone behind me again.
I waited, and there came this little boy.
I think he carried a bag of bop . . . I mean popcorn.
He ate them, as he looked at me.
Then he stretched out his arm to offer me some,
But as I reached for them, he had disappeared.

Instead there stood a huge, heavy man.
He wore some kind of a mediaeval coat.
I remember a picture of Henry VIII that looked a bit like him.

I was stunned at first.
Then I wanted to scream, but I had no voice.
So I started running downstairs again, taking two and three steps at a time.
But the man kept after me.
I had no time to look, but I could hear him panting.
Then, all of a sudden, the staircase ended before a deep abyss.
It was so dark now, that one could not see its bottom.
For a moment I thought I had lost the man.
But suddenly he grabbed my arm.
I screamed, wrested myself loose, and jumped.

I fell for a long time, but landed softly.
As I looked around I saw a narrow street before me.
I walked slowly through it.
I thought I was safe now.
It was dawn, and sunrise seemed to be close.
Then, out from a door I passed, a hand grabbed my arm again.
I screamed and woke up.
I noticed that I must actually have screamed.

There was another dream, but all I remember was that somebody with a huge
    mouth was eating an ice-cream cone.

*   *   *

Let us try to trace the major desires and defenses working in this dream, and
let us do so at first without recourse to anything that the patient may be able
to comment or elaborate on.

To begin with, there is a desire to be either on a spiral staircase or in a basement. Even the very first scene of a dream is already the product of desires. One
of the more general desires may be to be alone in a secluded place, another one
to go to the bottom of something. Yet if someone is coming behind her, she
cannot really have wished to be alone. She wants someone, as it turns out: a
male, to be with her in a secluded place or to go to the bottom with.

At the start she seems neither frightened nor anxious to obviate anything. In
other words, the desires are acceptable. She even stops and looks to find out who
is following her and she lets the person look at her.

First it is her father, although somewhat distorted. He has the hair and
complexion of another person. But he is dressed up as a priest or as a woman.
Hence he is no man, nor can he really act like one. This is what she may have
unconsciously concluded about her father long ago, since she could not arouse
his interests. He disappears. That means she makes him disappear. She throws
him out and tries another person.

This time it is a little boy eating bop . . . (or Bob . . . is that an allusion to the boy's name?) no, popcorn. And if it is a Bob, it might be her boy friend (whom she has been seeing sporadically these days) or her half-brother who has in the meantime grown into a big boy. Yet he may matter more as a little boy in her imagination, particularly since she had not even known her boy friend when he was little. Anyway, what he offers may be food or possibly something more pertinent to males. Yet she discards him too.

The next one she summons, however, is a person who takes over. Which means: whom she wants to take over or whom she picks because she knows he will, i.e. whom she had experienced in that capacity. He is a fat powerful man, somebody reminding her of Henry VIII (who would know how to get rid of women he loved no longer, but who, on the other hand, had loved them to begin with). That man could well be her psychological father, mother's husband, who had no use for another man's child. What he does in the dream or what she makes him do, however, is too much, although she is still tempted enough for a moment to be unable to scream. Then she runs, permits herself to hear him panting and even to grab her (the reader will remember that this resembles an incident between her and her step-father that she reported in her first session with the therapist), particularly since she has "turned off the light" in the dream and almost lost him on her flight. The grab, however, is again too much. She jumps into a deep abyss, apparently ready to risk her life rather than submit. Or is that what, according to her own phantasy, this man wants to do to her anyway? Kill her? Or go down with her?

She has obviated all of this. She has escaped the man and his advances, whether sexual or destructive, as well as her own wish for such a man. She is in the street. Sunrise is close (note her comment about mother's intervention in the incident reported). All of which is apparently harmless. Yet if she walks through this narrow street, she may be a "street-walker", and if sunrise is close, it has not quite come yet. In other words, she picks a scene in which the desire she tried to satisfy all along but got increasingly scared of as she came closer, would still have a chance to get satisfied.

This, incidentally, looks like a solution she has even practised in her real life. Since she failed to make much of an impression on her fathers, she was ready to run off with any boy who cared to. Her trouble with Bob was that he cared too much, that she was too seriously tempted into believing that she could make a lasting impression on a boy after all, that she had been wrong all along in thinking otherwise, wrong even in taking up with Bob, and that this very thing was impossible. She had to end the affair real quick and at all costs (or all unshed tears of the past would come over her at once; see also p. 29f). She herself was the one who did not want to marry, but live with him in sin instead and ultimately be punished for it, although there is also an element of punishing him in lieu of her fathers, and of punishing her fathers by having so many other men that they must become jealous at last, but also by being almost a prostitute and putting them to shame.

When, in the dream, her lurking desire is abruptly laid bare by another grabbing hand, she cannot handle the situation any longer except by waking up, that is by reinstating her full controls which had been released during sleep, because she was satisfying the oldest of all desires, sleep. All other desires are more or less stalled while a person is sleeping (see also p. 106 f). Those stalled the least are those that have been aroused during the preceding day. They are counter-cathected desires, to be sure. Otherwise they could have been satisfied during the day and would not have to be dreamt about. Yet both, desires and their counter-cathexes, may vary greatly in their psychological ages as well as in their intensities.

In the fragment of another dream the patient sees somebody with a huge mouth eat something small and delectable. As is to be expected—the dreams of one night tend to be dealing with the same, or closely related, problems—there is an element of being swallowed in the big dream too, when she is forced into the abyss and the darkness. She has been so bad and worthless that she deserves to be devoured. Yet there is also some hope that thereby she can satisfy that other person (who also grabs and holds her by the arm), and that this person may at last love her for it. She might even be caressed and kissed, by implication (licked like an ice-cream cone, landing softly after a long fall in the dark). However, these two scenes could also indicate her own wishes of oral exploration and perhaps even of oral revengeful destruction.

Analysis of the dream, i.e. exploring the patient's memories and ideas that come to her mind along with the events of the dream revealed further details. A few shall be given here. The strange spiral staircase reminded her of a similar staircase she had climbed with her father in the tower of a cathedral in K. (which they had visited as tourists). Her stepmother had been sick that day and had stayed in the hotel. When walking down again, she had to stop for a moment and her father bumped into her mildly. Somewhat later in therapy it turned out that as this happened she had felt something on her behind which could have been the contents of his pocket or, possibly, his sex-organs. Still later she remembered that, just then, she had had a fleeting, apparently meaningless and yet triumphant thought: "I am no virgin". But even the shape of the entire staircase, the column and the wall, may have had bearing on these matters.

The darker hair and the lighter complexion had probably been taken from the therapist. The first man in the dream was apparently a blend of him and her father. The gloating was connected with a new and somewhat daring dress that she had worn that day and about which she had wished to elicit some comment from the therapist, at least—she commented—when she was leaving. That as well as a man in his early thirties whom she had watched a little too conspicuously in the streetcar without, however, getting a response may have been the "day residues" that helped elicit the dream.

Two or three years ago she had discovered, she reports, that her half-brother Bob had become a rather handsome boy. He had also begun to look at her with different eyes. So she had thought, at least. Yet one day when she went to see her mother he was the only one home, behaved rudely, made no conversation and ate peanuts without offering her any. Once, however, she could notice that he looked at her rather than at the magazine he pretended to study and he did so almost wistfully. There was also a childhood incident that may have had bearing on the dream, a situation where she tried to change his diapers, but made a mess of it, but this came up only much later.

As for her stepfather, she did recall the incident mentioned before (see p. 333f), but realised that it may have implied much more than she had originally cared to remember. The abyss reminded her of the pit into which she had fallen, and of her stepfather's peculiar reaction. Also of a time when she and Bob, her boy friend, stood on top of a cliff to overlook the countryside. She had felt as close to happiness as she had ever come, and had had a wish to suggest to him: "Let us jump down." Not that she meant it, she claimed. Just to test him and also to tell him that, perhaps, possibly, things would go well and couldn't be better.

The narrow street she walked through after her fall reminded her of a similar street in K., the same city where she and father had climbed the tower. She had taken a walk by herself in the evening against the advice of her father. Her stepmother was well again. They and another tourist couple had got together for a card game. On this walk she was addressed by a man, invited to join him for a late dinner and quite tempted to see what it, and he, would be like. He was a handsome young man and didn't look dangerous. But she declined and rushed home. In this context it also turned out that the arm that grabbed her from a door was leaner than her stepfather's. It could have been that man's, her real father's, the therapist's or possibly even Aunt Patricia's arm.

As for the man with the ice-cream cone she remembered that, when a little girl, she had gone by a drug-store with a girl friend from school, first grade, stopped for a moment and talked about how nice it would be if they had money, because then they could buy some ice cream, strawberry, no vanilla, yes, but with whipped cream, etc. While they were talking, a white-haired old gentleman had stepped up to them, listened and given them the money, but made them promise that in return they would do something nice to somebody this very same day. They giggled and had their ice creams. When she mentioned the incident to Aunt Nellie, with whom she lived at that time, Aunt Nellie got very upset and made her and Joy, who had not even been in on it, promise never to accept anything from a man, because he could do terrible things to you. "What?" asked Elsa timidly. "Too terrible to talk about," was the reply. "He might even eat the child." Elsa also remembered that now she was not sure whether she should or should not do something nice to somebody, but after some musing threw the only coin she had in her piggy-bank out into the street so that a poor man may find it.

One more comment about dreams in general and their function in psychotherapy. They are only dreams—although one might say that anything anybody has ever achieved for the world, history, others or himself, has been a "dream" first—but as means to an end they have been called the "royal avenue to the unconscious", i.e. to all those desires and objects that a person has had to counter-cathect during his life. Yet the ultimate purpose of psychotherapy is not to interpret dreams, but to help the patient find out what it was *in reality* that he had wished for so badly and unsuccessfully that it would not leave him alone even in his sleep, and what he could actually do about it now.

As for the case reported, Elsa did improve considerably and finally married Bob, her boy friend who had in the meantime earned his engineering degree and found himself a better position than before. She was on the verge of leaving for another city and a fairly flimsy job offer when they had just become official fiancees with the approval and participation of both their families. When she did not—panic altogether, that is—she seemed to be pretty much over the hump and stopped coming for psychotherapy soon thereafter.

Epilogue

I HOPE I have accomplished to some extent what I announced in the preface. If the presentation has been too lengthy and elaborate in the first part, the Conceptual Introduction, the reader may have found it more concise in the second, The Theory at Work. If, on the other hand, the second part has been too loose and broad, the first part has perhaps been sufficiently rigorous so that the reader could still see and hold on to the theory proper.

I also hope to have given theorists of related fields a better idea of who their neighbor is. A certain isomorphism with a number of learning theories should not lead one to believe that one can replace the other. Psychoanalytic theory is capable of handling more complex conditions, say, having or not having a father, losing a person after various lengths and intensities of exposure, periodic separations from a person or a dear habit, the love for an institution such as one's college, etc., as *data*. Learning theorists do likewise, but they have usually left their theories behind, when they do so. They develop *ad hoc* assumptions of which they are sometimes not even aware. Psychoanalytic theory is also better prepared than most learning theories are to deal with the person as a whole and with all of his motivation, but, if you like, even with the rat and the entire system of *that* creature's motivation.

The same would hold for physiologists and neurologists wherever they are bordering on psychological phenomena, especially those of motivation. They have something relevant to say about the processes that constitute the constellations of nervous or cortical and sub-cortical excitation called "drives". They can come up with a theory of "memory" on the cellular and even molecular level. But like learning theorists they would have trouble accounting in their own theoretical terms for more complex *data*. That is true even for most aspects of psychopathology.

What about those who are not even neighbors but claim to occupy the same house: other "dynamic theorists"? Some of them call themselves even psychoanalytic or neo-psychoanalytic. They are dealing with the same subject-matter, but seem to be doing so less comprehensively, consistently, articulately and parsimoniously than one can by means of psychoanalytic theory proper (see also p. 296 f). This would at least be my impression after a careful study of the situation. That does not mean that those other theorists have not made contributions and valuable criticisms, nor that they cannot stand on their own feet. My

344

contention would be, however, that they stand less firmly and that all contributions as well as real criticisms could, in principle, be incorporated in psychoanalytic theory. Some criticisms, however, are not directed against psychoanalytic theory—as they claim to be—but against all theory of motivation. They sound somewhat like this: psychoanalytic theory is mechanistic, determinstic and presumptuous. It looks at man from the viewpoint of pathology. And it does not give full credit to the individual, his freedom and his creativity.

What these critics do not seem to know is that any theory must have a "grammar". Otherwise it is no theory. And once you have a "grammar", its exercise may well look mechanical and deterministic (see also Toman, 1954 b). According to them the theory's worst presumption is that it should apply to all mankind. Yet what good would a theory of human motivation and its development do, we might ask in return, if it applied only to some men and not to others. We would need a second theory to explain why that is so.

As for its alleged inclinations toward pathology, I am tempted to reply that the opposite is true. In learning and theorising, among other things, about the ways in which a person's development toward healthy adulthood can end short of its destination, we can appreciate the complexity and delicacy of psychological health much better than by talking about health in a kind of dream boat isolation.

And what tribute to the individual, his freedom and creativity, might be greater: that which presumes to have notions about the dimensions, in terms of which individuals differ, or those who are content to do no more than say incessantly: everyone is different from everyone else? As if Freud or psychoanalytic theory or anyone seriously engaged in the field had ever denied that. As for freedom, psychoanalytic theory maintains that more health means greater freedom and that a person loses freedom in proportion to the severity of psychological illness. Trying to understand how freedom grows and comes about is probably more productive than the refusal to discuss the problem. And as for creativity, psychoanalytic theory is perhaps the only one that can *derive* from its basic concepts that man is always in search of new things, new people and new aspects to deal with and to enjoy. What psychoanalytic theory cannot do is account in detail for the very different conditions under which creativity operates in different disciplines such as mathematics or physics on one hand (where so much conceptual work is necessary before a person can even begin to be objectively creative, i.e. to do something meaningful that nobody has done before) and, say, artwork on the other (where any little dot, lump, curve, word or punctuation sign, can qualify as objectively new, although not necessarily worthwhile). Other dynamic theories, however, can do no better than psychoanalytic theory.

Anthropology has used, but also abused or defied psychoanalytic theory in many ways, sometimes without even a fair understanding of their "tool" of inquiry. Several people have raised the argument that Freud has constructed his theory from his experiences with the middle class of Central Europe at the end of the Victorian era. Therefore it does not hold in social systems of other kinds and times. Yet Freud's theory was meant to be universal. Different cultural conditions may well lead to different patterns of inter-personal relationships, to be sure, but there is no culture where the child would not be exposed to some parent figures, usually a female first, a male later, but sometimes more than one of each kind. There is no society where children would not have to be nursed and otherwise taken care of, where they would not sooner or later experience their parents or parent-figures as powers that can force even their ways of cleanliness upon them. And every society whatsoever practises some kind of cleanliness and of waste disposal, even if they do no more than go out into the street rather than stay in the hut. Finally there is no society where children would not wise up to the fact that there are two sexes, in general and among the parents, that they themselves are of one sex only and that the parents belong more intimately to each other than they do to them, at least in some respects. And as they grow up the majority of them will learn that a relationship with a non-incestuous (i.e. not intimately familiar from childhood on) person of the opposite sex is among the best things life holds in store for them and that children generated will make things even better. The details of all this may vary, and psychoanalytic theory implies just that.

Other anthropologists, on the other hand, have gone out of their way to prove psychoanalytic theory by their own *data*. They are usually unaware of the general problems involved in such proofs. No matter how well their *data* might agree with what psychoanalytic theory would lead to expect, no single set of *data* can do any such "favor" to the theory. There are critical tests, to be sure. If it could be shown that deprivation for good of a well established desire or the loss of a dearly loved person would not create anxiety; that anxiety would increase rather than decrease as counter-cathexis of the desire or person involved is being established; that a state of extreme deprivation would increase the overall amount of concomitant cathexis, etc.; if that could be shown, the theory would have to be revised (see also Toman, 1954 b). But the vast majority of all anthropological *data* are not of this kind. Still other anthropologists have no such ambitions. They simply see everything according to their own misinterpretations of psychoanalytic theory. They might even manufacture *data* because they think it would make sense that way. Well, I don't know what that should be called, but it is not going to do much good to anybody. Which should not mean to say that, with a proper understanding of psychoanalytic theory, anthropologists might not be, and have not been, guided or helped in many ways. I am no critic of *true* cross-fertilisation.

Sociologists have often been more careful in those respects. They have not tended quite so much toward adopting psychoanalytic theory as such and embellishing it with some of their own frill-work. They have rather proceeded to construct their own theories from comparable, but not identical, premises and by a comparable grammar (see, e.g., Parsons). Isomorphism is about as much as one can reasonably hope for. Any claim beyond it should be treated with caution. That would at least be my recommendation.

My warnings include also those psycho-sociologists or socio-psychologists who take present sociological and psychological conditions to task and seem to appeal mainly to a certain kind of reading public. Not that they would not have valuable things to say. But they say questionable things along with it, have trouble keeping the two kinds apart, and above all they do not have, nor even attempt, a theory. At best they have a theorem, a hypothesis, and sometimes they do not even have that. They cannot show how they arrive at what they think they must say. Hence they usually get their followers for sentimental reasons rather than for what they, the followers, can learn and might ultimately be able to contribute themselves. These authors, however, may not even want any other followers. Those could put them on the spot, whereas with *their* kind they would remain unquestioned prophets who have God or at least their own "genius" at their absolute command.

May I have helped all the "neighbors" concerned and interested to understand better what psychoanalytic theory is about. May I have clarified obscure aspects of the theory and some of its conclusions even for the experts and daily users, if only for their teaching purposes. And may I have given any reader regardless of "creed" something to "take home" and apply with caution and care to themselves, their children, their friends and a few others. Only the readers' parents may have to be omitted. Often they can be "reformed" no longer, especially by their own children. And why should they ? In their own ways they have usually done their best anyway.

Bibliography

ABRAHAM, K., *Selected Papers on Psychoanalysis* (1924). Hogarth Press, London 1948.
AICHHORN, A., *Wayward Youth* (1925). Putnam London 1936.
ALEXANDER, F., *Psychosomatic Medicine; Its Principles amd Applications*. Norton, New York 1950.
ALEXANDER, F. and FRENCH, T. M., *Psychoanalytic Therapy; Principles and Application*. Ronald Press, New York 1946.
BETTELHEIM, B., *Love Is Not Enough*. The Free Press, Glencoe, Ill. 1951.
BOWLBY, J., *Maternal Care and Mental Health*, World Health Organisation, London 1951; *Child Care and the Growth of Love*. Penguin Books, Melbourne, London, Baltimore 1953.
DEUTSCH, F., (Ed.), *The Psychosomatic Concept in Psychoanalysis*. Internat. Universities Press, New York 1953.
DEUTSCH, F., (Ed.), *On the Mysterious Leap from the Mind to the Body*. Internat. Universities Press, New York 1959.
DEUTSCH, F., and MURPHY, W. F., *The Clinical Interview*. 2 vols., Internat. Universities Press, New York 1955.
DEUTSCH, Helene, *The Psychology of Women*. 2 vols., Grune and Stratton, New York 1944.
FENICHEL, O., *Psychoanalytic Theory of Neurosis*. Norton, New York 1945.
FREUD, ANNA, *The Ego and the Mechanisms of Defense* (1936). Internat. Universities Press, New York 1946.
FREUD, ANNA, and BURLINGHAM, DOROTHY T., *War and Children*. Medical War Books, New York 1943.
FREUD, S., *The interpretation of dreams* (1900). The Standard Edition of the Complete Psychological Works of Sigmund Freud, Hogarth Press, London 1953 etc., vols. 4, 5; *Three Essays on Sexuality* (1905). Stand Ed., vol. 7; *Formulations on the two principles of mental functioning* (1911). Stand. Ed., vol. 12; *Totem and Tabu* (1912–13). Stand. Ed., vol. 13; *The unconscious* (1913). Stand. Ed., vol. 14; *On narcissism; an introduction* (1914). Stand. Ed., vol. 14; *Instincts and their vicissitudes* (1915a). Stand. Ed., vol. 14; *Repression* (1915b). Stand. Ed., vol. 14; *Mourning and melancholia* (1916a). Stand. Ed., vol. 14; *Metapsychological supplement to the theory of dreams* (1916b). Stand. Ed., vol. 14; *A general introduction to psychoanalysis* (1916–17). Stand. Ed., vols. 15, 16; *Beyond the pleasure principle* (1920). Stand. Ed., vol. 18; *Group psychology and the analysis of the ego* (1921). Stand. Ed., vol. 18; *The Ego and the Id* (1923). Stand. Ed., vol. 19; *The passing of the Oedipus complex* (1924). Stand. Ed., vol. 19; *The problem of anxiety* (1926). Stand. Ed., vol. 20; *New introductory lectures on psychoanalysis* (1933). Stand. Ed., vol. 22; *Analysis terminable and interminable* (1937). Stand. Ed., vol. 23; *An outline of psychoanalysis* (1938). Stand. Ed., vol. 23.
GLOVER, E., *The Technique of Psychoanalysis*. Internat. Universities Press, New York 1952.
HARTMANN, H., KRIS, E., LOEWENSTEIN, R. M., Comments on the formation of psychic structure. *The Psychoanalytic Study of the Child* 1946, vol. 2, Internat. Universities Press, New York.
HARTMANN, H., KRIS, E., LOEWENSTEIN, R. M., Notes on the theory of aggression. *The Psychoanalytic Study of the Child* 1949, vol. 3–4. Internat. Universities Press, New York.
KUBIE, L. S., *Practical and Theoretical Aspects of Psychoanalysis*. Internat. Universities Press, New York 1950.

MENNINGER, K. A., *Man Against Himself*. Harcourt, Brace and Co., New York 1938.
MENNINGER, K. A., *Theory of Psychoanalytic Technique*. Basic Books, New York 1958.
PARSONS, T., *The Social System*. The Free Press, Glencoe, Ill. 1951.
PAVLOV, I. P., *Conditioned Reflexes*. Oxford University Press, London 1927.
RAPAPORT, D., (Ed.) *Organisation and Pathology of Thought*. Columbia University Press, New York 1951.
REDL, F. and WINEMAN, D., *Children Who Hate: The Disorganisation and Breakdown of Behavior Controls*. The Free Press, Glencoe, Ill. 1951.
RIESMAN, D., GLAZER, N., DENNEY, R., *The Lonely Crowd*. Yale University Press, New Haven 1950.
TOMAN, W., "Mental or psychic energy" and its relation to learning and retention: an experimental contribution. *Acta Psychol.* **10**, 317–350, 1954a; The conceptual structure of Freudian theory as related to experimental verification (14th Internat. Congr. of Psychology, Montreal 1954b). *Acta Psychol.* **11**, 124–125, 1955,; Repetition and repetition compulsion. *Internat. J. Psychoanal.* **37**, 347–350, 1956; A general formula for the quantitative treatment of human motivation (15th Internat. Congr. of Psychology, Brussels 1957). *J. Abnorm. Soc. Psychol.* **58**, 91–99, 1959; Die Familienkonstellation und ihre psychologische Bedeutung. *Psychol. Runds.* **10**, 1–15, 1959a; Family constellation as a basic personality determinant. *J. Individ. Psychol.* **15**, 199–211, 1959b; Family constellation as a character and marriage determinant. *Internat. J. Psychoanal.* **40**, 316-319, 1959c.

Other Recommended Reading
BRENNER, Ch., *An Elementary Textbook of Psychoanalysis*. Internat. Universities Press, New York 1955.
ERIKSON, E. H., *Childhood and Society*. Norton, New York 1950.
FROMM, E., *The Forgotten Language; an Introduction to the Understanding of Dreams*. Rinehart, New York 1951.
HALL, C. S., *A Primer of Freudian Psychology*. World Publishing Co., Cleveland, New York 1954.
HALL, C. S., *The Meaning of Dreams*. Harper, New York 1953.
HENDRICK, I., *Facts and Theories of Psychoanalysis*. 3rd ed., Knopf, New York 1958.
LINDNER, R. M., *The Fifty-Minute Hour; a Collection of True Psychoanalytic Tales*. Rinehart, New York 1954–55.
MARCUSE, H., *Eros and Civilisation*. Beacon Press, Boston 1955.
REIK, Th., *Listening With the Third Ear; the Inner Experience of a Psychoanalyst*. Farrar, Strauss, and Co., New York 1948.

Reading Recommended for Comparison
ADLER, A., *The Practice and Theory of Individual Psychology*. Harcourt, Brace, and Co., New York 1929.
ADLER, A., *Understanding Human Nature*. Greenberg, New York 1946.
ANSBACHER, H. L., and ANSBACHER, ROWENA R., *The Individual Psychology of Alfred Adler*. Basic Books, New York 1956.
JUNG, C. G., *The Psychology of the Unconscious*, Moffat, Yard, and Co., 1916.
JUNG, C. G., *Psychological Types*. Harcourt, Brace, and Co., New York 1923.
JUNG, C. G., *The Integration of Personality*. Farrar and Rinehart, New York 1939.
MASLOW, A. H., *Motivation and Personality*. Harper, New York 1954.
SULLIVAN, H. S., *The Interpersonal Theory of Psychiatry*, Norton, New York 1953.

Subject Index

351

Author Index